Dreamweaver® MX:
A Beginner's Guide

Dreamweaver® MX:
A Beginner's Guide

Ray West and Tom Muck

McGraw-Hill/Osborne

New York   Chicago   San Francisco
Lisbon   London   Madrid   Mexico City
Milan   New Delhi   San Juan
Seoul   Singapore   Sydney   Toronto

The **McGraw·Hill** *Companies*

McGraw-Hill/Osborne
2600 Tenth Street
Berkeley, California 94710
U.S.A.

To arrange bulk purchase discounts for sales promotions, premiums, or fund-raisers, please contact **McGraw-Hill**/Osborne at the above address. For information on translations or book distributors outside the U.S.A., please see the International Contact Information page immediately following the index of this book.

Dreamweaver® MX: A Beginner's Guide

1234567890 CUS CUS 0198765432

ISBN 0-07-222366-9

Publisher   Brandon A. Nordin
Vice President & Associate Publisher   Scott Rogers
Acquisitions Editor   Megg Morin
Project Editor   Jennifer Malnick
Acquisitions Coordinator   Tana Allen
Technical Editor   Massimo Foti
Copy Editor   Darren Meiss
Proofreader   Susie Elkind
Indexer   Jack Lewis
Computer Designers   George Toma Charbak, Lucie Ericksen
Illustrator   Melinda Moore Lytle, Michael Mueller, Lyssa Wald
Series Design   Jean Butterfield
Cover Series Design   Sarah F. Hinks

This book was composed with Corel VENTURA™ Publisher.

About the Authors

Ray West is coauthor of five books on Dreamweaver and UltraDev, including the best-selling *Dreamweaver UltraDev 4: The Complete Reference* and its successor, *Dreamweaver MX: The Complete Reference*. He is the Vice President and CIO of Workable Solutions, a company specializing in the Web-based administration of health-care alliances. Ray is also the publisher of *MX inSite* magazine and the founder of TODCON: The Other Dreamweaver Conference. Ray is a founding member of the Dreamweaver Team (www.dwteam.com) and the founder of Community MX (www.communitymx.com).

Tom Muck is coauthor of five Macromedia-related books including *Dreamweaver UltraDev 4: The Complete Reference* and *Dreamweaver MX: The Complete Reference*. He is an extensibility expert focused on the integration of Macromedia Web development tools with server-side languages, applications, and technologies. Tom has been recognized for this expertise as the 2000 recipient of Macromedia's Best UltraDev Extension Award. He also authors articles and speaks at conferences on this and related subjects. As Senior Applications Developer for Integram in Northern Virginia, Tom develops back-end applications for expedited electronic communications. Tom also runs the Basic-UltraDev site with coauthor Ray West (www.basic-ultradev.com) and is a founding member of the Dreamweaver Team (www.dwteam.com).

About the Technical Editor

Massimo Foti began using Dreamweaver on the very day the first beta was available, and he has used Dreamweaver ever since.

He has been a prolific extension developer since the pioneering days of Dreamweaver 1. He is the creator of www.massimocorner.com, and is a winner of the Macromedia Best Extension Developer award in 2000. His extensions are featured on the Macromedia Exchange for Dreamweaver and have been included in many books and magazines.

Massimo works at www.amila.ch developing database-driven Web sites using ColdFusion, PHP, and different kinds of databases. An avid reader of computer books, he works as tech editor, contributor, and reviewer for Osborne, New Riders, O'Reilly, and other publishers.

Contents at a Glance

Contents

PART II
Creating Web Applications With Dreamweaver MX

Acknowledgments

Ray's Acknowledgments

There have gotten to be too many people to thank as we continue to try and keep up with the production cycle at Macromedia. We will always forget someone, but that doesn't mean you aren't appreciated.

Thanks to everyone at Macromedia, especially Matt Brown, Dave Deming, Tom Hale, Niamh O'Byrne, Jessica Kutash, Susan Morrow, and Susan Marshall.

Thanks to the team at Osborne, who makes it possible for us to stay on track.

My thanks always to Tom, who keeps us doing cool stuff.

And mostly thanks to my family, who has been an unending supply of help and support.

Tom's Acknowledgments

This is our fifth book for Osborne about Dreamweaver, and the list of people to thank seems to grow each time. As always, the staff at Osborne has proven to be a big help during the entire process—Jenny is always right there with a foot in our behinds to keep us motivated. Thanks to Megg and Tana, and to Jim and Tim for getting the ball rolling. Also, good luck to Jim and Tim on your future endeavors!

Macromedia has given us much support over the years, and continues to do so. Thanks to everyone at MM, especially Matt Brown and David Deming.

Thanks to our tech editor, Massimo, who has edited all of our books and is one of the most respected names in the Dreamweaver community.

My daughter, Amber, has been a constant inspiration to me. She's getting to the age where she'll be learning these programs and teaching me how to use them.

Finally, my wife, Janet, is always supportive of my extracurricular activities. She is the best person I know and the reason why I wake up in the morning. Thank you, Janet, for everything you've done for me.

Introduction

A lot has changed in the year and a half since we wrote the first edition of this book, *Dreamweaver UltraDev: A Beginner's Guide*. The UltraDev program was completely folded into the Dreamweaver family, and now there is just one program: Dreamweaver MX. This new program is vastly more complex than any previous Web development environment that has come before it. This book shows you from start to finish how to build a simple Web application using Dreamweaver MX.

Despite its complexities, Dreamweaver MX is also vastly easier to use than its predecessor. That is due, in part, to the new interface the program sports. Dreamweaver MX has taken the best features of some of the other Web development software that has been developed or acquired by Macromedia, including Drumbeat 2000, Dreamweaver, UltraDev, Homesite, and CF Studio.

This is a book for beginners, and as such we will attempt to cover the necessities and building blocks. We will also try to move along at a quick pace, so that by the end of the book you will have an understanding of dynamic Web site creation using Dreamweaver MX.

Who Should Buy This Book

Anyone who is interested in building Web sites and is coming in with no prior knowledge will find this book to be a necessity. We do, however, make a few assumptions about you:

- You are familiar with basic Windows or Macintosh file manipulation.

- You have access to an application server and Web server, such as Personal Web Server or IIS.

- You have access to a database application, such as MS Access, mySQL, or MS SQL Server.

Conventions Used In This Book

The following conventions are used in the writing of this book.

Code references use the following monospaced font:

```
var strName = "Bob"
```

Sometimes code that is supposed to be on one line gets broken up because of the width of the page. In that case there will be a continuation character indicating that you should enter the code on one line. That character looks like this:

```
¬
```

When you are supposed to press keys, they will be represented like this:

CTRL-F10

Every attempt has been made to ensure that the code listings and content in the book are accurate. If you find any mistakes, please drop us a line so that we can correct future versions. Also, the code used in the book is available for download from www.osborne.com. The best way to go through the tutorials in the book, however, is to download the database used in the book and create your own files that interact with that database. Most of the examples use the built-in features of Dreamweaver and won't require any coding.

To really understand Web site creation, however, you will need to create your own. Do the exercises in each chapter; when you are finished with the book you will need to learn more about all of the different technologies used in Web site creation.

Special Features

Each module includes Notes, Tips, and Cautions to provide additional information wherever needed. You'll also find Ask the Expert boxes—question-and-answer sections to address potentially confusing issues—as well as step-by-step Projects to give you a chance to practice the concepts you've learned. Progress Checks also test what you've learned along the way.

Mastery Checks are included at the end of each module to give you another chance to review the concepts taught in the module. The answers to the Mastery Checks are in Appendix A.

We hope that, as you become more proficient in Dreamweaver and want to expand your knowledge even more, you'll seek out our book *Dreamweaver MX: The Complete Reference*, also by Osborne, which goes into much more detail than we are able to here in the Beginner's Guide.

We have an open-door policy at our Web site—if you have problems with anything you find in our books, you can send us an e-mail and we'll try to address the problem as quickly as possible. Also, feel free to drop us a line at www.dwteam.com if you have any suggestions.

Part I

Get Started with Dreamweaver MX

Module 1

Dreamweaver MX: Your Connection to the Internet

I have a little story to tell you. I recently had the privilege of taking guitar lessons from one of my all-time favorite players. During our first session, we had a good discussion about my background and my goals. He was insistent that the way to become the best player I could be was to study as if I were going to play for a living as a professional musician, and that meant going back and reviewing the basics.

Now, I have had more music theory than anyone should have to endure. I have played professionally on a variety of instruments since my college years. Nevertheless, within the context of the system my teacher developed, this review of the basics has helped my playing immensely. I went through it quickly, but I still picked up pointers that were new or that I had forgotten about.

So I say to you, the way to become the best Web developer and Dreamweaver user you can be is to study as if you plan to become a professional, and that includes a review of the basics. If you are an experienced developer and this book was purchased just to learn the particulars of Dreamweaver MX, you will get through this part quickly and may even pick up a few of those pointers. If you are new to Web development, do not believe that you can become accomplished without a solid understanding of the basics. No design tool can substitute for a good grounding in the way the Internet works and the protocols that make it up. Sure, you can skip ahead to the fun part, but it will mean much more to you if you hang around for a few minutes and learn the foundation of the job you want to perform.

CRITICAL SKILL
1.1
Understand the Internet and the World Wide Web

You can use Dreamweaver MX to build applications for your company on an intranet, for a kiosk, or even to run from a CD-ROM, but the most popular use is to build sites that run on the Internet; the world-wide network of computers that make information instantly available. In the scheme of things, the Internet is relatively new, but it is getting more powerful as each year passes. Dreamweaver helps you keep up.

The Internet

I suppose there was a time when questions went unanswered. A time when you would wake up at 3:00 A.M. wondering about the lyrics to that Styx song and there was nowhere to find the answer. But it is getting harder to remember that time. Somewhere around six or seven years ago, a little-known government research project began to gain popularity with the development of what would become the most useful software ever offered for free.

There have been several revolutions in world history that permanently changed the way people lived their lives. But none has occurred as quickly, ubiquitously, and nonchalantly as the Internet revolution. The Internet has affected every corner of our culture in profound ways. At home, at school, and at work, our lives are different, if not better, as we move into the Information Age.

It has been said that information is power, and if that is true, we are the most powerful we have ever been. From the theme ingredient on the next episode of Iron Chef to last-minute income tax filing forms to the complete text of pending legislation, there is almost nothing you can't find with just a little effort and access to the World Wide Web. It is interesting that one of the most exciting uses of twenty-first century technology is the exercise of ideals hundreds of years old. Speech and the flow of ideas have never been more free.

Our businesses have changed. The bookstore isn't necessarily down the street anymore— often it is at the other end of a *uniform resource locator (URL)* such as www.amazon.com or www.bn.com. People who could never have competed with the "big boys" now have all but equal standing and an unprecedented opportunity to market and sell their products.

We can communicate as never before. Whether it is parents to their kid in a school across the country, constituents to their representative, or a satisfied (or unsatisfied) customer to the CEO, we are more in touch with the world around us. The handwritten family letter of yesterday is today's smartly formatted electronic presentation complete with the latest pictures of the grandkids delivered instantly without a stamp. The Internet makes the world smaller than even Mr. Disney imagined.

But as with any medium with the potential of the Internet, those who choose to fill it with content bear a certain responsibility. Although the Web is full of sites and pages and words of incredible utility, it is also full of poor design, bad programming, and content of dubious validity. This book aims to help you learn how to use one of the most powerful Web design tools available so that you can make a positive contribution.

The Web is built around several key concepts and protocols. These are all interrelated, but serve very different purposes. Without any one of them, the Internet would not work as we know it. You will need to become well acquainted with these concepts and how they fit into the development cycle and the user experience. They are

- File Transfer Protocol
- World Wide Web
- TCP/IP
- Hypertext Transfer Protocol
- Hypertext Markup Language

File Transfer Protocol

The *File Transfer Protocol (FTP)* was one of the earliest methods of using the Internet. Its purpose is betrayed by its name: It is used to transfer files from one place to another, or from one computer to another over a distributed network. Originally, the Internet was used for the sharing of information by researchers and scientists. They would use FTP to transfer entire files of information back and forth. For instance, a researcher might compose notes about his or her current series of experiments. He or she could then upload them via FTP to a common repository where his or her colleagues could download them and comment on them or add to them with their own findings. FTP was a good way to connect users together and allow them to share their computer files.

Today, FTP is still one of the most widely used aspects of the Internet. If you have ever downloaded a shareware program or purchased an upgrade online, chances are you used FTP to do it. As a Web developer, you will find yourself using FTP primarily to place and retrieve the files that make up your sites on your remote server. This will make more sense when you understand how a Web site is constructed.

As a means of sharing information, FTP has been replaced by a more convenient, more dynamic, more appropriate method: the World Wide Web.

The World Wide Web

Just like FTP, the World Wide Web is well deserving of its name. It is truly a worldwide network, and the way it is constructed can best be described as an interconnected web of information that touches its surroundings like the balled-up string of quantum physics fame. You can start surfing at your favorite site and 30 minutes later there is no telling where you will end up.

The Web is distinct from FTP, though, and it works very differently. While the purpose of FTP is to allow the transfer of entire files of information, the purpose of the Web is to allow the viewing of the contents of those files without having to download them to your computer. Using the *Hypertext Transfer Protocol (HTTP)* and the *Hypertext Markup Language (HTML)*, the Web provides an infrastructure that allows the viewing of text content, graphics, images, and even movies and sound in a program called a *browser*.

You are likely familiar with the popular browsers such as Microsoft's Internet Explorer and Netscape Navigator. These programs are the means by which users connect to the content that is available to them on the Web. The current browser generations are a tremendous improvement over their text-based ancestors. The glitz and flash that they allow the user to experience is a prime reason for the exponential growth in the popularity of the Internet and the World Wide Web.

In order to develop the content that will make up your own little corner of the Web, you need to be familiar with the underlying concepts that make it work. These include the ways in which the vast number of computers and programs that make up the Internet communicate with one another, as well as the language of the Web, HTML.

1

TCP/IP

A key component of the infrastructure of the Internet is the communications protocol over which it operates. Actually a suite of protocols, *TCP/IP* is the several-tiered method by which data is packaged and sent across the wires that connect the world's computers together. It is made up of the Transmission Control Protocol and the Internet Protocol.

Internet Protocol

Although IP comes after TCP in the name of the protocol, IP is the communications core that makes the Internet work. You have likely heard of IP addresses, those sets of numbers separated by dots that are assigned to each host computer and domain on the Net (for example, 208.43.451.78). The Internet Protocol utilizes that numbering scheme to determine the path it should take across the routers and hosts that make up the Internet to reach the destination it is intended for. When you make a connection to a computer somewhere out on the Web, you are, in reality, connecting to any number of other computers and routers that forward your request in the most efficient way they can determine, given the millisecond they have to think about it. If you are interested to see how your requests are being routed, you can use the *tracert* (trace route) utility from a command prompt on your computer and see the connections, or *hops*, your request makes as it travels to the destination you provide (see Figure 1-1).

```
MS-DOS Prompt                                                    _ 🗗 ✕
 Auto      ▾  ⬜ 🖿🖻  🔲  🖫🗗  A

Microsoft(R) Windows 98
   (C)Copyright Microsoft Corp 1981-1999.

C:\WINDOWS>tracert www.basic-ultradev.com

Tracing route to www.basic-ultradev.com [63.96.26.230]
over a maximum of 30 hops:

   1    32 ms    53 ms    47 ms   adsl-20-119-1.mco.bellsouth.net [66.20.119.1]
   2    12 ms    11 ms    12 ms   205.152.111.65
   3    11 ms    11 ms    12 ms   205.152.111.248
   4    10 ms    13 ms    10 ms   Serial4-1-0.GW1.ORL1.ALTER.NET [157.130.65.157]

   5    22 ms    22 ms    21 ms   504.at-2-1-0.XR2.ATL1.ALTER.NET [152.63.84.46]
   6    31 ms    31 ms    32 ms   194.ATM6-0.GW3.ORL1.ALTER.NET [146.188.233.133]

   7   176 ms   149 ms   104 ms   63.74.97.33
   8   185 ms   135 ms   158 ms   www.basic-ultradev.com [63.96.26.230]

Trace complete.

C:\WINDOWS>
```

Figure 1-1 Running *tracert* to www.basic-ultradev.com returns a number of stops along the way.

Now, given that this is the way the Internet works, with each request you make being forwarded through a number of stops, consider what must happen when you download a large Web page, or even a 15MB program from a shareware site. Without the IP protocol, it might be necessary for the entire file to be copied to each node along the way until it reaches your computer. That could involve as many as 30 or more copies of the same file depending on where you and your destination site are located. Thanks to IP, your request and the response for the computer at the other end can be split up into small packets of data that travel easily across the network, following the most efficient path each of them can find.

NOTE

A number of things can affect the route a packet takes across the Internet, including bottlenecks and outages along the way. The ability of IP to dynamically route around these problems is a key factor in the stability of this kind of distributed network.

Consider how you might get a group of 12 friends across town to the movies. Unless one of you owned a bus, you would probably split up into three cars and head off for the theater. Perhaps one of the drivers likes the expressway, another knows a "shortcut," and the third doesn't have enough change for the tolls *and* popcorn and takes the normal route. Three cars are all taking different routes to the same destination, and each is liable to encounter things along the way that might speed their travel (such as no line at the toll booth) or slow them down (such as a wreck along the shortcut). Although each car left one after the other, there is no guarantee in what order or in what timeframe they might arrive at the theatre. One car might not even make it at all.

To make the point more clearly, suppose you ordered a book from Barnes and Noble, and, instead of shipping you the entire book at once, they sent the individual pages by different carriers with no page numbers. When and if you received all of the pages (and how would you know if you did?), you would be hard-pressed to get them back together in an order that was useful. This is pretty close to what happens to a file that is being transmitted across a network by the IP protocol alone. IP needs some help to make sure that things end up where they belong. That help comes from the Transmission Control Protocol.

Transmission Control Protocol

The *Transmission Control Protocol (TCP)* is like the big stack of envelopes that the shipping clerk at Barnes and Noble would use to send you all of those pages. Each envelope would be numbered in order and would indicate the total number of envelopes in the sequence—for example, 36 of 1,008. Each envelope would also give some indication of what was on the page inside so you could make sure that you got the right one. Using this scheme, you could receive all of the envelopes, put them back in order, and make sure you received what the store meant to send you. Then you could call Barnes and Noble and yell at them for sending you a book in such a stupid way.

But that's the way it has to work on the Web. Each packet created by the IP protocol is packaged up, numbered, and labeled so the receiving computer knows what to do with it. If the receiving computer is missing any packets, it knows to send back for them from the sending computer. And the TCP information indicates what the packet should contain so the receiving computer can identify corrupted data.

Together, the two protocols within TCP/IP provide the communications basis on which the Internet is built. But it can really only handle the connection between the computers over which the requests and responses of information are sent. Those actual messages are handled by the Hypertext Transfer Protocol.

Hypertext Transfer Protocol

There are basically four parts to any transfer of data over a client/server network (which is really what the Internet is). The first and last of these steps are the connection and disconnection of the two communicating computers, which is handled by TCP/IP. Sandwiched in between is the work of the HTTP (see Figure 1-2).

You have probably noticed the "http" that begins most Web addresses. Actually, most browsers now assume the HTTP protocol is being used when you type in an address, so the http:// designation is not strictly necessary. But rest assured, that is exactly what the browser is generating when it makes a request.

NOTE

Most browsers are also capable of sending FTP and news requests. If that is what is intended, the protocol must be specified or HTTP will be assumed.

Once a connection is made, a request for data is sent in the form of an address. This might be an IP address or it could be a fully qualified domain name such as http://www.dwteam.com/. That request is routed via TCP/IP to the host computer that can fulfill it, and the response is

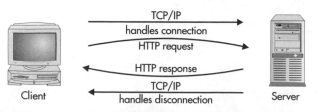

Client   TCP/IP handles connection   HTTP request   HTTP response   TCP/IP handles disconnection   Server

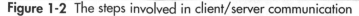

Figure 1-2 The steps involved in client/server communication

sent back as an HTTP response to the requesting computer. Once it arrives, the TCP/IP protocol again assists in putting the packets of information together so they can be used or displayed.

How that response is used when it gets back to the requesting computer depends on the content of the information sent. For these discussions, it is assumed that you are requesting the type of content that makes up most of the World Wide Web—HTML content.

Hypertext Markup Language

Hypertext Markup Language (HTML) is the foundation of the World Wide Web. It is a set of tags that describes to the client browser how a file should be displayed, which is the core purpose of the Web: displaying files of information.

The earliest HTML documents were just text. Often they were the text of scientific or research projects, and the way in which they were formatted was important. HTML provided a hierarchical means of organizing and displaying information so it could be viewed in a form

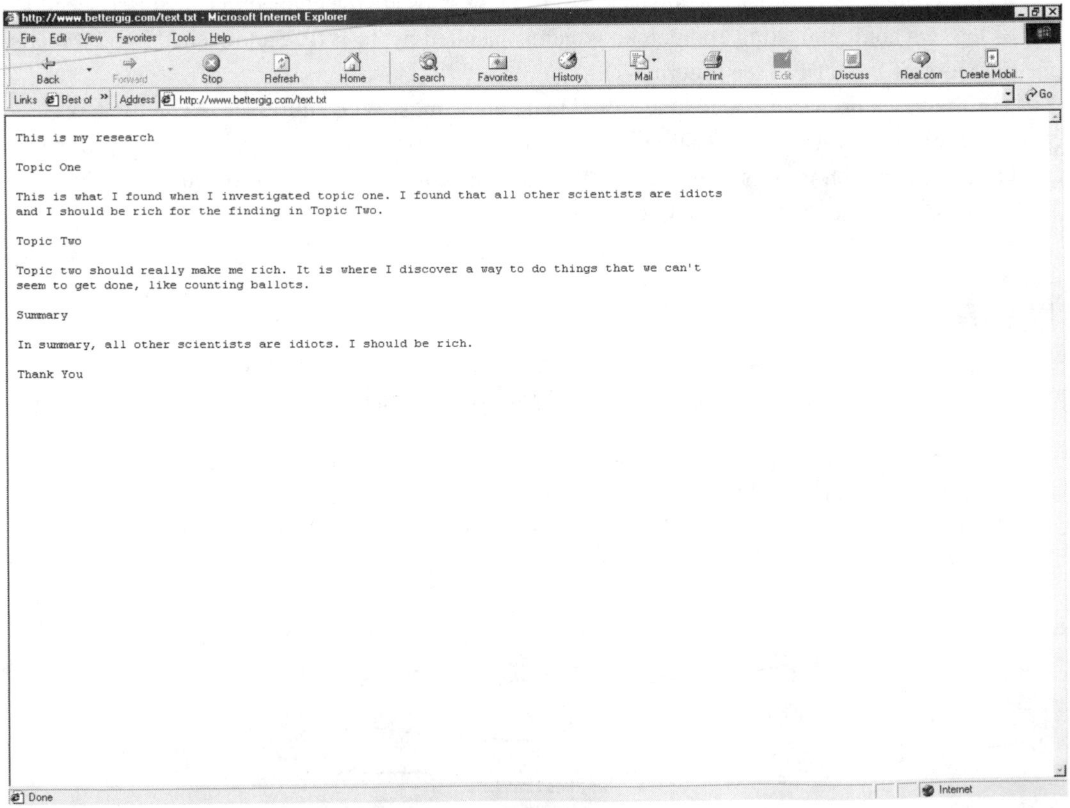

Figure 1-3 The sample text file viewed in a browser

that emphasized its structure more than its design. It does so by providing a selection of tags that mark up the raw text in ways the browser can understand.

For instance, you may want to display the raw text file shown in Figure 1-3 so that your fellow scientist can rip you apart for not following standard research guidelines.

But this file of simple text does not really allow you to organize your content in a way that will have the maximum effect on your colleague and let him or her know that you really do know how to write a good outline. HTML allows you to insert indicators such as the following directly into the text that tell the browser on the other end how to display the information:

```
<html>
<head>
<title>My Research</title>
</head>
<body>
<h1>This is my research<br>

</h1>
<h2>Topic One<br>
</h2>
<p> This is what I found when I investigated topic one.
I found that all other scientists are idiots<br>
and I should be rich for the finding in Topic Two.</p>
<h2> Topic Two<br>
</h2>
<p> Topic two should really make me rich. It is where
I discover a way to convince people that a tax cut means
they get to keep more of their own money.<br>
</p>
<h2> Summary<br>
</h2>
<p> In summary, all other scientists are idiots. I should
be rich.</p>
<p> Thank You </p>
</body>
</html>
```

To the end user, these indicators are invisible. They see only the finished product, as shown in Figure 1-4, after the browser interprets your instructions.

One of the great strengths of HTML is the ability to create and execute hyperlinks. *Hyperlinks* are directions built into the content itself that allow the user to be sent off to related material with a click of the mouse. For instance, suppose that your document discusses material for which you relied on the writings of another author whose work is also available on the Internet at its own document address. You could embed a portion of text referring to that work so that

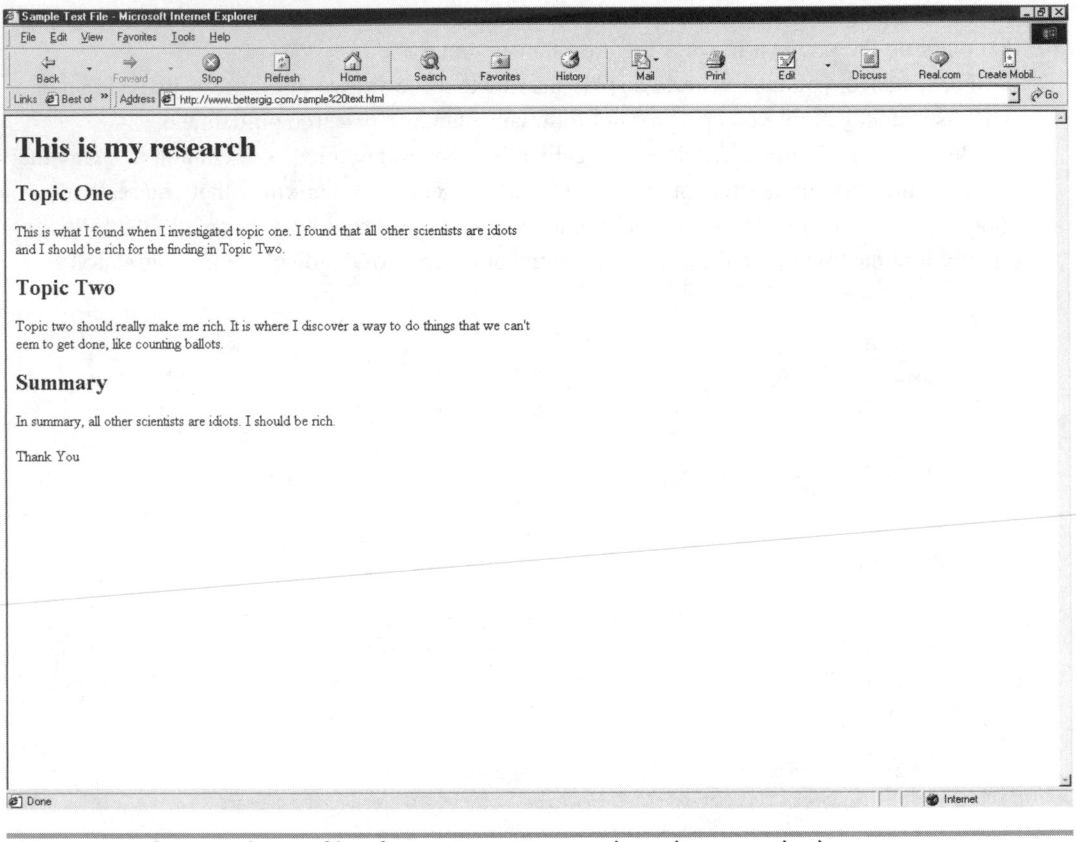

Figure 1-4 The sample text file after some HTML tags have been applied

when visitors clicked it they would be whisked off to that material, where they could properly appreciate how you had interpreted and extended that information in your own research. It is this interconnected structure that led to the coining of the term World Wide Web. The Web is truly a worldwide mesh of interconnected content.

CRITICAL SKILL
1.2

Understand Data-Driven Web Application Components

Everything covered so far makes up the component parts of your real interest in this book, which is the Web site. If you understand the stand-alone HTML document, you can consider the Web site to be a collection of those documents that makes up an interconnected web of information. What the entire Web is on a grand scale, the Web site is in its own little universe.

When you have a lot of content that you need to display, you have a couple of choices you can make. Believe it or not, some people actually choose to make one really long document that scrolls down forever. Although it eventually gets everything they wanted to say said, there is a more practical solution.

A Web site is formed when you bring together a collection of HTML documents that are related to one another and need to be displayed together. By organizing this content and providing logical ways to navigate it, you are turning your individual documents into a site that a user can use to find and access the information they need. There are three common layouts for such a site.

The first is the Table of Contents model that provides a front-end interface to a catalog of material. For instance, if you had a book or a report that was divided into sections, you might have a table of contents page that provided links to each section. As each section is completed, the user would return to the table of contents to determine the next section they wanted to access.

Second is the Web structure, where content is full of cross-referencing links. On any given page, you might have a number of links to other parts of the site connecting related material. The intent of such a structure is for the user to peruse the content of the site in a sort of stream-of-consciousness way, branching off to related parts of the site at will.

Third is the Web application. In a Web application, the user is typically guided through the site in a structured way by the way the pages are designed. For instance, if you were filling out an online insurance application, it would be important to complete each section of the application in order to be sure that everything was properly filled out. The user would depend on the site designer to guide them through the specific documents that needed to be completed.

Progress Check

1. What is the use of the File Transfer Protocol?

2. What are the two protocols that make up TCP/IP?

3. What is the language of the Web?

---

1. To transfer files to and from computers over a distributed network
2. Transmission Control Protocol and Internet Protocol
3. HTML

As you can see, there is a lot to learn during your journey toward Web stardom. The technologies and concepts that make up the Internet have been a while in the making, and if you are just now starting, you have a little catching up to do. But that is why we are here together.

So let's get started doing something practical by looking at the technologies involved in deploying a Web application. We start by installing Dreamweaver and then consider the related products you will need to access in order to successfully build your site.

1.3 Install Dreamweaver MX

Installing Dreamweaver itself could not be simpler. As a matter of fact, as long as you can double-click a mouse and respond to a few simple questions like "What is your name" and "Can you find your serial number," you should have no problem installing Dreamweaver on your computer.

But you are entering the world of Web development, and in this world the software you use to build your pages is only one small part of the set of programs you will need to be familiar with in order to successfully construct and deploy a data-driven Web application. You will need to make several decisions about the platforms and application you want to work with while constructing your site. Besides installing Dreamweaver, you will also need to arrange for access to one or more of the following:

- A Web server
- An application server
- A data store
- A staging server
- A live data server

Also, because Dreamweaver supports multiple development platforms, you will need to decide which of these you will be using and make sure that all of your choices are compatible with one another.

Let's look at your options.

The Web Server

You are likely familiar with the way the World Wide Web works, but a refresher never hurts (see Figure 1-5). When you create pages in Dreamweaver, no matter what platform you choose, you will use some kind of FTP program to upload them to a computer that is running a Web server. The Web server program is responsible for receiving and processing HTTP requests that are generated when a user types a URL into his or her browser.

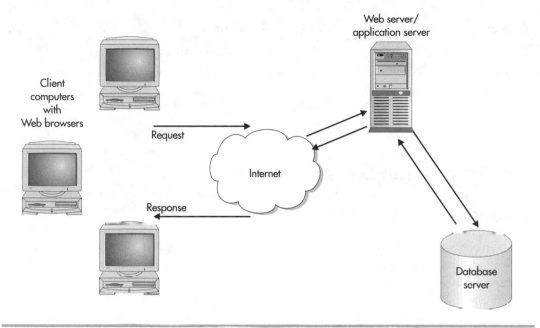

Figure 1-5 How the Web works

Depending on where your host machine is located and who owns it, you may or may not have much control over which Web server you use. There are quite a number available, and the kind of hardware and operating system you are using will narrow your choice to some degree. Some are free (or at least free with the operating system), such as Microsoft's Internet Information Server or Apache, and others you'll need to purchase. A list of some of the more popular Web servers and the platforms they support is in Table 1-1.

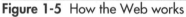

Web Server	Supported Platforms
Internet Information Server	Windows NT, Windows 2000, Windows XP
Apache	NetBSD, FreeBSD, BSDI, AIX, OS/2, SCO, HPUX, Novell NetWare, Macintosh, Be OS, Windows NT, Linux, Windows 95, Windows 98, IRIX, Solaris, Digital Unix
Lotus Domino Go Webserver	Digital Unix, AIX, OS/2, HPUX, Windows NT, Windows 95, IRIX, Solaris
Stronghold Secure Web Server	NetBSD, Digital Unix, BSDI, AIX, SCO, HPUX, Linux, FreeBSD, IRIX, Solaris

Table 1-1 Popular Web Servers and the Platforms They Support

Web Server	Supported Platforms
Oracle Web Application Server	HPUX, Windows NT, Windows 95, Solaris
Iplanet	HPUX, AIX, Solaris, IRIX, Windows NT

Table 1-1 Popular Web Servers and the Platforms They Support *(continued)*

The Application Server

Unless you're ignoring the powerful data features of Dreamweaver MX, you will have pages in your site that require more processing than the Web server provides. Pages that connect to databases will have extensions such as .asp, .jsp, .php, or .cfm. These pages require the attention of an application server that handles the code or tags in your pages that do the real work. The application server works closely with the Web server, however, to deliver pages that the user's browser can handle.

Some application servers are tightly integrated with a Web server. These include IBM's WebSphere, which can run with its own HTTP server or with another one such as IIS, or Microsoft's asp.dll, which requires IIS to run. Still others, like Cold Fusion, depend on an outside Web server. What combination works best for you depends on the specific features you are looking for.

The Data Store

Now that you are using Dreamweaver MX, you have an amazing array of powerful data features available to you. As you get better with the program, you are likely to want to connect to a database and make your site more dynamic. Theoretically, data can reside in a number of different kinds of files, including Excel spreadsheets and delimited text files, but as a practical matter, you will want the flexibility that a Relational Database Management System (RDBMS) provides. There are a number of database applications that qualify—from Microsoft Access, which can be had for a couple hundred dollars, up to enterprise-level server-based systems costing thousands of dollars and requiring significant hardware resources.

It is important to select and plan for your database application early in the planning process. Depending on the way you build your site, changing data stores midstream can be a frustrating, labor-intensive task.

The Staging Server

The Internet is a very public place. When you post something to it, people can and do look at it. When your company or your client depends on what the world reads about them, it is extremely important to get it right before it is made available on a live Web server. The more complex the sites you build, the more important it becomes to make use of a staging server in your development cycle.

A *staging server* is an interim publishing step that allows Web pages to be posted on a nonpublic server for review and quality control purposes. Depending on the size of your organization, this staging server could be an actual computer set up to serve that purpose on an intranet Web server, or it could just be a folder underneath the root of your Web site to which you can publish a copy of your site and any changes or maintenance items. These items can then be reviewed in a private setting, within the context of the entire site. Once approved, the new pages are then copied or replicated to the live Web site.

NOTE

What you don't want to happen is to be forced to put your test content up on a live site in order to debug it. Even if you just set up a hidden directory structure within your production domain, do something to allow the testing and review of your work.

CAUTION

Everything from the images you use to the grammar and spelling on your Web site make a statement about your company or your client. Use of a staging server to allow comprehensive review of the information you intend to post is vital to preserving your reputation.

The Live Data Server

One of the revolutionary parts of Dreamweaver MX is its ability to "bounce" data off of a live server and provide an editable design environment using actual data from your data store. Although we discuss this later, it is important at this point to consider how you will facilitate the use of this feature. For Windows users using the ASP model, it is easiest to use either Personal Web Server or a localized copy of Internet Information Server. Those using other technologies will want to identify a way to take advantage of this valuable design tool.

CRITICAL SKILL
1.4 Choose Server Technologies

Dreamweaver MX ships with five server models on which you can base your site: ASP, ASP.NET, JSP, PHP, and Cold Fusion MX. The decision which to use is guided by several factors and may guide other decisions that you need to make. It is important to make this decision early in your development cycle.

NOTE

Be careful when choosing which server technology you want to program for. Once you start generating pages, it's not easy to switch to a different one. Dreamweaver creates code based on the preferences you have set as you work. At this time, there is no facility for converting that code.

Active Server Pages

I would venture to say that the most common server language selection among Dreamweaver users will be ASP. Microsoft's technology is ubiquitous, easy to learn and use, and available on the many Windows-based servers currently used for Web site hosting. Although some would question its speed and scalability and its ability to keep up with the needs of a growing e-commerce site, it is certainly more than capable of providing tremendous functionality to all but the most complex applications.

If you are using a Windows NT or Windows 2000 server running Internet Information Server versions 4 or 5 to host your site, you are all set to include ASP in your pages. IIS4 supports ASP 2.0, which is the specification that Dreamweaver is designed to. IIS5 (shipped with Windows 2000) supports ASP 3.0. Although the standard Dreamweaver code will not take advantage of any of the newer features found in version 3, you can certainly hand-code portions of your application to do so.

If you are running Windows NT 4 and don't have IIS installed, you will need to get hold of the NT Option Pack. Included are several applications that you will find useful when running Web application, but the most important at this point are Internet Information Server and Microsoft Transaction Server (a must to run ASP). You can purchase an Option Pack CD or download it for free at this URL: http://www.microsoft.com/ntserver/nts/downloads/ recommended/ NT4OptPk/default.asp.

ASP on Non-Microsoft Servers

If you need to use a server that runs an operating system other than Windows or uses a Web server other than IIS, you can still use Active Server Pages for your site thanks to companies who have ported ASP to other platforms through their proprietary server applications.

ChiliSoft (www.chilisoft.com) makes a program called ChiliASP. ChiliASP provides complete ASP support on AIX, HP-UX, Linux, OS/390, Solaris, and Windows NT. They are willing to consider any other platform, and they invite visitors to their Web site to make suggestions about the next platforms they should support.

Instant ASP from Halcyon Software (www.halcyonsoft.com) promises to provide ASP support on any Web server, application server, or OS platform. It is a Java-based port of the ASP specification and is designed to allow the ultimate in portability. Instant ASP supports an impressive list of operating systems and Web servers, too many to list here. Complete information is available at their Web site.

The most difficult thing for non-Microsoft solutions to handle is the conversion of the COM components that make ASP so powerful. Most handle this by converting them to some sort of Java or JavaBean implementation.

ASP Scripting Languages

You'll also need to decide what scripting language to use in your ASP code. You will be writing code (or letting Dreamweaver write it for you) that is intended to run at the server (your Web server) and the client (your visitor's browser). Typically, the two choices are Visual Basic Script (VBScript) and JavaScript (or the Microsoft variant JScript). Which language to learn and use is an often-asked question.

VBScript

VBScript is a subset of the Visual Basic programming language. Because ASP is a Microsoft technology, it is not surprising that VBScript is the preferred language for ASP development. Because of this, most ASP tutorials feature VBScript, making example code easy to find. It is relatively easy to learn because its syntax resembles English, and there are tons of programmers with Visual Basic experience who find it a comfortable way to use ASP.

The downside of VBScript is that it is not practical as a client-side scripting language. Microsoft's Internet Explorer supports it for browser scripting, but Netscape's Navigator (the other major browser) does not. For this reason, some have concluded that using JavaScript for both the server and the client is a better alternative, especially for newer users who will only need to learn one language.

JavaScript

Anyone who does any serious Web programming will need to learn JavaScript. Although you may be most familiar with JavaScript as a client-side language used for things such as form validation and Dynamic HTML (DHTML) effects, it is actually a robust language that allows sophisticated object-oriented programming on the server side. Because it can be used for the client side and the server side, it is a logical language choice for the new user who can become productive by learning just the one language. And if you plan to write extensions for Dreamweaver, you will need to be intimately familiar with the entire JavaScript language.

However, JavaScript is more difficult to learn than VBScript. It has a less intuitive syntax, and example code is more difficult to find. It is more comparable to C or Java in its format, but it must not be confused with either of these; it is its own language. Those coming from a C or Java background may suffer a bit of confusion trying to remember which command goes with which, but having a good reference handy solves this quite nicely.

ASP.NET

ASP.NET is Microsoft's newest server-side technology. It promises to be the best of the other platforms rolled up into one, and to a certain degree, it has successfully integrated many of the ideas that have made other platforms superior to ASP. ASP.NET sports support for compiled code, broader and more powerful language choices, and total integration with the base Microsoft development platforms through the .NET framework. A good understanding of ASP is a real advantage when learning ASP.NET, and this book should prepare you to move into this new area.

Java Server Pages

Java Server Pages is Sun Microsystems' answer to ASP based on its popular Java programming language. Although it provides a scripting environment comparable to ASP, JSP is actually a small part of the Java 2 Enterprise Edition, Sun's enterprise application development framework. Included are the most popular Java technologies such as servlets, Enterprise Java Beans (EJBs), Java Database Connectivity (JDBC), and Java Naming and Directory Interface (JNDI).

One of JSP's claims to fame is its portability. While ASP is generally limited to the Microsoft platform, JSP is available on all major Web platforms. Even better, Web servers and application servers that support JSP are available from a number of manufacturers.

Like ASP, JSP is script-based, meaning that your pages are a mix of HTML and script that is prepared at the server and delivered to the browser in a form it can handle. The scripting in JSP is done in pure Java, so familiarity with the Java programming language and framework is a big help.

An advantage of JSP relates to its roots in the Java Servlet framework. The first time a JSP page is called, it is compiled into a Servlet that accepts requests from the user and returns a response output stream. The Java Virtual Machine in the browser then translates this precompiled code. By contrast, ASP pages are interpreted every time they are loaded. As big an advantage as this would seem to be, the interpretation of the JSP byte code and the interpretation of the ASP page take about the same amount of time, and well-written ASP and JSP usually run at about the same speed.

It is generally understood that it is a little more difficult to get a site running in JSP than in ASP, but there are definite advantages that may make the extra effort worth it for your site.

PHP

PHP (PHP Hypertext Preprocessor) is a popular choice among users of the Linux server platform. PHP is open source and freely available from the PHP Group. It runs on both the Windows and Linux platforms, but is most popular on servers running Linux with an Apache Web server and MySQL database. PHP is tightly integrated with the products and makes for an efficient development platform. Dreamweaver's implementation of PHP relies on its integration with MySQL.

ColdFusion MX

ColdFusion is Macromedia's proprietary server model. Unlike ASP and JSP, ColdFusion is tag-based, not script-based. This fundamental difference has made ColdFusion extremely popular among Web designers and HTML authors who are accustomed to tag-based programming. But ColdFusion is no less capable than its competition.

Using its set of built-in tags, ColdFusion can perform any function that you could script ASP or JSP to perform. Some are even significantly easier because ColdFusion has encapsulated functions that require external components in other languages (such as file upload). It is a compact language that often requires fewer lines of code to accomplish tasks than its counterparts.

You will need to obtain ColdFusion Server if you plan to develop ColdFusion applications. It is available in both standard and enterprise versions, and also a developer edition, which is free and limited to one connection at a time. It is a great way to build and test ColdFusion application locally.

ColdFusion Server is currently available for Windows, Sun Solaris, and Linux, making it as portable as it is powerful. For those needing to run a non-Microsoft server, Cold Fusion presents a popular, scalable, and very capable option.

Progress Check

1. What are the five server models supported by Dreamweaver MX?

2. What is the purpose of a live data server?

3. What is the purpose of a data store?

CRITICAL SKILL
1.5 Install and Configure Microsoft Internet Information Services

Because this is a beginner's guide, I've had to make several assumptions about the platforms you are likely to be using. We stay pretty close to the core product without a lot of hand-coding, so the application platform you select is not as important. And you will likely be operating in a

---

1. ASP, JSP, ColdFusion, PHP, and ASP.NET

2. To provide a Web server that Dreamweaver uses to display actual database output in a design environment

3. To provide a place to store the data with which your Web application will be designed to interact

Ask the Expert

Q: Which server technology should I use with Dreamweaver MX?

A: That is a personal decision based on several factors. Two important ones to consider are: what kind of hardware and software you have available, and what programming experience you have.

If you are operating in a hosted environment, you may be able to select an ISP that provides the services necessary for whichever model you would like to try. If, however, you or your company have a substantial investment in existing infrastructure, you may be limited by that.

With the popularity of Visual Basic, many developers find they can leverage their knowledge well in an ASP environment. Then again, Java is also a popular language and JSP is gaining popularity as a result. Cold Fusion offers a tag-based language that is very comfortable for those with lots of HTML experience.

Q: If I am just starting out, which server model would be the least expensive to implement?

A: That, again, is a many faceted consideration. While ASP is free with a Windows server installation, you have to buy Windows, and that can run several hundred dollars. Cold Fusion costs a little over a thousand dollars, but it is available to run on operating systems that can be obtained for free or for very little investment. JSP has operating systems and application servers available that can be freely downloaded, but it is also the most complicated to configure, and that is a real consideration. In a hosted environment, though, many of these considerations disappear. You may be able to find hosted ASP, JSP, PHP and ColdFusion service for roughly the same cost.

hosted environment, meaning that you are paying somewhere between $0 and $100 or so per month for server space and maintenance, so you don't need a lot of information about setting up your servers. The most important part of this discussion from a technical standpoint, then, is the development environment you will be using.

Windows XP is taking hold of the PC community. By the time you read this, chances are good that you will have upgraded from your Windows 98 platform. Windows ME is certainly not suitable for Web programming. It doesn't even technically support a development Web server like Personal Web Server. Windows 2000 Professional (or XP Professional) is a more robust environment, and I recommend that you use it if at all possible. In addition, it has the advantage of supporting a development version of Internet Information Server, which provides a professional testing environment for your work. Although we do not wish to appear Microsoft-centric in our approach to Dreamweaver, this combination of development tools is extremely popular, and we center our discussion around it. Rest assured, however, that very little of what is covered is specific to that environment, and you will have no trouble adapting the information to another set of tools or even a Macintosh development machine.

Project 1-1 Installing and Using Internet Information Services

Although Internet Information Server 5.0 (IIS) ships with Windows 2000 Professional, it is not installed by default. Follow these steps to install and configure IIS for your development machine.
   By the end of this project, you will have

- Installed Internet Information Services on your development computer
- Prepared your computer to send e-mail using the IIS SMTP server and CDO mail

Step by Step

1. Select Start | Settings | Control Panel from Windows.

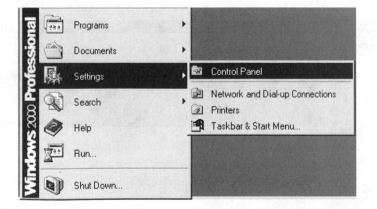

(continued)

2. In the Control Panel, double-click the Add/Remove Programs icon.

3. Select Add/Remove Windows Components.

4. After a brief pause, the Windows Component Wizard will appear. Check the box next to Internet Information Services (IIS) and click Next.

5. You may be prompted for your Windows 2000 CD.

(continued)

6. Windows will keep you posted as to its progress in copying the IIS files to your computer.

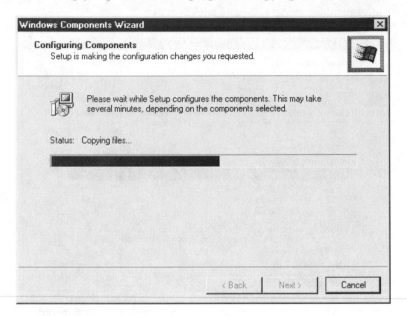

7. When finished, you will see the following screen indicating a successful installation of IIS:

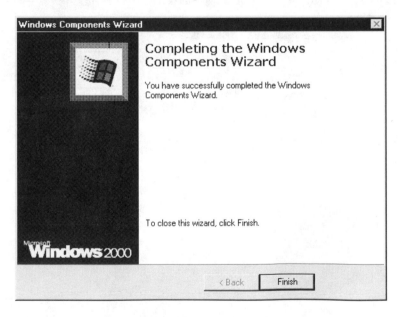

8. Close the Windows Component Wizard, but leave the Control Panel open. In the Control Panel, double-click the Administrative Tools icon.

9. Double-click Computer Management.

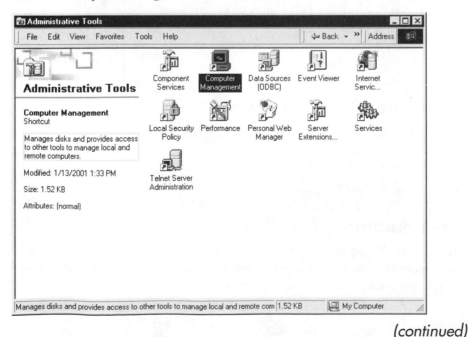

(continued)

10. Click the plus (+) sign next to Services And Applications and then the plus sign next to Internet Information Services. You will be presented with the components of your IIS installation. Using these, you can configure your server to respond the way you want it to.

There are three parts to the IIS installation:

- The default FTP site
- The default Web site
- The default SMTP virtual server

Project Summary

This project has helped you to install and configure Internet Information Services on your development machine. The knowledge you have gained by completing this process will help you in your understanding of the concepts that follow.

CRITICAL SKILL
1.6 Understand the Components
of an IIS Installation

Once you have Internet Information Services installed, you can learn more about the components that make it up and how they can be configured.

The Default FTP Site

FTP is the Internet protocol used to transfer files back and forth between machines, as you could probably tell from its name. It is used when getting a complete file from computer A to computer B is more important than viewing the contents of the file over the Web. For instance, when you create and save Web pages as HTML files on your development computer, they are only accessible once they are placed on a server that is connected to the Internet. If that server is a machine other than your development computer, you will use an FTP program, either within Dreamweaver or from a third party, to transfer those complete files to the appropriate directories on the server. From there, their contents can be viewed over the Web by browsers everywhere.

The default FTP site is the directory that has been created for this machine. Accessing FTP using this computer's name or using its default IP address will map you to this directory for uploading your files. There are a few things that you will want to do in the FTP site properties to complete the setup. You can access the FTP properties by right-clicking on the default FTP Site and selecting Properties from the pop-up menu.

Figure 1-6 shows the Default FTP Site Properties window. It has several tabs, only a couple of which are important to us at this point. The FTP Site tab lists the description and the IP address for this FTP site. You can change this description to anything you like.

The default setting for the IP address for this site is All Unassigned. That means that any FTP request that arrives at this machine for which a specific IP address has not been assigned will end up here. This is important if you are running multiple FTP servers on a single machine. Because you can run only one FTP site on IIS in Windows 2000 Professional, this is a less important setting. You can leave it as is or change it to one of the IP addresses that are assigned to your computer, either for your internal network or by your Internet connection.

Click on the Security Accounts tab and you will see the Properties window, shown in Figure 1-7.

There are two important settings on this page. The first is at the top where Allow Anonymous Connections has been enabled by default. If you want people to be able to log in to your FTP server anonymously and download things, you can leave this setting as is. But considering that this is going to be your development directory and not a site dedicated to downloadable files, you will probably want to disable anonymous connections for this server.

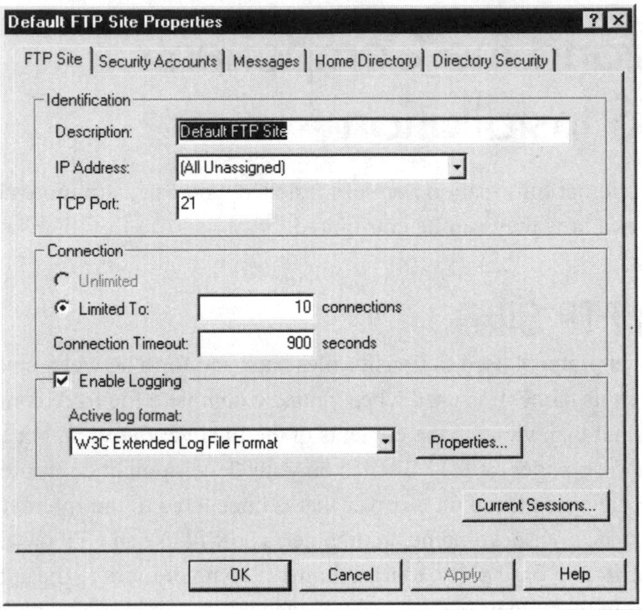

Figure 1-6 The Default FTP Site Properties window

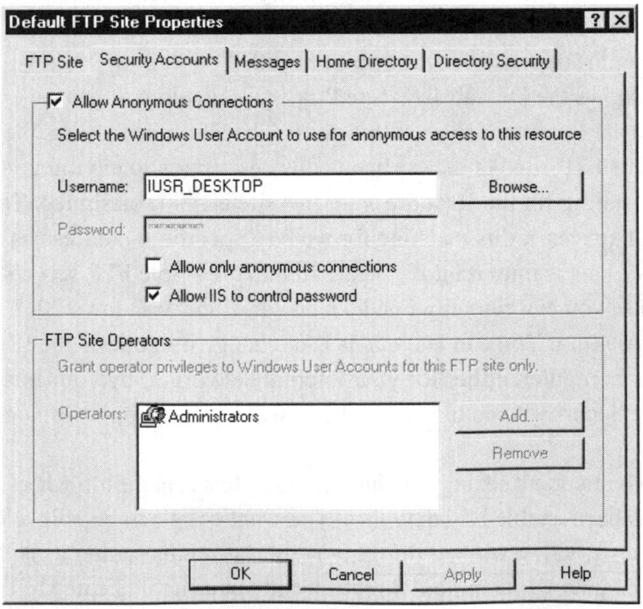

Figure 1-7 The Security Accounts tab of the Default FTP Site Properties window

NOTE

Allowing anonymous connections can be especially dangerous if you allow users to write files to the FTP site in the Home Directory tab, which will be discussed in a moment. A malicious user could then upload files that contained viruses or other damaging code. Although you need to be able to write to the FTP site in order to upload your Web pages, allowing an anonymous user to do so may very well result in the commandeering of your computer by an unscrupulous hacker.

Disabling anonymous connections means that only those users who are listed in the FTP Site Operators in the lower half of the screen can access the FTP server. The Administrators group is listed by default. You can leave it like this, add users explicitly, or add users to the Administrators group to allow access to only those people who need it.

Finally, look at the Home Directory tab, shown in Figure 1-8.

Although you can change the physical directory that is accessed by this FTP site, it is not really that useful to do so because you can have only one FTP site set up. You should, however, check the Write option so you can upload files into the directory from within Dreamweaver.

After you have made these simple changes, you are left with a basic, yet very useful FTP server that can be used to test the site you develop.

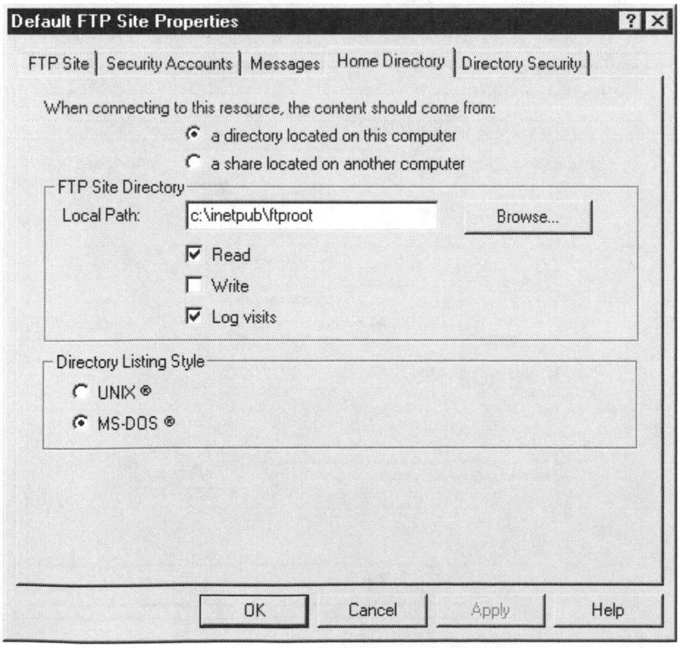

Figure 1-8 The Home Directory tab of the Default FTP Site Properties window

The Default Web Site

As with the ftproot directory in the FTP site setup, your server has a wwwroot folder that can serve as a default Web site. Any sites that you publish to this directory are available by browsing to http://machine_name/ or this server's default IP address if browsing from a local area network (LAN), or to http://localhost/ or http://127.0.0.1/ if the browser is actually on the server machine. Once you upload your pages using the FTP site defined earlier, you can view them using this default Web site.

NOTE

In addition to managing your IIS installation from the server itself, IIS allows you to perform many administrative tasks remotely over the Internet. See the IIS documentation for help setting up this capability.

As with the FTP site, there are a few things you are going to want to change in the default setup. Right-click on the default Web site in the Internet Information Services section of the Computer Manager and select Properties. The window shown in Figure 1-9 will be displayed.

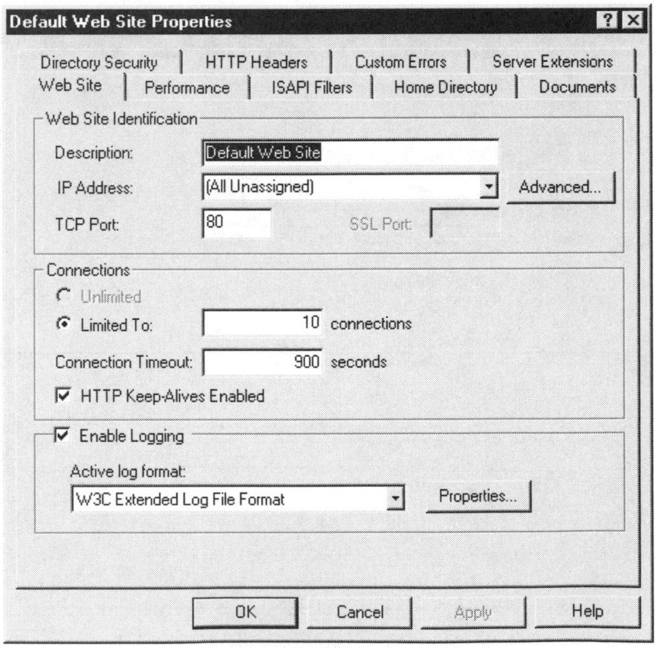

Figure 1-9 The Default Web Site Properties window

Just as with the FTP site properties, you can change the description and IP address if you like, but it is not necessary. Likewise, you can change the default directory (see Figure 1-10) if you like, but leave the checked options as they are until you learn more about the ramifications of changing these settings.

The information presented on the Documents tab (shown in Figure 1-11) is important to consider.

The page names listed here are the documents that IIS will consider as valid default pages for your site. Whenever you visit a site by typing just the domain name, such as www.dwteam.com, you are actually leaving off an important part of your request: which page from that site you want to see. IIS makes an assumption in this case based on the information in this tab. Starting from the top, IIS looks for pages that match these names, and when it comes to one, that is the page that is displayed by default for that directory. If a matching page is not found, and directory browsing has not been enabled, the user will get a permissions error stating they are not allowed to see information from the directory.

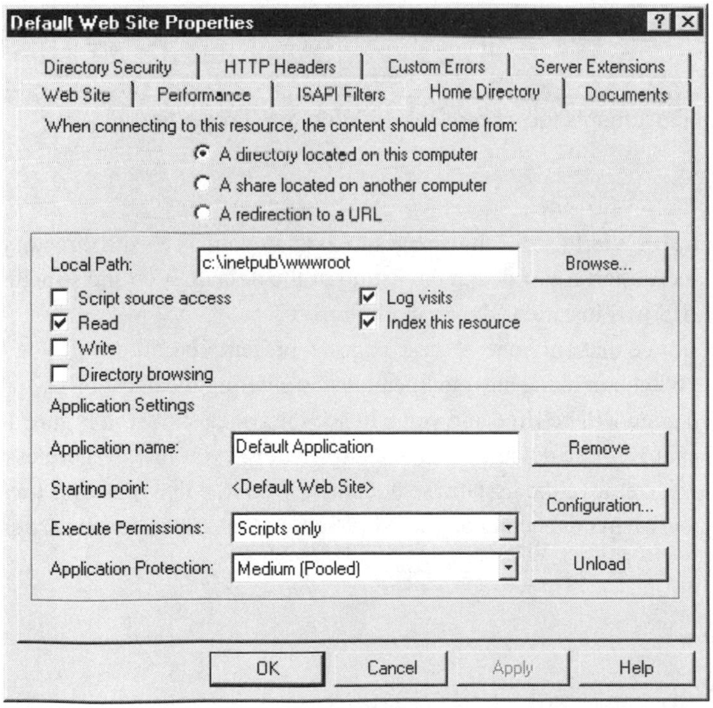

Figure 1-10 The Home Directory tab of the Default Web Site Properties window

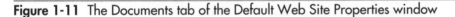

Figure 1-11 The Documents tab of the Default Web Site Properties window

By default, IIS will look for three pages to exist in your Web site directory: Default.htm, Default.asp, and iisstart.asp. Look at the listing of the default Web site structure that was created when IIS was installed, shown in Figure 1-12.

You will notice that only one of these pages is present, iisstart.asp. If you try to connect to your Web site without making any modifications by entering localhost or 127.0.0.1 in a browser, the iisstart.asp page will be fired and you will see the pages shown in Figure 1-13.

You can change these default documents to whatever you like. Regardless of what you choose, however, remove the iisstart.asp document from the list. You don't want the default pages to display when connecting to your site. Some common selections are shown here:

- Home.asp
- Home.htm
- Home.html
- Index.asp
- Index.htm
- Index.html

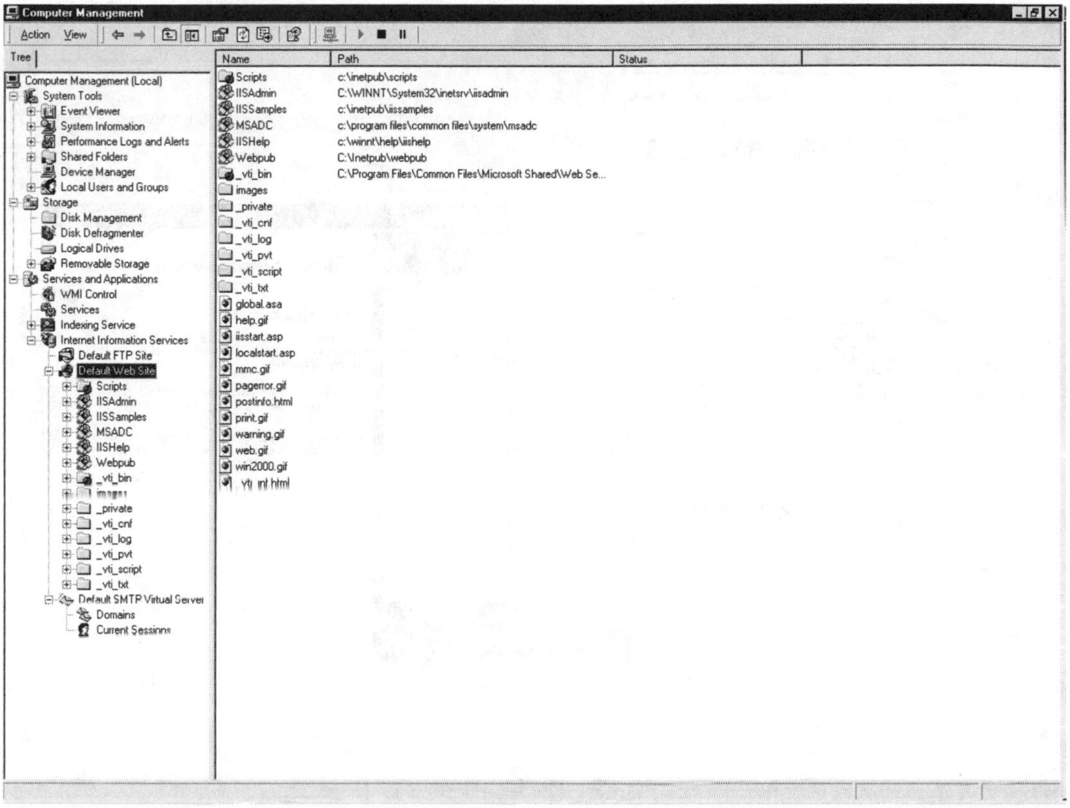

Figure 1-12 IIS's default Web site structure

- Default.asp
- Default.htm
- Default.html

Note that you can add as many of these documents as you would like, but the more that your site has to search through to find the page it is supposed to display, the longer it will take to get around to displaying it.

The Default SMTP Server

Although the default SMTP server is not strictly a part of setting up IIS to work with Dreamweaver, sending mail within Web applications is a very popular topic of discussion. We cover some preliminary setup so you can use both this SMTP server and CDO mail in our later examples.

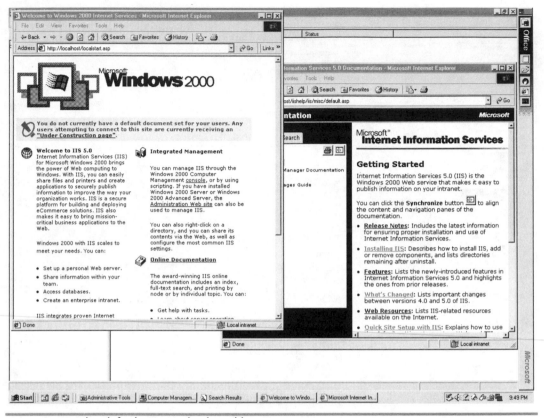

Figure 1-13 The default pages displayed by IIS

Simple Mail Transport Protocol (SMTP) is a very simple, as the name implies, way to send and receive mail across the Internet. With the advent of POP3 and IMAP, SMTP is not used much for mail retrieval, but it is still the standard for sending mail. The IIS installation installs an SMTP server along with IIS, so you can use your Web server to send mail, or you can use another mail server that you control, such as Exchange or Lotus Notes. All you have to know is its IP address and security settings. Let's take the simple route and set up the local Web server to send mail for you.

Two components are necessary to get CDO mail running on your server: the cdonts.dll file and an SMTP server. CDO for NTS1.2 is a lightweight version of the full Collaboration Data Objects that works with Microsoft Exchange. It comes with IIS5 and should be on your server if IIS is running, but it may not be registered.

To make sure cdonts.dll is registered, select Start | Run. In the Run dialog box, type **regsvr32 c:\winnt\system32\cdonts.dll**.

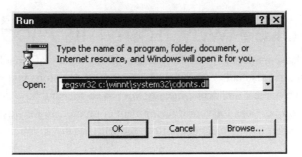

NOTE

You should use the path of your system folder in place of c:\winnt\system32. This is the default installation path for Windows 2000.

If the registration completes successfully, you will get a confirmation dialog box like this:

IIS will create a default SMTP virtual server and a drop directory where mail will be kept. See the IIS documentation for information on setting up additional remote and alias SMTP servers.

That should do it. Your server is now set up with a default SMTP server and the necessary CDO files. We make use of this in later examples.

Progress Check

1. What components are required to use CDO mail in your IIS installation?

2. Why should you enable the Write check box in your FTP Site Properties?

3. What is a default document?

---

1. cdonts.dll and an SMTP server
2. So you can upload files to your site's directory
3. The page that is loaded when no specific page is requested in a Web site URL

What to Take Away from This Module

You should now have a fairly good understanding of the history of the job you are about to undertake. You should also better understand the kinds of decisions you will need to make to prepare for the development and deployment of your Web site, and how to install and customize Internet Information Services for your development computer. In the next module, we take a tour of Dreamweaver so you can get comfortable with the environment in which you will be working.

✓

Module 1 Mastery Check

1. The series of numbers that are assigned to every host on the Internet is known as an _____.

2. Which of the following is the scripting language that you would use with the ASP server model?

   A. Visual Basic Script

   B. Perl

   C. C++

   D. JavaScript

   E. Tcl/Tk

   F. Java

3. The protocol used to send mail over the Internet is _____.

4. What features of Cold Fusion make it a popular choice for those with experience building static Web pages?

5. What is the protocol that is used to provide communications for the World Wide Web?

6. A collection of HTML documents that are related to one another and need to be displayed together form a _____.

7. What type of server provides a place to post your pages for review before they go live?

   A. A Testing server

   B. A Staging server

C. An Interim server

D. A Push server

8. Which protocol is responsible for making sure that all of the packets of a Web transmission have arrived?

   A. Transmission Control Protocol

   B. File Transfer Protocol

   C. Internet Protocol

   D. Hypertext Transmission Protocol

9. Name three server-side languages that could be deployed on a Linux Server.

10. What programming language is supported by JSP?

Module 2

The Dreamweaver MX Environment

Dreamweaver MX is the combination of what was Dreamweaver and UltraDev, plus a whole lot of new functionality. Because of the integration of these products, it is now possible for the resulting version of Dreamweaver to be developed with the entire product in mind. Where UltraDev seemed, in places, like functionality tacked on to an HTML editor, Dreamweaver MX has been redesigned to work more like an application development environment.

And you are presented with evidence of the thought that went into this new version from the moment you run the program for the first time. Although the Dreamweaver 4 interface is still available, the PC version of Dreamweaver MX offers two flavors of its new MDI (Multiple Document Interface) environment. In many ways, it is easier to use, especially on single monitor setups, but the sheer volume of it can be intimidating. The good news is that Dreamweaver goes out of its way to allow you to customize your working environment. A little practice will allow you to make good use of whichever interface you choose.

Let's spend some time getting to know the new Dreamweaver MX environment.

CRITICAL SKILL
2.1 Learn to Work with Dreamweaver MX

Dreamweaver MX offers what is essentially a three-pronged approach to Web development. Using the tools it provides, you can enter information such as text directly onto the page, have information inserted for you with built-in objects and behaviors, and go behind the scenes to work directly in the underlying code that makes up your page. To construct a site of any substance, you will almost certainly utilize a combination of these methods.

When you first launch Dreamweaver, you are presented with a selection of interfaces. Select the Dreamweaver MX interface for now. We look at changing that choice a little later. The Dreamweaver MX interface is shown in Figure 2-1. This default configuration can be customized to meet your needs. We discuss setting your preferences later in the module. The defaults will serve us quite nicely as we get started with Dreamweaver.

CRITICAL SKILL
2.2 Use the Site Panel

In Dreamweaver 4, the Site Manager was the center of much of your activity. In Dreamweaver MX, the Site Manager, while still important, is relegated to its own panel, making it more accessible during page design. It is also easier to get now that Dreamweaver supports the editing of multiple pages, which you can select with tabs along the bottom of the design area. But the Site Manager, shown in Figure 2-2, still provides a powerful command center from which to manage all of your Web sites. Using it, you can define the characteristics of each site so that they can be administered efficiently, even if they use different server models and reside

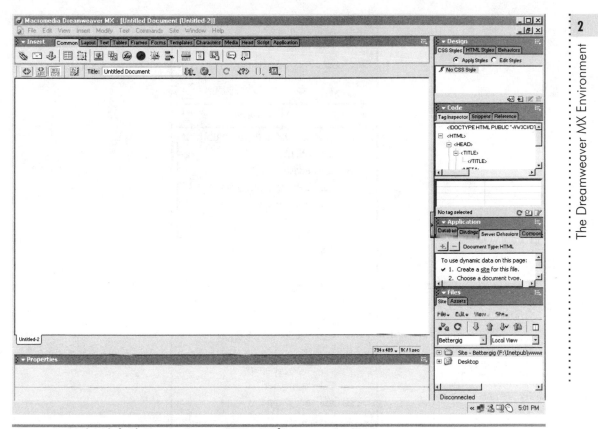

Figure 2-1 The default Dreamweaver MX interface

on different servers around the Internet. You can use Dreamweaver's built-in FTP program to send and receive files from any of your sites. And you can manage the growth of your site by adding pages, editing pages, and structuring the directories and pages that make it up. But in order to manage a site, it must first be defined.

NOTE

You can expand the Site Manager to its full size with local files on one side and remote on the other by clicking the Expand/Collapse button (the far right icon). Click the same icon on the expanded Site Manager to return to the regular design view.

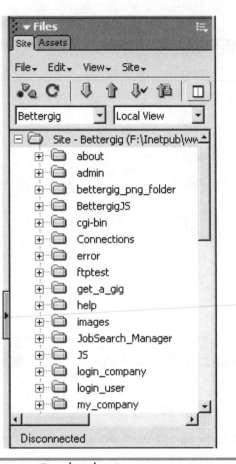

Figure 2-2 The new Site Manager Panel makes it easy to access your files as you edit pages.

On the toolbar of the Site Manager is a drop-down list box that lists all of your currently defined sites. If you are using a fresh installation of Dreamweaver, you will have Macromedia tutorial sites in the list. Selecting a site in the list makes that site active. Its directories and pages are then presented in the window below the toolbar.

Next to the site selection drop-down is another drop-down that allows you to select which view is presented in the Site Manager panel. You can select from four options:

- **Local View** Shows the files that currently exist in the local computer folder that you define as the repository for this site

- **Remote View**   Shows the files that currently exist on the production server you defined in the site setup

- **Testing Server**   Shows the files that currently exist on the testing server that you defined in the site setup

- **Map View**   Shows a graphical representation of the site files and their relationships to one another based on the links that Dreamweaver is able to identify

NOTE

Selecting a site and connecting to its remote server will change your Site Manager view to Remote view. This is important to remember as you begin to work. Make sure you are opening and editing the file that you intend to.

We cover defining your new site in Module 4.

CRITICAL SKILL
2.3 Work in the Document Window

Dreamweaver is a WYSIWYG (What You See Is What You Get) development tool. Although you can certainly build a Web page in a text editor such as Notepad and view the results after you have finished, the Web is, at its core, a presentational medium, and it's nice to actually see what you are doing while you're designing for it.

Development in Dreamweaver centers on the Document window, as shown in Figure 2-3.

The Document window is the graphical palette on which you will build your site. When first opened, a new window offers only a white background onto which you will place the text, images, and other elements that make up your site.

Underneath the design area is a status bar region that provides access to information and properties about the page you are working on.

The Tag Selector

At the left side of the status bar, just above the Property Inspector, is the Tag Selector. HTML files are made up of tags that describe the hierarchy of the content on the page. The Tag Selector provides a way to view and select that hierarchy as you edit your pages.

When a new page is created, the <body> tag is all that appears in the Tag Selector. As you add content, additional tags appear. If you place a table on the page, a <table> tag is generated. As you add rows and cells to that table, <tr> and <td> tags appear to represent those portions of the page. You can select an element on the page, and the appropriate tag becomes bold to indicate what is selected. You can also select a specific tag in the Tag Selector, and that

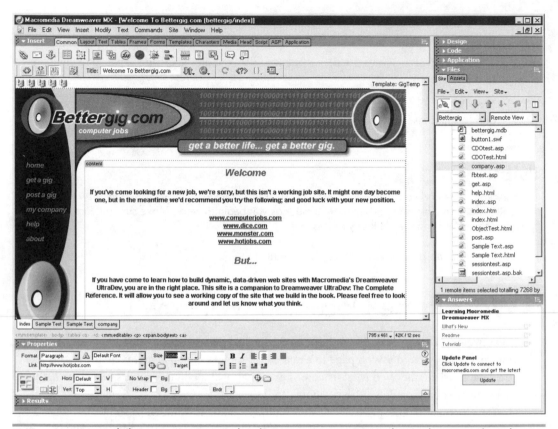

Figure 2-3 Several documents open in the design space. You can choose between them by using the tabs at the bottom.

portion of the page becomes selected. Once a tag is selected, it can be easily edited or deleted. This method of selecting specific portions of a page comes in especially handy when pages grow very complex and selecting the proper portion in Design view is difficult.

NOTE

The Tag Selector is dynamic, depending on what you have selected on the page. While nothing is selected, you will see only high-level tags, such as the <body> and <table> tags. As you select these tags or their graphical representations on the screen, their system of child tags will appear in the Tag Selector. This method of isolating portions of the page as you navigate it makes for a very elegant way to manage complex pages.

The Window Size Pop-Up Menu

When you are developing sites for public consumption (as opposed to a captive audience such as a corporate intranet), you must be constantly aware of the variety of client hardware and software your pages will encounter. Some users will have the latest processor with a high-resolution, 21+-inch monitor that does justice to their graphical masterpieces. Others, whose attention may be just as important to you or your client, may not know how to set their video cards to a resolution greater than 640×480 with 256 colors. Dreamweaver helps you develop a variety of settings with the Window Size pop-up menu.

```
592w
536 x 196   (640 x 480, Default)
600 x 300   (640 x 480, Maximized)
760 x 420   (800 x 600, Maximized)
795 x 470   (832 x 624, Maximized)
955 x 600   (1024 x 768, Maximized)
544 x 378   (WebTV)

Edit Sizes...
```

This menu lists some of the more common dimensions available to users, depending on what screen resolution they are using. By selecting an option, you can resize your screen to those dimensions and see a representation of the content area that your users will see. Some developers set their screens to a target dimension and design all of their content to conform to that size restriction. Others simply use this menu to check that their content scales gracefully on a variety of platforms.

Dreamweaver comes configured with several popular screen sizes. The first time you try them, you may feel quite closed in, especially in the vertical setting. Remember, though, that most browsers have chrome that you need to deal with. *Chrome* consists of the menu, button and address bars, and any advertising that may appear at the top of the interface, robbing you of screen real estate in which to place content. Although these default sizes do represent a reasonable selection of the circumstances you are likely to encounter, an Edit Sizes option is available in the menu that allows you to add, delete, or edit screen sizes to suit your needs.

NOTE

The Window Size menu works only when your page is not maximized in the design area. Maximized pages allow the tab system to work to switch between pages, but because use of the Window Size menu changes the dimensions of the page, it will work only when pages are "undocked" into the design area.

The Download Indicator

Just as you will encounter a variety of screen sizes and resolutions, you will also encounter a variety of bandwidth issues, including the connection speed over which your visitors view your pages. From the home user with the 28.8K modem, to the corporate users with a T1 or faster connection, you need to be prepared to serve content in a manner that keeps your audience's attention. On the Web, that generally means optimizing your content to load as quickly as possible over slower connection speeds.

Optimization tools are not perfect, because they cannot take into consideration things such as line quality, bandwidth saturation, and bottlenecks in the Internet backbone itself, but the download indicator can give you a pretty good idea of the average download time your users will experience. By taking the size of all of the elements represented on your page and dividing it by the number of bits per second in the connection speed you select, the status bar gives you an indication of how long this particular configuration will take to load. Thoughts on the proper download time of the average page vary, but you should certainly keep pages with normal content within a 10- to 15-second window if you can help it. Much longer, and your visitors are going to go looking for speedier pastures.

You can alter the download speed indicated in the status bar in your Preferences, which we cover shortly.

Organize Your Workspace with the Dreamweaver Panels

To the side of your design area, or surrounding it depending on where you choose to put them, are panels and toolbars that provide access to some of Dreamweaver's most powerful features. The objects, behaviors, commands, and other extensions that make up the core of Dreamweaver's functionality are primary reasons for its popularity in the Web development world.

NOTE

Extensions are add-in pieces of code that allow Dreamweaver to perform certain tasks. An important feature of the product is the fact that the extensibility model is documented. This allows anyone with the requisite programming skills to build extensions and distribute them to others, which makes Dreamweaver more powerful all the time. You can learn how to create extensions in *Dreamweaver MX: The Complete Reference* (McGraw-Hill/Osborne, 2002), also by Ray and Tom.

By default, Dreamweaver presents you with the panels shown in Figure 2-4. Additional panels are available in the Window menu.

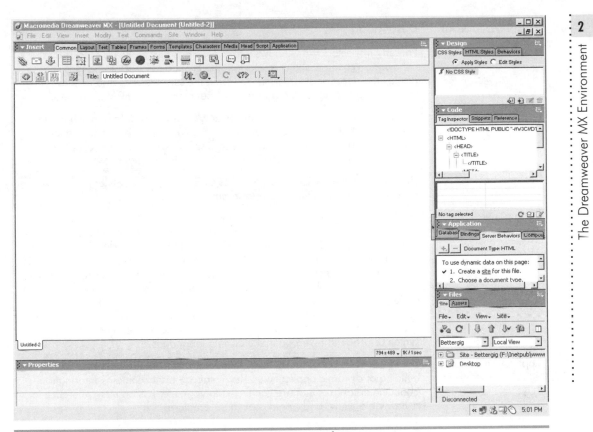

Figure 2-4 The default panels in the Dreamweaver interface

A list of the default panel groups and toolbars is shown in Table 2-1

Panel or Toolbar	Description
Insert toolbar	Objects are generally snippets of HTML code that are applied to your page. Many objects provide a user interface that allows you to set properties of the tags themselves, such as the number of rows or columns in a table. Others are simple HTML inserts such as the Horizontal Rule object. New to Dreamweaver MX are the Application Objects, which provide functionality that is specific to each of the server models. The Insert toolbar is dynamic—it changes what is offered to you depending on what kind of page you are editing.

Table 2-1 The Dreamweaver MX Panels

Panel or Toolbar	Description
Property Inspector	Property Inspectors are windows into the settings that make up objects and behaviors. When an object is selected, the Property Inspector changes to display the appropriate information about the selected item and to allow you to change properties and tag values without entering the HTML code itself.
Results panel	The Results panel is new to Dreamweaver MX and consolidates much of the information that Dreamweaver outputs about your site into one convenient area. A number of tabs are available to display search results, validation reports, browser and link checks, and other log information.
Design panel	The Design panel contains tabs, such as CSS Styles, HTML Styles and Behaviors, that affect the design, or client side of your site.
Code panel	The Code panel holds the Tag Inspector, Snippets, and Reference panels. The Tag Inspector shows an overview of the structure of your site by displaying the HTML tags that make it up. You can use it to add tags and edit the properties of the tags on the page. Many of the tag properties can access dynamic elements such as recordset fields so that they can be set on the fly by your application. Snippets are reusable chunks of code that you can add to your page. They are useful for storing lines of code that are used over and over again in your sites. You can add your own snippets to those provided with Dreamweaver. The Reference tab holds language references so that you can easily check syntax or usage in several popular coding languages.
Application panel	The Application panel group holds four panels that are important to the building of dynamic applications. The Database panel contains information about the databases that are connected to your site. It is an easy reference to review table, view, and stored procedure structures. The Bindings panel lists the specific recordsets that have been designated for the current page. It can also hold server-specific dynamic elements such as ASP request and response objects. You can drag and drop elements from the Bindings panel onto your pages. The Server Behaviors panel allows you to add, remove, and edit server behaviors such as repeat regions and dynamic navigation. Server Behaviors are chunks of server-side code that take parameters from the developer and use them to perform common server-side operations.
Files panel	The Files panel group houses the Site panel and the Assets panel. We have been working with the Site panel extensively. The Assets panel is a list of the various types of assets, such as images, templates, movies and scripts, that exist in your site folder. Dreamweaver searches the entire folder and caches the location of these support files for easy access.
Answers panel	The Answers panel is Macromedia's attempt to make Dreamweaver a truly self-supporting development environment. From within the Answers panel, you can search the Macromedia support site, get new tutorials, and even download extensions, all without leaving Dreamweaver.

Table 2-1 The Dreamweaver MX Panels *(continued)*

A numbers of other panels are available in the Window menu and can be selected and displayed wherever you like in the interface.

It is important to remember that you are not locked in to the default panel configuration. You can edit, move, dock, float, and create panels at will. In fact, some of the best new third party extensions coming out for Dreamweaver MX are new toolbars and panels that you can add to your environment.

You can dock and undock panel groups by dragging them around the screen. There is a little five-dot gripper in the upper-left corner of each panel group that you can use to grab the panel group with your mouse and reposition it on the screen. You can also use the right-click context menu to rename, maximize, and close panel groups.

Panels cannot be dragged and dropped. Instead, Macromedia has added a menu-based grouping function to the context menu of the panels. Right-clicking on any panel tab and selecting the Group With menu item lets you select an active panel group to add this panel to. The panel will be added to the tight end of the panels in that panel group. A little manipulation is necessary to get things in a specific order.

From the Group With menu, you can also create and name a new panel group, which the selected panel will be added to. This is actually the only way to close and remove a particular panel from a panel group. You must create a new panel group and then use the context menu to close that panel group.

NOTE

Make sure to take notice of the button on the panel group divider to the right of the design area. This rectangle button with the arrow on it collapses all of the panel groups and re-expands them with one click—a great feature when you need extra screen space.

CRITICAL SKILL
2.5
Learn Dreamweaver's Menu System

As you work in the Document window, you will access many features through the status bar and Dreamweaver's system of panels. The main Dreamweaver set of menus duplicates much of this functionality, but some features can only be accessed through menu and shortcut options. Following is a description of Dreamweaver's default menus.

The File Menu

The File menu contains menu items that relate to file management and page-level features. Table 2-2 describes the menu choices available in the File menu.

Menu Selection	Description
New	Opens the New Document window from which you may select the type of document that you wish to open
Open	Allows you to browse to and open a file
Open in Frame	Opens a selected file into the current frame
Close	Closes the current window
Save	Saves the page with the current filename replacing the currently saved version
Save As	Displays a Save As dialog box
Save As Template	Saves the current page as a template file in the Templates folder for future use
Save All	Saves all of the currently open pages
Revert	Disregards current changes and reloads the most recently saved version of the current file
Print Code	Print the code from the Code view of the current page
Import—Import XML into Template	Creates a new page with XML data inserted inside a template
Import—Import Word HTML	Opens an HTML file generated in Word and cleans up the code
Import—Import Table Data	Imports delimited data to form a new table
Export—Export Template Data as XML	Saves the editable regions in the current template as an XML file
Export—Export CSS Styles	Uses the current page's style sheets to create an external style sheet file
Export—Export Table	Exports table data as a delimited file
Convert—3.0 Browser–Compatible	Converts the current page to a format that is compatible with version 3.0 browsers
Convert—XHTML	Converts the current page to XHTML-compliant tags
Preview in Browser—Edit Browser List	Allows you to add, subtract, and configure the list of browsers loaded on your machine
Preview in Browser—Browser List	Lists the currently loaded browsers that Dreamweaver can use as preview browsers
Debug in Browser	Enables you to debug JavaScript within a local browser session, using any breakpoints you may have set

Table 2-2 File Menu Selections

Menu Selection	Description
Check Page	Provides a variety of page checks such as Accessibility, links, target browsers, and validation
Design Notes	Displays the Design Notes dialog box in which you may enter notes for the current page
Previous Files List	Displays up to four recently opened files for easy access
Exit	Closes open files and exits Dreamweaver

Table 2-2 File Menu Selections *(continued)*

The Edit Menu

The Edit menu provides you with commands that make page editing easier and allow you to recover from mistakes, as shown in Table 2-3.

Menu Selection	Description
Undo	Reverses the last action taken
Redo	Re-executes a reversed action
Cut	Removes the current selection and places it on the system keyboard for use elsewhere
Copy	Copies the current selection to the system clipboard for use elsewhere
Paste	Inserts clipboard date at the current cursor position
Clear	Removes the current selection
Copy HTML	Copies the current selection onto the system clipboard with the HTML tags
Paste HTML	Pastes the clipboard data to the page with the HTML tags
Select All	Highlights all of the tags and elements on the current page
Select Parent Tag	Selects the tag that surrounds the current selection
Select Child	Selects the first tag within the current selection
Find and Replace	Displays a dialog box in which you can enter the text you want to find on the page, and lets you enter text with which to replace the found instances
Find Next	Finds the next occurrence of the search string
Go to Line	Allows you to jump to a particular line in Code view

Table 2-3 Edit Menu Selections

Menu Selection	Description
Show Code Hints	Turns on the Code Hints window in Code view
Indent Code	Indents a selected line of code
Outdent Code	Outdents a selected line of code
Balance Braces	Checks to see that the braces that surround sections of JavaScript are balanced, that is, that each opening brace has a closing brace
Set Breakpoint	Sets a point at which execution of code will pause for debugging purposes
Remove All Breakpoints	Removes any breakpoints you have set
Repeating Entries	Options for editing repeating regions
Edit with External Editor	Launches an instance of the text editor you have configured in your preferences
Keyboard Shortcuts	Enables you to set, remove, and edit keyboard shortcuts that perform menu operations
Tag Libraries	Opens the Tag Library Editor where you can review and edit the various tags in all of the Dreamweaver-supported languages
Preferences	Displays the Preferences dialog box in which you can set numerous Dreamweaver properties

Table 2-3 Edit Menu Selections *(continued)*

The View Menu

The View menu controls what you see on the page in the design environment, as you can see in Table 2-4. These menu items toggle page elements to allow you to customize your work environment.

Menu Selection	Description
Code	Switches your working window to Code view, where you can view your page's underlying code
Design	Switches your working window to Design view, where you can view your page's visual layout
Code and Design	Divides your working window into two sections containing the Code view and the Design view onscreen at once

Table 2-4 View Menu Selections

Menu Selection	Description
Switch Views	Switches whichever view you are currently in (Code or Design) to the other available view
Refresh Design View	Reloads the page to properly display any changes you have made
Design View on Top	When using the Code and Design option, enables you to choose whether the Code view or Design view is in the top frame of the split screen
Server Debug	Allows you to debug Cold Fusion MX pages from within Dreamweaver
Live Data	Toggles live data on and off
Live Data Settings	Displays the Live Data Server Configuration dialog box
Head Content	Displays categories of information inserted into the head of the current page
Table View	Enables you to switch between Standard view and Layout view
Visual Aids	Provides a selection of layout and design aids, including whether borders are displayed on tables and layers, and whether image map overlays are visible
Code View Options	Provides a selection of Code view options such as Word Wrap and Line Numbers
Rulers—Show	Toggles the visibility of page rulers
Rulers—Reset Origin	Resets the 0,0 coordinates to the upper left of the page
Rulers—Increments	Controls the measurement that the rulers are incremented by
Grid—Show	Toggles the visibility of the design grid on the current page
Grid—Snap To	Controls whether design elements placed on the page snap to the grid lines
Grid—Edit	Displays the Grid Settings dialog box
Tracing Image—Show	Toggles the visibility of a tracing image
Tracing Image—Align with Selection	Aligns the top-left corner of a tracing image with the top-left corner of the current selection
Tracing Image—Adjust Position	Allows a tracing image to be positioned with the cursor keys
Tracing Image—Reset Position	Places the tracing image in the upper left of the current page
Tracing Image—Load	Allows the selection of a tracing image to be placed on the page

Table 2-4 View Menu Selections *(continued)*

Menu Selection	Description
Plug-ins—Play	Plays the currently selected plug-in
Plug-ins—Stop	Stops the currently playing plug-in
Plug-ins—Play All	Plays all plug-ins on the current page
Plug-ins—Stop All	Stops all plug-ins from playing
Hide Panels	Hides all panels except for the Design window
Toolbar	Toggles the visibility of the Document and Standard toolbars

Table 2-4 View Menu Selections *(continued)*

The Insert Menu

The Insert menu provides easy access to the wide variety of objects that are available to you in Dreamweaver. These objects automate the inclusion of HTML into your page using predefined modules of code. See Table 2-5 for menu choices.

Menu Selection	Description
Tag	Opens the Tag Selector to allow the selection of any available tag
Image	Allows the selection of an image that will be placed on the page
Image Placeholder	Inserts an Image Placeholder for early design purposes
Interactive Images	Provides a selection of interactive images such as Flash Buttons, rollover images, and Fireworks HTML that can be inserted in the current page
Media	Provides a selection of media such as Flash files and Java applets that can be inserted in the current page
Table	Inserts an HTML table with the selected properties
Table Objects	Inserts objects that are a part of tables, such as <tr> and <td> tags
Layer	Inserts a layer
Frames	Provides a selection of frame configurations to be added to the current page
Template Objects	Insert objects that are a part of templates, such as editable and repeating regions
Form	Inserts a form tag

Table 2-5 Insert Menu Selections

Menu Selection	Description
Form Objects	Provides a selection of form elements such as edit boxes and Submit buttons to be added to the current form
E-mail Link	Inserts an e-mail link at the current selection
Hyperlink	Inserts a hyperlink
Named Anchor	Inserts a named bookmark
Date	Inserts a static client-side date at the current selection
Horizontal Rule	Inserts an <hr> tag
Text Objects	Text objects allow you to apply formatting to text such as list parameters, HTML text markup and comments
Script Objects	Script objects let you include blocks of script and Server Side Includes in your code
Head Tags	Inserts head tags such as Meta and Keywords tags
Special Characters	Inserts special characters such as foreign currency, trademark, and copyright, and nonbreaking spaces
Application Objects	Contains server-side objects that are specific to the different server models supported by Dreamweaver
Get More Objects	Takes you to the Macromedia Exchange, where you can download additional objects

Table 2-5 Insert Menu Selections *(continued)*

The Modify Menu

The Modify menu allows you to make changes to the properties of selected elements on your pages, as you can see in Table 2-6.

Menu Selection	Description
Page Properties	Displays properties of the current page, such as Page Title, Background Image, or Link Colors
Template Properties	Displays the properties of a template
Selection Properties	Toggles the visibility of the Property Inspector
Edit Tag	Displays a dialog box with the available properties of the selected tag

Table 2-6 Modify Menu Selections

Menu Selection	Description
Quick Tag Editor	Toggles the visibility of the Quick Tag Editor
Make Link	Displays the file browser for selecting a file to link to
Remove Link	Deletes the currently selected link
Open Linked Page	Opens the linked page
Link Target	Sets the target of a link to the current window, a new window, or a particular frame
Table	Provides a variety of edits and properties for a selected table
Frameset	Provides a variety of edits and properties for a selected frameset
Navigation Bar	Modifies properties of a Navigation bar
Arrange	Sets the z-order of a layer in relation to other layers
Align	Aligns selected layers to one another
Convert	Allows you to convert tables to layers and layers to tables
Library	Adds and updates library items
Templates	Adds, updates, and modifies template files
Timeline	Adds, updates, and modifies timelines on the current page

Table 2-6 Modify Menu Selections *(continued)*

The Text Menu

The Text menu provides a variety of ways to control the display of one of the most important parts of your site, as you can see in Table 2-7.

Menu Selection	Description
Indent	Indents the current selection using the <blockquote> tag
Outdent	Removes the <dir> or <blockquote> tag to cancel indentation
Paragraph Format	Provides a variety of text-formatting options
Align	Provides a variety of text-alignment options
List	Provides a variety of list options such as numbered list and unordered list

Table 2-7 Text Menu Selections

Menu Selection	Description
Font	Provides a variety of text-formatting options
Style	Provides text style options such as bold and italic
HTML Styles	Provides a variety of HTML styles
CSS Styles	Provides a variety of CSS styles
Size	Allows the specific sizing of text
Size Change	Allows for relative sizing of text using + and −
Color	Allows you to choose the color of the currently selected text
Check Spelling	Runs a spell checker

Table 2-7 Text Menu Selections *(continued)*

The Commands Menu

Commands provide streamlined ways to traverse and alter code in your site. The Commands menu provides access to loaded commands and allows you to record your own commands in a macro-like fashion, as you can see in Table 2-8.

Menu Selection	Description
Start Recording	Records a series of steps to be saved as a command
Play Recorded Command	Plays the recorded command
Edit Command List	Edits the list of existing commands
Get More Commands	Navigates to the Macromedia Exchange, where you can obtain additional commands
Manage Extensions	Runs the Extension Manager
Apply Source Formatting	Uses the Source Formatting Profile to structure the current page
Apply Source Formatting to Selection	Uses the Source Formatting Profile to structure the currently selected chuck of code
Clean Up HTML	Removes HTML that does not conform to the options you select
Clean Up Word HTML	Removes HTML that does not conform to the options you select, with special emphasis on HTML added by Word

Table 2-8 Commands Menu Selections

Menu Selection	Description
Add/Remove Netscape Resize Fix	Adds a function that forces the page to reload when a Netscape browser is resized, fixing a bug in Navigator with pages that contain layers
Optimize Image in Fireworks	Displays the Optimize Image dialog box using Fireworks
Create Web Photo Album	Creates a photo album site using a directory of images
Set Color Scheme	Allows you to select a color scheme for the current page
Format Table	Enables a table format to be applied to the current table
Sort Table	Displays table sorting options

Table 2-8 Commands Menu Selections *(continued)*

The Site Menu

The Site menu provides access to features that control site-level aspects of your site, such as the Site Manager, site definitions, and FTP commands, as shown in Table 2-9.

Menu Selection	Description
Site Files	Displays the Site window
Site Map	Displays the Site window with the Site Map enabled
New Site	Opens the Site Definition window for creating a new site
Define Sites	Opens the Site Definition window where you can create a new site or edit existing sites
Get	Gets a file or files from a remote server
Check Out	Checks out a file for editing
Put	Places a file on the remote server
Check In	Checks in a file after editing
Undo Check Out	Reverses a file checkout
Locate in Site	Selects the current document in the sitefile list
Reports	Provides a series of workflow and HTML reports that contain information about your site
Deploy Supporting Files	Uploads Data Connection support files for the ASP.NET server model

Table 2-9 Site Menu Selections

The Window Menu

The Window menu provides show and hide access to all of the panels that make up the Dreamweaver design environment. It is unnecessary to list them all here, but any window or panel in the program can be made visible or invisible by selecting it in this menu.

The Help Menu

The Help menu provides access to Dreamweaver help files and a variety of online support services at Macromedia.

CRITICAL SKILL
2.6 Learn About Dreamweaver MX Objects

When you start Dreamweaver, you should notice the Insert toolbar at the top of the interface. The Insert toolbar contains several tabs, each of which contains several icons representing the various things you can do, as shown in Figure 2-5. These tabs represent categories that enable you to keep objects organized by functionality or by their source, or by any other method that makes them easy for you to use.

In concept, objects are fairly simple. Their main purpose is to accept input from the user and place it as HTML code in the body of the page they are applied to. In practice, every object works a little differently. With practice, you will learn what to expect from each of them. The following sections look at three objects that vary in the way they are implemented.

The Horizontal Rule Object

The simplest type of object is represented by the Horizontal Rule object on the Common tab of the Insert toolbar. A horizontal rule is simply a line that rules horizontally across the page. Although it does have properties that can be assigned to it, a Horizontal Rule object can be represented with nothing more than an <hr> tag. At the point on the page where that tag appears, a line will be placed on the page. Place your cursor at the desired location on the page, locate the Horizontal Rule object on the Insert toolbar, and click it. The horizontal rule will appear on the page.

Figure 2-5 The Dreamweaver Insert toolbar

After your object is placed on the page, you may want to edit its properties to change, in the case of the Horizontal Rule object, the height or width, the color, or the alignment. When you select the Horizontal Rule object, its details appear in the Property Inspector panel. The Property Inspector displays the standard properties that apply to the object that is selected. For instance, when the Horizontal Rule object is selected, the Property Inspector looks like Figure 2-6.

On the Property Inspector for the Horizontal Rule object, you can set the name of the Horizontal Rule object, the width in pixels or percent, the height, the alignment, and whether the line is shaded or not. Those are the basic settings and represent the most-used attributes for this object. A complete list of attributes can be accessed in the Tag Inspector panel in the Code panel group.

The Tag Inspector provides a high-level look at the tag structure of your site. You can use it to review your page's tags, add tags, and most importantly, set the attributes of the tags in the complete properties list provided. If you select the horizontal rule on your page with the Tag Inspector open, the inspector will jump to and highlight the <hr> tag. You can use the list in the bottom portion of the panel to view and set properties.

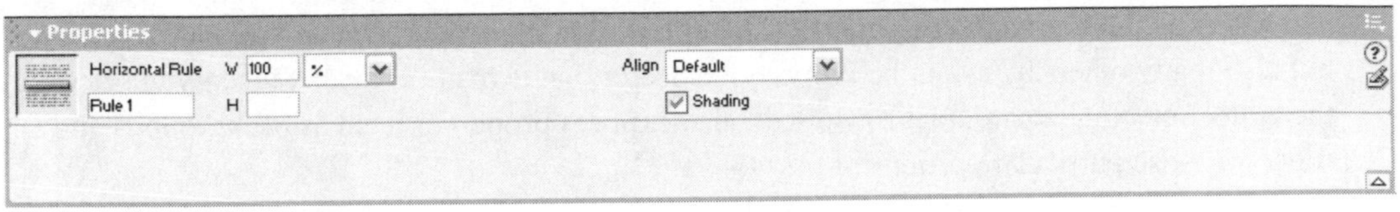

Figure 2-6 The properties of the Horizontal Rule object

The Horizontal Rule is the simplest kind of object. It asks for no input from the user to place the basic object, and then it enables you to set properties afterward.

NOTE
The Horizontal Rule object and the Table object (discussed next) are both dependent on your cursor position. They will place the object at your cursor's position.

The Table Object

If you have spent any time at all with HTML, then you are familiar with the Table object. Originally designed to allow the display of information in columns, Table objects have evolved into a primary means of allowing more complex visual designs on HTML pages. The Dreamweaver Table object enables you to build complex table structures to accommodate your design.

NOTE
Tables have become a popular method of display because they are lightweight and are supported by the earlier browser versions. The technically preferred method of creating pixel-perfect designs is the use of layers. Layers, however, are not supported prior to the version 4 browsers, and then not even consistently across brands. Additionally, old habits die hard, and many designers still prefer to use tables.

The Table object is much like the Horizontal Rule object in that it is dependent on your cursor's position. It will place a table on your page consistent with the properties you set; but in this case, you are asked by the Insert Table dialog box to set some of the properties up front.

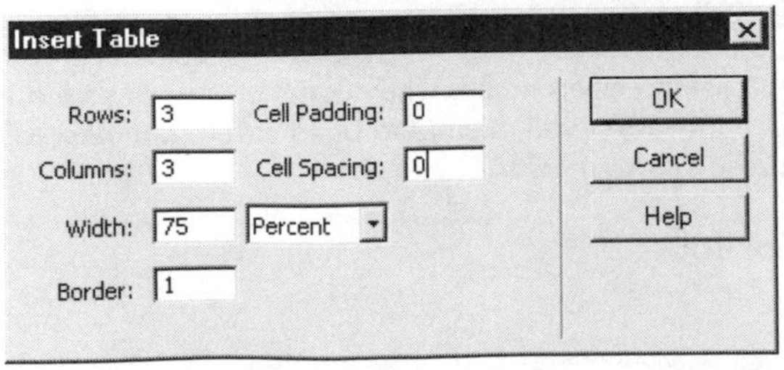

After the table is on the page, you can alter not only the properties that you set originally, but also many others by using the Property Inspector that is made available when you select the table. Selecting a particular row or cell also exposes properties such as backgrounds and fonts for those particular portions of the table.

The Layer Object

Whereas the Horizontal Rule and Table objects are dependent on the position of your cursor within the current HTML, the Layer object is a part of the newer Cascading Style Sheets (CSS) specification that allows absolute positioning of items on your page. When you select the Layer icon on the Insert panel, your cursor changes to crosshairs. Using your mouse, you may draw the layer at the position and to the size that you desire.

NOTE

Actually, drawing a layer in this fashion is only one of three ways to insert a layer into your page. You can also select Layer from the Insert menu and set it precisely using numeric settings. Or, you can use a CSS definition to set the properties of a new Layer object.

After your layer is on the page, you can use the Properties Inspector to alter any of the available Layer properties, including positioning and the HTML tag that is used to create the layer.

These three examples represent the diverse ways that you may be asked to interact with objects. Just remember that objects are intended to save you work by taking your input and turning it into HTML. Each object may ask for your input in a slightly different way, but you will get used to it with a little practice.

Table 2-10 lists the groups of objects available in the Insert bar.

Insert Bar Tab	Contains
Common	The most common of the HTML elements, such as hyperlinks, images, tables, and layers. The Common tab also contains objects such as Fireworks HTML and Flash files.
Layout	Elements from the Layout View option in Version 4 of Dreamweaver. These objects allow you to draw layers on the screen as you might in a desktop publishing environment. They can then be converted to layers, and Dreamweaver will attempt to build a very complex table structure that preserves your layout.

Table 2-10 The Insert Bar Tabs

Insert Bar Tab	Contains
Text	A number of objects related to text markup. The objects here are divided between the font-based and the HTML-based manipulation of text. You will learn in Module 12 that it is wise to utilize the HTML elements and control their appearance with style sheets, but other options are available to you here.
Tables	The Table object (as on the Common tab) and each of the individual elements that make up tables, such as the <tr> and <td> tags.
Frames	A selection of common framesets that can be dragged onto the page.
Forms	The Form object itself and all of the elements that are used to construct forms, such as buttons, text field, menus, and radio buttons.
Templates	A collection of objects to create templates and nested templates and to create editable regions, optional regions, and repeating regions.
Characters	A host of special characters, including line breaks, copyright, and foreign currency characters.
Media	Flash, Shockwave, Java, and ActiveX elements.
Head	Elements that are common to the head of an HTML document, such as metatags, keywords, and descriptions.
Script	Script, NoScript, and Server Side Include objects.
Application	Server-side objects common to the server models, such as recordsets, repeat regions, recordset navigation, and master-detail pagesets.
Server Specific	Each server model has its own set of unique objects. Depending on which server model you have chosen for the current page, a dynamic tab will appear presenting you with a selection of objects applicable to your page.

Table 2-10 The Insert Bar Tabs *(continued)*

Ask the Expert

Q: Can I get more objects than the ones that come with Dreamweaver?

A: Yes. Additional objects, behaviors, commands, server behaviors, and other items (known as extensions) can be downloaded from Macromedia's Web site and from other places around the Web.

(continued)

Q: How can I build my own extensions?

A: Anyone with a good knowledge of JavaScript can learn to create all of the extensions in Dreamweaver. An exact description of how to do so is beyond this book, but you will find detailed instructions In *Dreamweaver MX: The Complete Reference* and in *Building Dreamweaver and UltraDev Extensions.*

CRITICAL SKILL
2.7 Learn About Dreamweaver MX Behaviors

Objects are designed to place code within the body of your HTML page, usually as HTML tags with a series of attributes. But, sometimes you need to do more complex things on your page. Often, your desired effect requires the use of JavaScript functions triggered by events on the page. Behaviors are Dreamweaver's way of handling these issues.

The Behaviors Panel resides in the Design panel group by default. Behaviors are used for client-side events. Because of this, and because different browser brands and versions implement client-side code differently, it is important to apply behaviors that are meant to work in your target browser.

A successful behavior has three parts: an object, an event, and an action. The object is the part of your page that the event will occur against. For instance, you may have a button that will trigger an action when it is clicked. The button is the object, the click is the event, and the response is the action.

To illustrate, follow this example. On a new Dreamweaver page, place a Form button from the Forms tab of the Insert bar. Make sure the Behaviors panel is visible and select the button. The title bar of the panel will indicate the object to which you are about to apply your behavior. This indication actually shows the tag that is selected. By default, the Form button is created as a Submit button, so you will notice that the title of the Behaviors panel says <submit> actions. If you change the button type to Reset, the title bar will read <reset> actions; and if you change it to None, it will read <button> actions.

Click the plus (+) button on the Behaviors panel to view a list of available behaviors. Select the Go To URL Behavior. In the resulting dialog box, set the URL that you want to go to. Now, whenever this button is selected, your Go To URL Behavior will appear in the list of behaviors on the panel.

Next, select an event by selecting it in the list and clicking the down arrow. A list of available events is presented. Select the *onClick* event to cause your action to be followed when the button is clicked.

Now, take a look at the HTML source window to see what this behavior did in your code:

```html
<html>

<head>

<title>Untitled Document</title>

<meta http-equiv="Content-Type" content="text/html; charset=iso-8859-1">

<script language="JavaScript">

<!--

function MM_goToURL() { //v3.0

  var i, args=MM_goToURL.arguments; document.MM_returnValue = false; _

  for (i=0; i<(args.length-1); i+=2) eval(args[i]+".location='"+args[i+1]
    +"'");

}

//-->

</script>

</head>


<body bgcolor="#FFFFFF">

<form name="form1" method="post" action="">

  <input type="button" name="Submit" value="Submit"
onClick="MM_goToURL('parent','www.bettergig.com');return
 document.MM_returnValue">

</form>

</body>

</html>
```

Note that the behavior did two things in the preceding code, one in the body of the page and one above the body. To the basic button tag, the behavior added the *onClick* event and the parameters you set within a call to a function called *MM_goToURL*. That function was also inserted above the body, ready to be called by the click of the Submit button.

Table 2-11 lists the behaviors that are available in Dreamweaver.

Behavior	Associated Action
Call JavaScript	Enables you to define a JavaScript routine that will be run when the associated event occurs
Change Property	Enables you to dynamically alter the properties of several high-level HTML tags, such as Span, Form, and Layer
Check Browser	Allows the determination of a visitor's browser type and subsequent redirection to suitable content
Check Plugin	Checks for the existence of a required plug-in (such as a Flash Player) on a visitor's computer
Control Shockwave or Flash	Supplies external controls to allow the control of Flash and Shockwave files
Drag Layer	Allows the creation of a variety of effects based on a user dragging and dropping layers and their content
Go To URL	Allows the variety of events available to trigger redirection to a URL
Hide Pop-Up Menu	Allows you to set an element on your page to hide a Dreamweaver- or Fireworks-created pop-up menu
Jump Menu	Enables you to edit an existing jump menu
Jump Menu Go	Adds a Go button to an existing jump menu
Open Browser Window	Opens a new, customized browser window when the associated event is triggered
Play Sound	Plays a sound file of a variety of types when the associated event is triggered
Popup Message	Triggers a JavaScript alert (a pop-up message box) to display a message to your user
Preload Images	Causes all images to be preloaded when the page loads; especially useful for rollover buttons and images that are initially hidden

Table 2-11 Standard Dreamweaver Behaviors

Behavior	Associated Action
Set Nav Bar Image	Enables you to edit an existing navigation bar
Show-Hide Layers	Gives you control over the visibility of layers based on the triggering of certain events
Swap Image Restore	Restores an image to its original state after an event has triggered a Swap Image
Swap Image	Swaps an original image for another image when an event occurs
Validate Form	Validates the contents of form fields before submission
Set Text	Sets the text property of the status bar, a layer, a text field, or a frame
Show Pop-Up Menu	Allows the editing and creation of Dreamweaver and Fireworks pop-up menus and the assignment of the *Show* method to an element on your page
Timeline	Provides a variety of controls to manipulate an existing timeline

Table 2-11 Standard Dreamweaver Behaviors *(continued)*

The Dreamweaver MX Environment

2

Progress Check

1. The components of Dreamweaver that insert the standard HTML constructs into your pages are known as what?

2. Which menu is used to toggle the visible panels while using Dreamweaver?

3. Which menu selection provides access to the properties of the current page, such as its background color and margins?

---

1. Objects
2. The Window menu
3. Modify | Page Properties

Set Your Dreamweaver MX Preferences

As alluded to previously, Dreamweaver goes out of its way to allow you to customize your work environment. Selecting the Preferences option from the Edit menu presents you with 20 categories, covering everything from color schemes, to style formats, to which tag is used when you insert a layer. The preference settings are fairly self-explanatory, so we won't cover them all here. Just keep in mind that any time you want something to work a little differently in Dreamweaver, you can probably change it in the Preferences menu. Spend some time here when you first begin using the program. It will acquaint you with what Dreamweaver can do for you to make your development experience go more smoothly, whether you're customizing the way code is displayed or adding browsers to the preview list.

One preference of note is the ability to change the Dreamweaver Environment in which you are working. On the General tab, you will notice a button called Change Workspace. Clicking that button displays the same dialog box that you used to select your interface when Dreamweaver ran the first time. You can use it anytime to select between the three environments. Once you restart Dreamweaver, your new selection will be implemented.

Project 2-1 Setting Your Dreamweaver MX Preferences

There are a number of preferences that you can set, and your setup is likely to be different from anyone else's. It is most important at this point to understand the kinds of things you have control over in the Preferences dialog box.

Project Goals

By the end of this project you will have

- Set some basic properties
- Learned your way around the Preferences dialog box in Dreamweaver

Step by Step

1. Choose Edit | Preferences. The Preferences dialog box will appear.

2. Check the top box on the first panel, Show Only Site Window On Startup. This will cause Dreamweaver to display the Site Window without opening a new untitled document every time you start the program.

3. If you want Dreamweaver to open new files into new design windows, leaving other current documents open, leave the next option, Open Files In New Window, checked. If you prefer files that you open to replace the currently open page, uncheck this box.

4. Select the Preview In Browser category from the left side of the Preferences dialog box.

5. Click the Plus (+) button at the top to add installed browsers to your list.

6. When the dialog box opens, provide a name for a new browser, such as Netscape or Opera, and use the browse button to navigate to the executable file that runs the browser.

7. You may also set this new browser as a primary or secondary browser so that you can use the F12 hotkey to view the current page in a browser with one keystroke.

8. Click on the Status Bar category.

9. In the Status Bar section, set a new browser size. These browser sizes are available in the status bar of your design window and alter the design window size to keep your design constrained within certain proportions.

(continued)

10. Click near the bottom of the Width column and enter **700**.

11. Click near the bottom of the Height column and enter **500**.

12. Under Description, enter Standard for this page size.

13. Once you save, this page size will be available to you in your status bar.

Project Summary

This project has familiarized you with the Preferences dialog box in Dreamweaver. Now that you are able to find your way around and make changes to the settings, feel free to experiment with the settings represented here and see how your working environment is affected by your changes. You may find settings that help you work more efficiently.

Progress Check

1. If you were having trouble with the way your custom code was being rendered in Dreamweaver, where would you first check to try to remedy the problem?

2. How do you access the Properties panel in Dreamweaver MX?

3. On what page of the Properties panel can you tell Dreamweaver which browsers you have loaded?

What to Take Away from This Module

There is a lot to the Dreamweaver interface. An incredible amount of thought has gone into its design and layout, especially considering all of the advanced tools that are now integrated into the program. The consolidation of panels into panel groups and extremely useful additions like the Results panel allowed Macromedia to end up with a very concise and useful interface that is efficient for both designers and programmers. In Module 3, we put these tools to good use as we begin building pages in Dreamweaver MX.

---

1. The Code Rewriting page of the Properties panel
2. From the Edit | Properties menu
3. The Preview In Browser page

✓ Module 2 Mastery Check

1. What are the three prongs of Dreamweaver's approach to Web page construction?

2. What are the three parts of the implementation of a behavior?

3. What is the main purpose of an object?

4. Many of Dreamweaver's features, such as objects, behaviors, and commands, are made available on _____.

5. What are the four views available on the Dreamweaver Site Panel?

6. The _____ provides a way to view and select the page hierarchy as you edit your pages.

7. _____ Mode allows you to draw tables and cells on your page.

8. Extensions that place javascript actions onto your page are known as _____

9. What is the purpose of the Download Indicator?

10. You can test your page at different screen sizes using the _____

Module 3

Creating a Web Page

Now that you have seen some of the interesting features of Dreamweaver and know how to create a site, it's time to start creating pages. The easiest way is to dive right in and create a new document.

3.1 Open, Edit, and Save a Web Page in Dreamweaver MX

As with most programs, Dreamweaver has the standard File menu that you've seen a million times. Inside this menu are the commands you'll need to create, open, and save your Web page. When you open Dreamweaver and choose the File menu, this is what you'll see:

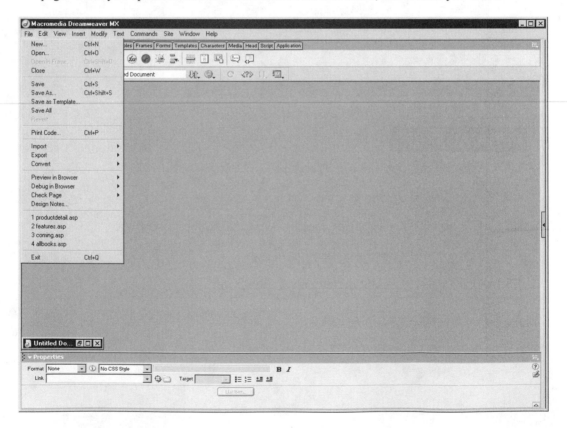

Most of the standard items that you would expect to find in a File menu are there:

● **New** Create a new document.

- **Open**   Open an existing document.

- **Save**   Save the current document.

- **Save As**   Save the current document and give it a filename.

There are quite a few other commands in the File menu, which we discuss later, but for now all you need to concern yourself with are the four commands just shown and one more, Preview In Browser. This command will allow you to preview the current page in the browser of your choice, which you should have set up in Module 2. Also, it is a good idea to get into the habit of using keyboard shortcuts. These are great time-savers for repetitive tasks, such as saving a document or previewing the Web page. To save your document, you can either choose File | Save, or you can press CTRL-S (COMMAND-S on the Macintosh). To preview your Web page using your primary browser, you can press F12, or CTRL-F12 for your secondary browser.

Naming Your Page

When you open Dreamweaver, you may notice that a blank new document is already created for you. The document is open, but it has not been saved and, therefore, it has no filename. The first thing you should do when designing a new page is to save it. If you get in the habit of saving the page immediately, you will be spared headaches in the event of computer crashes, program crashes, power failures, or other mishaps. The first time you try to save a page, the Save As dialog box will pop up and prompt you for a filename.

You should develop a system for naming your pages that will make it easy to determine the purpose of the page. Also, make sure you follow standard Web naming conventions so your pages will be viewable by anyone and any browser:

- **Don't use spaces**   Some browsers, such as Netscape, won't be able to load your page.

- **Use only letters, numbers, underscores, or dash characters**   Avoid all special characters.

- **Be aware of case-sensitive systems**   Some systems are case sensitive, such as Unix-based servers. If you name your page Home.jsp, a user who types in http://www.yoursite.com/home.jsp may not be able to find your page.

NOTE

The same naming conventions apply to images or any other files that you might be using in your Web site.

Editing the Page

With a new page open in Dreamweaver, you are free to insert text, images, form elements, or whatever type of content you want to include in your page. The first thing you'll notice about Dreamweaver is that when you type something on the page, it appears in the top left corner of the page. This is one of the hardest concepts to understand for the newcomer to Dreamweaver. You can't put your cursor in the middle of the page and start typing. Many desktop publishing programs and some Web page editors work this way. Dreamweaver needs to be told exactly where to put the text. But we get to that later. For now, if you type some text on the page and then browse the page, the text will show up in the top left corner.

Another thing you may notice about typing in your text is that you can only use one space—if you try to hit the spacebar a second time, nothing will happen. This is because a Web browser ignores all spaces beyond the first space. You can put spaces into your source code freely without worrying that they will appear on the Web page. This allows you to format your source code easily. You can try this out by going into HTML source view and clicking Show Code View.

If you place a bunch of spaces and carriage returns in the text that is on the page, and then go back into Design view, you'll see that it makes no difference. Also, if you browse the page, the spaces won't show up on the page.

So how do you get a space to appear? By holding down SHIFT and CTRL and pressing the spacebar. This inserts a *nonbreaking space* into your document. This is a special kind of space that is Web-friendly and will display as a space in the browser. If you look at the nonbreaking space in the source code, you'll see that it is represented by a special character: * *. These Web-safe special characters begin with an ampersand character and end with a semicolon. Some other useful special characters are shown in Table 3-1

Character	Description	Code
©	Copyright character	*©*
®	Registered	*®*
™	Trademark	*™*

Table 3-1 Special Characters in the Dreamweaver Insert Menu

Character	Description	Code
£	British pound	£
¥	Japanese yen	¥
•	Euro dollar	€
"	Left quote	“
"	Right quote	”
—	Em dash	—

Table 3-1 Special Characters in the Dreamweaver Insert Menu *(continued)*

These characters are all accessible from the Insert menu, and also from the Insert bar in the Characters tab.

CRITICAL SKILL
3.2 Add Text to a Page and Format It

Your text probably looks a little drab if you are just typing it in, but it's easy to apply different font characteristics to the text using Dreamweaver. Although there are many ways to apply styles to your text, the easiest is using the text Property Inspector. The Inspector is the panel that generally appears at the bottom of the screen (although you can place it anywhere) and allows you to change properties for whatever selection was made in the Dreamweaver environment. If you have an image selected, an image Property Inspector will appear. When you select some text, a text Property Inspector will appear.

As you can see, there is quite a bit of built-in functionality on the Property Inspector. Much of this functionality is also available from the contextual menu. Like the Property Inspectors, the contextual menus can be different depending on your selection. When you highlight some text on the page and right-click (CONTROL-click on the Macintosh), the standard text contextual menu will be shown. If you happen to have an image highlighted, the contextual menu will change and display items that pertain to images.

The text formatting available on the Inspector and contextual menu will add <font> tags to your text. For example, if you highlight some text and then add a font style of Arial and click the B button on the Property Inspector to make the text bold, this is what you'll see in Code view:

```
<b><font face"Arial, Helvetica, sans-serif">
This text is Arial and bold </font></b>
```

This is certainly an acceptable way to add text formatting, but you should be aware that the current trend is toward the acceptance of cascading style sheets (CSS) instead of <font> tags. Style sheets also make it much easier to define global changes to your page or your site. For example, let's say you have three paragraphs on the page and each paragraph has a heading. The heading could be formatted with an <h1> tag or something similar. The text in the paragraphs could be formatted as Arial with a size of 3. Now what happens when you want to change the heading style to an <h2> tag instead? Or what if you want to change the text style from Arial to Verdana? You would have to find all three instances of the style on the page and make the change. Compound this over 100 or more pages and you can see the problem. With a CSS style, you simply redefine the style that you used for the heading or the paragraph text, and it will magically change in all places and in all pages.

Not only are CSS styles just plain easier to use, <font> tags are deprecated by the W3C, which means that they are being phased out in favor of style sheets. Also, when you become proficient with CSS, you'll soon be able to perform style manipulation and customization with JavaScript.

Style sheets can be defined for the page or for the entire site. Dreamweaver has a special panel that makes it easy to find your styles and use them.

To create a new style, you can click the + icon in the CSS panel, or you can use the contextual menu and choose the New CSS Style item.

Paragraph Format	▶
List	▶
Align	▶
Font	▶
Style	▶
HTML Styles	▶
CSS Styles	▶
Size	▶
Templates	▶
Edit Tag <body>...	Ctrl+F5
Insert HTML...	
Edit Tag Code <body>...	
Make Link	
Remove Link	
Open Linked Page	
Target Frame	▶
Add to Color Favorites	
Create New Snippet	
Cut	
Copy	
Paste	
Design Notes for Page...	
Page Properties...	

CSS Styles submenu:

| ✔ None |
| New CSS Style... |
| Edit Style Sheet... |
| Attach Style Sheet... |
| Export Style Sheet... |
| Design Time style sheets... |

Either method will bring up the following dialog box:

New CSS Style   ✕

Tag: |.unnamed1 ▾| OK

Type: ○ Make Custom Style (class)   Cancel
       ● Redefine HTML Tag
       ○ Use CSS Selector

Define In: ● |(New Style Sheet File) ▾|
           ○ This Document Only   Help

The style will be unnamed by default, but you should give it a name that means something to the application. If your CSS style definitions are readable, your code will be self-documenting, and you will find that it is easier to read the code listings and make changes when necessary. For example, you might have a list of styles like the following:

- MainHeading
- SubHeading
- BodyText
- CodeListing
- FinePrint
- MenuItems

You can create a new style sheet file, or you can simply add a style to the current page. In most cases, it's a good idea to define an external style sheet. This page will work with any page that includes the following line:

```
<link rel"stylesheet" href"mystyles.css" type"text/css">
```

The program adds this line automatically when you attach a style sheet to the page.

Project 3-1 sample.css

To practice the addition of a custom style sheet to a site, let's create one in Dreamweaver and see how styles can affect the text that you type onto a Web page.

By the end of this project, you will have

- Created a new style sheet in Dreamweaver
- Applied styles to text in Dreamweaver
- Edited your style sheet and observed the effects on your Web page text

Step by Step

1. Create a new style sheet by either using the contextual menu and choosing New CSS Style, or by clicking the + icon in the CSS panel (on the Design Panel Group).

2. In the New CSS Style dialog box, choose Make Custom Style under Type and then choose (New Style Sheet File) under the Define In set of radio buttons.

3. Create each of the following styles in turn:

- MainHeading, Arial, 24 pixel, bold
- BodyText, Arial, 14 pixel
- FinePrint, Arial, 9 pixel, italic

4. After creating the styles, put a dummy heading on the page and apply the MainHeading style to it and then look at the resulting HTML in Code view.

5. Place a paragraph of dummy text under the heading and then apply a BodyText style to it.

6. Place some dummy fine print text after the paragraph and apply the FinePrint style to it.

7. Open the CSS panel, select the Edit Styles radio button, and double-click the MainHeading style.

8. Edit the MainHeading style to change the font size to 36 pixels. Notice the changes that occur to the page in Design view.

9. Go back into Code view and look at the page again and note any change to the page. There shouldn't be any.

10. Edit each of the styles in turn and then look at the Code view for the document. You shouldn't see any changes in the document.

11. After you've played with the styles for a while, open the CSS file and look at it in your text editor of choice. You should see the three style definitions in the file.

Project 3-1

sample.css

Project Summary

This project has taught you the basics of cascading style sheet creation and application on a simple Web page. As we create more complex pages, you will grow to appreciate the power of style sheets. It will become apparent that the extra "up-front" work is worth it for the ease of maintenance that CSS affords.

NOTE

A new mode of the text Property Inspector allows you to set CSS styles from the Inspector itself.

Progress Check

1. What is the keyboard combination for saving a document?

2. How do you make a nonbreaking space in Dreamweaver?

3. What are some advantages of using CSS as opposed to <font> tags?

Understand the Types of Images Available to the Web Page

Text doesn't get you very far these days on the Web. Although the Web started off as a method to read research papers using hypertext, the ability to view visual content soon became a necessity. Images are the most basic form of visual content available to the Web. When we refer to images, we are referring to clip art, logos, pictures, backgrounds, and any other kind of static visual content that you can imagine.

Images can be inserted in the Dreamweaver environment in one of four ways:

- From the Insert menu, simply click Image.

- Drag an image to the page from the Assets panel.

- Use the Common tab of the Insert Bar and click the Image icon.

- Use the keyboard combination CTRL-ALT-I (COMMAND-OPTION-I on the Macintosh).

After performing one of these actions, the Select Image Source dialog box will pop up, as shown in Figure 3-1. From this box, you can browse to the folder where the image is stored and choose the image to be inserted into the document. You can also get your image location from a database by choosing Data Sources instead of File System from the Select Filename From radio button selection.

As you choose an image to insert, you'll notice that the image is previewed in the right side of the dialog box. Directly under the image preview is a handy size meter that tells you the height and width of the image in pixels, the file size in kilobytes, and the approximate

---

1. CTRL-S (COMMAND-S on the Macintosh)
2. Hold down CTRL-SHIFT and press the spacebar
3. Easier to make global changes, <font> tags are deprecated, JavaScript manipulation

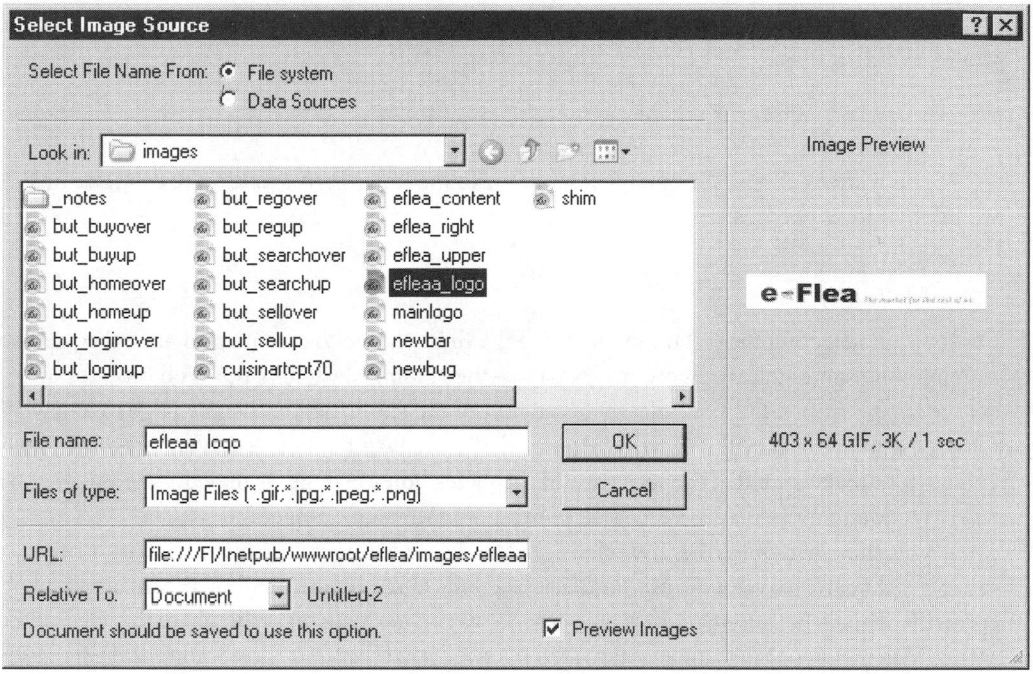

Figure 3-1 The Select Image Source dialog box allows you to choose an image to insert.

download time using a 28.8 modem. These numbers can help you decide whether you need to do further optimization on the graphic. The image preview can be turned off by unchecking the Preview Images check box.

Relative and Absolute Image Paths

After selecting the image source file, you can choose to display the image as an *absolute* URL, where the path is fixed, or as a *relative* URL. A URL can be relative to the document or relative to the site root. The concept of absolute and relative paths might be better understood with an illustration of the principles behind them. Let's say you have a Web site, http://www.e-flea.cc/, and the home page is named index.asp. You might decide to save the images in a folder under the site root named images. When you insert the image on the page, you can choose to make the file link source absolute, relative to the document, or relative to the site root. If you were to insert an image named eflealogo.gif into the index.asp page, for example, the *absolute* path to that image would be:

```
http://www.e-flea.us/images/eflealogo.gif
```

If you took that same image, and the path was made relative to the document, the link would look like this:

```
images/eflealogo.gif
```

If you were to choose the final option, to make the link relative to the site root, the link would then look like this:

```
/images/eflealogo.gif
```

Now, in selecting the last option, making the link relative to the site root as in the previous example, the same link will work in any page—the leading slash tells the Web browser to get the image from a location relative to the root of the site. If you move the page to a new folder, the image link will still work. However, if you make the link relative to the document, you have to make sure that the locations of the pages don't change. If they do, the image links won't work any more because the relative position will have changed.

If you choose to make the link relative to the document, and the document hasn't been saved yet, Dreamweaver will insert a file:///C| prefix to the image to allow the image to display correctly. This is because Dreamweaver has no way of knowing exactly where the file will be saved. You can avoid this unnecessary step by always saving your files before inserting any images. You should get in the habit of saving the blank document as soon as you start working with it.

If the image you are inserting happens to be located somewhere outside the site root, Dreamweaver will ask you if you want to copy the image to your site, as shown in Figure 3-2. This step should always be done unless you intend to create an absolute URL for your images.

To create an absolute URL, you'll have to type it in. An absolute URL is more work for the Web browser and more work for the server, but it has advantages in certain situations. For

Figure 3-2 If an image that you insert is located outside the site root, Dreamweaver will prompt you to save it within the current site.

one, the page can be saved by a user to his or her local machine and all of the image links will still work, because they point to the server. Another use of absolute links is inside an HTML e-mail message. If you don't want to send the entire image along with the e-mail, you can set your image links to be absolute. If you remember in this example, to make an absolute link, all you have to do is type in the actual link to the image:

```
http://www.e-flea.us/images/eflealogo.gif
```

NOTE

An absolute URL for an image source won't allow Dreamweaver to render the image. All you will see in the Dreamweaver environment is a blank image placeholder.

CRITICAL SKILL
3.4 Format and Align Images on the Page

Images for the Web are generally one of two different formats: GIF or JPEG. The GIF image is a standard format, developed by CompuServe in the late 1980s, and has been widely adopted since then. GIF stands for Graphics Interchange Format. JPEGs came along a little later and were developed by a joint committee. In fact, JPEG stands for Joint Photographic Experts Group. The file extension on a PC is JPG, without the "E."

The most common reasons to use a JPEG image are the following:

- Millions of colors are possible.
- Photos look better as JPEG.
- There is a high compression rate.
- It's a standard format across platforms.

The best reasons to use a GIF format are the following:

- Transparent backgrounds are possible.
- Solid colors (such as in clip art) look better.
- GIFs can be interlaced, meaning they will show up a little at a time in full view, giving the person a preview as it loads in.
- GIFs can be animated.

NOTE

In addition to GIF and JPG, the PNG format has gained popularity over the past few years. PNG was developed as a replacement for the GIF format and has many advantages over that format. Unfortunately, PNG has not yet gained the browser support necessary to make it a viable alternative for most Web sites.

Images for the Web can be created in your favorite image-editing application, such as Fireworks MX, Paint Shop Pro, or Photoshop. Most of the latest generations of these programs have Web capabilities built in. However, one program stands out as the program of choice for many Web designers using Dreamweaver MX: Fireworks MX.

Fireworks is Macromedia's image- and graphic-editing program that was built from the ground up with the Web in mind. It has many features that make it perfect for building your Web graphics, and also includes several features that help write the HTML and JavaScript code for rollovers and menus. The integration is so good between Dreamweaver and Fireworks that you can actually write extensions for either program that enable the two programs to communicate with each other.

Ask the Expert

Q: **Fireworks stores its images in a PNG format. Can I use these images as-is on the Web page?**

A: You could, but in general you are better off exporting the image as a Web-safe image in either a GIF or JPG format. The PNG format that Fireworks uses stores extra information that keeps track of the different parts of the image, such as the layers and vector information. Also, it is best to keep copies of any Fireworks PNG files in a separate place as a master file. When you save an image as JPG or GIF, the quality of the image is reduced, and you will never be able to re-create the original image. So save the PNG, but export the image as a JPG or GIF for use in your Web page.

Q: **What is the advantage of using a relative path to an image in a Web page?**

A: Absolute paths require the browser to do more work, because they require that the URL be resolved by the browser to get the image. It naturally follows that an image addressed with a relative path will download faster. Relative paths also have the advantage of making your documents more portable, by allowing you to transfer whole folders with files and related images. Absolute paths have advantages also, such as the user being able to save an HTML file anywhere and still have the image work in the browser, as long as the user is connected to the Internet.

Progress Check

1. What are the two main image formats used on the Web, and what do the letters stand for?

2. What are the differences between image URLs that are relative to the document versus image URLs that are relative to the site?

3. What is the best image format for displaying photos on the Web?

4. What are the four methods for inserting an image in Dreamweaver?

CRITICAL SKILL
3.5 Use Tables to Position Elements
on the Page

Tables can be simple row/column structures, or they can be complex structures containing cells that have been merged with each other. It is even possible to have tables inside tables. Tables are built from rows and columns, with the individual units of the table called *cells*. If you have a list of names and e-mail addresses, you might put them in a table like Table 3-2.

Tables were once thought of simply as a way to format data so that it could be aligned on the page in a readable format. Their use and structure were well suited for the Web as a way to display data. However, when the Web quickly grew from its hypertext beginnings, new ways of aligning elements on the page were needed to create more complex layout structures for the

ID	Name	E-mail
1	Jim Jehosephat	jjehosephat@jehosephatlodge.com
2	Jake Snake	jakesnake@jakethesnake.com
3	Freddy Freeloader	fred@freeloader.com

Table 3-2 Simple Table Structure for Displaying Data

---

1. GIF (Graphics Interchange Format) and JPEG (Joint Photographic Experts Group)

2. Document-relative URLs are linked to the document in such a way that if the document location changes, the image link won't work anymore. Site-relative URLs work for any page in the site in any location and have a leading slash character.

3. JPG

4. From the Insert menu; drag an image to the page from the Assets panel; use the Common tab of the Insert bar and click the Image icon; keyboard combination of CTRL-ALT-I (COMMAND-OPTION-I on the Macintosh)

Web page. Thus, the use of tables was expanded, and soon they were used for everything from displaying data to creating navigation bars to organizing complex graphical displays of images.

Inserting a Table in Dreamweaver

Dreamweaver MX offers two different modes for working with tables: Layout view and Standard view. Standard view allows you to insert a table using a dialog box. Layout view allows you to draw the table on the page. You can insert a table in Dreamweaver in one of several different ways:

● Choose Insert | Table (disabled in Layout view).

Insert	
Tag...	Ctrl+E
Image	Ctrl+Alt+I
Image Placeholder	
Interactive Images	▶
Media	▶
Table	Ctrl+Alt+T
Table Objects	▶
Layer	
Frames	▶
Template Objects	▶
Form	
Form Objects	▶
Email Link	
Hyperlink	
Named Anchor	Ctrl+Alt+A
Date	
Horizontal Rule	
Text Objects	▶
Script Objects	▶
Head Tags	▶
Special Characters	▶
Application Objects	▶
ASP Objects	▶
ASP.NET Objects	▶
ColdFusion Basic Objects	▶
ColdFusion Flow Objects	▶
ColdFusion Advanced Objects	▶
JSP Objects	▶
PHP Objects	▶
Get More Objects...	

- Click the table icon from the Common tab of the Insert Bar (disabled in Layout view).

- Drag the table icon to a location on the page (disabled in Layout view).

- Draw a table with your mouse while in Layout view (disabled in Standard view).

● Enter the raw HTML in Code view (can be used in either mode).

When you choose to insert a table using the Insert menu or the Insert Bar's Common tab while in Standard view, the following dialog box is shown:

The dialog box prompts you for the basic table attributes of rows, columns, width, border, cell padding, and cell spacing. After you enter the numbers, a table is inserted at the insertion point (the place where the cursor is currently located on the page). After the table is inserted on

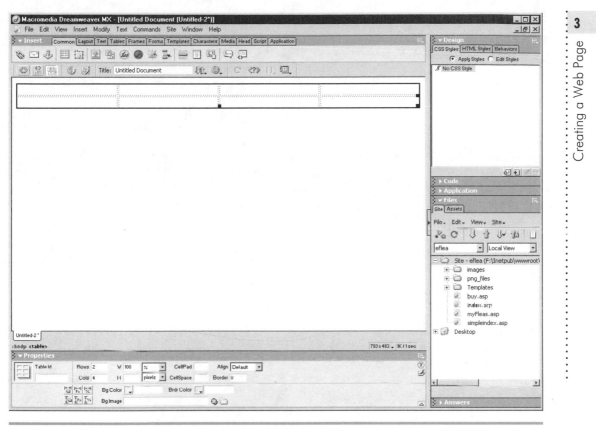

Figure 3-3 The newly inserted table can be adjusted by hand or with the Property Inspector while in Standard view.

the page, you can change its attributes by using the Property Inspector (shown in Figure 3-3), dragging the table border, or changing the code in Code view.

Layout View

Layout view allows you to draw the table and the cells on the page, allowing for greater flexibility when designing your Web pages. To draw the table on the page, you must click Draw Layout Table on the Layout Tab of the Insert Bar.

This allows you to position your cursor on the page and draw the outline of a table.

If you are starting with a blank page, the table will be inserted starting at the top left corner of the page. This is in keeping with Dreamweaver's adherence to standard HTML rules—HTML is read by the browser from top to bottom and left to right. When you've inserted the table, you'll see that you have one large table cell. You can then click the Draw Table Cell icon in the Insert bar to draw cells within your table.

By combining the Draw Table Cell method with the Draw Table method, you can create some really complex tables in a fraction of the time that it would have taken to do so manually or in Code view.

Adding Spacer Images

One thing that has been a thorn in the side of Web developers is the variation in the way that different browsers interpret a Web page. The two primary browsers—Netscape and Internet Explorer—have different ways of interpreting tables. Netscape in particular has a hard time with table cell widths not being interpreted properly. Web developers created a technique that works around the problem by inserting a transparent GIF image inside table cells and then stretching it to the desired width of the cell. This eliminates the cell width problem by forcing the table cell to the width of the transparent GIF. This has no visible effect on how the page looks to the end user, because the image is transparent. One of the other benefits of using such a spacer image is when you have a section of the table that can expand and contract depending on the size of the browser window. Spacer images in the other cells will ensure that they don't change along with the cell that is supposed to change.

Dreamweaver MX makes inserting transparent GIF images automatic when you are in Layout view. Simply click the little down arrow icon next to the table column width in the table layout bar and choose Add Spacer Image from the menu.

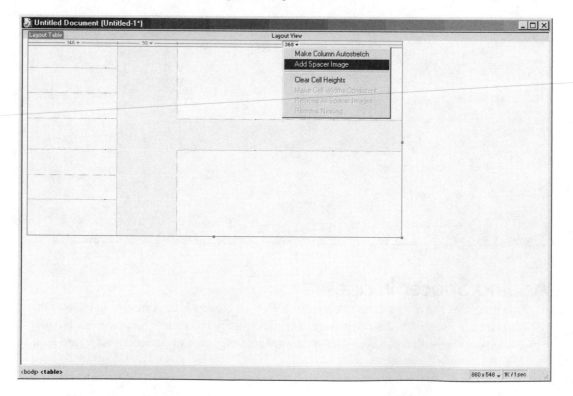

If this is the first time you've inserted a spacer image in the site, a dialog box will pop up asking if you want to create a new spacer image or use an existing image. If you have a predefined spacer image, you can choose it now or choose to create a new image.

Dreamweaver will create a spacer image named spacer.gif at a location of your choice, and it will prompt you for a location. From this point on, Dreamweaver will use this image for all table cell spacer images and you won't be prompted any more. Also, you should note that the table layout bar now looks a little different—the column you applied the spacer image to will now show up a little differently with a larger graphical representation of the column width.

It's always a good idea to include spacer images in your tables to ensure cross-browser compatibility. Dreamweaver doesn't add these by default, but provides you with the tools to make it extremely easy to add them to your table layout.

Additional Layout View Features

The tab that surrounds the table in Layout view is handy while you are building the tables, but can get in the way when you are doing your actual page design. The tab can be turned off by choosing View | Table View | Show Layout Table Tabs.

The layout tabs can be turned on again by going to View | Table View | Show Layout Table Tabs once again. The menu item will have a check mark next to it if it is enabled.

Dreamweaver creates the table cells with fixed column widths and row heights, but you can change both of these easily. To remove all of the row heights, you can click the little down arrow icon on the Layout tab and choose Clear Cell Heights.

The fixed column width can be changed to an *autostretch* column. This is a Dreamweaver term for a 100 percent width table cell. This allows your Web page to fit to the width of the end user's browser window. Generally, you will want to put your text content into an autostretch cell to allow it to fall into place regardless of the screen size of your end user.

When you choose to make a column autostretch, the spacer image is removed from the table column. If you decide to go back to a fixed width column, you'll have to add the spacer image back into the column.

Nesting Tables

Nesting means putting a table inside another table, and it's used frequently when designing Web pages to allow the content of the inner table to be unaffected by the outer table. For example, if you wanted to include a navigation bar on the left side of your page, you could include it as a separate table inside a larger table that holds the design of your entire page. To nest a table in Layout view, you can draw your layout cells in the larger table and then draw a layout table around the cells. This will completely remove the cells from the outside table and place them into the new table.

Tables can be nested inside other tables inside other tables. There is really no limit to the nesting you can do, but you should carefully consider any consequences of nesting and keep your table design as simple as possible. Nested tables can be difficult to maintain if you have to modify your page in the future. One tag out of place can wreak havoc with the design of the page and may be difficult to trace.

Layout View Preferences

The Preferences option in the Edit menu allows you to set up some user preferences for your table layouts. Click Edit | Preferences | Layout View to access this dialog box.

The preference items are as follows:

- **Autoinsert Spacers**   Allows Dreamweaver to automatically insert spacer images whenever you have an autostretch column.

- **Spacer Image**   Allows you to assign the spacer image file for your sites. You can choose a site from the drop-down box.

- **Image File**   Allows you to pick the spacer image or create a new image for the site chosen in the drop-down box.

- **Cell Outline**   Allows you to assign the color used to draw the cell outline in Layout view. This item (and the next three items) will have no effect on the final page. They are for the colors you see in the design environment when in Layout view.

- **Cell Highlight**   Allows you to set the highlight color of the cell when you move the mouse over a cell or choose that cell.

- **Table Outline**   Allows you to set the outline color of the table.

- **Table Background**   Allows you to assign the background color of the table in the Document window.

Customizing Tables

Tables are easily customized in Dreamweaver. There are several methods available to you to change the table once it is on the page, both in Layout view and in Standard view. We've described a few methods of using Layout view, but most of the table customization can be done in Standard view as well.

When you are in Standard view, you can select multiple cells or rows by clicking your mouse inside a cell and then dragging the mouse across other cells. This technique is important later when you have to apply Repeat Regions to areas of tables for server-side formatting. Here we've added a table to the page and selected the top row by clicking inside the first cell and then dragging the mouse across the cell next to it.

When a cell or row is selected, the Property Inspector changes so that formatting can be applied or removed from the selected cells. The top half of the Inspector allows you to form at the text within those cells. The bottom half of the Inspector shows the attributes that can be applied directly to the cells of the table that are selected. Some of these attributes will be applied to the <tr> tags (table row) if the row is selected or the <td> tags (table cell) if individual cells are selected. These attributes include the following:

- **Horizontal position**   Left, center, or right (which is actually the *align* attribute of the row or cell).

- **Vertical position**   Default, middle, top, bottom, baseline (the *valign* attribute).

- **W and H**   Width and height of the cell or cells.

- **No wrap**   Sets the *nowrap* attribute for the cell so that your text doesn't wrap within the cell.

- **Bg**   There are two bg items that allow you to apply either a background image or color to the cells.

- **Border**   Allows you to set the border color of the cells.

- **Header**   Make the selected cells into header cells (changes the <td> tags to <th> tags).

- **Merge selected cells**   Clicking the icon shown in Figure 3-4 merges selected cells.

- **Split cell into row or columns**   Clicking the icon shown in Figure 3-4 splits the cell.

In addition to the Property Inspector, you can customize a table by using the contextual menu (right-click on a PC and CONTROL-click on a Macintosh). The contextual menu for the table is available if your cursor is inside the table or if any part of the table is selected. You can even select the entire table by placing your mouse inside the table and choosing Select Table from the table contextual menu.

The menu items available from the table contextual menu are as follows:

- **Merge Cells**   Selected cells are merged into one cell

- **Split Cell**   Splits a cell into two or more rows or columns

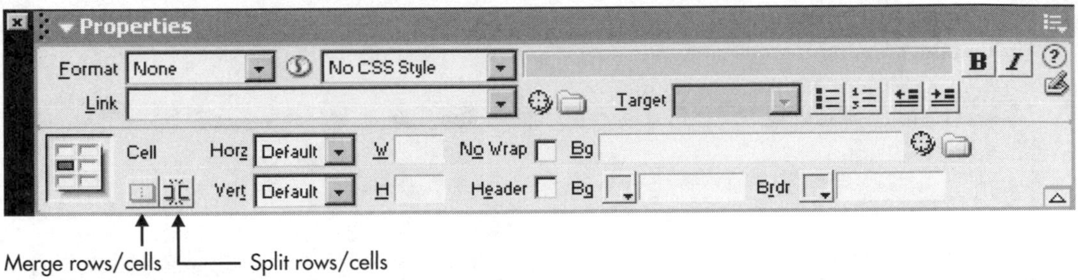

Merge rows/cells └─── Split rows/cells

Figure 3-4 The Property Inspector for table cells or rows allows you to set their attributes.

- **Insert Row**   Inserts a row above the currently selected cell

- **Insert Column**   Inserts a column before the current cell

- **Insert Rows or Columns**   Inserts one or more rows or columns either before or after the current selection

- **Delete Row**   Deletes the row where your cursor is located

- **Delete Column**   Deletes the column where your cursor is located

- **Increase Row Span**   Merges the cell with the cell directly below it

- **Increase Column Span**   Merges the cell with the cell directly next to it

- **Decrease Row Span**   Splits the cell into rows, if the cell spans two or more rows

- **Decrease Column Span**   Splits the cell into columns, if the cell spans two or more columns

Using these commands by themselves, you can create some complex table structures without ever using Layout view.

Using Tables in Code View

Of course, all the great features of Dreamweaver make building and editing tables a snap, but if you don't know the underlying HTML, you will soon be lost. You can get by knowing only a little HTML, but you can get a lot more out of Dreamweaver if you know your way around HTML.

Tables are made up of rows and columns, but more precisely, HTML tables are made up of rows and cells. Following are the three basic tags that belong inside a table:

- **<table> </table>**   The main table tag is used to start and end the table.

- **<tr> </tr>**   The table row tag is used to start and end a new row in the table.

- **<td> </td>**   The table cell tag is used to block out individual cells within the rows.

In addition, a fourth tag is sometimes used instead of <td> tags to denote a table header row: <th> </th>. These special cells will center and bold any text items contained in them and are not used much since the advent of CSS. Here's a simple table with two rows and two columns (four cells total):

```
<table>
 <tr>
  <td>Row 1, Cell 1</td>
  <td>Row 1, Cell 2</td>
 </tr>
 <tr>
  <td>Row 2, Cell 1</td>
  <td>Row 2, Cell 2</td>
 </tr>
</table>
```

As you can see, the <tr> tags (table rows) are indented one level and the <td> tags are indented one more level for readability. If your own tables need to be formatted for readability, you can click Commands | Apply Source Formatting, and all tables (and other HTML) will be formatted nicely. Also, note that all opening tags have a corresponding closing tag. This is not strictly a requirement, but it's a good practice. Some browsers will not render a table properly, if at all, if tags are not closed.

Progress Check

1. What are the three different views for working with tables in Dreamweaver?

2. How do you make a column autostretch in Dreamweaver?

3. Name two methods of merging table cells in Dreamweaver.

What to Take Away from This Module

You should now know how to open, create, and save a page in Dreamweaver. In addition, you should know how to add text to a page and format it using both HTML elements and cascading style sheets (CSS). Furthermore, you should know how to put an image in the page and know

---

1. Layout view, Standard view, Code view
2. By Clicking the menu item Make Column Autostretch on the Layout Table tab
3. Clicking the Merge Selected Cells in the table row or table cell Property Inspector; using the Merge Cells command from the contextual menu

about the different types of images available for use on the Web. Finally, you should have some understanding of the use of tables in setting up the layout of a page. In the next module, we start building a sample site beginning with the site definition.

✓

Module 3 Mastery Check

1. What are the legal characters that you can use in a Web page name?

2. Which of the following are deprecated by the W3C?

   A. CSS

   B. <font> tags

   C. <table> tags

   D. <b> tags

   E. ASP

   F. Java

3. The two most widely used image formats are _____ and _____.

4. Which image format is better for photos and which format is better for graphics?

5. What are the tags used for tables, table rows, table headings, and table cells?

6. Dreamweaver includes a special mode that allows you to draw complex table structures on your page. It is called _____.

7. A transparent graphic used to keep table cells at the proper width is called a _____.

8. What is a newer graphic format that shows great promise but is not yet supported in all browsers?

9. Dreamweaver will open with a new Untitled Page created for you. What is the first thing you should do before working with this page?

   A. Name it.

   B. Save it.

   C. Add a background image.

   D. Put a table on it.

   E. Switch to Layout view.

10. For what reason are sections of code indented in Code view?

Module 4

Creating a Web Site

Now that you understand the basic elements that will make up your Web pages, it is time to learn about how Dreamweaver MX organizes and handles all of the individual files that make up a Web site. Rather than forcing you to deal with the parts of your site individually, Dreamweaver MX allows you to define a site structure that allows the sharing of assets and connections so that your pages work together as an efficient application.

CRITICAL SKILL
4.1 Define a New Web Site in Dreamweaver MX

There is more to the modern Web site than a collection of static pages. Today's sites contain pages that work together and are dependent on one another. Dreamweaver MX allows you to define Web applications that organize your files and assets and allow you to treat them as a whole for development, deployment, and synchronization.

The Site Manager, shown in Figure 4-1, is the central organization point for your site in Dreamweaver MX. From here you can define sites, each with its own unique properties, and

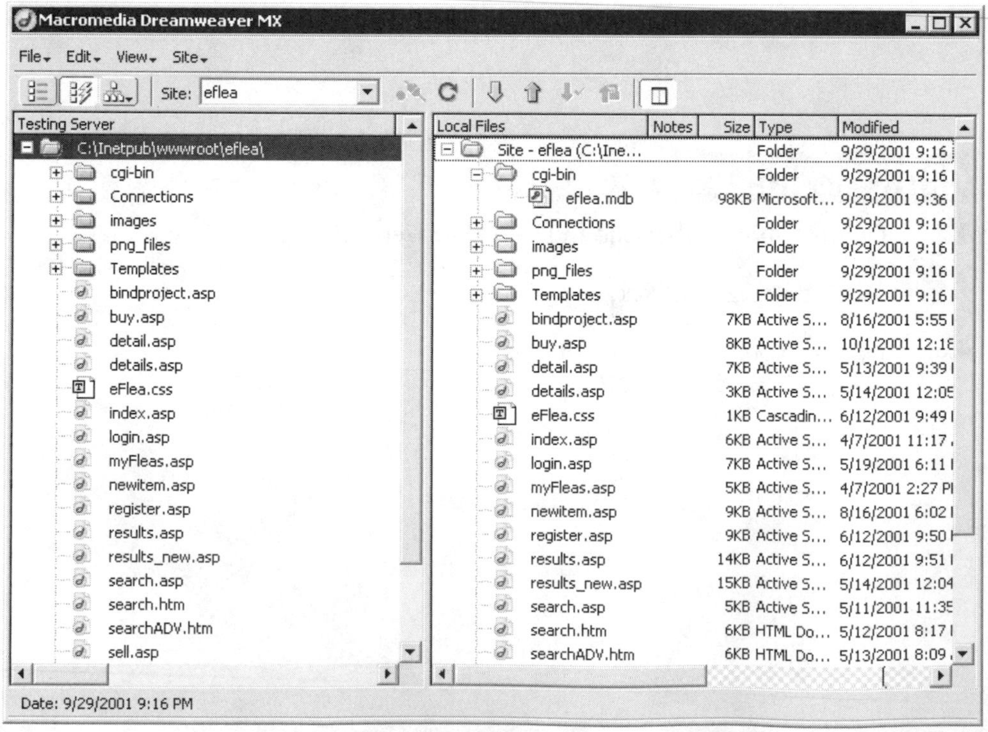

Figure 4-1 The Site Manager in Dreamweaver MX

easily switch between sites, even if they use different server models and reside on different servers around the Internet.

If you are using the new integrated workspace of Dreamweaver MX, the Site Manager is collapsed into the Site panel, shown in Figure 4-2. By clicking the Expand/Collapse button, the Site panel will expand.

You can use Dreamweaver MX's built-in FTP program to send and receive files from any of your sites. Additionally, you can manage the growth of your site by adding pages, editing pages, and structuring the directories and pages that make it up. However, in order to manage a site, it must first be defined.

On the toolbar of the Site Manager is a drop-down list box that lists all of your currently defined sites. If you have UltraDev installed, the sites that were defined in UltraDev will show up in Dreamweaver MX when it is installed. Selecting a site in the list makes that site active. The site's directories and pages are then presented in the windows below the toolbar (see Figure 4-3).

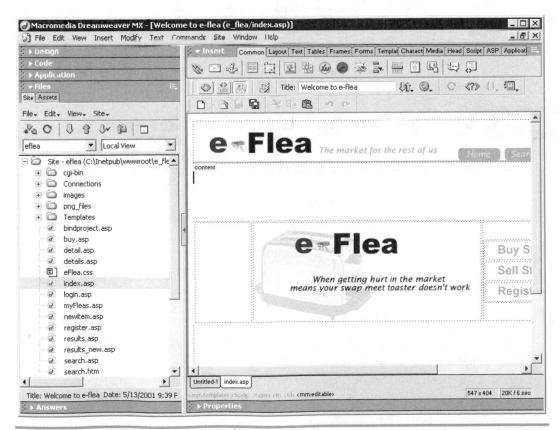

Figure 4-2 The unexpanded Site panel

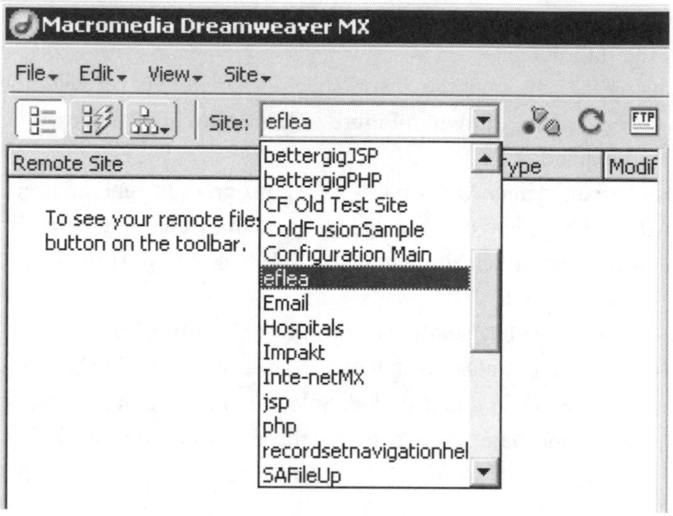

Figure 4-3 Select the site you wish to manage from the list provided.

In Project 4-1, you will create a new site definition for the sample site covered in the upcoming modules.

Project 4-1 Create a Site Definition for eFlea

You will be building an online classified ad and flea market site called eFlea. eFlea is a place where users can list items they want to sell. A potential buyer can then search the available items and contact the seller with an offer. It is not a complex site, but it does represent much of the basic functionality available in Dreamweaver MX and provides a real-world look into the features that you might find at a site like Amazon or eBay. Defining a new site will set up the area in which you will work while constructing your site.

By the end of this project, you will

● Understand the parts of Dreamweaver MX's Site Definition dialog box

● Have created a site definition for the eFlea Web site

There are several ways to get to the screens you will use to define your sites. You can double-click a site displayed in the drop-down list of the Site Manager to edit the definition for that site. The main menu bar of Dreamweaver MX also has a Site menu with options to create a new site or edit existing sites. Or, you can select the Define Sites option at the bottom of the list, and the following screen will appear, allowing you to select a site to edit, create a new site, or delete a site:

Step by Step

To define a new site, follow these steps:

1. From the drop-down list of sites in the Site panel, select Edit Sites to define a new site. The Site Definition screen will open.

2. If the Basic tab is not selected, select it now. This presents the Site Wizard, which is an easy way to add a site definition to Dreamweaver MX. The wizard will present a series of questions that you will answer with your site settings.

3. The first question is, "What would you like to name your site?" Type **e-flea** and click Next.

4. The next question asks you if you want to connect to a server-side technology. You can choose from a list of what is available in Dreamweaver MX: ASP JavaScript, ASP VBScript, ASP.NET C#, ASP.NET VB, ColdFusion, JSP, PHP MySQL. Choose the one that you plan to use for the tutorial. Click Next.

5. Now you have to choose the situation that you are in: Where are your files located and where is your testing server? The choices are these:

   ● Edit and test locally

   ● Edit locally and upload to a remote testing server

(continued)

- Edit directly on a remote testing server using the local network
- Edit directly on a remote testing server using FTP or RDS

6. Select a local root folder for your site. This folder will be a directory on your local hard drive or local network. All of the HTML pages, images, media, and scripts that make up your site will be stored in this folder and its subdirectories. You can use the file icon to the right of the text box to browse your hard drive for this folder. We have selected the following directory on our C drive: C:\inetpub\wwwroot\eflea. You should put your own files in a dedicated Web directory on your machine. This can be in your Web root folder (such as C:\inetpub\wwwroot) or in a virtual directory that you have set up in your Web server. Click Next.

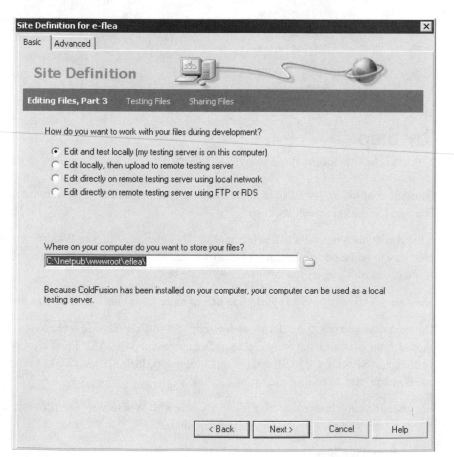

7. Now you are asked the following question: "What URL would you use to browse to the root of your site?" If you are testing locally, this will probably be something like http://localhost/eflea. If you are developing on a remote server, the address might be an IP number, like http://192.168.100.1/eflea. There is a Test button on the wizard that you should use before you go any further. If you have a good URL, you'll see the following box:

```
┌─────────────────────────────────────────┐
│ Macromedia Dreamweaver MX         [×]    │
├─────────────────────────────────────────┤
│   (i)   The URL Prefix test was successful. │
│                                          │
│              ┌────────────┐              │
│              │     OK     │              │
│              └────────────┘              │
└─────────────────────────────────────────┘
```

8. After clicking Next, you are asked if you want to transfer your files to a remote server. You should answer this in a way that matches your situation. If you are testing everything locally, you can answer this with a "No." Click Next. How you answered the question determines the next few steps. If you answered No, you can skip to step 12.

9. Choose your method of connection to the remote server. This can be Local/Network (meaning "local machine or network drive"), FTP, RDS, SourceSafe Database, or WebDAV.

   • **Local/Network drive**   Choose a folder where the files will go.

   • **FTP**   Dreamweaver MX lets you manage your local and remote site files from within the Site Manager if you select the FTP option. Enter the URL of your FTP site in the Host name box. Possible entries might be www.eflea.cc or ftp.eflea.cc. Do not include the protocol in the address, such as ftp://ftp.eflea.cc. Enter the folder name where your files will go. Enter the username and password that have been established for you at this FTP site. Dreamweaver MX will automatically save your password for future use. Uncheck the Save box if you want to be prompted for a password each time you connect to the FTP server.
   In most cases, you will be using an FTP server to access your Web site. For RDS, SourceSafe, or WebDAV options, consult the Macromedia documentation. These advanced settings require that you have RDS, SourceSafe, or WebDAV set up for source control.

10. Select or deselect the Refresh Local File List Automatically check box. If selected, the list of files in the Site Manager will refresh automatically every time a file is added, subtracted, or edited. Deselecting this box allows Dreamweaver MX to run faster, because the screen is not refreshed every time a change is made, but you will have to refresh the file list manually.

(continued)

11. The next screen allows you to choose the Check in/Check Out features of Dreamweaver MX. This is very helpful when working in a team environment. If you choose to use the features, you can enter your name and e-mail address here as well:

Site Definition for e-flea

Basic | Advanced

Site Definition

Editing Files   Testing Files   **Sharing Files, Part 3**

Do you want to enable checking in and checking out files, to ensure that you and your co-workers cannot edit the same file at the same time?

⦿ Yes, enable check in and check out.

○ No, do not enable check in and check out.

When you open a file that isn't checked out, should Dreamweaver check it out, or do you want to view a read-only copy?

⦿ Dreamweaver should check it out.

○ I want to view a read-only copy.

What is your name?

`tom`

What is your email address?

`tom@dwteam.com`

< Back | Next > | Cancel | Help

12. The final screen shows all the choices you've made. If you have any mistakes in your settings, you can go back into the wizard and change them. If not, click Done and your site is now set up.

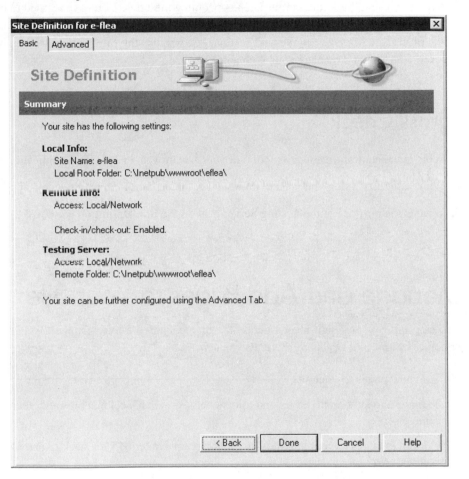

(continued)

Project Summary

Once you have successfully completed this project, you will have created a site definition that you will use to build the sample site in upcoming modules. You have learned to complete a very important task in Dreamweaver MX and are on your way to taking advantage of the power of the Site Manager. In the next section, you will use the Site Manager to begin to add pages to your site and manage your Web application.

Progress Check

1. What is the central organization point of your Dreamweaver MX Web application called?

2. What is the first thing you need to do when beginning development on a new application?

3. What is the purpose of the Testing Server page in the Site Definition window?

CRITICAL SKILL
4.2 Manage and Add Pages to Your Site

You can control many high-level aspects of your site using the Site Manager. With menu options, buttons, and keyboard shortcuts you can

- Add new pages to your site.

- Manage and synchronize files and folders between your local machine and your remote server.

- Control changes to your site files by using Dreamweaver MX's Check In and Check Out features.

- Check links.

- View a graphical representation of your site using the Site Map Layout.

- Cloak certain files or folders.

---

1. The Site Manager
2. Define the site in the Site Manager.
3. To allow the choice of server model for your site and to configure your connection to your remote server

Add New Pages to Your Site

Dreamweaver MX offers several methods of adding pages to your site:

- Select File | New. You can then choose the type of document you want to create, and a new document window will appear. This new document window is not strictly related to your site at this point. You must select File | Save and save it in this site's folder with a unique filename.

- Select File | New File. A new file will appear in either the local or remote side of your site, depending on which was selected when the menu option was selected. This new file's name will be highlighted with a default name such as *untitled1.cfm*, ready for you to give it a unique name.

- In either the Local or Remote side of the Site window, right-click to display the pop-up menu. Select the New File option from the menu. This option works just like the New File option in the File menu.

- Click the New button on the Common toolbar.

No matter which method you choose, you will create a new page to which you will need to add content. If you chose to create a new page from a template, you will have a page with some elements on it, and you will need to fill in only the content areas that were defined when the template was created. If you chose any of the other methods, you will have only a blank page, and you will need to add all of the content that will make up the page.

Once a new page is created, you can use a combination of the available Dreamweaver MX methods to add content to it. You can type text directly onto the page. You can use objects and behaviors to visually add HTML elements to the page. You can go behind the scenes and add code and HTML elements in the Code view.

Experiment with adding content to some sample pages until you get a feel for how things work. Be sure to save any pages that you want to keep. Once you do this a few times, you will end up with several files in the local side of your site manager. Before we get into actually adding pages to the sample site, let's take a look at how Dreamweaver MX allows you to manage your files. A preliminary understanding of these issues will assist you in the next module, when we begin building an actual site.

Adding New Directories to Your Site

A Web site can become a large, sprawling collection of files. The best way to manage these files is to organize them into directories. The Dreamweaver MX Site Manager makes it very easy to add new directories (folders) to your site. After you have directories in your Site Manager, you can drag and drop files or entire directories inside the Site Manager. This is usually the best way to manage your files.

As you drag a file from one folder to the next, Dreamweaver MX will scan your file to make sure there are no relative links that will need to be changed. It will also tell you if there are any other files in your site that reference the file that you are moving. Dreamweaver will then ask if you want the links to be updated. This can be very handy when you are moving files that contain images, links, includes, CSS, or other files that have relative links. You don't have to worry that your files will have broken images or bad links—it is all taken care of for you.

To add a new folder to your Site Manager, click Site | New Folder or use the context menu within the Site Manager and click New Folder. This will create a new folder with the folder name selected and awaiting your input to give it a new name.

CRITICAL SKILL
4.3 Publish Your Site to the Internet

In the Site Files view in the expanded Site panel, the Site Manager is divided into two halves. By default, the left half of the screen displays information from your remote server. These are the files that reside in the remote folder that you specified in your site definition. The right side is the Local view and displays the files that reside in the local folder that you specified in your site definition. If everything is going well, the two sides should be pretty close to the same. It is the Site Manager's job to keep it that way. The buttons on the Site Manager toolbar aid in the management of your site:

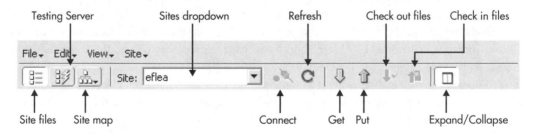

The Connect and Disconnect Buttons

When you have created pages and are ready to upload them to your remote server, you will need to establish an *FTP (File Transfer Protocol)* connection. Use the Connect button to initiate a connection to the FTP server that you designated on your site definition. Once an FTP session is started, the Connect button becomes a Disconnect button that allows you to end the session whenever you want.

TIP

You can monitor the activity in your FTP session by using the FTP Log, located by clicking Window | Results | FTP Log (CTRL-SHIFT-F12).

Getting and Putting Files

The main function of an FTP program is to transfer files back and forth, as you might have guessed from the name. When you have files on your local machine that you need to transfer to your remote server, use the Put button to place them there. When you need to receive files from the remote server, use the Get button to get them and save them in your local folder.

To get or put specific pages or files, select them and click the Put or Get button. To get or put an entire site, select the root folder at the top of the file list, and the entire site will be transferred.

TIP

The Get and Put commands are also available from the Site menu in the main Dreamweaver application, and also from the Document toolbar.

When you transfer a page, there may be dependent files such as images, Flash files, or include files that need to go with it. Dreamweaver MX will prompt you for whether you want those files to transfer with the Dependent Files dialog box, shown here:

Dependent Files	☒
Include Dependent Files?	Yes
☐ Don't show me this message again	No
	Cancel

The Refresh Button

The Refresh button allows you to update your view of your site files to include the most recent changes. It is very useful when you are working as a part of a design team. When others make changes to files or add or delete pages to the site you are working on, you may not have the most up-to-date list in your remote view. Refreshing on a regular basis ensures that you are always aware of the changes that are happening as you work.

Synchronizing Your Site Files

If you do any work offline, or if you are away from a site while others are working on it, you will end up with copies of files in your local window that are out of sync with the versions on your remote server. You may need to place newer versions that you have created offline onto the server, or you may need to bring your local copies up to date.

To synchronize specific files, select them in the local or remote pane of the Site Manager and select the Synchronize option from the Site menu.

When you select the Synchronize menu, the following dialog box is displayed, allowing you to choose how your files are synchronized.

In this box, you can select whether to synchronize the entire site or only the files you have selected. You can also choose whether to put newer files from your local folder into the remote server, get newer files from the remote server, or do both, which generates up-to-date versions of the site in both locations.

If you have deleted files on your local machine, you can enable the Delete Remote Files Not On Local Drive option, and they will be deleted on the remote server also.

CAUTION

Be very careful when setting the Delete Remote Files Not On Local Drive option. If you are working with other developers, it is likely that someone will create a new page that would then be deleted by your synchronization because it does not yet exist on your machine.

Check In and Check Out

There is hardly anything more exciting than working on a big project with several developers. And there is hardly anything more frustrating than having your work overwritten by a careless coworker. Dreamweaver MX allows you to work safely in a collaborative environment with its Check In and Check Out features.

Checking files out is Dreamweaver MX's way of letting other developers on your team know that a file is in use and is likely being edited. It is a warning that, should another developer decide to edit it as well, someone's changes will get overwritten. Consider the amount of work that could be lost if you were to open a page and, while you were making major revisions to it, a coworker opened the same page to make a simple typo correction. If you saved your file, and then your coworker saved his or her old version on top of it, your changes would be lost and the site would be left with an old, albeit correctly spelled, version of the page.

When you check out a page, a check mark is placed next to the page name on the remote server and your name, or whatever identifying name you entered in the Check In/Out category of your site definition, is placed to the right of the filename. A green check mark indicates a file that you have checked out, and a red check mark indicates a file that someone else has checked out.

TIP

You can also use Dreamweaver MX's Check In/Out feature when you are the sole developer on a project. Many developers work from more than one computer, such as a home PC and a work PC. By selecting a name that identifies the computer that opened a file rather than the person, you can always track down the machine on which the file is opened.

Dreamweaver MX uses a small text file with a .lck extension to lock a file that is checked out. When this file is present on the server, that file is not available for others to access and edit until you check it back in. Once you have edited a file and checked it in, that file is made read-only on your local machine, forcing you to get the file from the server in order to edit it. This will keep you from editing a local copy of the file and inadvertently uploading it over a newer version of the file.

NOTE

You can turn off this read-only setting in the File menu or the right-click pop-up menu by selecting the Turn Off Read-Only option. You should carefully consider the consequences of doing this, however, and be careful not to overwrite newer versions of the page on your remote server.

CAUTION

This method of locking the remote file is not foolproof. Applications other than Dreamweaver MX will not realize the significance of the .lck file and will allow these pages to be overwritten.

Checking Links

Dreamweaver MX provides a powerful method of verifying the links within your sites. Links are those places in your pages where you offer the end user an opportunity to navigate to another page, either within your site or in another site somewhere on the Internet. If those links are broken, either because the pages they point to no longer exist or because they are mistyped, the usability of your site is severely impacted. Checking your links with Dreamweaver MX identifies broken links in your site, reports external links so you can verify them manually, and finds orphaned files.

Dreamweaver MX can verify links that point to other pages in your site. If the pages represented in these links do not exist or cannot be found, Dreamweaver MX reports them as broken.

NOTE

In order for Dreamweaver MX to be able to identify links as internal, it is important that you set the URL of your site under Link Management Options in the Local Site category of your site definition. If this value is not set, Dreamweaver MX will likely report a large number of your internal links as external links and will not verify them.

If links to external Web sites exist on your pages, they will be reported to you so that you can verify them manually; Dreamweaver MX has no facility for verifying external links and depends on you to do it.

Orphaned files are pages in your site that have no other pages pointing links to them. Because the Web is a hyperlink environment, it is unlikely that a visitor would ever find their way to a page in your site without following a link there. Orphaned pages serve little purpose because users will probably never see them.

You can check links in a specific page, a set of pages, or your whole site. To check a page or several pages, select them in the Site Manager and right-click to display the pop-up menu. The Check Links selection in the menu has two options: Selected Files/Folders and Entire

Site. You may also check the entire site by selecting the Check Links Sitewide option from the Site menu.

After Dreamweaver MX verifies your links, a dialog box appears that reports its findings. You can use the drop-down list to filter the results that you need to view, and you can even save the report information so it is easier to refer to when making changes to the site to fix broken links and orphaned files.

The Site Map

Dreamweaver MX's site map offers a graphical view of your site in which you can add pages, open pages for editing, create links between pages, and change page titles. The site map allows you to perform many Dreamweaver MX functions in a visual manner, such as selecting a group of pages by dragging across them and adding pages to your site by dragging them from Windows Explorer. Lines between files indicate link relationships, and icons represent things such as broken links within pages.

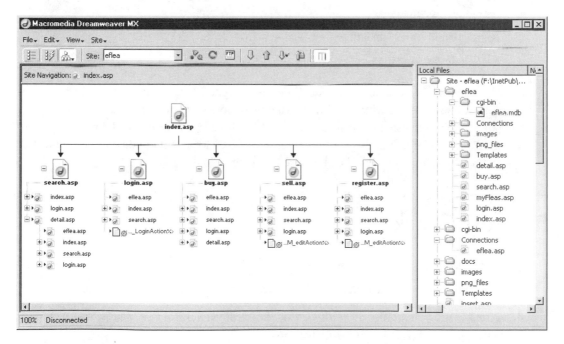

As discussed earlier, you can adjust the way the site map is displayed by altering the number of columns and the column width in your site definition.

Cloaking Files and Directories

This feature allows you to turn off certain operations of the Site panel to certain file types or folders. The operations affected are

- Put and Get
- Check In and Check Out
- Reports
- Select newer local
- Select newer remote
- Sitewide operations (such as search/replace)
- Synchronize
- Asset panel contents
- Template and library updating
- Automatic link updating

Cloaking cannot be done to individual files, but only to file types and folders. For example, if you want to exclude PNG files from these operations, you can enable cloaking and put the PNG extension in the list of cloaked files. Folders can be cloaked directly from the Site Panel, and not from this configuration screen. To cloak an individual folder, right-click on a folder in the Site Panel and choose Cloaking | Cloak.

Progress Check

1. Uploading and downloading files in the Site Manager is known as _____.

2. What Dreamweaver MX feature would you enable to facilitate team development?

3. To make sure you are always working with the latest versions of your pages, you should regularly invoke what function of Dreamweaver MX?

---

1. Getting and putting.
2. Check-in and check-out
3. Synchronize

Ask the Expert

Q: How can I work on files directly on the remote server in Dreamweaver MX?

A: You can't work on remote files directly in Dreamweaver MX. To work on a remote file, you need to create a site and then access the remote file. You can double-click the remote file and it will download to your local site; you will then be in "edit" mode, but when you save the file, it will be saved only to your local machine. You have to put the file to the remote server using the put arrow key on the toolbar or the Site panel. You can also set up Dreamweaver to automatically put the files upon saving by checking Automatically Upload Files To Server On Save in the Remote Info tab of the Site Info dialog box.

Generally speaking, it is unwise to edit files directly on your remote server. This is especially true when you are in a shared hosting environment. One bad section of code can freeze up a server and bring everyone else's sites down with yours. It is always better to test and debug your pages locally or on a testing server than to try to edit live pages on your remote server.

Q: What is the best way to organize files in a site?

A: There is no correct answer for this, but there are several good methods. If you have a small site, you can organize it in such a way as to have each menu item in your main directory point to its own directory. For example, you might have the following menu items:

- Home
- Sales
- Products
- Contact
- About

Each one of these items can be a subfolder in your main site. Inside of each of these subfolders would be an index file, or default file, that would be set up in your Web server as a default document. A default document might be index.htm, index.asp, index.jsp, default.php, or some other document name that can be standardized across your site. If you organize in this way, your links can be shorter and more easily typed by your end users, such as http://www.myspiffywebsite.com/sales. Then you can store other site assets in separate folders as well, such as an images folder or a Flash swf files folder.

What to Take Away from This Module

Dreamweaver MX provides you with a very powerful interface in which to design your applications. But with that power comes the necessity that you spend a little time learning how the program is organized. Once you get comfortable with how Dreamweaver MX treats your site structures and the files within them, you will realize how efficient a model it is. Dreamweaver MX packages together all of the tools you need to easily build and publish your Web applications.

In the next module, we discuss how to plan your site.

✔ *Module 4 Mastery Check*

1. What setting in Dreamweaver's Site Definition panel can be used to increase performance during development?

2. True or False: You should always set your default page extension to the server model you are using for the site.

3. Dreamweaver's Check Links feature can identify pages that have no other pages linked to them. These pages are known as _____.

4. A graphical representation of the site can be viewed using the _____.

5. To put a file means what?

6. What is the purpose of site synchronization?

7. How is the site panel expanded and collapsed?

8. True or false: Check-in and check-out allows Dreamweaver users to lock files from being edited by other programs.

9. True or false: It is a good idea to edit remote files directly.

10. The .lck files created by Dreamweaver are used by which feature?

11. True or false: Get and Put are only available from the Site panel.

12. True or false: Dynamic pages like ASP, CFM, or PHP can be browsed in a browser from the file system, like c:\inetpub\wwwroot\mypage.asp.

Module 5

Adding Content
to Your Site

I f you are anything like us, this is the module you have been waiting for. You may have even flipped straight to it when you got the book. Although the importance of the preceding modules cannot be overstressed, it is certainly time to start building some pages.

In this module, you will learn how to create a simple page using the features of Dreamweaver. You'll then see how to build more complex page designs using Fireworks, another Macromedia product. Finally, you'll examine the creation of templates in Dreamweaver and how you can use them to give your site a consistent look and feel.

Build a Home Page in Dreamweaver

If you completed the projects in the preceding modules, you should have a pretty good idea of what you want your site to look like. That doesn't mean you have to have the entire look and feel worked out—sometimes that takes a while staring at the monitor to accomplish. But you should have some of the basics in mind. You may have a logo you want to use and you may have seen a Web site or two that you would like yours to emulate.

Prepare Your Assets

One of the first things you need to do if your site will contain any graphics is create them and put them where you can make the best use of them. You might use Fireworks, Photoshop, or Paint Shop Pro to create your graphics, or they might be supplied by your graphic designer or your client. However you get them, you should have a few graphics that you want to use on your pages.

Graphic images are one of the categories of items known as *assets* in Dreamweaver. You can think of your site's assets as all of the things that you can put to work to make up your pages. These include images, colors, links, Flash files, movies, Shockwave files, templates, scripts, and library items. Assets are organized and accessed from the Assets panel, shown in Figure 5-1.

To start with, you need to store your images within your site structure so that the Assets panel will pick them up and make them available to you. Technically, any appropriate image file types (such as .gif and .jpg) anywhere in your site folder will be displayed in the Assets panel, but it is better to stay more organized by placing your images in a folder created just for them.

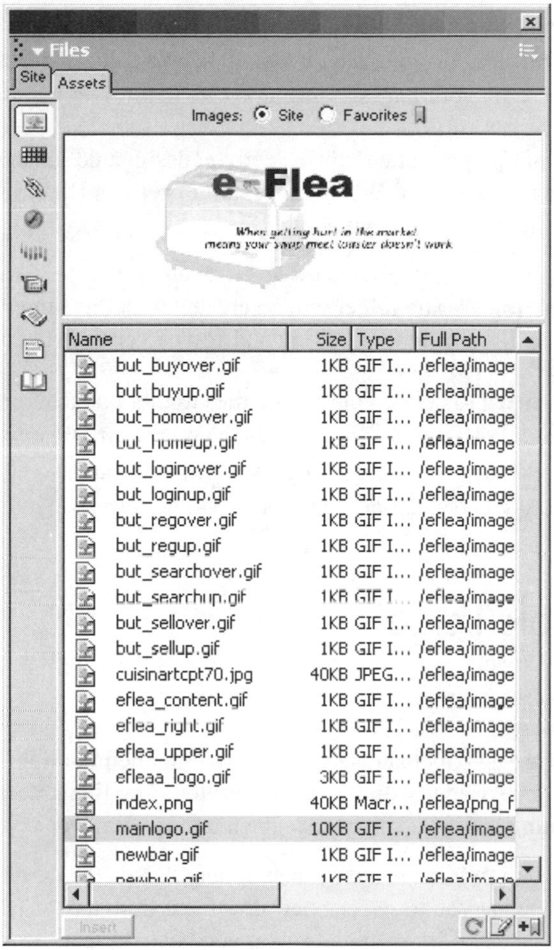

Figure 5-1 The Dreamweaver Assets panel

NOTE

Different designers have their own preferences about where their images are stored. Some prefer everything in one image folder at the root level of the site. Others create multiple image folders within the subdirectories that make up the site and store images pertinent to each area of the site in its unique folder. How you organize yourself is up to you, but do develop some method to keep track of your files that fits efficiently into your workflow.

When you defined your site in Module 4, you created a folder on your hard drive and selected it as the root folder for your site. You will need a folder within that root to house the images you plan to use on your pages. You can create that folder a couple of different ways:

- In Windows Explorer, navigate to the folder you designated for the site and create a new folder called Images within it. When you restart or refresh Dreamweaver, your new folder will appear as a subdirectory in your site.

- Right-click in the Site panel in Dreamweaver. The pop-up menu that appears will allow you to add a new folder. The folder will be created with the name Untitled, but the name will be automatically selected for editing and you can change the name to Images.

Now you simply need to create your image files to this Images folder or use Windows Explorer to copy existing image files into it. When you restart Dreamweaver, the Assets panel will find the image files in your site and display them. You can also click the Refresh button at the bottom of the Assets panel, and your assets will be refreshed and your images will be displayed.

Create a Simple Page

To create a page in Dreamweaver, you first need a document window to work with. There are a couple of ways to create a new document window:

- Right-click in the Site panel and select the New File menu option. A new file will be created in your local folder with the name Untitled. The filename will be automatically selected for editing, and you can change the name to whatever you like.

- From the File menu, select the New menu option. A New Document Wizard will appear on the screen allowing you to select a new document from any of Dreamweaver's available document types or any of the templates that you have defined for your sites. Until you save the page, it is not technically a part of your site, so links and file paths may be represented strangely. Be sure to immediately save your page within the current site structure to avoid this problem.

At this point, creating a page is done with a combination of three things:

- Text
- Assets
- Dreamweaver objects

Text

As snazzy as most modern Web sites are, most are still made up of a good deal of plain HTML text. There are several reasons for this:

- Plain text can be easily indexed for site searches.

- Plain text is easily categorized by search engines.

- Plain text is easily edited as information on your site changes.

You will still find sites around the Web that are almost exclusively text, but most are some combination of text and other elements such as images, which are classified as assets in Dreamweaver.

Assets

Assets are the images, Flash files, links, colors, and other elements that can be used to make up your site. When you save files of these types inside your site structure, Dreamweaver's Assets panel will find them and make them available. You'll see in the upcoming project how easy it is to build a page using these assets.

Objects

In addition to text and assets, there are several HTML items that you will use to build your sites. These include tables, frames, layers, forms and form fields, and many of the other items that Dreamweaver was created to simplify. Dreamweaver's representations of these HTML elements are called objects. You will most certainly be using objects in conjunction with text and other assets to build a well-organized site.

Project 5-1 Using Dreamweaver to Create Your First Web Page

If you have Dreamweaver open, and you have placed some graphic images inside your site's folder, you are ready to begin building your first Web page. The upcoming project steps you through the construction of a simple page. Feel free to follow along using the images supplied with this book or use your own content. Either way, you will learn many of the Dreamweaver features you can use to quickly create Web pages.

Project Goals

By the end of this project, you will have

- Built a simple Web page using text, assets, and objects

- Previewed your page in Dreamweaver

(continued)

Step by Step

1. In Dreamweaver's Site panel, select the site you created from the Site drop-down box.

2. Create a new document by selecting File | New. Select the Basic Page category and the HTML page and click Create.

3. Save the new document in your site by using File | Save As. Make sure that you save the page in the folder that serves as your site's root directory. Save the page as firstpage.html.

4. Your new page will have a default title of Untitled Document. In the menu bar at the top of the page, give your page a title.

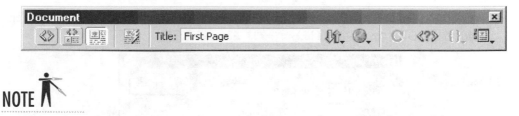

NOTE

Always remember to title your pages as you build them. Take a quick look around the Web and you will see pages at prominent sites with the default Untitled Page title. Such lack of attention to detail is not a confidence-building experience for your clients.

5. Dreamweaver's default page properties give the page a white background and a small margin at the top and left of the page. You can change these and other page-level properties by selecting Modify | Page Properties.

Page Properties	
Title: First Page	OK
Background Image: [ ] Browse...	Apply
Background: [ ] #0000FF	Cancel
Text: [ ] Visited Links: [ ]	
Links: [ ] Active Links: [ ]	
Left Margin: [ ] Margin Width: [ ]	
Top Margin: [ ] Margin Height: [ ]	
Document Encoding: Western (Latin1) ▼ Reload	
Tracing Image: [ ] Browse...	
Image Transparency: ————————— 100%	
Transparent Opaque	
Document Folder:	
Site Folder: C:\eflea2\	Help

6. Select a background color using the color picker on the Page Properties dialog box. Set the left margin and top margin properties to 0 to remove the default margin. Click OK to apply your changes and return to the document window.

(continued)

7. Click on the Table object in the Common tab of the Insert panel.

8. In the Table dialog box, set the new table's properties to 1 row, 2 columns, and 75 percent width. Click OK to insert the table.

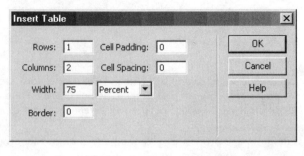

9. Click on the table to select it. In the Property Inspector, choose Center in the Align drop-down box to center the table on your page.

10. You need a logo on your page. If the Assets panel is not already open, select Assets from the Windows menu to display it. Click on the top icon near the left edge of the Assets panel to display the images that are available in your site. Scroll down to your logo file and click on it. A thumbnail of the logo will appear in the top section of the Assets panel.

11. Double-click and hold your mouse button on the thumbnail image to select the logo image. Drag your mouse onto the development window and into the left cell of the table. Release the mouse to insert the image in the table cell.

12. Click on the image to select it. In the Property Inspector, click the Center button to center the image in the cell.

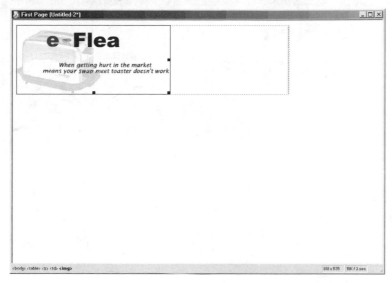

Project 5-1

Using Dreamweaver to Create Your First Web Page

(continued)

13. Click in the cell on the right. Type a title or welcome message for your page into the table cell.

```
First Page (Untitled-2*)                                    _ □ ✕

    e ⁻ Flea

          When getting hurt in the market          Welcome to e-Flea
       means your swap meet toaster doesn't work




<body>                                          777 x 508 ▾ 11K / 3 sec
```

14. Starting with the cursor in the right table cell, press the TAB key on your keyboard eight times. This will leave you with the original table row and four additional rows beneath it.

```
First Page (Untitled-2*)                                    _ □ ✕

    e ⁻ Flea

          When getting hurt in the market          Welcome to e-Flea
       means your swap meet toaster doesn't work




<body>                                          777 x 508 ▾ 11K / 3 sec
```

15. Either hold down the SHIFT key and click the left cells in the third, fourth, and fifth table rows, or click and drag over the cells. This area will serve as a place to display a paragraph of text, and you want it to be one cell that you can type in. With all three cells selected, click the Merge Cells button on the Property Inspector.

16. Type a welcome message or instructions in the cell you have created. You may use the default text settings or change the font and color properties in the Property Inspector that appears when you select the text you entered.

17. You will use the three cells that remain to the right for navigation links. Since you are building a simple version of the eFlea site, your links will be Buy Stuff, Sell Stuff, and Register. You can use other links and add more than three if you need to. Type the text for your links in the right table cells.

(continued)

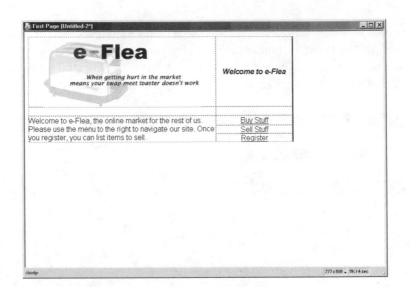

18. Once your text is entered, you need to make each one into a link to another page. Highlight the text in the first right cell. In the Property Inspector, type the path to the page you want your user sent to when they click on this link. It could be a link that is external to your site, in which case you need to type in the fully qualified path, such as http://www.somewhere.com/. It could be a page within your site, in which case just the page name or directory and page name is sufficient. If this is a page you have already created, you can click the file folder icon next to the link text box and select the page you want to link to from the resulting dialog box. Do this for all the links you have entered in your table.

19. Although you may have used different graphics and text, your page should look something like the following illustration. Save your page by using File | Save or the ALT-S keyboard shortcut.

20. To preview your page, make sure the following things have been done:

   - You have created a virtual directory in your Web server for the site you are working in.
   - You have entered the correct URL prefix in your site definition (usually http://localhost/).
   - At least one browser is set up in the Preview In Browser section of your Dreamweaver Preferences.

21. With your page open, press F12 or select the browser you want to preview in from the Preview In Browser option in the File menu. Remember that your links will work only if they refer to pages that actually exist. If the pages exist, you should be able to test out your page and see that you successfully created working navigation links.

Project Summary

Although the end product may not be as fancy as you wanted, you learned some important techniques in this project. You can add tables to your page and use their properties to help you position items where you want them. You learned how to merge table cells to create asymmetric regions within your table, a very important technique in more advanced design. You added navigational links to text you have placed on your page. You learned how to use the Assets panel to add images to table cells. And you used Dreamweaver's Preview In Browser feature to see your work as it will appear to an end user. Experiment with these techniques (adding text, objects, and assets) in different combinations to get comfortable with the Dreamweaver interface and with the properties that are available for each item.

CRITICAL SKILL
5.2 Use Fireworks to Design a Page and Use It in Dreamweaver

Creating graphic designs in Dreamweaver is certainly possible. You have all of the tools necessary to painstakingly build complex table structures and plug in carefully cropped image pieces to make up what you hope will be a coherent display. But there is an easier way, using another Macromedia product, Fireworks.

Project 5-2 Creating a More Complex Design

Fireworks is a professional graphics package that specializes in creating images for the Web. Using it, you can design entire pages and export them for easy use in your Dreamweaver sites. The specific features of Fireworks are beyond the scope of this book, but this project will teach you a lot of what you need to know to use Fireworks to design the look and feel of your site.

(continued)

Project Goals

By the end of this project, you will

- Learn to slice and export a Fireworks design for use in Dreamweaver
- Learn to use Fireworks slices to create rollover images in Dreamweaver

Step by Step

1. In Fireworks, create a new graphic. If you are targeting 800×600–resolution browsers, you can make your graphic 700×500 and it should work nicely. Use the Fireworks tools to create a page design. Unfortunately, there is not room to teach you all about Fireworks, but there are several excellent references available. Once you see how easy and powerful this combination is, you will certainly want to learn more about it.

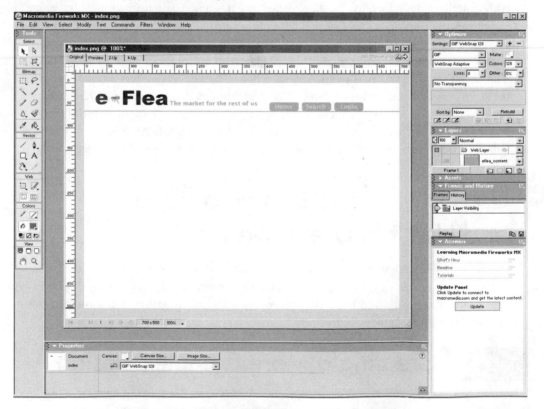

2. Once your graphic is created, the goal is to export it in a fashion that makes it useful in Dreamweaver. Rather than loading the design as one big image, you can divide the page up into logical sections using Firework's Slice tool. Locate the Slice tool on the Fireworks toolbar.

3. When you select the Slice tool, your cursor changes to crosshairs. You can use the cursor to draw rectangles on your image. These rectangles will become individual graphics files when the design is exported. As you draw, Fireworks will compensate for the choices you make by defining additional slices to complete the image. The slices show in a special Web layer indicated by a green hue.

4. How you slice your image is very important. You want to be sure and take into account things like blocks of text that may change, logos, and images that will become navigational buttons. Following is how the eFlea image was sliced. The logo was kept intact, the navigation buttons were made into individual images, and a large content area was defined in the lower part of design.

5. Fireworks will automatically assign names to each of your slices. They are not terribly descriptive, though, so you are better off renaming them. You can name them whatever

(continued)

you like, but keep one thing in mind. The three slices around the buttons in the top right are intended to be rollover images once they are placed in Dreamweaver. Rollover images are graphics that change or respond in some way to the action of your mouse either hovering over them or clicking them. Because these initial images represent the original state of the rollover images, name each of them to indicate this. Ours are named using _up as a part of the name to indicate that these particular images will be used for the "up" state of the button, when the mouse is not hovering over it. With any slice selected, look at the Properties panel in Fireworks You can rename slices in the text box to the left.

6. Once all of your slices are created and named with names that will help you identify the images, it is time to export the design. Exporting will create two things: an HTML file with a table structure that mirrors the slices you created, and a directory of images, one for each of the slices. Select File | Export.

7. An Export dialog box will appear asking you to select a directory for your export and make a couple of other decisions. First, select a directory where the images that the export creates will be placed. This will probably be the Images directory of the root folder that you defined for your site.

8. Next, select a base name for the HTML page that will be created. If this is your home page, you might use index.html.

9. Make sure that the Slices option is set to Export Slices.

10. In the HTML box, select Export HTML File.

11. The Put Images In Subfolder option can be set so that the images are placed in the directory of your choice. Because you will likely create your index page in the root of your site folder, check the Put Images In Subfolder box and browse to the images folder of your site. This will create a common directory structure where the index.html page resides in the root folder with its associated images one level down in an Images directory.

12. Click Save to complete the export operation.

13. Now open the eFlea site in Dreamweaver. Within the directory you created, you should now have an index page that was created when you exported your graphic from Fireworks. When you open this page in Dreamweaver, you will find that it contains a table structure that mimics the slices you made in your image. Each table cell contains a reference to a portion of that graphic (a slice) in the Images directory.

14. To make the navigation buttons into rollover images, you'll need to create the graphic that will be displayed in the button's "over" state, when the mouse hovers over the button. Changing the image in some small way provides an added level of interaction for your user by indicating that the button is meant to be clicked. Return to your graphic in Fireworks.

15. You will notice the green layer that represents your slices prevents you from editing the graphic underneath. Because you need to make changes to the image, you'll need to get past this layer (known as the *Web layer*). In the Layers panel, you should see Layer 1 and Web Layer. Both are visible (the eye icon is showing in the left column). Click on the eye icon for the Web layer, and the green slices layer will be hidden, allowing you to work on the image underneath.

16. The change you make to the portions of the image that will become rollover buttons is up to you. You can change the colors, add an accent graphic such as an arrow, or you can simply change a font color, as was done in the eFlea example. With the Web layer turned off, double-click each word on the three navigational buttons and change their font color to white. When the user rolls over each button, the text will change from the more muted color to white, indicating that this is a button to click.

(continued)

17. Next, click the eye icon next the Web layer again, making the green slices layer visible. Select each of the three navigation button slices, and rename them as in Step 5, using _over as the last portion of the name. This will enable you to easily identify these images in the Images directory when building the actual rollover images in the following steps.

18. Right-click on the first of the three navigation button slices and select Export Selected Slice from the pop-up menu. This operation will export a .gif file just like before, but only this particular slice will be exported. Click Export in the Export Preview dialog box that appears. Make sure that the eFlea Images directory is selected in the resulting Export dialog box. The base name should be the new _over name you gave this slice, and the HTML style should be None. Click Save to export this version of the image to the Images folder. Repeat this step for each slice that you altered in Step 17.

19. When you return to Dreamweaver, you are ready to convert your existing navigation buttons to rollover buttons. First, select the table cell that contains the first image. You will notice in the Property Inspector for this cell that the _up version of your button is listed in the image source. Delete the image from the table cell, leaving the cell empty.

20. From the Insert menu, select Interactive Images | Rollover Image. The Insert Rollover Image dialog box will appear. You have five choices to make:

- First, name the rollover image. Give it a name that will be meaningful to you if you end up needing to refer to the image in another code.

- Next, use the Browse button to locate the _up version of your navigation button image. This will be the Original Image that is displayed when the mouse is not hovering over the table cell.

- Do the same for the Rollover Image, selecting instead the _over version of your graphic.

- Leave the Preload Rollover Image box checked. This will cause both graphics to load into your user's browser when the page is first opened, allowing for better performance as each image is rolled over for the first time.

- Finally, type in or browse to the page that you want your user directed to when this button is clicked. Because you are just starting to build your pages, you will likely type this page name from the list of pages that you know will be created as you continue.

21. Click OK to save these selections. Repeat these steps for each of your navigation buttons.

22. When you preview this page in a Web browser, you will see the images as you created them, looking surprisingly like the Fireworks image you first designed. Your rollover images will respond to your mouse. Save your page in Dreamweaver.

Project Summary

Using this method of page creation allows you to transition complex designs from image editing software like Fireworks into HTML pages. Although you may want to spend time tweaking the final HTML version, there is no doubt that this is an extremely efficient way to get started with fancier graphic designs in Dreamweaver. The time it would take to build the table structure for this and even more complex layouts can be spent on other things.

Progress Check

1. When you export a Fireworks image into Dreamweaver, each Fireworks slice is represented as what in Dreamweaver?

2. What image size should be used in Fireworks to accommodate an 800×600 browser resolution?

3. Name three kinds of assets.

CRITICAL SKILL
5.3

Create Templates in Dreamweaver

Templates are special files in Dreamweaver that can be used to create pages in your site that share a common design. When a template is created (or actually, when a regular Dreamweaver document is saved as a template), it contains those parts of the site's design that you want to remain consistent. In Project 5-2, you created a basic site design with navigation buttons that will remain consistent throughout the eFlea site. Each page, no matter what its main content, will have this same graphic design and navigational buttons.

To accomplish this, you will need to prepare the index page that was exported from Fireworks to be a template and then save it so that it can be used as a template in Dreamweaver. In order to prepare the page to be a template, you need to do three things:

- Identify a content area
- Prepare the content area
- Mark the content area

---

1. A table cell
2. 700×500
3. Images, links, and templates (colors and Flash files are other types of assets)

Identify a Content Area

A template is made up of two kinds of areas on the page: parts that cannot be edited and parts that can be edited. It is the parts that cannot be edited that allow the template to enforce a design scheme on the entire site. When templates are used in the construction of regular site pages, these areas will resist any attempt to edit them, making the site's look and feel consistent.

But it is the parts that you can edit that give each page a reason for its existence. There is no need for a bunch of pages that all look the same. You need pages that contain different information or serve different purposes depending on where they exist in the site, while maintaining a common look. It is important to carefully consider what portions of a page can be edited in the construction process. You should choose sufficient area so that the page can be useful without compromising the consistency of the site's overall graphic design.

These areas that you will allow to be changed during the page design process are known as *editable regions*. They are identified in Dreamweaver by special tags within the page code. When you are creating pages from templates, only the sections of HTML within these special tags can be edited.

Each page that is created from a template has one editable region by default: the title tag (called doctitle). This editable region allows you to use the Page Properties dialog box or the Title text box in the document window of Dreamweaver to set a unique title for each page.

Other editable regions must be chosen and designated by you when the template is created. The eFlea template will be created from the index page you created in Fireworks. It is a simple design, with the graphics confined to the top portion of the page. This leaves a rather large area beneath those graphics that is well suited for each page's unique content. We will designate it as the editable region for this template.

NOTE

You can have as many editable regions as you would like in a template as long as you give each one a unique name. Be careful not to litter your page with editable regions, though. If you find yourself needing to have more than two or three, you may want to rethink the page's design and the complexity of the graphics you are using.

Prepare the Content Area

Preparing the content area is as simple as making sure that it is empty space. In the eFlea page that is being prepared to become a template, the content area is the large table cell beneath the graphics. Although it may look empty, when you select the table cell, you will see that it actually contains a large white square. This is a side effect of the export function in Fireworks. Although you may not have actually placed anything in that portion of the image, the processing of flattening your image in a GIF file and exporting it makes every slice contain something, even if it is just a big white square representing the white background of the original image. Delete the image, leaving an empty table cell where you want the content area to be.

At this point, save the page as a template by selecting File | Save As Template. A Save As Template dialog box will appear. Make sure the eFlea site is selected. Give the template a name in the Save As box and click Save. This page will be saved as a template in a special folder called Templates underneath your site root. This folder will be created if it does not already exist.

You will notice that the Save As Template box gives you a list of existing templates for the site you are working with. It is important to note that different areas of your site may warrant different designs, and you can create a variety of templates to accommodate your needs.

Mark the Content Area

In order for Dreamweaver to know that this area will be an editable region, you must mark it as such and name it so it can be referenced. Once your page is saved as a template, you are able to access additional template menu items that allow you to mark up the page as needed.

NOTE

When you first save a page as a template, it is left open for you to do additional work with, such as creating editable regions. If you try to close the page without creating any regions, you will be warned that the page contains no editable regions and will be of little use as a template.

With your mouse in the table cell that you want to mark, right-click and select New Editable Region from the pop-up menu. A New Editable Region dialog box will appear. Name the region Content and click OK. A label will appear in the table cell marking the region. Save the page and your template is ready to be used to create other pages in your site.

Use Templates to Add Pages to Your Site

As you prepare to create pages from your template, it is important to consider what is happening when you do so. A page that is created from a template or that has a template applied to it actually contains a reference back to the template file. This is a very important point and is a key factor in the usefulness of templates. Not only do they allow you to build a site using a consistent design, they also allow you to keep that design consistent even when you need to make changes to it. Whenever a template file is edited, you will be given the opportunity to update all of the pages that contain links to that template so they reflect the changes that were made. This is a much easier proposition than going through page by page making changes that you or your client may decide upon. One template update can cascade those changes for you.

There are actually a few ways to apply a template to a page. Here are three popular methods:

- Create the page from the template initially

- Apply a template to an existing page

- Drop a template onto a page from the Assets panel

Create the Page from the Template

Select File | New and select the Templates tab of the New Document window. Select the e-Flea site and the template you created and click the Create button. This will create a new page containing the template's design in the document window. The editable regions will be marked, and you can begin to add that page's unique content or database references.

Apply a Template to an Existing Page

If you already have a page that contains information, and you then decide to apply a template to it, you can use a set of selections in the Modify menu to assist you. Select Modify | Templates and a submenu will be presented that allows you to perform several operations. The first is Apply Template To Page. This selection will allow you to choose from the available templates for the current site and will apply the template you select to the page.

There is an important thing to remember if the page to which you are applying the template already has something on it. The existing content of the page can be moved into an editable region of the template, but into only one editable region. When you apply the template, you will be asked which editable region should house the existing page elements. Your options are to pick one region to hold the content or to have the content deleted. If you need the existing content to be displayed in more than one editable region of the template, have it placed into one of the regions and divide it up by hand once the template is applied.

The Templates menu selection also allows you to detach a page from a template. Doing so does not remove the content that was inherited from the template; it simply removes the reference to the template so that future edits to the template file will not affect the design of this particular page.

In addition, you can use the Template menu selection to open the template file that the current page is attached to. This can be a convenient way to locate and edit the template file if something that needs editing is hampering your ability to construct the current page properly.

Drop a Template onto a Page

Choosing the templates icon to the left of the Assets panel allows you to view a thumbnail of each of the available templates. When you find the one you want to apply, you may simply grab it with your mouse and drag it onto the page you are currently editing. The same existing content constraints that were discussed in the previous section apply to this method as well.

What to Take Away from This Module

Although Dreamweaver is a powerful data-centered application development environment, its design features make it a powerful platform for all aspects of site construction. This module has covered some of the basics of site design. Using this foundation, you can quickly begin the population of your site with data-driven content. Remember, though, that even hard data must be presented in a manner that is appealing to the end user.

Module 5 Mastery Check

1. What three methods can be used to apply a template to a page?

2. When exporting a page design from Fireworks to Dreamweaver, the Fireworks graphic is divided into portions called _____.

3. An image that responds to a user's mouse contacting it is known as a _____.

4. What happens to existing content when a template is applied to a page?

5. A combination of what three things is used to create pages in Dreamweaver?

6. When creating slices in Fireworks, the programs will automatically name them for you. You can change the assigned names on the _____.

7. When creating a Dreamweaver template, you will identify a content area known as an _____.

8. Templates are used primarily to give your site a _____.

9. Creating a simple page in Dreamweaver is done with a combination of what?

10. If a link on your page leads to a page outside your site, you should make sure to use what?

Part II

Creating Web Applications With Dreamweaver MX

Module 6

Planning the Site

Web designs are growing increasingly complex, and keeping a visitor's attention is getting harder and harder. Thinking about it from the perspective of a Web surfer, there are a few key things to consider:

- When you visit a site, how long do you wait for a page to load before you become impatient and close down the window?

- How much are you willing to read on a page before it becomes too "wordy?"

- How many times can you watch the same spiffy graphic on a page before it becomes boring?

- What color combinations quickly become irritating or hard to read?

CRITICAL SKILL
6.1 Plan and Design Your Site

When you begin to build data-driven sites, it becomes more important than ever that you take the time to plan and design your site. Too many people jump right into building pages without properly considering the details of what they plan to do. Not only will a lack of planning impact the quality of your final product, it may get you into a sticky situation with a client whose ideas about the site were different than yours. Building a Web page is easy, but building a Web application, possibly with a database back-end is no trivial task, and proper planning is a necessity. From the server type to the database type to the language you are going to use, these are all considerations when planning out your Web site. You might have a background in Visual Basic, but decide that the features of a ColdFusion site make it more cost-effective to do the site in ColdFusion. Or maybe you have access to JSP and MySQL, but only know ASP. Dreamweaver works with five server technologies, so the environment is friendly to whichever server you choose.

Once you've decided on a course of action, however, you can't easily change midstream. Dreamweaver doesn't have any built-in functionality for changing from one server technology to another or from one language to another if you are building an ASP site. It pays to plan your site in detail before building the pages. Although the techniques for building the pages are the same, the code that's used in creating the functionality in the five server models is completely different.

 TIP

You can't change midstream to another server technology in a site, but you can go back and re-create the functionality in another server model by simply starting from scratch with a page and applying the same server behaviors with the same parameters.

Some of the things you need to consider when planning your site are

- The purpose and goal of the site
- Your target audience
- The tools and platforms available to you and your client
- The site's design
- Your navigation scheme
- Development time and cost

CRITICAL SKILL
6.2 Establish the Purpose of the Site

It should go without saying that you need to understand the purpose and goal of the site you are designing, yet too little attention is paid to this basic element of Web site creation. There are several questions you must answer to truly understand the purpose of the site you are creating:

- Is this an information, education, entertainment, or commerce site?
- Is the site intended to display cutting-edge technique or to reach a broad audience?
- Will the site service a company, regional, or global community of users?
- How will the site be used?
- How will traffic be driven to the site?
- What competition is there for the niche this site will service?

When you can answer these questions, you will be well on your way to developing an understanding of the work you are about to undertake. However, it is important that your answers to these questions are the same answers as your client's. Too often, a designer spends hours on a snazzy Flash introduction only to find that the client doesn't like Flash. Work with your client to discover the answers to these questions.

The Focus of the Site

The focus of your site will cross the lines between information, education, entertainment, and commerce. Many sites, like Pepsi's at www.pepsi.com, seek to entertain while educating their visitors about their products and generating sales. Still, whether your site will have a single focus or a combination of purposes, you should be able to boil them down to a statement or two that will serve as the "mission statement" under which you will work.

For instance, let's consider the site that we are going to work on in this book. The site is for a fictitious online company called eFlea.us. eFlea.us is a site that will serve as a "flea market" or "swap meet" on the Internet. Users will be able to post things for sale and make purchases of items for sale. It will be sort of like eBay without the bidding—everything has a price. Naturally, the business model consists of the site being able to keep a small percentage of each sale.

We can also make some assumptions about the site. Because this will be a corporate presence for eFlea.us, we can assume that it should be a professional presentation. People should feel safe and secure that anything they place on the site for sale will bring together reputable sellers and buyers together in secure transactions. Buyers should feel safe that anything they buy will have the eFlea.us stamp of approval on it. This kind of Web presence can take time to establish, but we'll assume for the purpose of these exercises that the Web presence won't be a problem.

To tie all of this together, we might come up with the following "mission statement" to guide us through the development of this site:

"The eFlea.us Web site will be a central marketplace for the average consumer to be able to buy and sell used or new merchandise, as in a flea market or swap meet. Sellers will have to sign up and establish a history with eFlea so that the buyers can feel secure in buying merchandise from them."

This statement may change as we go, but it is a good place to start, and it provides a cogent picture of the site.

How the Site Will Be Used

Just as different sites have different purposes, visitors use sites differently. Some sites are free flowing, allowing navigation to any page from any page. Others guide the user through a series of steps toward a goal, and to allow deviation from that series of steps would interrupt its effective use.

The eFlea site, as with many sites, is a combination of these. Although the casual visitor may jump from place to place browsing the products for sale, a user who decides to participate as a seller will need to be walked through the steps necessary to create an online presence and establish credentials as a qualified merchant of eFlea.

Competition

Unless you are one of the rare few who create an industry, your site will likely have competition, and you are well advised to pay attention to it. It is entirely acceptable to offer services in a different way than your competition, but it is not acceptable to do so without a clear purpose. Learn everything you can about what is happening in your industry. It can only help you serve your customer base better.

Your Target Audience

The need to understand your target audience cannot be stressed enough. In the big world of the Web, it is likely that any one site will appeal to only a small percentage of users. If you do not know who is in your percentage, you have no hope of finding them and getting them to your site. There are several things you need to know about your target audience before you can figure out how to reach them over the Internet:

- Does my audience have computers?

- How much time do they spend on the Web?

- What browsers do they use?

- How do they hear about new Web sites?

- How computer savvy are they?

CRITICAL SKILL

6.3 Make Basic Site Construction Decisions

When you are working on sites for your own use, you are free to use your choice of development tools and platforms. This consideration becomes more important when you begin constructing sites for clients that already have ideas about the way they want things done. Often, you will be called upon to maintain or add to existing architecture. Convincing a client that has a considerable amount of work done in, say, ColdFusion, that they should allow you to do your part in ASP is a tough sell, and even if you can sell it, the client is often dissatisfied with the final product.

Although many developers work quite successfully in a number of languages, you will certainly want to build some space into your design plan if you will be working on a platform that is less than familiar to you. Dreamweaver makes the transition from one server model to another much easier, however, because the one tool works with five different server technologies and makes the transition between them almost invisible. Applying a server behavior to a JSP page is identical to applying the same server behavior to an ASP page or a ColdFusion page. Even with that in mind, the extra time involved in working outside of your primary language should be built into the cost.

The Site's Design

Although you will likely begin to formulate the actual look and feel of the site only when you sit down at the computer and start fiddling with it, there are some decisions you can make at this point in the process that will help you when you get there.

Will the Site Be Based in HTML or in Graphics?

Sites based in HTML are typically made up of HTML text over a colored background or a tiled or image background. This technique can be used very effectively and gives a simple, no-nonsense interface when the information is the most important thing.

Sites based in graphics generally use a more intricate interface that is designed and imported from a graphics program such as Fireworks or Photoshop. The links are often graphic text overlaid with hotspots rather than text anchors.

Will You Use Frames?

Although frames were all the rage for a while, they seem to have fallen into some disfavor of late. There are certainly opportunities to make good use of frames, but you will typically find it cleaner to avoid them and the temptations they present. Too many sites end up framing in other sites, which frame in other sites, and the result is just a big mess.

Which of the Common Layouts Will You Use?

Several basic page layouts seem to work best on the Web. Although designers are forever looking for ways to differentiate their pages, the most usable pages seem to adhere to two or three basic layouts: the navigation bar on the left, the top navigation bar, and the page of links where the entire page is made up of columns that house links to other places. A few sites use a navigation bar on the right, but users seem to have grown used to these other three layouts and find them to be the easiest to navigate.

Commit to Avoiding the Design No-Nos

Although you probably don't need to hear this, it is such an annoying problem that I need to say it. Text is unreadable when placed over a tiled image of your dog. Light yellow text is unreadable on anything except a solid black background. I'm sure the 1960s were a lot of fun, but tie-dyed page backgrounds are annoying.

Take care that you do not spend your time creating something that is unusable or annoying to your visitors. A quick tour around the Web will provide you with a great many examples of this. If you need help to determine appropriate design, seek it out on the many great Web design newsgroups or from a knowledgeable colleague.

Progress Check

1. What are the two main styles of site navigation?

2. Can you easily change from ASP to ColdFusion after the site is halfway completed in Dreamweaver?

3. How many server technologies does Dreamweaver MX natively support?

CRITICAL SKILL
6.4 Add Pages to the Site with the Site Map

The design of your navigation scheme goes hand in hand with the site design you consider using. But as you begin to consider your site's navigation, it is appropriate to start sketching out the pages that you will need to create for the site. Start with the home page and begin adding pages in your drawing and indicating links. Tools such as Microsoft's Visio and Rational Rose can assist in this process. You will be amazed how much more quickly your site will come together when you have planned the pages that make it up and how they connect to one another.

---

1. Navigation link across the top and navigation links along the left side of the page

2. No, there is no built-in conversion capability. This should be taken into consideration before site construction begins.

3. Five

Site Map Layout

After creating the general navigation concepts for your site, you can use Dreamweaver's Site Map to help in the process of building the pages and links. The Site Map can even be saved as a PNG or BMP file so you can open it up in your image editor.

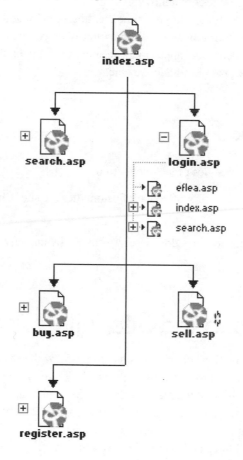

The Site Map is a visual representation of the linking in your site. For instance, if you have a home page with links to six pages, the Site Map will show the home page with six arrows pointing to the six files that the home page links to. Each link in those six pages will have a corresponding arrow pointing to pages that the link points to. The Site Map Layout dialog box contains these following attributes to help define the Site Map:

- **Home Page**   This is your site's home page. You can either fill in the complete path or browse to it by clicking the folder icon. The Site Map won't work without having a home page defined.

- **Number of Columns**   This is the number of columns in the top level of the Site Map. For instance, if you have a home page that links to five pages under it, you might set the number 5 for Number Of Columns.

- **Column Width**   This is a number between 70 and 1,000 to define the width of each column in the Site Map. If you make your columns wider, you will be able to fit more items in each group, but you may have to scroll left and right to see the whole map.

- **Icon Labels**   These two radio buttons are labeled File Names and Page Titles. You can choose one or the other for the label of the page on the Site Map.

- **Options**   These two check boxes allow the following:

    - **Display Files Marked As Hidden**   Allows you to display pages such as template files, which are generally hidden from view.

    - **Display Dependent Files**   These are files that may not be linked to a page, but are dependent on the page via a form action or some other means. This box allows these pages to be shown as well.

Project 6-1   The Site Map

Module 4 allowed you to create the site definition for the eFlea site. In this project, you'll add some blank pages to the site by using the Site Map. The Site Map is a good place to create your files and links. Module 4 listed several ways to add pages to a site, but this project will allow you to work with the Site Map to create the basic outline of the site. The Site Map allows you not only to add pages, but to create the navigation scheme as well.

(continued)

6

Planning the Site

Project 6-1

The Site Map

Step by Step

1. Open Dreamweaver and make sure the current site is the eFlea site that was set up in Module 4. The site should be blank at this point, or it may contain a few files that you have been practicing with.

2. Open the Site Definition dialog box again. You can do this by clicking Site | Edit Sites and then clicking Edit on the resulting dialog box to edit the eFlea site definitions.

3. In the Category box, select the Site Map Layout option. This will bring you to the following page:

4. Set the Number of Columns to 1. This will be the width (in pages) of your Site Map. As you become more familiar with the program, you'll find that there are settings that work well depending on how your navigation is set up.

5. If the home page hasn't been defined yet, type **index.asp** (or index.jsp, index.cfm, index.aspx, or index.php depending on your server model). If the page doesn't exist yet, Dreamweaver will ask if you want to create it. You can click OK to this.

6. After a few seconds, the Site Map will open with the new index.asp page displayed in the center.

7. Right-click (CONTROL-click on a Macintosh) on the index.asp page in the Site Map. This should bring up a list of options, as shown here:

```
View as Root
Link to New File...
Link to Existing File...
Change Link...
Remove Link
Show/Hide Link
Open to Source of Link
Open
Open With                   ▶
Add to Favorites

Get
Check Out
Put
Check In
Undo Check Out

Preview in Browser          ▶
Check Links                 ▶
Check Target Browsers...

Design Notes...
```

(continued)

8. Click Link To New File, and another dialog box will pop up asking for three things, which you should fill in as follows:

- **File Name** search.htm
- **Title** Search eFlea
- **Text of Link** Search page

9. Do the same thing (from the index.asp page for each one) for register.asp, login.asp, buy.asp, and sell.asp.

10. Open the index.asp file now and take a look at it. It should have the five links at the top of the page for the new pages you've set up. More importantly, the five pages have been created with titles, and the navigation scheme has been roughed out. It may change later, but now you can open the index page and be able to browse any of your other pages from there by clicking a link.

11. Now look in the Site window (not the Site Map) and create a new file there by right-clicking and selecting New File. Call it test.htm. You'll notice that it doesn't show up in the Site Map.

12. Go back to the Site Map and select the index page again. You'll notice a small globe-shaped icon next to it. Click on this globe and—holding the mouse button down—drag the line that it creates right to the test.htm file and drop it on the file. This will create a link on the index page to the new test.htm file. You'll also notice that the test.htm file now shows up in the Site Map.

Project Summary

The Site map provides a good way to visually framework your site and the relationships between its pages. You may find it useful to describe the pages that you plan to include in your site and how they will link together by using the site map early in the site creation process.

Understand Basic Design Concepts

It's all about packaging, really. The days of single color or tiled backgrounds with simple text on them are not gone, as a quick tour around the Web will show, but they are going. Your competition has great looking sites, and if you want to have a chance to distinguish your sites among them, you need great looking sites, too.

Ask the Expert

Q: I am a designer. Do I need to learn all of this server-side information?

A: Dreamweaver is an excellent tool for the designer aspects of site construction, and you may find that your particular responsibilities limit you to that part of the program. But the Web is moving from static sites to managed content, and users refine their needs and seek out the most helpful and informative sites. Whether or not you ever have to write a SQL query, it is assured that you will have to work on sites that use server-side technologies. The more you understand about them, the more valuable you will be to the development team. Dreamweaver makes it simple to ease into server-side work.

If we could teach you in a few paragraphs how to become a world-class graphic artist, we would be rich, and you would have paid a heck of a lot more for this book. But there are a few things you can learn from this book.

Navigation

Navigation is the means by which you allow your user to get around your site. As we said earlier, there are times when you will want to allow the users to move freely to and from any page that strikes their fancy, and there are times when you need them to remain on a set path in order to complete the task they have set about. We will use both in the eFlea Web site.

If there is one rule that applies to navigation in general, it would have to be to keep it clear, keep it simple, and don't overdo it. (Okay, so that's *three* rules.)

Keep It Clear

When users look at your site, they should be able to tell two things rather quickly: where the navigation links are (how to get around) and where those links will take them. There is a trend in Web development that has been dubbed "mystery meat navigation." Mystery meat navigation is when the designer presents you with image-based links with little if any indication where they lead. At best, you can hover over the image link (if you can find it) and get a tool tip with a hint as to where you might end up if you were to click on it. Although this kind of navigation might lend itself to the look and feel of the art you are trying to create, it is frustrating to the user and leads more to visitors moving on to a site that clearly presents the information they are seeking than it does to them fawning over your design sense.

Keep in mind that most Web sites are for the purpose of communicating with visitors. Use links that are text-based (either HTML or graphic text) or images along with text that identify the links. Although it may offend your design sense, it will keep your visitors at your site longer because they can clearly see how to get around.

Keep It Simple

Your site may be 200 pages. There may be something very interesting on each and every page which you are excited about sharing with everyone who drops by. But 200 links on your home page is going to overwhelm them and drive them away in frustration.

Keep your navigation simple. Design a hierarchy of concepts within your site that leads visitors to areas of interest, and then offer additional pages that fall within that area. Keep the number of links on your home page reasonable. What is reasonable? That is for you to decide. But if you are feeling the need to put much more than ten navigational links on it, you may want to rethink your site structure. If every one of those pages is so unrelated to the other pages around it that it has to have its own link from the home page, you have a maze on your hands that few people will want to wade through.

NOTE

These "rules" are generalizations. They are good generalizations, but they may not apply to your specific circumstance. If you are designing a portal site, for instance, like www.yahoo.com or www.cnet.com, there may be a good reason to make your home page a mass of links. As always, rules are made to be broken, but you must know what rules you are breaking and why.

Don't Overdo It

Another disturbing trend in page design is repeating links. Almost as a means of filling space, designers will put identical links in a navigation bar on the left, as an image in the body of the page or at the top, and as a text link at the bottom of the page. Unless your pages are extremely long and you are concerned that users will get lost in them, you don't need to provide duplicate links all over the place.

Usability

It can't be said enough: Web sites are for the communication of information to your visitors. It does not matter if you are tired of making sites with left-hand navigation. If that is what your visitors expect to see, if that is what will keep them at your site, then that is what you need to give them.

The following rules are fairly accepted usability practice:

- Keep your page-load times limited to 10 to 20 seconds on a 56K modem.

- Don't pop up new windows on your visitors.

- Frames are not the best idea. If you do use them, don't frame in other sites. It is annoying to your users and to the people whose site you are framing in.

- Always provide a link back to your home page.

- Make sure that your site's features work in the available browsers. Make sure you know going into a project what browsers you are targeting so that you can test for degradation, especially if you plan to use cascading style sheets (CSS).

Media

"Media" is a pretty broad term. It can relate to anything from the images on your site to sound files to extravagant Flash files. Here is a list of things to remember when choosing and using media on your site:

- **Use the appropriate file type for images.**   JPEG files are often preferred for photographs, but they are lossy and can be large if you are not careful. GIFs are good for graphics and graphic text.

- **Only use transparency when it is needed.**   Don't make part of an image transparent and then stick it on a white background. It bloats the file unnecessarily.

- **Optimize your graphics.**   A product like Fireworks will allow you to optimize your files by selecting different numbers of colors or different quality settings and observing how picture quality is affected.

- **Size your images properly before putting them on your page.**   Resizing in HTML takes a long time and produces questionable quality.

- **Flash is really cool, but use it cautiously.**   Although the Flash player is becoming ubiquitous, bandwidth that can handle the files is not. If you do use it, give your visitors a way out—a way to skip the file or never start viewing it in the first place.

- **Do not load MIDI files with your home page that start playing as soon as the page loads.**   They usually sound terrible. If you are forced to use one, provide a prominent Off button.

Use Collaborative Development

In addition to the physical specifications of the Web site, such as server type, database type, and server language, there are other decisions as well. If there is more than one person involved with the site design and implementation, you will need to decide on the workflow and who handles the different aspects of the site. A carefully thought-out plan designed in advance is going to eliminate confusion between the collaborators. If everyone's task is spelled out—including the completion dates for each aspect—the process will be much smoother.

Design and Development

Dreamweaver is typically the development tool of choice for designing Web pages. If different people are doing the design and server-side programming, Dreamweaver makes it easy to work side by side and not interfere with each other's workflow. Dreamweaver allows designers and developers to communicate well with each other, allowing for a collaborative development process.

TIP

Dreamweaver offers the capability to have more than one designer or programmer working on a site by using check-in and check-out features, as shown in Module 4, and including design notes in the site. By checking Enable File Check In And Check Out in the Site Definition dialog box, this feature is enabled in your site. When a page is "checked out" by a user, it is marked as such in the site window, and it will be locked from editing by another user.

In addition to the collaboration features, Dreamweaver makes it easier for programmers and designers to work together because they can both work from the same program. The server-side code will be unobtrusive to the designer, as most of the code will have *translators* that make the design environment easy to work with.

NOTE

A translator is a Dreamweaver extension that is able to take a section of code and translate it into something that's meaningful to the developer. For instance, a translator for a recordset column translates the code into a readable "{Recordsetname.columnname}" that shows up in the design environment.

Design Notes

One way to communicate with others on your team is by using "sticky notes." These notes are typically pasted to the desktop or monitor of the person that the note is intended for. Dreamweaver has its own version of the sticky note, called a *design note*. Design notes can be attached to any page in the site by using the Site window or Site Map.

View as Root
Link to New File...
Link to Existing File...
Change Link...
Remove Link
Show/Hide Link
Open to Source of Link
Open
Open With ▶
Add to Favorites
Get
Check Out
Put
Check In
Undo Check Out
Preview in Browser ▶
Check Links ▶
Check Target Browsers...
Design Notes...

The design notes for the site are stored in the _notes folder under your site root. The actual note file is an XML file with a .mno file extension that Dreamweaver will read internally. Each page that has a note attached to it will cause a file to be generated in the _notes folder on the remote site (and the local site). Here is a typical note:

TIP

Design notes are a great way to log changes to a page so that other people working on the site can follow what is going on. If everyone is religious about adding notes every time they make a change, the design process can be a lot smoother.

Design notes can be set to open automatically when you open a file. This is especially handy when working in a collaborative environment. If your teammate has made a change to the file, he or she can leave a design note attached to the page. You will be able to see the note the next time you open the page. This way, it is less likely that any changes in the page will be overwritten by another person.

File View Columns

Another way to use design notes is to create your own file view columns in the Site window. Clicking File View Columns in the Site Definition window allows you to configure the look of the Site window by allowing you to pick and choose the columns that you are going to show, and even define your own columns. For instance, you could have a Programmer column to show the name of the person responsible for a given page, or a Date Due column listing specific due dates for pages. An Important Message column could allow you to place a short message that will be seen by everyone on your team when they open the site. You can use your imagination and create columns that pertain to your own situation and add the appropriate design notes to each page.

This is done by defining your column with a column name and then associating it with a design note. When you create a design note, you can give the note a name/value pair that will cause it to show up in the column.

TIP

You can be creative with your file view columns. If there is anything that you want to keep track of for each page, a file view column is a good place to put it.

You can add a new column by clicking the plus (+) button above the column list, or delete a column by clicking the minus (–) button. The up-arrow and down-arrow buttons allow you to arrange the columns in a particular order. The attributes associated with the File View Columns window are as follows:

- **Enable Column Sharing**   This is a check box that enables the columns to be shared between users. In other words, the columns you see are the same columns that the rest of your design team will see.

- **Column Name**   This is a unique name that will be the column heading in the Site window.

- **Associate with Design Note**   This is the name of the design note that the column will get its information from. For instance, if you have a design note named Important Message, whenever the Site window is opened, every page that has an Important Message note attached to it will show the actual contents of the message in the column.

- **Align**   This can be Left, Right, or Center and is the alignment of the data in the column.

- **Options**   There are two options:

  - **Show**   Allows you to turn off certain columns if you don't want them to show in the Site window.

  - **Share with All Users of This Site**   This check box determines whether the column is something that will be stored on the server for all users to see, or if it's only to be seen on your particular computer.

CRITICAL SKILL
6.7 Use Site-Wide Find/Replace

Dreamweaver is a Web application development tool. When you use Dreamweaver, you will be working on one document at a time, but the *whole site* should be your focus. One feature that you may find very handy is the Find/Replace dialog box.

Find/Replace has become a standard feature in most computer programs, and one of the most often used features, as well. One thing you might not be aware of, however, is that in Dreamweaver you can do the searches on a site-wide basis. This makes it especially handy for changing something that is on every page in the site, such as a color.

The Find/Replace dialog box has several unique features that bear mentioning.

Find In

This drop-down list gives you several options for finding text and code within your site:

- **Current Document**   This is a standard search in the currently open document.

- **Entire Local Site**   This option allows you to do a site-wide search and replace.

- **Selected Files in Site**   This option allows you to multiselect files in the Site window and restricts your search to certain files.

- **Folder**   This option allows you to do searches on any folder on your hard drive. In effect, it turns Dreamweaver into a powerful search-and-replace tool that you can use outside of Dreamweaver.

Search For

This is a drop-down list that gives you four options for items you may want to search:

- **Source Code**   This option allows you to search throughout the source code of your page—scripting, server-side code, tags, and actual text all fall under this category. In short, if it's in the document in any form, you can find it with this option.

- **Text**   This option narrows the search to the actual text that is viewable on the page. For instance, if you want to search for the word "color," but you don't want to match the instances of the word in the HTML, you could use the Text option.

- **Text (Advanced)**   This option allows you to refine your search to text that is contained within certain tags or outside of certain tags. There are further refinements and several other options that can be accessed by clicking the plus (+) button.

- **Specific Tag**   This option not only allows you to search for specific tags, but also allows you to search for attributes within those tags and even set the attributes for a tag site-wide. For example, if you wanted all <td> tags to have a mouseover attribute set to a certain function, you can do it here. Or, if you wanted all <font> tags with a size of 2 to have their size attribute changed to 3, you could do it with this feature.

Options

The options for the dialog box are shown as check boxes and are as follows:

- **Match Case**   This allows you to match only those words that match the case exactly, so "font" wouldn't match "Font."

- **Ignore Whitespace Differences**   This allows you to do searches where spaces, line feeds, and tabs have no effect on the outcome of the search.

- **Use Regular Expressions**   If you know how to use regular expressions, you can take advantage of the powerful RegExp features of the Search/ Replace dialog box. For example, to search for all instances of things contained within quotes, you could use the following RegExp, which searches for a quote and then finds all characters up to and including the next quote character that it finds:

```
"[^"]*"
```

If you were to search the source code of your document, and the document contained the following tag:

```
<table width"100%" border"1">
```

your search using the regular expression above would find two matches:

```
"100%"
"1"
```

What to Take Away from This Module

You should now know a few things about creating navigation schemes. You learned some of the generally accepted principles of site design. The Site Map was used in a project to show you a method of developing a graphical representation of your site, while at the same time creating the links for the site navigation. Some of the collaboration techniques available in Dreamweaver were outlined, including the use of design notes. Finally, the Find/Replace dialog box was explained.

Module 6 Mastery Check

1. Will the Site Map feature of Dreamweaver work without a home page?

2. How are design notes stored in Dreamweaver?

3. Does Dreamweaver's Find/Replace work outside the site you are currently working on?

4. Do all the files in your Site Window show up in the Site Map?

5. What is a regular expression?

6. Name two site design no-nos.

7. What are some questions that you need answered about your target audience?

8. What collaboration features help make sure that team members do not overwrite each other's work?

9. Page load times should be limited to about _____ on a 56K modem.

10. What is a translator?

Module 7

Essential Language Components

Each of the server models has specific language components and syntax that you will need to become aware of if you plan to do any serious Web programming work—with or without Dreamweaver MX. Dreamweaver MX is a visual tool, but like any visual tool, the visual part only goes so far. If you come to a point where the built-in functionality doesn't do what you need it to do, you'll have to look under the hood and see what's powering the pages. In a static site, this is just the HTML and JavaScript code that you can see by viewing the source in the browser. In a dynamic site, the underlying functionality is provided by server-side code that the end user will never see. In the case of Dreamweaver MX, this code can be VBScript, JScript, Java, PHP, VB, C#, or CFML.

We introduce some of the key elements of server-side scripting by discussing the ASP object model, and then briefly cover Java, PHP, ASP.NET, and CFML and the ways they might differ from ASP.

CRITICAL SKILL
7.1 Learn the Basics of ASP

Although ASP is often spoken of as an entity unto itself, it is actually a combination of technologies that work together to deliver dynamic page content. At the base is the HTML that serves as the static framework of the page. To that is added a series of ASP objects that can be manipulated by scripting languages such as VBScript and JScript. Finally, ASP can include a number of active server components, from Microsoft's ActiveX Data Objects (ADO) for data access to custom COM components that you develop in-house or get from third parties. Integral to the process are the ASP objects that tie together the client and the server.

ASP code is contained within <% %> tags. These tags tell the ASP server that anything contained within them is to be executed on the server before the page is sent to the browser. You can freely mix ASP code with HTML code, and only the resulting HTML is seen by the end user.

The *Request* Object

When a browser makes a call to a server to retrieve a Web page, it is said to be making a request. In addition to the name of the page it wants, the browser sends a variety of other information to the server. The added information may be intentional, such as a form post or a query string, or it may be the standard information that is passed in by the browser behind the scenes whenever it communicates with a server. Either way, the ASP *Request* object grabs all of that information and makes it readily available to the server. The *Request* object has five collections from which it gathers this information:

- The *QueryString* collection
- The *Form* collection

- The *ServerVariables* collection

- The *Cookies* collection

- The *ClientCertificate* collection

We look at three of these.

The *QueryString* Collection

You are no doubt familiar with the uniform resource locator (URL) used to direct your browser to the site you wish to visit. A URL contains a protocol (such as http://) and a fully qualified domain name (such as www.macromedia.com). It may also contain a reference to the specific page you are looking for. A query string is additional information that is passed to the page you request. The information is passed in name/value pairs following a question mark (?). For example, if there were a page called login.asp at the Dreamweaver Team site, you would access it with the following URL:

http://www.dwteam.com/login.asp

That page might expect a username and password to be passed in so that your visit can be validated. That username and password could be passed in a query string like this:

```
http://www.dwteam.com/login.asp?name=jim&pass=huffy
```

Notice the extra information in this version of the URL. Following the ? are two name/value pairs. The parameter names *name* and *pass* are assigned the values *jim* and *huffy*, respectively. Each pair is separated by an ampersand (&).

You can pass parameters into any page like this. If the page doesn't expect them, they are ignored. But if the page knows what to do with this information (or even requires it to work properly), it can make use of it within the page's code. The *Request* object allows you to retrieve and manipulate these parameters.

To retrieve the value of a name/value pair, you can simply place the following line within ASP tags on your page:

```
<% myVariable = Request.QueryString("name")%>
```

The query string is a convenient way to pass information between pages. It can allow you to use a single page destination for multiple purposes by passing in a parameter that indicates where a user came from or where he or she wants to go. Remember, though, that the query string is available to the user in the address bar of his or her browser. He or she can see what you are passing, and can even fiddle with it by changing parameter values and resubmitting the page. This can cause a security nightmare if you do not consider ways to make sure that visitors see only information that should be available to them.

The *Form* Collection

The *Form* collection works much like the *QueryString* collection, except that its name/value pairs come from the elements of a form that is posted to an ASP *action* page. The action attribute of the form element is set to the action page, where you can then process the data. Although the query string is a great way to pass parameters that you can control, a form is much more suited to collecting input from your user and capturing it for manipulation within your code. To retrieve a form variable passed to a form action page, you could retrieve it like this:

```
<% myVariable = Request.Form("myFormElement") %>
```

The *Cookies* Collection

There has been much hoopla over the use of cookies over the past several years. Apparently, people want a highly interactive Web experience, but object to the tiny files that help make that possible. Let's be clear, cookies play an important role in a site's capability to offer a personalized experience for its users. They make the Web more interesting and more convenient for most users. The risk of a security breach is overblown, which becomes obvious when you understand how cookies work.

Cookies are nothing but small text files that reside on your user's computer. Each browser has a special place where it keeps cookies. As a result, a computer may have more than one directory of files each associated with a particular brand of browser. These files store information about a user that relates to the site that creates the cookie. It could be a username and password or the user's choice of a colored background he or she prefers when visiting the site. Anything that can be expressed as a name/value pair in a small text file can be written to a cookie by an application and later retrieved.

An important point to remember is that a Web application can only read the cookies that it wrote itself. So a rogue application cannot read the information on the user's computer and glean password information for another site.

Cookies are read using the *Request* object, much like the other collections. Use the following format to read a cookie that was set previously:

```
Request.Cookies("cookiename")
```

The *Response* Object

What the *Request* object is to receiving information, the *Response* object is to sending it out. Whether you need to simply write information into the user's browser or direct them off to another location, you can send information and commands back to your visitor's browser by using the *Response* object. We cover two of the four main methods of the *Response* object: *Write* and *Redirect*.

The *Write* Method

Now that you know how the HTML stream works, you will be interested to know how you can use ASP to insert items into it based on the processing of your page. The *Write* method of the *Response* object can be used to insert information into your pages. For instance:

```
<%
Dim X
X=53
Response.Write "The value of X is " & x
%>
```

This will concatenate the string of text with the variable *x* to end up with an actual text line like this:

```
The value of X is 53
```

NOTE

Because we are using VBScript here, we used the & character to concatenate my strings. In JScript or JavaScript, you can do the same thing using the + operator.

You can also use a shortcut method of *Response.Write* to write the value of a variable like this:

```
<% = X %>
```

This line would simply write 53 to the browser. Needless to say, this method is best used when the data you are writing is self-explanatory, such as *<% = Now %>* to write the time, or when it is in conjunction with other formatting that makes the values you are displaying meaningful.

The *Redirect* Method

There will often be times when you need to send users to other pages within your application based on their input or the processing of the data they submit. The *Redirect* method of the

Response object allows you to do server-side redirection to the page of your choice. For example:

```
<%
Response.Redirect("home.asp")
%>
```

The *Session* Object

Essentially, the Internet operates on what are known as stateless protocols. What that means is that the basic HTTP protocol does not maintain a record of who is currently connected to it. Each request is handled by the server as if it were the only time that particular client had asked for something.

Contrast that to the way local area networks work. If you have ever rebooted your computer in a networked setting you may have seen a warning message that tells you that a certain number of computers are currently connected to yours and that shutting down will disconnect them. Your local network protocols are maintaining the state of those users that are connected to your computer.

Application servers such as ASP provide an elegant solution to the problem of maintaining state in Web applications. The *Session* object can hold information about your user in a way that is unique, secure, and easy to use. The *Session* object is actually a set of variables that you define that are stored on the server. As long as your visitor remains connected to your site (meaning that he continues to make requests without pausing longer than the timeout value set for the *Session* object), those variables persist and can be used to identify and track them. The *Session* object makes use of a unique session ID for each user. This ID is written to a cookie on the client computer and serves to identify which set of session variables should be associated with that user. So, if the user has cookies disabled in their browser, the *Session* object will fail.

To write a value to a session variable in ASP, you could do the following:

```
<% Session("username") = Request.form("txtUsername") %>
```

This would retrieve a form value named *txtUsername* and place it into a session variable named *username*. To display the variable on the page, you could use the shorthand form of the *Response.Write* method:

```
<%= Session("username") %>
```

The *Application* Object

What the *Session* object does for the individual user, the *Application* object does for the entire site. Variables can be set in much the same way, like so:

```
<% Application("users") = Application("users") + 1 %>
```

The difference is that this variable is accessible by any user at any time. Any page within your application can then access the *users* variable and display the number of people who are currently logged in.

The *Server* Object

The *Server* object is a low-level object that can be used to perform several tasks within ASP. The most common use is to create instances of server-side components using the following syntax:

```
Set InstanceName = Server.CreateObject("ClassName.ComponentName")
```

To create an instance of the CDO *Newmail* object in order to send e-mail from your page, you might use:

```
Set Email = Server.CreateObject("CDONTS.NewMail")
```

The object referenced by the name *Email* can then be manipulated as the class itself, adding properties and calling methods. You will see more examples of object creation and manipulation when we cover database recordsets in Module 11.

The ASP Languages

There is no way that we can cover all of the intricacies of languages as powerful as VBScript and JScript (or JavaScript) in this space. But there are a few things we can look at that will help you with some light-duty scripting:

- Variables
- Conditional statements
- Loops

Variables

Variables are simply representations of other things to your computer program. You can no doubt remember a time when you grabbed a few rocks to draw out the battle plan for storming the neighbor kids' tree fort, or even when you played Monopoly and you chose a die-cast token to represent you on the board. You didn't actually become the car or the shoe, but everyone knew what space you occupied on the board by locating the token you had selected. Every time they saw your playing piece, they saw you within the scope of the game. Now, the next time the game was played, someone else might have chosen the same token, and this time around it represented them. The tokens are variable in their representation, taking on the value of whoever selected it in it the minds of the players.

Program variables are the same, except you are not limited to eight or ten little pieces of metal to hold your values. You can make up pretty much whatever character combination you'd like to represent other things to the computer. For instance, you could select the letter *i* to represent the age of your user. A 25-year-old who visited your site would then have the value 25 assigned to the letter *i*. Then, every time the computer came across the letter *i* in your code, it would really see the number 25. You could add 1 to *i* and the computer would respond with 26. Or you could add *i* to another *i* and get the answer 50.

But if a new user came along who was 40 years old, his or her instance of the application would assign the number 40 to *i*, and all of his or her calculations would be altered accordingly. That is the power of variables. One set of code can be reused regardless of the actual values that need to be manipulated because the representation, the variable itself, is always the same. You just tell the computer what to see when they come across the variable by assigning a value to it.

This concept is consistent in both VBScript and JavaScript, but the implementation is slightly different.

VBScript

Here is a sample VBScript that we can examine:

```
<%
Dim name
Dim address, city
name = "Joe"
address = Request.Form("address")
city = "Orlando"
Response.Write "Your name is " & name & ".<br>"
Response.Write "You live at " & address & ", " & city
%>
```

The first two lines take care of a process known as *declaring* variables. Although declaring your variables is not absolutely necessary, it is good practice that will prevent innumerable debugging headaches down the road. You should get into the habit of declaring your variables.

In VBScript, this is known as *dimensioning* variables and uses the *Dim* keyword. Because all variables in ASP are variants (meaning that they can hold any data type), there is no need to specify that one is an integer or another is a string. VBScript assigns the variable the most logical way it can and manipulates it according to its best interpretation of the instruction you give it.

Next, we assign values to the variables. We assigned hard-coded string values to one and used a *Request* for another. When we are ready to output our variable values, it is most meaningful to the end user if they are displayed within the context of how they are being used. We can concatenate (string together) literal string output with our variable values by using the & operator. When used with string values, the & operator tells VBScript to put the values together into our output string.

JavaScript

The script for JavaScript is much the same. There are only slight differences in how the variables are declared and then concatenated with the string output:

```
<%
var name;
var address, city;
name = "Joe";
address = Request.Form("address");
city = "Orlando";
Response.Write "Your name is " + name + ".<br>";
Response.Write "You live at " + address + ", " + city;
%>
```

You will notice three major changes. First, the keyword *var* is used to declare the variables instead of *Dim*. Second, the + operator is used to concatenate the string values. Finally, the line ends with a semicolon.

NOTE

The + operator has different uses in JavaScript. When used with numerical values, it does addition, as you would expect. If any of the values are strings, however, it concatenates instead.

Conditional Statements

Conditional statements are ways of testing what is going on in your application and responding differently to the variety of situations you may encounter. For instance, you may want to send your visitor to one site if they are from the North and another if they are from the South, and yet another for the West. You could use a conditional statement to gather information and determine what action to take. Consider this VBScript code:

```
<%
Dim region
region = Request.Form("region")
If region = "North" Then
    Response.Redirect("North.asp")
ElseIf region = "South" Then
    Response.Redirect("South.asp")
Else Response.Redirect("West.asp")
End If
%>
```

In this script, we dimension a variable to hold the region and then assign a value to it that is gleaned from a form submitted by the user. We then enter a conditional statement that tests the value of the region variable and sends the user off accordingly.

The *If* keyword begins by checking to see if the value is "North". If it is, the redirect to the North.asp page occurs. If it is not, the next line is invoked, which asks again if the value is "South" by using *Else If*. *Else If* begins another test for the value of *region*. If the value is not "North" or "South", our script assumes it must be "West" and uses the *Else* keyword to invoke the only remaining option, which is to send them to the West.asp page. The *End If* statement is required to demarcate the entire conditional statement so the script knows when to stop testing conditions and return to regular code.

The JavaScript version of this script is somewhat different:

```
<%
var region;
region = Request.Form("region");
if (region == "North") {
    Response.Redirect("North.asp");
}else if (region == "South") {
    Response.Redirect("South.asp");
}else {
    Response.Redirect("West.asp");
} %>
```

Each *if* conditional in JavaScript is contained within parentheses. If the condition within the parentheses is evaluated to *true*, the response for that condition is then enclosed in braces beneath it. The double equal sign (==) is the equality comparison operator. Also, there is no *End If* statement in JScript or JavaScript. The closing brace acts like the *End If* in VBScript. This is really just a syntactical difference, and the concept of conditionals remains the same in the two languages.

Loops

Loops are places in your code where you will want to run a set of instructions a number of times. It may be a set number of times, such as 100, or it may depend on some criteria that you won't even know until the program runs, such as once for every record in a recordset. Although there are a number of different ways to manipulate a *for...next* loop, the basic idea is that you determine a starting number, an ending number, and an increment.

Let's say that we wanted to perform an operation on all of the even numbers from 1 to 100. The first even number is 2, so the starting number is 2. The last even number is 100, so the ending number is 100, and even numbers occur every two numbers, so we want to increment by two at each pass. Consider the following VBScript code:

```
<%
Dim i
For i = 2 to 100 step 2
Response.Write i * i
Next
%>
```

Here, the variable *i* is dimensioned to hold where you are in the loop. You then begin the loop in the next line, which says that you want to run the code that is coming up once for each value of *i* that is between 2 and 100, stepping up 2 each time. The code then outputs the current value of *i* times itself and calls the *Next* keyword to begin the process again with the next value of *i*.

The concept is the same in JavaScript, with a bit of a syntactical difference:

```
<%
var i;
for (i=2; i<=100; i=i+2){
    Response.Write(i * i);
}
```

The JavaScript code in this case uses the same parentheses and bracket construct that we saw earlier. After the *for* statement, the three portions of the statement in parentheses establish the starting, ending, and incremental value of the variable, then the code within the brackets runs until the ending conditional is no longer true. Also, it should be noted that the JavaScript code is case-sensitive, whereas the VBScript code is not.

Progress Check

1. What is the syntax for requesting a form element on an action page?

2. How is the shorthand version of *Response.Write* used to write a session variable to the page?

CRITICAL SKILL

7.2 Learn the Basics of JSP

One of the most popular programming languages that emerged from the Web era of the late 1990s is Java. Although Java has been around for several years, it is only in the last few years that JSP has come into prominence. JSP was built upon some of the same ideas as its predecessor, ASP, but was able to avoid some of its shortcomings by taking the best ideas of ASP one step further.

JSP is a mixture of Java code within the constructs of an HTML page. The Java code is enclosed in *<% %>* server tags, like ASP code, but the code is compiled into *servlets* on the Web server when the page is browsed for the first time. Upon each successive hit, the code doesn't have to be compiled again—the compiled version remains on the server. In fact, the entire page is compiled, not merely the code that is between the server tags.

Java is a language based in part on the C language. It started as a small language that could be used in a wide variety of appliance hardware. It quickly grew, however, into a robust, platform-independent language that enabled Web developers to include *applets* in their Web pages. Applets are mini-applications that exist client-side and can be executed from a browser by invoking the Java of that browser. Applets can exist server-side as well.

From applets, to servlets, to JSPs and Enterprise JavaBeans (EJBs), Java has steadily evolved over its short lifetime. Applets have been considered somewhat of a failure to most Web developers, because the technology never really took off as anticipated. JSP, however, now has a solid foundation and a large user base that is continually growing. Macromedia has its own JSP server named JRun.

The Java Programming Language in JSP

Java offers many advantages compared to other programming languages. For starters, it's an object-oriented programming language, and offers a full set of standard classes for most tasks.

---

1. *Request.Form("formelement")*

2. *<%= Session("variableName")%>*

Java is also portable, having the capability to run on most platforms using the same code. One advantage it has over C++ is automatic garbage collection. C++ programmers have to take care of their own memory management. In addition, Java is multithreaded, which allows the programmer to run different tasks at the same time.

JSP pages are HTML pages with a .jsp file extension and Java server-side code mixed in. There are three types of scripting contained in JSP pages: scriptlets, expressions, and declarations. Java snippets, called *scriptlets,* are contained inside *<%* and *%>* tags. The code inside the tag is compiled and run on the server, and the resulting HTML code is sent to the browser. A Java scriptlet in a JSP page might look like this:

```
<% out.println("Greetings " + request.getParameter("firstname");%>
```

Another type of JSP scripting is called, simply, an expression. A JSP expression looks like the shorthand *Response.Write* expression in ASP, but is in fact a member of the *out* object rather than the *Response* object. The *out* object is another name for the JSPWriter, which writes directly to the output stream. For instance, the following code displays a session variable named *Username*:

```
<%=(session.getValue("Username"))%>
```

When the JSP server sees the =, it's telling the server that the following expression is to be evaluated and sent to the browser as text to be displayed. Additionally, if the parameter inside the expression isn't a string, the JSP server converts it to a string to allow it to be displayed.

Another type of JSP tag that you might see is the declaration. The declaration is used to declare a method, variable, or field. A declaration tag will have *page* scope, meaning that anything declared within the tag will be available to the whole page. A JSP declaration looks like this:

```
<%! int i = 1000; %>
```

One thing you must be mindful of when writing Java code is that everything is case-sensitive. The following lines might look the same to someone not familiar with Java, but the first is correct, and the second will cause an error:

```
<%=(session.getValue("Username"))%>
<%=(session.GetValue("Username"))%>
```

The latter code snippet will cause the JSP server to throw an error message that "No method named GetValue was found." Java developers must pay strict attention to the case of the code they write. This applies to functions, variables, properties, methods, events—in short, the whole language has to be thought of as being 100 percent case-sensitive.

Variables in Java

Java is strictly *typed* when it comes to variables. Type, in the case of variables, refers to the kind of data the variable will contain. In ASP—both JavaScript and VBScript—you can get away with declaring variables without worrying about the type. The ASP variable type is a *variant*. In Java—and in JSP—you have to declare the variable type when you declare its name, as in these examples:

```
<%
boolean myFlag = true;
boolean isLogged = (session.getValue("Username")!=null);
    //evaluates to true
String myFirstName = "Tom";
int myCounter = 1;
%>
```

NOTE

String is a special Java class, and not a variable type per se. The string is actually an array of characters, so the Java string represented by "Tom" is actually a Java object of type *String* having the value of the quoted character array. The *String* object has special methods that you can use to operate on strings.

If you try to use a variable before it's declared, the JSP server will throw an error. Also, if you try to put a value into a variable of the wrong type, the JSP server will throw an error. This forces the programmer to maintain strict coding practices. Java developers consider the nontyped ASP languages to be "lazy" languages, allowing the programmer to develop bad programming habits by not typing the variables.

In addition to declaring the variables with the proper type, you can't change types or mix two variables of different types in the same expression without first *casting* the variable. Casting refers to "changing" the variable type for the expression. The actual variable isn't changed, but the way that the server "sees" the variable is changed. For instance, to cast a session variable as an integer, you might use an expression like this:

```
<% int myUserID = (int)session.getValue("UserID");%>
```

The rules for casting variables are described in the Java API or any good Java reference. For example, a Boolean value can't be cast into another type. If you are planning to do any JSP development, you should have a good Java reference handy at all times. Table 7-1 shows the different variable types that are available to the Java developer.

Type	Range of Values	Description
byte	−128 to 127	Byte-length integer (8-bit)
short	−32768 to 32767	Short integer (16-bit)
int	−2147483648 to 2147483647	Integer (32-bit)
long	−9223372036854775808 to 9223372036854775807	Long integer (64-bit)
float	+/−3.40282347e38 to +/−1.40239846e-45	Single-precision floating-point number (32-bit)
double	+/−1.79769313486231570e308 to +/−4.94065645841246544e-324	Double-precision floating-point number (64-bit)
char	Single character	A single 16-bit Unicode character
boolean	true or false	A true/false value

Table 7-1 Variable Types and Their Ranges in Java

You can also declare more than one variable on a line of code, as in this example:

```
<%
int i=1, j=100, k=1000;
boolean isAllowed, isNewUser, isAdmin = false;
char newLine = '\n', answerYes = 'y', quoteChar = '\u0022';
%>
```

Variables must be named according to Java conventions, which also apply to functions, classes, and packages. They may contain upper- or lowercase letters, digits, underscore characters, and the $ character. Although upper- and lowercase letters are allowed, Java is case-sensitive. For instance, the variables *myCounter* and *MyCounter* would be completely different variables.

Expressions

Java is an expression-based language, like C. Java expressions represent computations, declarations, and flow of control. The simplest of Java expressions is a variable declaration, as in the following:

```
int i = 0;
```

A more complicated expression would be a computation, which can use any of the Java operators listed in Table 7-2.

Operator	Type	Function
+	Arithmetic	Add
−	Arithmetic	Subtract
*	Arithmetic	Multiply
/	Arithmetic	Divide
<	Relational	Less than
>	Relational	Greater than
<=	Relational	Less than or equal to
>=	Relational	Greater than or equal to
==	Relational	Equal to
!=	Relational	Not equal to
+=, −=, *=, etc.	Compound assignment	Expression on the right used as the first operand

Table 7-2 Operators in Java

The following statements are examples of legal expressions in Java:

```
int a = 1 + 2; // Addition
total += subtotal; // Compound assignment:
        // total is equal to total + subtotal
boolean c; // Set c as a Boolean variable
c = a > b; // C takes a value of true or false
```

The last example illustrates a Boolean value being assigned to the Boolean variable *c* as the result of a comparison between *a* and *b*. In Java, unlike some other languages such as C and JavaScript, a comparison yields a true or false (Boolean) value rather than a one or a zero.

The integer types (*int*, *long*, *short*, and *byte*) can be operated on in combinations. Type casting is automatic, and the result is always type-cast into the higher of the values. For instance, if you add a byte variable to an *int* type variable, the result would be an *int* type. This allows you to work with different integer data types without worrying about casting the variables into the same type beforehand.

Strings can also be operated on with a plus sign (+), which effectively concatenates the variables, as in this example:

```
<%
String myFirst = "Fred";
String myLast = "Periwinkle";
String myName = myFirst + ' ' + myLast;
out.println(myName);//the result would be "Fred Periwinkle"
%>
```

Strings also allow the use of compound concatenation, as in this example:

```
theCode += '\n';  //add a line feed to the end of the code
```

Some Common JSP Objects

JSP has many of the same objects as ASP, but the syntax is a little different. Here are some of the more common object calls on a JSP page.

request.getParameter()

The *Form* and *QueryString* parameters can be retrieved from the client by using the following syntax:

```
request.getParameter("myFormElement")
```

or

```
request.getParameter("queryStringVariable")
```

Because Java is case-sensitive, it expects the *request* object to be in lowercase. The *getParameter()* method covers both *GET* and *POST* processes of form submission. To display the contents of a form or *QueryString* variable, you can use the shorthand version of JSP expression evaluation, which displays the result in the browser, similar to the *Response.Write* object in ASP:

```
<%=request.getParameter("myVariable")%>
```

response.sendRedirect()

This statement is similar to the *Response.Redirect* in ASP or the CFLOCATION in ColdFusion. Provided the headers haven't been sent to the browser yet, this method will redirect the user to a page specified in the string, as in this example:

```
<% response.sendRedirect("error.jsp");%>
```

The *out* Object

Also known as the *JSPWriter* (the buffered form of the *PrintWriter*), this object sends a stream of output to the client's browser. This object is used in scriptlets and is usually accessed by using the *println* method, as in the following example:

```
<%
out.println("Your book is " + request.getParameter("title"));
%>
```

This is similar to the *Response.Write* method in ASP.

The *session* Object

To access the session object in JSP, you have to set a name and a value to a variable. In JSP, the session variable name is referred to as a session *attribute.* You have to explicitly set the attribute and the value when you create a session variable, as in this example, which uses the *setAttribute()* method of the *session* object:

```
<%
session.setAttribute("Username",request.getParameter("Username"));
%>
```

In the example, you are setting a session variable named *Username* to the value retrieved in either a query string or a form variable (recall that the *getParameter* method of the *request* object can take either type). You could also have used the *putValue* method of the *session* object, as in this example:

```
<%
session.putValue("Password",request.getParameter("Password"));
%>
```

You can retrieve the values by using the attribute (variable name) in the *getAttribute()* method of the session object, as in this example:

```
<input type="text" value="<%=session.getAttribute("Username")%>">
```

The previous example combines HTML with a JSP expression that will put the value of the session variable named *Username* into the text field before it is sent to the browser.

Progress Check

1. True or False: Java is case-sensitive.

2. What is the equality operator in Java?

3. What is a ternary operator?

---

1. True

2. The double equal sign ==

3. It's a shorthand version of if/else, so that you can evaluate an expression and return one of two values depending on the condition of the expression.

CRITICAL SKILL
7.3 Learn the Basics of ColdFusion

Dreamweaver MX comes in many flavors of server models, the tastiest of which is ColdFusion, because it is Macromedia's own server. ColdFusion offers the best qualities of JSP and ASP, has the extensibility of ASP.NET and JSP, but also offers the accessibility of HTML.

ColdFusion is a tag-based language, like HTML, but offers a rich set of over 70 tags that are executed on the server—unlike HTML, which is executed on the client. When you execute the CFQUERY tag, for example, the server interprets the tag and executes a connection to the database and a return of information from the database. A single CFQUERY tag offers the same functionality as eight to ten lines of ASP or JSP code.

NOTE

ColdFusion tags use name/value pairs, just as HTML tags do. The tags, however, should be thought of as server-side script blocks.

In addition, ColdFusion has just about everything you need built right into the language, including such functionality as database manipulation, e-mail distribution and retrieval, file manipulation, directory manipulation, and anything else you might need to get your site up and running. In ASP and JSP, much of this functionality involves add-on components or hand-coding of complex scripts, beans, applets, and objects. ColdFusion programmers can realize the complexity of a data-driven site by implementing tags that are similar in style to HTML tags.

A ColdFusion page is called a *template*. This is not to be confused with the Dreamweaver template, which is a design-time element. The ColdFusion template is an HTML page with ColdFusion tags mixed in that are executed and replaced on the server.

The ColdFusion Server

In addition to the ease of programming, ColdFusion offers a powerful server that is able to scale to the most demanding of Web applications. It offers load balancing, just-in-time compiling, security, dynamic caching, and failover. The server is robust and capable of high volume using multithreaded processing. Also, it is easily integrated with other programming technologies—such as ASP, XML, COM, CORBA, EJB, Java, and C++—and with application technologies, such as databases, mail servers, file systems, and a host of others. The server is also easily clustered and offers unparalleled server administration features that enable you to administer the server remotely—including your database connections.

NOTE

The latest version of CF server is called ColdFusion MX. It works well together with Dreamweaver MX and Flash MX.

In addition to its Windows functionality, ColdFusion can be deployed on Solaris, HP-UX, and Linux, making it quite versatile as an option for a non-Windows system. The Linux version of ColdFusion has become quite popular since its release in late 2000.

Dreamweaver MX is shipped with a single-user license of the ColdFusion Server Enterprise version. The server will run on Windows 98, NT, and 2000. Different levels of the ColdFusion server are available, with the Enterprise version being the top of the line. The version that ships with Dreamweaver MX contains all the advanced features of the Enterprise edition, but can be accessed only locally—that is, through http://localhost or through the default 127.0.0.1 IP address.

CFML: The ColdFusion Programming Language

ColdFusion Markup Language (CFML) isn't a traditional programming language, per se. CFML is a tag-based language, which is somewhat different than the script-based ASP languages and the object-oriented Java language. ColdFusion has a script language built into it—CFScript—but the majority of ColdFusion programming involves the use of tags. A page that contains CFML is saved with a .cfm or .cfml file extension. Any page with a .cfm or .cfml extension that is requested from the Web server will be parsed by the ColdFusion server before being sent to the browser.

A tag is nothing more than a command that is flanked by the < > symbols, like the HTML tags that Web developers are accustomed to seeing. A typical ColdFusion statement might look like this:

```
<cfoutput>#form1.Username#</cfoutput>
```

The CFOUTPUT statement is similar to *Response.Write()* in ASP or *out.print()* in JSP. The pound signs (#) are signals to the ColdFusion server that the code contained within the signs is to be evaluated by the server. In this particular case, a Form variable named *Username* will be evaluated and directed to the browser.

ColdFusion tags all begin with the <CF prefix. Those three characters act as a signal to the server that the current tag is to be executed by the ColdFusion server. It's similar to the <% prefix found in ASP and JSP or the <? prefix found in PHP. Some of these tags come as

a "set," with an open tag and a close tag, such as the preceding CFOUTPUT tag. Others, such as the CFFILE tag, exist as one tag. Generally speaking, a ColdFusion tag contains a series of name/value pairs that provide the server with the information needed to execute the tag. The following CFFILE tag is an example:

```
<cffile action="Delete"
 file="c:\inetpub\wwwroot\images\#form.filename#">
```

The ACTION attribute of the tag is set to "Delete", the FILE attribute is set to the c:\inetpub\wwwroot\images directory, and the filename is set to an incoming Form variable named "filename." When the ColdFusion server reads this tag, it will execute the tag—which, in this case, will cause a file named in the form element to be deleted from the server. Using the same CFFILE tag, you can create a file upload by setting the ACTION attribute to "Upload":

```
<cffile action="Upload"
 filefield="Filename"
 destination="c:\inetpub\wwwroot\images\"
 nameconflict="Overwrite">
```

In this case, a FILEFIELD attribute of "Filename" is specified, which will be the name of the incoming Form variable. The DESTINATION attribute is the folder on the server in which the file will be stored, and the NAMECONFLICT attribute instructs the server what to do if the name happens to conflict with a file that already exists on the server.

As with most ColdFusion tags, the CFFILE tag has some required attributes and some optional attributes. The NAMECONFLICT attribute in the preceding CFFILE tag is optional. Whenever an optional attribute is included, the server follows a default behavior if the attribute isn't contained in the tag. In this case, if the NAMECONFLICT attribute isn't defined, the default behavior is to throw an error if a file already exists.

ColdFusion tags all behave differently and all have different degrees of complexity. For instance, a CFABORT tag exists by itself, and has an optional attribute of SHOWERROR. You can put it on the page like this:

```
<cfabort>
```

If the ColdFusion server encounters this tag, it will simply stop processing the page. If you give it a SHOWERROR attribute, as in this example,

```
<cfabort showerror="You have to be more careful!!!">
```

the page will execute and the error page will display the message. A CFABORT tag is useful in a conditional statement to stop processing the page if a certain condition exists.

The Core ColdFusion Tags

These are the tags that are considered "required" for any ColdFusion developer. Coincidentally, all of these tags are included in the free ColdFusion Express package.

CFSET and CFPARAM

These two tags enable you to set variables and parameters in ColdFusion. What's the difference between them? With a CFSET tag, you are simply assigning a value to a variable, as in the following expression:

```
<cfset Session.UserID = myQuery.userID>
```

Here, you are assigning the *userID* value from a query to the *Session* variable *UserID*.

With CFPARAM, you have three choices. You can check for a parameter's existence by using the NAME attribute, check to make sure that a variable is of a specific type by using the TYPE attribute, or set a DEFAULT value for a possible variable:

```
<cfparam name="form.username" default="newuser">
```

In this instance, you have a Form variable of *username* that is expected on the page. But what if the user types in the link by hand and doesn't use the login form? In that case, there is a risk of errors on the page, because your ColdFusion functions are expecting a Form variable named *username*. With this statement in place, if the Form variable doesn't exist, it's given a default value. If the variable *does* exist, the CFPARAM statement doesn't do anything. It's only there as a safeguard to give a value to a parameter that may or may not exist. You can use it with any of the variable types, as in this statement:

```
<cfparam name="url.userid" default="baddata">
```

In this case, your page is expecting a URL variable named *userid*. If, for some reason, the URL variable doesn't come through, the default value of "baddata" is assigned to the URL variable.

TIP

When addressing variables on the ColdFusion page, an error will be thrown if the variable is referred to and it doesn't exist. You can either check for the variable's existence before using it, or you can set up a CFPARAM to give it a default value.

You can also use ColdFusion functions within a CFSET or CFPARAM declaration. The CFSET in that statement will assign a date that is seven days ago from the current server date to the variable named *Lastweek*:

```
<cfset Lastweek=DateFormat((Now()) - 7)>
```

The following statement sets a variable equal to the filename of the current page without the file extension such as *mypage* if the path was c:/inetpub/wwwroot/bettergig/mypage.cfm:

```
<cfset CurrentPage = GetFileFromPath(GetCurrentTemplatePath())>
<cfset CurrentPage = Left(CurrentPage,Len(CurrentPage)-4)>
```

You can also declare variables in CFSCRIPT, like this:

```
<cfscript>
CurrentPage = GetFileFromPath(GetCurrentTemplatePath());
CurrentPage = Left(CurrentPage,Len(CurrentPage)-4);
</cfscript>
```

CFOUTPUT

The CFOUTPUT tag is the multipurpose bull worker of ColdFusion. It does many things besides display text, which you've seen in a few examples. In general, it's used to interpret ColdFusion functions and expressions so that the result can be output to the browser. It also acts as a loop when you specify the QUERY attribute. The QUERY attribute can be the result of a database query, or it can be the name of a CFPOP, CFDIRECTORY, or other tag. You can use it in the body of the document to display text in the browser, or to dynamically apply a value to an HTML element. Here are a few examples. The following simply displays the current server time in the browser:

```
<cfoutput>The time is now #TimeFormat(Now())#</cfoutput>
```

This example shows the CFOUTPUT tag used to insert a value returned from a query into a hidden form element:

```
<input type="hidden" name="hiddenAccessCode"
value="<cfoutput>#UserAccessQuery.AccessCode#</cfoutput>">
```

The next example populates an unordered list (bulleted list) with the results of a CFQUERY tag, which can be one row or a thousand rows. The results are limited only by the capacity of the browser. In actual practice, you'll break up the queries with the MAXROWS attribute.

The CFOUTPUT QUERY acts as a loop by itself and does not need any other programming to construct a loop, such as a *for/next* or *do/while* construct:

```
<ul>
<cfoutput query="myQuery"><li>#FirstName# #LastName#</li>
</cfoutput>
</ul>
```

CAUTION

When using the CFOUTPUT QUERY, you have to consider everything that you are looping over. If there is a line break in the code, the line break will be output in the loop as well. In the example, the open CFOUTPUT tag was placed on the same line as the <li> tags so as to not introduce an extra line break into the resulting HTML source code.

CFIF/CFELSE/CFELSEIF

These tags are used in ColdFusion to implement conditional logic. The CFIF tag enables you to check for a condition before executing a statement. The CFIF tag has a corresponding closing tag that you must use. Here's an example:

```
<cfif form.password NEQ rsCustomers.password>
    <cflocation url="FailedLogin.cfm">
</cfif>
```

NOTE

The NEQ statement means "not equal to" and is the same as <> in VBScript or != in Java, PHP, and JavaScript. ColdFusion uses EQ for "equal to" in comparisons. In ColdFusion, you are also allowed to spell out "not equal to" and "equal to."

You can use the CFELSE and CFELSEIF tags in the conditional statements to construct more complex conditions. You must use them within a CFIF code block. Here's an example using both:

```
<cfif form.location EQ "Buffalo">
    <cfset session.location = "NY">
<cfelseif form.location EQ "Rochester">
    <cfset session.location = "NY">
```

```
<cfelse>
     <cfset session.location = "not valid location">
</cfif>
```

CFQUERY

If you are familiar with ASP or JSP, you know that you must create a recordset object to retrieve a *resultset*. In ColdFusion, you don't create a recordset, per se—you define a CFQUERY tag giving a datasource and a *Select* statement, and the ColdFusion server does the rest. Here's an example that simply retrieves all columns and all records from the Customers table of the Bookstore database:

```
<cfquery name="rsCustomers" datasource="Bookstore">
Select * from Customers
</cfquery>
```

The only two required parameters for the tag are NAME and DATASOURCE. The query needs a name so that it can be referred to on the page when displaying the information. For instance, a FirstName column can be referred to like this:

```
<cfoutput>#rsCustomers.FirstName#</cfoutput>
```

The DATASOURCE parameter is simply a system DSN that has been previously established in the ODBC Administrator on the machine (in CF 5 or earlier), or in the ColdFusion Administrator interface.

The CFQUERY tag can pass commands to your database in the form of valid Structured Query Language (SQL). These commands can be simple *Select* statements, as in the previous example, or they can be *Insert*, *Update*, or *Delete* statements—or even stored procedures. You can think of the CFQUERY tag as an interface to the database.

TIP

Although the CFQUERY tag will perform all the required database interactions, other ColdFusion tags are targeted for inserts, updates, and stored procedures and make those tasks easier.

Other attributes are available to CFQUERY, such as MAXROWS, which make it easy to set up pages that show partial resultsets. Consult the ColdFusion documentation for a full explanation of the CFQUERY tag.

CFLOCATION

The CFLOCATION tag is similar to the *Response.Redirect* statement in ASP or the *response.sendRedirect* statement in JSP. When the ColdFusion server finds this tag, the processing of the page stops and the user is redirected to another page:

```
<cfif Not IsDefined("form.username")>
    <cflocation url="error.htm">
</cfif>
```

ColdFusion Functions

In addition to the many available ColdFusion tags, over 200 built-in functions are available. These functions consist of everything from basic string-handling functions—such as *Len(string)*, which returns the length of a string—to complex functions, such as *QuotedValueList*, which will convert a column returned from a database into a comma-separated list with the values enclosed in single quotes. The functions are grouped into these categories:

- Array functions

- Authentication functions

- Date and time functions

- Decision functions

- Display and formatting functions

- Dynamic evaluation functions

- International functions

- List functions

- Mathematical functions

- Query functions

- String functions

- Structure functions

- System functions

- Other functions

The functions have to be contained within a ColdFusion tag to be recognized. Also, in some instances, they will be contained within the pound signs. These functions don't begin with <CF like the ColdFusion tags—they are simply descriptive names of the functions they represent. When the ColdFusion server sees a function, the code is executed on the server and the result of the function is returned. In this example, the *RepeatString* function returns a string of 20 nonbreaking spaces:

```
<cfoutput>#RepeatString(" ",20)#</cfoutput>
```

You can also combine and nest ColdFusion functions, creating some pretty complex statements:

```
<cflocation url="#IIF(ListFind(ValueList(
    myquery.username),form.username),'Page1.cfm','Page2.cfm')#
</cflocation>
```

This statement uses a query named *myquery*, which contains a *resultset*. The resultset is transformed into a list with the *ValueList* function; then, the *form.username* is checked against that list with the *ListFind* function. Finally, the IIF function performs an *if/else* statement, depending on whether the username is found in the list returned by the query. The CFLOCATION tag sees only the result of the function—either Page1.cfm or Page2.cfm.

TIP

All the ColdFusion functions are available to the built-in scripting language as well—CFScript. User-defined functions are also available in CF 5.0 and later.

ColdFusion contains some truly powerful functions that make the development process much quicker. For instance, some list and array functions are available that make working with lists and variable arrays much easier. Some system functions also are available, such as the *DirectoryExists* function, which determines whether a given directory exists on the server; and the *GetCurrentTemplatePath* function, which returns the path on the server to the current page that's being served.

The Pound Signs in ColdFusion

If you're unfamiliar with the CFML language, then you're probably wondering about the use of the pound signs (#) around certain expressions. A lot of rules apply to the use of pound signs; but in general, they are used when something is to be evaluated before being sent to the browser, and they are placed around an expression that the ColdFusion server is to differentiate from regular text. For instance, in the following expression, the pound signs signify to the server that the name "username" should be replaced by the value that's stored in the variable named "username":

```
<cfoutput>Welcome #username#</cfoutput>
```

The pound signs aren't limited to use in text that is to be written to the Web page, however. They can be used inside of any ColdFusion tag to allow a value to be replaced by the current value of the variable:

```
<cfquery name="myQuery" maxrows="#maxrows#" datasource="#myDSN#">
```

In this case, assume that two variables have been set up in advance: *maxrows* and *myDSN*. The *maxrows* variable holds the data that the MAXROWS attribute of the CFQUERY tag needs in order to process the tag. The *myDSN* variable holds the name of a data source name that was set up in advance as a variable. What the ColdFusion server is doing, in essence, is evaluating the areas between the pound signs first, then substituting the results of the evaluation in the expression, and then evaluating the expression.

If you are using a function, you have to place the pound signs around the entire expression, as in this example—which simply converts the value in the variable *username* to uppercase:

```
<cfoutput>Welcome <b>#Ucase(username)#<b></cfoutput>
```

This example also shows that you can put HTML tags inside of a CFOUTPUT statement. Whatever is inside of the CFOUTPUT statement will be sent to the browser.

The pound signs aren't always used, however, which may be confusing to some people. In this expression, for instance, the variable name is enclosed in quotes:

```
<cfif IsDefined("Form.username")>
```

Here, you are verifying that the Form variable named *username* exists—you aren't interested in the value. In general, when you are using the variable itself in the expression, and not the value, you don't use the pound signs.

The ColdFusion Administrator

The ColdFusion Administrator is the interface that enables you to administer the ColdFusion application server. In the Administrator, you'll find the functionality to change security settings, add database connections, administer log files, schedule tasks, and set up debugging, among other things. If you have a full version of the server installed (not the single-user version), you can administer the server from a remote location through a Web browser.

Learn the CFML Language

It is not required that the ColdFusion server be installed on your local machine to use Dreamweaver MX with ColdFusion, but it makes life easier. In general, you'll be able to debug your pages more quickly locally if you don't have to upload them to the server each time and maintain a connection to the remote server. Also, it is a wise move to use your local machine as a development server with a similar configuration to your remote server. This way, you aren't testing and debugging on your production server—a dangerous thing to do.

CFML is a robust language and is relatively easy to use—especially for the Web developer who is already familiar with HTML. The ease of use, however, doesn't imply that the language is any less powerful than ASP or JSP. In fact, many consider it more powerful because of all of the built-in functionality. Whatever your background, ColdFusion is a viable way to get your data-driven site to the Web, and Dreamweaver MX is the perfect way to combine the designer-friendly environment of Dreamweaver with the server-side functionality of ColdFusion.

Progress Check

1. How do you display a variable in a browser in a ColdFusion page?

2. What is the use of a CFQUERY tag?

CRITICAL SKILL
7.4 Learn the Basics of ASP.NET

ASP has been around for several years and is one of the most popular application servers there is. The large number of Windows servers mean that ASP is available to the millions of people that use shared hosting. It is powerful and relatively simple to learn. UltraDev made it even easier to use. There is a large base of ASP programmers—and they all need to consider making a change.

Microsoft recently released its new .NET Framework. The .NET Framework is an expansive revision of the way that most of Microsoft's development tools work. In much the same way that Macromedia is streamlining and building integration into its MX product line, Microsoft is uniting its development tools within .NET. Visual Studio is now Visual

---

1. *#variableName#*

2. It is the ColdFusion method for connecting to a database and delivering a SQL query to retrieve a resultset.

Studio.NET. Visual Basic is now VB.NET. There is still C++, but there is also a brand new language called C# (C sharp) that was created just for .NET.

There are still a large number of Windows servers, and the .NET Framework is still free to run on them. Luckily, .NET was solidified just in time for Macromedia to implement it in Dreamweaver MX, which makes it easier to use and provides a much needed design environment. But it is not as easy to learn.

.NET represents a significant shift in the way you must think about programming Web Applications. Microsoft has learned well from its competitors and has implemented a wealth of new features. It is powerful, well supported, flexible and its object model is thorough and expansive. It may take some time to get your head around .NET, but it will be time well spent.

Make the Move from ASP

If you have not read the section on ASP, we recommend you do so before reading this section. Some of the object model in ASP.NET is inherited from ASP, though it may work a little differently now. This section makes reference to these similarities, but tries not cover them over again. A good understanding of ASP is helpful in grasping how the basics of ASP.NET work.

ASP, as it is typically used, is an inline scripting language. VBScript or Jscript is used within the HTML of your pages to insert dynamic data in the stream that becomes the browsed file. ASP.NET represents a paradigm shift in the way that your pages are constructed. Its core languages (VB.NET and C#) can still be used in a messy inline scripting format, but the entire design of ASP.NET encourages you to do it differently. In ASP.NET, everything is an object all the way up to the page itself, which has its own properties and events. Although you may be used to the concept of events from client side JavaScript, you must now get used to the idea of server-side events, things that the user does on a page that trigger the firing of events back at the server.

Some things are the same, or are basically the same with a .NET twist. ASP has a global.asa file, ASP.NET has global.asax. *Response*, *Request*, *Application*, and *Session* objects are all present, and work essentially the same, though there are some stricter usage requirements. VBScript users should become comfortable with VB.NET fairly quickly. But there are a bunch of new things that you need to become familiar with. Web controls, user controls, server-side events, the CLR, Web services, and the Web.config file are just a few of the changes that await you inside ASP.NET.

Differences Between ASP and ASP.NET

On the whole, a move to ASP.NET is a fundamental change in the way things work. That does not mean, however, that it is totally unrelated to the methods that you may be familiar with in traditional ASP. There are several things that we can compare that should help you get your head around the things that have changed and the reasons that they did so.

Interpreted vs. Compiled Code

The most obvious difference in ASP and ASP.NET pages, and the one that tells you what a particular site is using, is the page extension. ASP files use the .asp extension, and ASP.NET files use .aspx. But the difference is more substantial than the simple addition of a letter. Because both ASP and ASP.NET pages can run on the same server, this page extension signals exactly how a particular page will be processed.

ASP pages are interpreted at run time. They contain scripting code that must be parsed out from HTML each time a page is called on the server. This is done by the asp.dll utility, which does not have much of a memory. If ten people call a page, that DLL will parse the page independently for each of the ten visitors like it was the first time it had seen the file. This builds an inherent lag into the delivery of your content, and although an ASP server is pretty quick about its work, there comes a time at which this methodology will bog down a busy server.

ASP.NET compiles its pages into native code to improve performance. The first time a page is called, it is compiled to an intermediate language (IL) and then the compiler in the .NET Framework will compile that IL code into native code. This compiled page is then cached by the server and used each time the page is requested. The cached file remains available until you make changes to the page or the cache expires.

You don't have to do anything for this to happen; you don't even have to know that it is happening. The .NET Framework takes care of it for you and dramatically improves the performance of your site.

Namespaces

ASP.NET contains a massive collection of objects that are arranged into Namespaces. These namespaces are the way in which you include and reference functionality. For instance, HTML controls exist in the *System.Web.UI.HtmlControls* namespace, and server controls exist in the *System.Web.UI.WebControls* namespace.

You can find complete references to the classes in the .NET Framework using the .NET Framework Class Browser. There are several copies around the Web. You can access the class browser at this address: http://samples.gotdotnet.com/quickstart/aspplus/doc/classbrowser.aspx. Click the Run Example link to run the browser and explore the available classes.

NOTE

The Class Browser is expansive because the object model in the .NET Framework is expansive. Don't let that deter you. Most of what you will need is located in the *System.Web* namespaces. Get familiar with what is there and you will be a long way down the road.

Events

If you have done any HTML and JavaScript programming, you are familiar with events. Events, such as *onClick* and *onMouseOver*, are actions that can be responded to. They may be triggered by the user or by code, as in the *onError* events. They indicate that something has happened that can be used to determine what direction the application should go next.

ASP.NET extends the events that you are familiar with by creating server events. For instance, a button might have an *onClick* event, at which an alert box is to be displayed or a URL is to loaded. Now in ASP.NET, a button could have an *onServerClick* event indicating that action needs to be taken on the server. This button will exist within a form with the attribute *runat=server*. This indicates that the actions taken by the elements within the form require the form to be posted to the server so that its events can be handled. These elements that utilize the server for their functionality are called Server controls.

Server Controls

Server controls have a lot in common with the HTML controls you are used to. They are ASP.NET versions of text boxes, drop-down menus, and buttons that you use to build forms on your pages. But Server controls have a couple of differences.

Server controls run at the server. They do this for a couple of reasons. First, this enables them to call server-side functions rather than just browser functions. That means that you can trigger almost any kind of code through your form elements. Second, running at the server offers automatic state management, allowing the server to handle and forward form information as your user progresses through your application. Because of this, server controls will always have the *runat=server* attribute and will exist in a form with the same attribute.

XML

XML is an important part of the .NET Framework. Even the configuration of your .NET server is handled through an XML file called web.config. While ASP Server takes much of their configuration from server-level settings, or page-level directives, the web.config file allows you to set your configurations specifically and separately for each application. Dreamweaver uses the web.config file to store connection settings to your databases.

Method Calls

Method calls in ASP.NET must always be in parentheses. For instance, in ASP you could shortcut a *Response* call like this:

```
Response.Write Request("name")
```

In ASP.NET, you must include the () for the *Response* object.

```
Response.Write(Request("name"))
```

Page Rendering

In ASP, you could mix your HTML and ASP code by switching in and out of ASP tags to create page rendering as follows:

```
<html>
<% If logged = 1 Then %>
Hello <%= Session("name") %>. Thanks for coming.
<%End If%>
</html>
```

In ASP.NET, the HTML output should be generated from within the code using a *Response* call like this:

```
<html>
<% If logged = 1 Then
Response.Write("Hello " & Session("name") & " Thanks for coming. ")
End If%>
</html>
```

Functions

In ASP, functions were defined within the <% %> tags of the page, indicating that they were server-side functions that ran on the back end of the site:

```
<%
Sub Add()
Response.Write(2 + 2)
End Sub
Add
%>
```

Because the page is an object in ASP.NET, functions are defined within script tags:

```
<script language="VB" runat=server>
Sub Add()
Response.Write( 2 + 2)
End Sub
</script>
<%
Add()
%>
```

Languages

You can no longer use more than one language on a page, like switching between VBScript and Jscript. It was never a great idea in ASP anyway, but it is not allowed at all in ASP.NET.

File Extensions

ASP pages used the .asp file extension. In ASP.NET, you are liable to see one of three file extensions:

- **.aspx**   Normal ASP.NET files

- **.ascx**   ASP.NET user controls

- **.asmx**   ASP.NET Web services

ASP.NET Concepts

In addition to those things that can be expressed as differences between ASP and ASP.NET, there are some concepts that are brand new to the .NET Framework.

User Controls

We have talked a little about server controls. User controls are nothing more than server controls that are created by you, the user. User controls can be as simple as a bit of HTML or as complex as the best code that you can write. They are stored with a namespace that you create and reference on your pages just like the inherent ASP.NET objects. This makes the class-based architecture of the .NET framework quite extensible. You can create your own sets of reusable code and save them as .ascx files or compile them into DLLs.

The BIN Directory

Each application has a BIN directory. It is literally a folder at the root of your Web site called /bin. The name refers to an abbreviation for "binary," as a folder where the binary files were stored in CGI days, or to a bin where you throw stuff, depending on your perspective.

The BIN directory holds the supporting files that are used in your ASP.NET pages. User controls (.ascx files) and compiled DLLs are two things you will see here often. When using ASP.NET in Dreamweaver MX, there is a file called DreamweaverCtrls.dll that is a DLL that contains functionality for Macromedia's .NET implementation. This file must be deployed for each .NET application that you do. We cover that shortly.

The *PageLoad* Event

The *PageLoad* event is an event that fires any time the page loads into a browser. Within that event, you can place code and functions that perform any tasks that you want completed when a page is viewed. In contrast to an ASP page, which runs from top to bottom, this event-driven model allows you to better organize your code.

In the *PageLoad* event, you might have code that creates connections, or sets up datasets, or populates arrays for use on the page. Using it and its related functions, you can precisely control when certain things happen in the page creation process.

PostBack

PostBack is a methodology in ASP.NET that allows for its server event–driven functionality and also allows for much of the state management that is provided by .NET. PostBack is the act of posting a form back to the page on which it resides rather than posting it to a separate page. All forms with the *runat=server* attribute (forms that contain server controls) must post back to themselves.

Each time a page loads, a function called *isPostBack* evaluates to determine if this is the first time the page is loading, or if it is posting back to itself. You can utilize a conditional statement (*if isPostBack()*) to determine functionality that runs only if the form is being posted back, meaning that the server controls should now have information in them that has been evaluated. .NET handles all of this for you. It will know all by itself whether the page is loading for the first time or not. You just need to know how to respond to its answer.

Dreamweaver's .NET Implementation

We are beginning to see, with Dreamweaver MX, a divergence in the way that the included server models work. This is actually a good thing, because it allows Dreamweaver to take advantage of the strengths of newer models such as ColdFusion MX and ASP.NET without being worried that each of the server models contains exactly the same functionality and works exactly the same.

This is especially true of the ASP.NET server model. ASP.NET works differently, and so does Dreamweaver's implementation of it. In fact, Dreamweaver's implementation works differently than most people would code ASP.NET. That is not necessarily a bad thing. Macromedia has taken advantage of the extensibility of the platform and created the DreamweaverCtrls.dll control, which we mentioned earlier, to facilitate the development of ASP.NET in Dreamweaver. The following sections cover a few things you need to know.

Deploy Your Support Files

Whenever you create an ASP.NET site in Dreamweaver, you need to deploy the DreamweaverCtrls.dll file from Macromedia so that your Data Binding will work correctly. Macromedia exposes the data layer through this DLL so that it will work with the server behaviors and objects that make up Dreamweaver.

Select Commands | Deploy Support Files. A dialog box will ask you where your BIN directory is. Point it to the root of your application, where a BIN directory will be created. The support files will be deposited here.

The DLL and its source, which you should become familiar with if you plan to do advanced development or extensions in .NET, can be found in your configuration folder here:

X:\Program Files\Macromedia\Dreamweaver
MX\Configuration\ServerBehaviors\Shared\ASP.Net\Scripts

Interestingly, any files placed in this folder get deployed when you choose to deploy support files. This means that extension developers will be able to create .NET extensions based on user controls and have them automatically deployed by Dreamweaver. This opens up a tremendous opportunity for both the creators and users of extensions.

Perhaps more than any other, it is necessary for you to have a pretty good grasp of ASP.NET while using Dreamweaver to create an application. It can make it easier and provide great design time tools that are not available anywhere else, but it is not as intuitive to use as the other server models. Unfortunately, it takes volumes of books to teach .NET, and we have only a limited space to allot. There are a couple of books coming out dedicated to Dreamweaver MX and ASP.NET. This information should get you started, though, as you make a transition to ASP.NET.

Progress Check

1. What are the two languages of ASP.NET that Dreamweaver MX supports?

2. What is a PostBack in ASP.NET?

CRITICAL SKILL
7.5 Learn the Basics of PHP

PHP, Personal Home Page, has come into prominence in the last few years as a low-cost alternative to JSP, ASP, and ColdFusion. The cost of ownership of PHP is generally thought of as being much lower than the other server models because it can run on a free (or minimal

---

1. Visual Basic.NET and C#

2. PostBack is when the form submits back to itself. The ASP.NET controls take care of the details of determining whether the form has been posted or not.

cost) server platform such as Linux, whereas ASP requires a high-cost Windows server, and ColdFusion requires the purchase of an application server license.

Dreamweaver MX supports only the combination of PHP with a MySQL database in a default installation, but other options are available through third parties.

PHP can run on Linux, Unix, or Windows operating systems. Also, because Mac OS X is Unix-based, a PHP server can run on a Macintosh as well. If you are using a Linux box, the best way to set up a PHP server is to download the source code and compile the binaries yourself, but for Windows, installers are available from www.php.net that streamline the installation process.

The PHP Programming Language

If you are familiar with Java, Perl, C, C++, or JavaScript, you should have no trouble transferring your skills to programming with PHP. The language is similar to those, but it also has many noticeable differences, particularly in the way in which you refer to variables.

PHP was designed for ease of use. Many things that are expensive add-ons to other servers, such as e-mailing, file uploading, dynamic PDF creation, image creation, and database access, are built directly into the language or in easy-to-find modules that you can add to PHP. Direct database access is provided for many popular database servers, and add-ons are available that create classes for database access so that you can call databases generically.

PHP Templating

PHP pages are HTML pages with a .php file extension and PHP server-side code mixed in. The code is enclosed in *<? ?>* server tags, but there are other options as well. PHP can run in ASP mode, whereby you can use the more standard *<% %>* tags. Also, XML mode allows you to use *<?php ?>* style. There is also a script style of tags, but that is rarely used, except when you have an HTML editor that has trouble displaying the other standard PHP tags. A typical PHP statement might look like this:

```
<?php echo("Greetings ".$HTTP_POST_VARS["firstname"]);?>
```

In this case, a form variable named *firstname* is evaluated along with a string expression ("Greetings") and then "echoed" to the page, which is much like the *Response.Write* expression in ASP or CFOUTPUT in ColdFusion.

The page structure is much like the other server models. HTML tags and PHP tags can be mixed freely on the page. The PHP server (or preprocessor) executes the code within the PHP tags, and the result is an HTML page that can be sent to the browser.

Variables in PHP

Variables in PHP are preceded by a dollar sign. A typical variable in PHP might look like this:

```
$username
```

A letter or underscore, and any combination of letters, numbers, and underscores can follow the dollar sign. To PHP, a letter can be a–z or A–Z or any of the ASC characters between 127 and 255. Variables are also case-sensitive, so the variable name *$UserName* would be a different variable from *$username*. Dollar signs are also permitted within variable names; you should avoid them, however, because of *variable variables*, which we describe later.

Variable names should not conflict with any of the 2,500+ built-in PHP functions. If you have a specific naming convention, such as using your company initials in all variable names, you will be less likely to run into any conflicts.

Scoping

Variables are not always scoped in PHP the way that other application servers reference variables. In PHP, there is a switch in the PHP.ini file that determines how the variable scope will be utilized. In PHP, if the *register_globals* switch is set "on" in the PHP.ini file, you can refer to variables without any scope prefix, like this:

```
$username
```

The *$username* variable could be a form variable, local variable, request variable, or any number of other variable types. The *register_globals* switch is set to "on" by default in PHP servers prior to version 4.2.0, but its practice is discouraged. If the switch is not set, you have to scope your variables with the appropriate collection, such as *$HTTP_POST_VARS* for *post* (form) variables and *$HTTP_GET_VARS* for *get* (form or query string) variables.

PHP variables do have a scope in reference to the page, however:

- Variables used at the page level have a global scope.
- Variables used inside a function are local to the function.
- Variables declared as global inside a function are global to the page.

What this means is that you can have a page-level variable named *$username*, but if you use a variable named *$username* inside of a function, it is a completely different variable.

Expressions

PHP is an expression-based language, like Java. PHP expressions represent computations, declarations, and flow of control. The following statements are examples of legal expressions in PHP:

```
$a = 1 + 2;
$total += $subtotal;
$firstname = 'Tom';
$fullname = "$firstname Muck";
```

Strings can also be operated on with a dot character (.), which concatenates the variables, as in this example:

```
<%
$myFirst = "Fred";
$myLast = "Periwinkle";
echo $myFirst.' '.$myLast;//the result would be "Fred Periwinkle"
%>
```

Strings also allow the use of compound concatenation, as in this example:

```
theCode .= "\n";  //add a line feed to the end of theCode
```

Built-In Functions in PHP

PHP has a vast number of available built-in functions, and the number is ever increasing as new versions of the server come out. PHP v 4.1.*x* has over 2,500 functions available. You can find a current list of functions at www.php.net/quickref.php. Some of the functions that you may see inside of Dreamweaver MX's generated code, as well as some other general purpose functions, are shown in the following sections.

date(format,[timestamp])

The *date* function allows you to format a date timestamp (or current timestamp if the second parameter is not given) using a format that you selected. For example, if you want to display a date in the format of "Mar 22, 2003," you can use the function like this:

```
<?php echo "Today is ".date("M j, Y"); ?>
```

In that example, "M" references a three-letter month abbreviation, "j" is a day of month with no leading zeros, and "Y" is a four-digit year. For a complete listing of the date formats available, check the PHP Web site.

die(message)

The *die* function causes the page execution to cease, but also passes a message to the page. It is used frequently as an error-handler, as in the following:

```
$connEflea = mysql_pconnect("localhost", "eflea", "eflea")
  or die("There was an error connecting to Eflea");
```

This type of statement works because of *short-circuit evaluation*. The theory behind this is if the first statement before the *OR* operator is executed successfully, the second statement will never be executed. If the first statement fails, because there is an *OR* operator, the PHP application server will attempt to execute the second statement, which is the error handler.

file(filename)

The *file* function is rather useful: It reads a file (or Web page from a URL) into an array, with the line breaks of the file as delimiters that split the file into the array. Once the file is in the array, you can use array techniques to access the parts of the file. This is useful for parsing CSV files, Web pages, or log files.

getdate(timestamp)

The *getdate* function is great for turning a timestamp into a useful array of its component parts. The function returns an associative array of seconds, minutes, hours, mday (day of month), wday (day of week), mon (numeric month), year (numeric year), yday (day of the year), weekday (full text of day of week), month (full text of month).

intval(number)

intval returns the integer part of a number.

isset(variable)

The *isset* function tests a variable to see if it has already been defined, to avoid potential errors. In PHP, depending upon the *error_reporting* setting inside of the PHP.ini file, you can't always use a variable that isn't defined yet. A common programming practice is to use *isset($myVar)* to return a true/false value.

nl2br(string)

One of the most often used functions when returning data from a database, this function inserts a *
* tag before every new line character (ASCII 10, or \n) so that the text retains its formatting in a Web browser.

split(pattern, string [, limit])

The *split* function is similar to the *explode* function—it splits a string into an array. The difference is that with the *split* function you can use multiple delimiter characters or patterns through the use of a *regular expression* pattern. Consult www.php.net for information on regular expressions.

stristr(string, string to find) and strstr(string, string to find)

These functions find a string within another string and give you a substring consisting of all characters from the first occurrence of the match to the end of the string. If no match occurs, the function returns false. The *strstr* function is case-sensitive, whereas the *stristr* function is case-insensitive.

strlen(string)

strlen simply returns the integer length of a given string.

User-Defined Functions

PHP allows you to declare functions on your page, similar to the way you can in JavaScript or Java. You declare a function with the *function* keyword and the name of the function, followed by the list of incoming parameters (if any) inside of parentheses, followed by your function body inside of curly braces:

```
function makeSearchWordsBold($string, $word) {
    $temp = str_replace($word,"<strong>$word</strong>",$string);
    return $temp;
}
```

After declaring the function, you can use it within your code in the same way that you would use any of the built-in functions.

PHP with MySQL

PHP has a rich tradition of being utilized with the MySQL database server. MySQL has been criticized for not being a true relational database management system. It doesn't have such things as referential integrity that a true RDBMS has. Still, MySQL is very popular and is in fact the most popular database for PHP. It is lightning fast for simple data display.

Dreamweaver MX is configured to work seamlessly with MySQL. All of the generated code that Dreamweaver MX produces uses PHP's built-in MySQL functions. In fact,

Dreamweaver MX by default will work only with the MySQL database. This was done to minimize the complexity of building compatibility for PHP into Dreamweaver, but also because the vast majority of PHP Web sites utilize MySQL databases.

MySQL is freely available for most operating systems, including Windows, Linux, and Mac OS X. The product is covered by the GNU license, like PHP. It has a command-line interface, but many third-party programs are available that make the database administration a little easier for the Windows user who is less comfortable in a command-line environment than a point-and-click environment.

After installing MySQL, you need to do a few things:

- Add a password to the root user.

- Delete the anonymous user.

- Start the service and make sure it's set up to run automatically.

- Create a database.

MySQL has a privilege system that you'll have to learn in order to work with the database. Essentially, all users can have specific privileges on the databases, tables, columns, and SQL statements. You should never use the root user, or an administrative user for your Web application. You should always set up a specific user for each Web application that has permission granted only to the areas that the Web application is going to use. For example, your Web application would probably never need the *CREATE* statement for databases or tables, so you would be wise not to allow it. Also, you might not need the *DELETE* statement for your Web application. If not, don't allow the user to have *DELETE* privileges. If your Web application displays data only, grant only *SELECT* privileges on the tables needed.

To grant privilege to a user, you can type the following into a command line (from your MySQL prompt):

```
mysql> grant select, insert, update
->on eflea.*
->to tom identified by 'myuserpassword';
```

PHP is a popular server because of its ease of use and because it's available as a free download for most of the popular server platforms. PHP is even preinstalled with Macintosh OS X, making it a perfect choice for someone who wants to build a dynamic Web application in an all-Mac environment. PHP is also probably the most popular server platform for Linux servers, and ties in well to the Apache Web server and MySQL database server on that platform.

Progress Check

1. What is the safe method of looping over an array in PHP?

2. What SQL keyword allows you to set permissions for users?

Project 7-1 Server Model

We'll go through a checklist of pros and cons of the three standard server models and decide which one would be best to use with your site.

Step by Step

1. Have you chosen a location for your Web site yet? If you haven't, it's time to ask your Web host what server model they support— ASP, JSP, ColdFusion, PHP, or ASP.NET. This should narrow your choice down. Start a sheet of paper numbered 1 to 5. Write down the list of server choices available under number 1.

2. Do you have your choice of databases? If you already have content located on a central database, is it something that is adaptable to your Web server? Many hosts offer SQL Server access for a small fee. This might be the most logical choice for an ASP or ColdFusion server, however, a very small site could utilize an Access database. Many databases need third-party drivers in JSP. Check into this as well, because third-party components can often be costly. Write down the list of choices you come up with under number 2.

3. What is on your development machine, what can you install, and what are you willing to install? If you are running Windows, you have many choices, but if you are on a Mac, you might not be able to run an ASP, ASP.NET, or ColdFusion server locally. This may not be a consideration, but it is a frequent time-saver to have a local development server.

4. Do you have a background in one of the programming languages—VBScript, JavaScript, ColdFusion, or Java? If not, do you have knowledge of another language, such as Perl, C, C++, or Visual Basic? PHP is similar to Perl, C and C++ are similar to Java and JavaScript (JSP or ASP), whereas Visual Basic is similar to VBScript (ASP). Do you know HTML,

---

1. Using the *for/each* construct
2. Grant

(continued)

but no server-side languages? If so, ColdFusion would be a good choice. Write your language choice or choices down under number 3.

5. What is your application going to do? If there is e-mail or file access involved, you may need third-party components. You should check into this with your Web host as well, because most Web hosts might have only one of the available components installed for your use. Many things like this are built into ColdFusion and PHP.

6. After asking yourself these questions, examine your results and see if your original choices seem logical.

Project Summary

In this project, you evaluated your needs and chose an appropriate server model based on several factors: your needs, your skills, the platform you are developing for, and the database you will be using. These will be considerations for each site you develop.

What to Take Away from This Module

In this module, we've given a brief overview of the different server models of Dreamweaver MX: ASP, JSP, PHP, ASP.NET, and ColdFusion. You learned a few basic facts about each one and were given a brief overview of the syntax of the server models.

Ask the Expert

Q: **What's the best language for developing Web applications?**

A: There is no "best" language. Each of the languages has its strong points and should be evaluated based on your needs and your current situation. An ASP server is usually a free component of a Windows-based machine, however, the cost of a ColdFusion server can be quickly recouped in a production environment because of its speed of development time. Also, add-on components are frequently needed in an ASP site. Maybe your Web host has these components available already, but maybe they don't. A JSP server can be complex to learn and implement, but can offer a powerful enterprise-level environment to the experienced programmer. PHP can be a nice option if you are on a budget.

✓

Module 7 Mastery Check

1. What do letters in ASP, JSP, PHP, and CFML stand for?

2. What does the query string do?

3. Which of the following languages are case-sensitive: Java, VBScript, JavaScript, CFML, PHP, C#?

4. Which languages have typed variables of the languages mentioned?

5. Can a server retrieve a cookie that was set by another Web site?

6. Can PHP be run on a Windows server?

7. Can ColdFusion be run on a Linux server?

8. What database does Dreamweaver MX allow you to use with PHP?

9. Which of the following server technologies allows you to send e-mail using the core language components: PHP, ASP, ColdFusion?

10. True or false: Sessions in ASP require that cookies be present on the client machine.

11. What does EJB stands for?

12. True or false: Always use the root user when accessing a MySQL database from a Web application.

13. True or false: ASP pages work without change in ASP.NET.

14. What is the string concatenation character in PHP?

15. True or false: PHP can run natively on the Macintosh.

Module 8

Creating a Database

225

The heart of a data-driven Web application is the database that stores your information. If you are going to store something, especially a lot of something, it is a pretty good idea to have a system for storing it that lets you find it and get it back out of storage when you need it. Filing cabinets have alphabetical folders, the library has the Dewey Decimal System, and databases have the Relational Design Model.

In 1970, E. F. Codd, then a researcher at IBM, published a paper that was the first conception of what we now know as the Relational Database Design Model. Codd was concerned with the mechanics of storing and retrieving data in large database applications. His model stood in contrast to the models that were in use at the time, which were more reliant on the physical storage of the data and were significantly less flexible than Codd's vision.

NOTE

Many people think that Codd's design model is called "relational" because of the way that tables are "related" to one another when querying a database. Actually, Codd's terminology was somewhat different than today's. What we call a table, Codd would call a relation because, by definition, that table should hold information about individual items that are in some way related to one another. What we call tables, columns, and rows, Codd would call relations, attributes, and tuples.

Since that time, Codd has revised and expanded the rules that govern relational database design. The last 30 years have proven the validity of the relational concept, and it is the model on which most modern databases are built. In order for you to access data from an application built with Dreamweaver MX, you are going to need to design that data store.

The design of a data store is really a separate issue from how you connect to the database or how you query data from it. Although closely related to your overall goal, database design is a discipline all to itself. In this module, we cover the points that you need to know to design a database that will be flexible and powerful enough to serve your application well.

CRITICAL SKILL
8.1

Understand the Basic Database Components

Perhaps the best way to think of a database is like a big filing cabinet that you have squeezed onto the hard drive of your computer. In that filing cabinet, you have file folders. In those folders, there is paper and on that paper is information. If you plan carefully when you set up your filing cabinet, it can be a quick and easy way to put your hands on the data you need.

Suppose that you needed to collect information about all of the players in a golf tournament you have started. For the most part, you need the same information about each player. You might want to collect the following information:

- Name

- Address

- Phone number

- Payment method

- Handicap (a method of tracking average score related to par, and thereby skill level)

- Team number (which team of four players this person is assigned to)

- Score (this team's score for the tournament)

- Ranking (the ranking of this team in relation to other teams in the tournament based on their score)

- Notes (any miscellaneous information you may need to store about this player)

To collect this information, you might whip up a quick form in your favorite word processor and print off a copy for each player you expected to register. Once you had filled out the form (which, keep in mind, is identical for every player) with each player's individual information (which is obviously different for each player), you can store those forms in a file folder for future reference. To make sure you could always find this information, you would place this folder in a drawer in your filing cabinet.

So, in the current example, there are five items that are necessary to collect and store information about the players in your golf tournament: a filing cabinet, a filing drawer in the cabinet, a file folder, a basic form design, and an individual form for each player. These physical items relate directly to the basic parts of a modern database system. They are

- The database management system

- The individual database

- Tables

- Columns

- Rows

NOTE

There are other parts of a database, such as stored procedures and triggers, which are beyond the scope of this discussion. The elements listed here represent the basics and are sufficient for this discussion. When you are ready to move on to more advanced topics, there are many books and Web sites where you can get more information on database design's advanced topics.

The Database Management System

Microsoft Access is a file-based database that is perfect for learning database concepts and languages. It also integrates very well with Dreamweaver MX in most of the server models from a Windows environment. For the remainder of the book, we use a sample Access database, which is available from www.osborne.com, to illustrate database principles.

The database management system is the overall application framework within which you design, house, and manage all the databases you create for your individual projects. Access does not provide what can technically be considered a database management system, but you can achieve some of the same effects through the basic Access program. Rather than truly managing databases within a management environment, you will use Access to find and open individual files on your computer, each of which represents a self-contained database, as shown in Figure 8-1.

In the current example, the Access database application represents the filing cabinet in which your filing drawers are kept. You may have several drawers in the cabinet, but they are all available to you right there in the filing cabinet along with the rest of the data.

NOTE

In a filing cabinet, you have only so many drawers, usually two or four. One of the great things about a database system is that you can keep adding drawers (databases) as you need them to hold more data.

The Individual Database

Within Access are the individual databases you have created. An individual database is a set of components and data that serve a particular purpose for a particular project. Although it is possible to keep shoving data into one expanding database to serve multiple purposes, such a database will quickly become disorganized and useless. It is highly advisable to create separate databases for each project, and sometimes even more than one for a project if the project is of sufficient size and scope to require it.

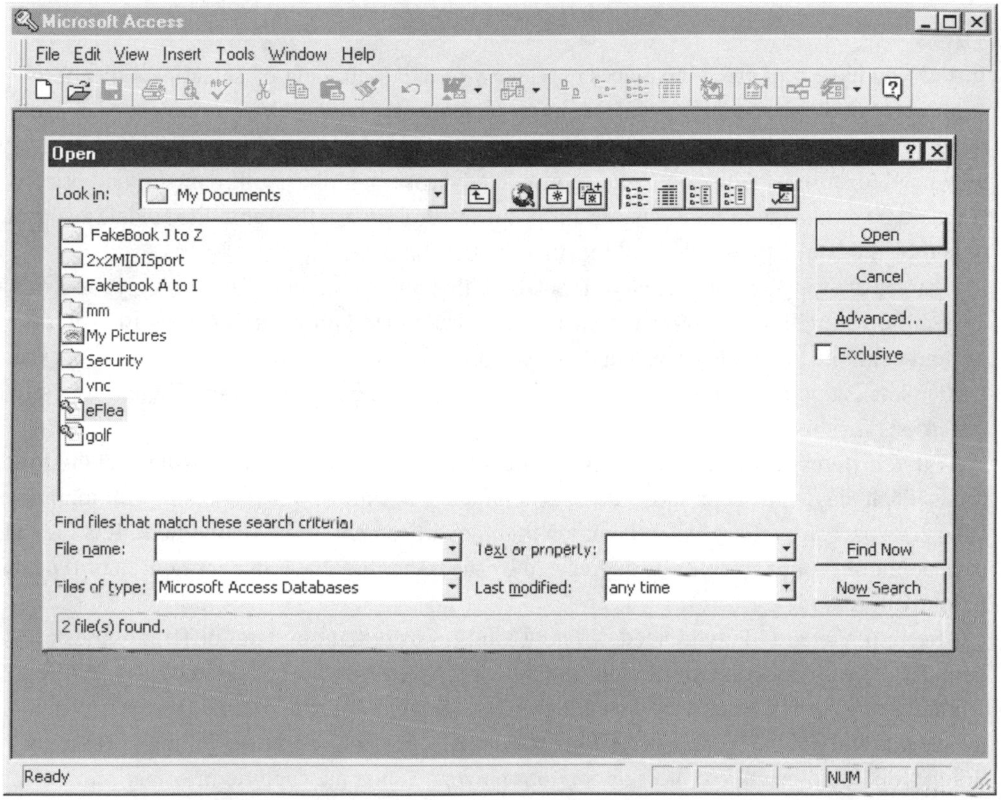

Figure 8-1 Use Access to manage your database

NOTE

The decision of how many databases are required to service a project is a many-faceted consideration. Factors such as security, performance, maintenance, and data compatibility need to be investigated in the design stage in order to make a reasonable determination.

In the current example, the individual database is represented by the file drawer. The file drawer is housed in the filing cabinet, just as the database is housed in the database application. Just as you might designate a drawer in your file cabinet for financial information, or contracts, or golf tournament participation, you would create and populate individual databases for each type of data you need to store.

Tables

Just as you have organized the places in which you will store data by selecting a database application and creating individual databases to segregate related data, you must organize the data being stored in each database. In addition to the players in your golf tournament, you may need to store information about sponsors, advertisers, judges, golf courses, and prizes. It would be a mistake to try and store all of this information in the same file folder, just as it would be a mistake to jumble it all together in your database.

Tables are the components of your database that are responsible for holding your data. Typically, you will have a table for each set of related data you need to store, just as in the present example you would create a different form on which to write information about the participants, advertisers, and golf courses if you were doing this on paper. There are a couple of reasons for this.

First, different forms for each type of contact make it easier to identify the data the form holds. Each player has at least one thing in common: They are all players in this golf tournament. Likewise, each advertiser has in common their advertisement at the tournament. It is logical to keep those groups of contacts segregated by the thing they have in common: their type of participation in the event.

Second, you are likely to need different kinds of information about different kinds of contacts. The information you might need about the players was discussed earlier. While it would be silly to put a place to store the team assignment or score of an advertiser, you would need a place to put the type of advertisement, the rate they paid, and their billing information—things you do not need to collect about your players. When the specific information that you need to collect and store differs to this degree, it is a strong indication that it should be stored on two different forms or in two different database tables.

NOTE

Looking back up the chain of data constructs we are creating, you can clearly see the relation that each has to the other. No matter how many tables you create, they all relate to your golf tournament, and hence belong in your golf tournament database. That golf tournament database, in turn, is one of your projects and, therefore, belongs in the database management system that houses your projects.

Figure 8-2 illustrates the tables you might create in your golf tournament database.

Columns

On the form to hold information about the players in the golf tournament, several pieces of information were identified that needed to be collected about each player. This information

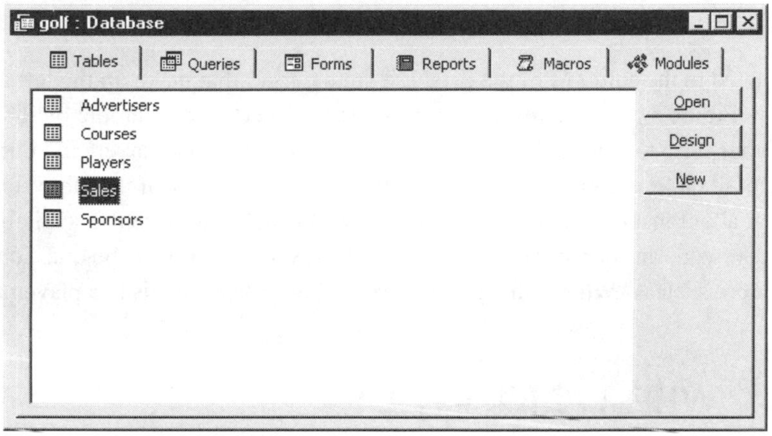

Figure 8-2 The tables in the golf tournament database

represents attributes of the individual players. These translate to your database table as the columns of the table. Although these attributes are not always represented as columns, the datasheet view, a common way of looking at data, looks much like a spreadsheet with the attribute, or field, names listed across the top. You can see this in Figure 8-3, which makes it clear why "columns" is the common name for this part of the table.

In essence, each column represents a question about the topic of the table. For instance, in the players table, each column relates to one of the attributes of the player. In filling out each column for each player, you are, in effect, answering a question about that player that represents information your database needs to know to manage the tournament effectively.

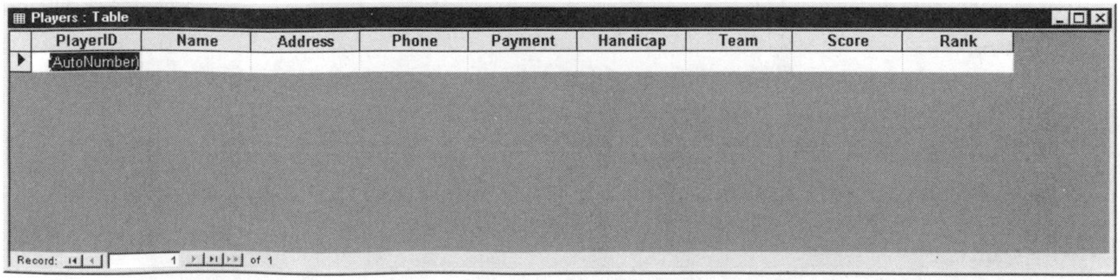

Figure 8-3 A database table showing the column names across the top

Rows

Closely related to the columns of the database are the rows that make up the left axis of the datasheet in Figure 8-3. These rows are represented in the current example by the individual copies of your form that hold the information about the individual players in your tournament. In the database table, each player is entered on his or her own row of the table. That row holds information about that player and only that player. On each row, a field is available for each column where you can enter information about that player that answers the question represented by the column, such as "What is this player's name?" or "What team is this player assigned to?"

CRITICAL SKILL
8.2 Work with Data Types

Before we look at the design of a database, it is important for you to understand data types. *Data types* are the way that programs identify what kind of information is being stored and how it will be manipulated.

A good example of the importance of data types is 1. What is 1? Is it a number? Yes, it could be identified as a number. It could also be identified as a character or a piece of text. What difference does it make? A lot when you start doing things with it.

For instance, what do you get when you add 1 to another 1? If they are both numbers, the mathematical function for addition controls the transaction and you get the answer 2. If, however, they are textual characters, a text function called concatenation might be invoked and the answer would be 11. Not really the number 11, but a piece of text that is two ones placed next to each other.

Another example is U.S. ZIP codes. Although you might be tempted to store a five-digit ZIP code (like 32811) as a number, some ZIP codes may be stored with their four-digit extension (like 32811-1234). If you try to store this as a number, you will either get an error or you will get 31577 (32811 minus 1234). Neither is the result you expected, so these types of numbers are better stored as text.

Access has eight basic data types:

- Text
- Memo
- Number
- Date/time
- Currency
- Autonumber

- Yes/no
- OLE object

Text

The text data type is for storing data such as names and addresses that can be represented in lengths up to 255 characters. You can specify a length in Access so that the user is limited to fewer characters. This is advisable if you are storing things that have set lengths, like Social Security numbers, because anything over 11 characters (###-##-#### in this case) would never be used and the database would just be wasting space by allotting more characters for the field. An additional benefit is that if anyone tries to enter more than 11 characters for a Social Security number (obviously an error), the database will not allow it, and the user must enter something that is at least the correct number of characters.

You can also set additional properties, such as a default value and whether the field is required.

Memo

The memo field is used when you need to store blocks of text that exceed 255 characters. For example, if you are storing movie reviews or descriptions of items for sale, you can provide a more free-form method of text entry by using a memo field.

Number

Some databases have several different data types for dealing with numbers, and so does Access, technically speaking. You can select the number data type for any kind of numerical data and then set a subtype in the Access properties. The subtypes include the following:

- Byte
- Integer
- Long integer
- Single
- Double
- Replication ID

If you will be using this field as an ID that will be joined to an autonumber data type in another table, you must use a long integer data type.

NOTE

The replication ID data type creates a globally unique number used when performing database replication. It is most useful when using Access as a stand-alone database application rather than as a Web data store.

Date/Time

The date/time data type stores exactly what you would expect, dates and times. It is important to use this data type to store dates rather than the text data type (which works in a display-only environment) if you plan to do any date manipulation using DateAdd. For instance, if you want to determine how many days have elapsed between dates, it is important that the database knows that you are dealing with a calendar and not just text data.

Currency

Currency is a special numeric data type that forces all numbers to a two-decimal-place representation for storing money data. Regular floating point (non-integer) numbers are prone to rounding errors when doing calculations because of the way that these numbers are stored in the computer. A currency data type is not prone to the rounding errors when doing floating-point calculations.

Autonumber

The autonumber data type is designed to provide an incrementing ID field in a table. It is often used to provide a unique ID for a user or a product. The fact that the database handles the insertion of the data in this field (you cannot enter anything into it yourself) guarantees that no two records will have the same ID. The autonumber datatype is unique to Access, although other database systems have similar data types (identity column in SQL Server, for example).

Yes/No

The yes/no data type stores one bit of data, either a 1 or a 0. A 1 equates to yes, or true; a 0 equates to no, or false. Data from check boxes is often stored in this data type. You can use it when your field is storing the answer to a question that is either yes or no, such as, "Is this user over 18?" or "Is this person active in the system?"

OLE Object

An OLE object is a binary data type, such as an image or a sound. It is *not* recommended that you store data like this in your database. It causes significant performance problems to move around large files in your database. It is better to store a path to the image or sound in the database and use that path to point the user's browser to the correct file.

Proper use of data types can solve a myriad of problems when designing your database. As you complete the next section, the importance of planning this part of your application will become clear.

Progress Check

1. A long integer is a subtype of which basic Access data type?

2. Which database components make up the top and left axes of a database table?

3. What creation of E. F. Codd forms the basis for database design to this day?

CRITICAL SKILL
8.3 # Design a Relational Database

Some people's filing cabinets are nothing but collection areas for excess paper they can't decide what to do with. The drawers barely open and close, and they quickly become useless space wasters. If you are not careful, your database will end up the same way: no organization, overstuffed, useless, and difficult to open and close.

Despite all that computers can do for you, sometimes it is a good idea to set them aside and start with a pencil and a piece of paper. When you begin to sketch out the functionality of a computer project, and especially a database schema, it is often best to get out a good #2 pencil and a legal pad and try to get your thoughts organized so that the job of actually implementing the database can be done right the first time.

NOTE

If you are new to programming, the importance of doing things right the first time cannot be overemphasized. True, you will almost always have bugs that need to be fixed and maintenance to perform, but you can significantly reduce these and eliminate more major problems by spending the time to design your application properly.

---

1. Number
2. Columns and rows
3. The Relational Database Design Model

There are several questions you need to answer before you can begin constructing your database:

- What kind of data will you be storing?

- How will the database be accessed?

- Will your users need to add and change things in the database or just look things up?

- What changes might you need to make in the future?

Your Data

What kind of data you will store in your database is an important consideration both in selecting the database management system (or application) you will use and how its structure is defined. If, for instance, you will be storing only text information, such as names and addresses of clients and simple product information, you are pretty safe in an assumption that any modern system can accommodate your needs. If you need the ability to store things like BLOBs (binary large objects) such as images and sounds directly in the database tables (rather than just storing references to them), you will need to do some extra research to make sure that your database selection supports them and determine whether they require any special considerations.

An important point in this day and age is the security level of the information you will be storing. Financial, medical, and other personal information is stored in databases all over the world. If you will be handling information of this nature, you will need to pay special attention to the security scheme you implement to ensure that the data remains secure.

Access Your Database

Determining how your database will be accessed is also an important consideration. For instance, will this database service only a Web site, and only one Web site, or will it need to be accessed by multiple applications? This scenario might involve a sales site, an administration site and an internal office application written in another language (such as Visual Basic) that your sales staff might use to query information and maintain the site's data.

Also, think about how the different uses of the database might affect your security needs. It is unlikely that a stand-alone Access database that lets users look up ZIP code information, for instance, would pose the same security risk as a large database management system operating at a financial institution. Likewise, a database that allows only office users to access it may not need the same level of security planning as one that makes data available over the Web. Because you are contemplating data access over the Internet with Dreamweaver MX, it is likely that you will need to spend some time in this important area.

NOTE 🏃

It is not possible here to adequately cover database security. Security is a complex matter with differences in implementation depending on the software you need to use. If you are unsure as to the steps required to successfully secure your data, please seek competent help before you attempt to place sensitive information in a Web-connected database.

Use of the Database

The purpose for which your database will be used is also an important point to consider. Earlier, a ZIP code lookup function was mentioned. In such an application, the user would most likely be providing some simple information on which a database query would be constructed. The database would return information to the user based on the input they had provided. For example, if the user supplied a ZIP code, the application might tell them for which city that ZIP code was valid. The functionality could likely be accomplished with only a table or two of data. Such a database would be used to query data from the tables, but it is unlikely that you would ever allow a user to add or change ZIP code information. That kind of information is updated by official sources on a periodic basis, and your own maintenance procedures are all that should be allowed to alter any data in the tables.

However, the golf tournament database discussed earlier required several tables to store all of the data. Not only will you and visitors to your site need to query data out of this database, but some of these tables will need regular updating as new players and advertisers sign on and team assignments and scores are updated. Designing a database of even moderate complexity like this can take careful consideration.

For example, it is important to keep data that needs to be updated separated from static or private data, so that users do not inadvertently change something they shouldn't. You can also save a significant amount of space and simplify maintenance of your site if you use properly normalized data, which is discussed shortly.

Database Maintenance

The last item on the list of considerations when designing a database is the methods you will use to perform maintenance. Ideally, there will be as little maintenance as possible, but the real-world fact is that you will end up performing some maintenance on your database as you go. Careful planning will help minimize the number of alterations you need to make, but the sheer complexity of some sites means you are bound to either miss something or experience an honest to goodness change in how you need the database to work.

One of the primary concerns about altering databases once they are in use is if you find yourself needing to add or change fields (or columns) in a table. In either case, you will likely have existing data that will be affected by the change, and you will need to carefully consider

Ask the Expert

Q: How large a Web site can Microsoft Access handle?

A: That is not an easy question to answer. It depends on what your users will be doing on your site. If they are just searching and displaying information, it can handle quite a bit of traffic. If, however, you need users to insert, update, or delete data, table locking will be invoked. Table locking is the means by which Access makes sure that more than one person is not overwriting a single record at the same time, and it takes database resources. In this case, about 20 people can make concurrent connections to the database before you start to see a degradation in performance. But 20 truly concurrent connections probably represents several times that number of visitors to your site, because people do not hit the database at exactly the same time.

Q: When should I upgrade to an enterprise database such as SQL Server or Oracle?

A: Without sounding trite, the answer is as soon as you can afford it. There are advantages to a real database management system that supercede simple performance, and even the smallest site can recognize significant benefits. From security to ease of maintenance, you will want to be on a server platform as soon as you can if you plan to grow your site at all.

Although a full license of this software can be expensive, many ISPs offer access to SQL Servers for only $25–30 a month.

how your changes will impact that data. Give special notice to how existing data will react if you need to change data type, such as changing a field from a text data type to an integer, for instance. Also, think about existing records if you must add a field to a table. Consider what it will mean if all the existing records have had no data inserted into that new field, and how you can best address collecting and inserting the appropriate values for each existing record.

CRITICAL SKILL
8.4 Integrate Uniqueness and Keys

Suppose you had several bills of U.S. currency of different denominations in front of you, from a $1 bill up to a $100 bill. If someone asked you to hand them the bill that had a U.S. president's picture on it, how would you know which one they meant? Not all U.S. currency has presidents on it (Benjamin Franklin was never president), but certainly more than one denomination has a president on it.

Luckily, there is unique information on the bills. Each has a different denomination that can identify the bill uniquely when compared to other bills. But even that would not be sufficient in, say, a stack of $10 bills. In that case, you would need to resort to the serial number on each bill to be sure that you could identify each bill uniquely.

The records in your database are much the same. Many of them may have information in common. Just as many U.S. bills have presidents on them, many of the players in your golf tournament may live in Georgia. You can go a level deeper and look only for the players from Atlanta. That may work, just as you may only have had a single $10 bill, but it is just as likely that you could have multiple players from Atlanta. To be sure you can identify a single player without question, it is necessary to have information that is unique to them. Although we are not collecting this information in our example, you might think of something like a Social Security number, which is guaranteed by an outside source to be unique to each person. Although it may be inappropriate to demand players' Social Security numbers just so they can play golf, you can approximate the role of the Social Security number by telling your database to assign a unique identifier to each entry in the database.

Think about why table uniqueness is so important. First, from a common sense standpoint, how much sense does it make to store multiple copies of identical data in your table? If there is nothing different about a second or third record, there is no reason to waste space storing them.

Second, and more importantly, when you attempt to update or delete a database record, the database must be able to identify exactly which record you are trying to operate on. If it can't do so, the database will likely throw an error rather than risk corrupting your data by altering the incorrect record. Records can be identified by the use of three kinds of keys:

- Candidate keys

- Primary keys

- Foreign keys

Candidate Keys

A candidate key is a set of one or more columns in your database that are unique across all occurrences. For instance, consider the following table:

ZIP Code	City
32811	Orlando
32835	Orlando
34749	Ocoee
32789	Winter Park
32790	Winter Park

In this sample, there are two possible candidate keys based on their uniqueness. The first is the ZIP Code column. Because no value repeats, it can be considered a candidate key. In addition, although the city names in the City column do repeat on occasion, the combination of the ZIP Code and City columns together never repeat, providing another possible candidate key. The City column does repeat and has no value of itself for identifying unique records.

NOTE

Just because the values in these columns do not repeat in the sample data does not necessarily mean they never will. The designation of a candidate key is based on your knowledge of the data that will be placed in your tables, and your knowledge that certain combinations of columns should remain unique. Once designated, this decision will be enforced in your database to call attention to attempts to duplicate data that you have identified as a candidate key.

Another consideration when identifying a candidate key is where it is possible for a particular record to be null for a key column. Because null values cannot be guaranteed to be unique, no candidate key can contain nulls.

Primary Keys

A primary key differs from a candidate key only in that it has been arbitrarily designated as the primary key from the selection of candidate keys already defined. Although primary keys, in the current thinking, are not strictly necessary in your tables, they are quite useful, especially because of their minimalist nature.

NOTE

There is another kind of relational key called an alternate key. An alternate key is simply any candidate key that has not been designated as the primary key for a table.

Although a given candidate key may be up to several columns in complexity, a primary key is often designated as a single column that uniquely defines a row in the database. Sometimes this single column has no real relationship to the actual data being stored, other than the fact that you have designated it as an arbitrary identifier. Developers will often use an autonumber or identity function to have the database itself create a random or incremental integer or whole number that is used as the primary key. In many cases, you can construct the database so that number becomes meaningful for the data in question, such as making the generated number a group or account number, but this is not strictly necessary. Primary keys are of the greatest use when used to refer to table data being referenced from a foreign key.

Foreign Keys

Foreign keys are not strictly keys at all in that they do not typically have any impact on the uniqueness of a particular record. The job of a foreign key is to refer to the primary key (or candidate key, to be proper) of a table that holds more detailed information about some topic that is related to the current record.

For an example, return to the golf tournament database from earlier. In that database, a table was created to hold information about advertisers at the golf tournament. Suppose that this year the tournament is becoming quite an event, and you must hire some salespeople to handle the transactions with your advertisers. You have promised those salespeople a commission, so you must, of course, track the sales they have made. To do this, you will need to add a table to hold data about your sales staff. Consider the Sales table:

PK	SalesID	Integer
	Name	Text
	Address	Text
	Phone	Text
	Social Security	Text
	Commission Rate	Integer

Note that we designated the SalesID column as a primary key for the table. The SalesID is a unique value that is automatically assigned by the database when a new sales rep is entered. As mentioned earlier, this autonumber field has been given significance by making it the sales representative's identification number.

Now look at the structure of the Advertisers table:

PK	AdID	Integer
	Name	Text
	Address	Text
	Contact	Text
FK	SalesID	Integer

The Advertisers table also has a primary key assigned. In addition, the SalesID field has been designated as a foreign key. When you enter a new advertiser into the table, the ID of the sales rep who sold the transaction is entered in the SalesID column. By relating the SalesID foreign key column from the Advertisers table to the SalesID primary key column in the Sales table, you gain a couple of distinct advantages. First, information about your sales staff has to be stored only once and then referenced by a simple integer from wherever else in your database you need this information. This saves space in the database as well as data entry time. Second, you can very easily assign multiple accounts in the Advertisers table to the same sales rep, creating a one-to-many relationship between the tables. Table relationships are discussed next.

CRITICAL SKILL
8.5 # Know the Different Table Relationships

There are three types of relationships between database tables:

- One-to-one
- One-to-many
- Many-to-many

One-to-One Relationships

A one-to-one relationship between two tables means that for each record in the first table, there can be one and only one related record in the second table. This type of relationship is rarely used and, when it is used, it's usually because of some limitation of the database application that requires a piece of information unique to one record to be stored separately, perhaps because of its size.

One-to-Many Relationships

One-to-many relationships are, by far, the most common in relational databases. A one-to-many relationship means that one record in the first table may have multiple related records in the second table, usually identified by a foreign key. The golf tournament database is a good example of this. In it, there is one record for each sales representative. The sales representative's ID, however, might show up in multiple records in the Advertisers table if one sales rep sold advertisements to many different companies. The one-to-many relationship is the most useful type of relationship and is a core component of the relational database model.

Many-to-Many Relationships

A many-to-many relationship exists when there are many records in one table related to many records in a second table. In reality, this relationship cannot be properly illustrated using the relational database model. To do so would require the use of several overlapping one-to-many relationships. In actual practice, you would have a table that relates two primary keys in two different tables, such as a categories table that relates several categories to each record. This third table, also known as a *lookup* table, would be able to relate to two other tables providing a many-to-many relationship.

CRITICAL SKILL
8.6 Use Database Normalization

An in-depth discussion of database normalization could take many modules, and indeed it has in some books. For our purposes, it is important that you understand that normalization is a process of organizing data to reduce duplication. This is most often accomplished by separating data into two or more related tables. When done properly, advantages include gain in storage space, performance, ease of use, and maintenance.

There are at least five normal forms that can define how data is laid out in a database. The most common form through which databases are normalized is the third normal form.

NOTE

The third normal form represents a good compromise between performance and design considerations and the total eradication of data duplication. When you get beyond the third form, the recommendations for how data can be organized get rather absurd and unworkable in the modern environment.

The First Normal Form

The first normal form holds that each field in a database table must contain different data. For instance, in the golf tournament Players table, you could have only one field in which the score was entered. Also, each field should contain only one value. It would be wrong to store information in a comma-separated list in one field. Finally, each group of related data should be in its own table.

The Second Normal Form

The second normal form says that no field of data may be derived from another field. For example, if in the Players table you were storing the date of birth of the players, it would be improper to have a second field that stored the year of birth alone. That data would be redundant in that it is available in the birthdate field.

The Third Normal Form

The third normal form says that duplicate information is not allowed in the database. The third normal form is what was achieved in the golf tournament foreign key example. Instead of storing information about the sales rep for an account directly in the Advertisers table each time the sales rep sold a new account, a Sales table was created to hold that information, which was then referenced by a foreign key in the Advertisers table.

Progress Check

1. What are the three types of database keys?

2. Before placing sensitive data on the Web, it is important that you become familiar with what subject?

3. Which normal form holds that each field in a database table must hold different data?

Create the eFlea Database

The real test of all of this information is whether we can put it to use in even the simplest of databases. In reality, the eFlea application can be served quite well by only two tables. But within those two tables, you will see much of what we have just talked about.

Project Goals

By the end of this project, you will

● See how the database theory we just discussed applies to an actual database design.

● Have designed the eFlea database.

● Have created the eFlea database in Access.

Step by Step

1. The first thing you need to do when designing your database is answer the questions that were discussed in this module:

● **What kind of data will you be storing?** The eFlea database is intended to bring buyers and sellers of used items together. As such, there will be two types of data that will be stored: users' information and item information. Most of this data will be simple text, so you won't need any specialized functionality that cannot be handled in Access.

● **How will the database be accessed?** Because this is a Web-only application, the database will be accessed from your Web site. There will not be any need for the data

---

1. Candidate, primary, and foreign
2. Database security
3. The first normal form

to be accessed from additional Web sites or from an internal application. Again, this is good news if you are planning to use Access.

- **How will your users use the database?**   Your users will be adding their personal user information and information about the items they want to sell to the database, so you will need insert functionality. They may also need to change information about themselves or their products, so you will need update functionality. And, of course, users will want to be able to search for what is available for purchase, so you will need search functionality. You could also include the capability for users to delete their account or their items. As simple as this application is, it contains the entire gamut of database functionality.

- **What changes might you need to make in the future?**   A well-designed database and application will limit the amount of maintenance that you have to perform. However, you will likely find yourself wanting to add features to your site after it has been up for a while and you have gotten feedback from your users. When using Access, the only way to make changes to the database itself is to download the current copy, make your changes, and then upload it again. Any information that is inserted into the database while you are working on it will be wiped out when you upload your changed version on top of it. It is best, then, to temporarily shut down your site while performing maintenance. This is one of the biggest disadvantages of using a file-based database like Access.

2. What you have learned from answering these questions is that, at its most basic, your database needs two tables: one to hold user information and one to hold item information. The next decision to make is what specifics you need to store about each.

3. You will want to store the following information about your users:

   - A user ID to uniquely identify each user
   - The user's name
   - The city they live in
   - The state they live in
   - Their e-mail address
   - A username used to log in and add or change items for sale
   - A password to go with the username
   - What group the user is in (administrator, user, and so on)

4. You will want to store the following information about the items that your users want to sell:

   - An item ID to uniquely identify each item
   - The ID of the user who has listed this item
   - The name of the item

(continued)

- A description of the item
- The date the item was entered into the database
- The asking price of the item
- Any keywords that might assist in a search for the item
- Whether the item is currently active, so that it can be turned off when it is sold

5. Using this information, you can construct your database. Open Access on your development machine. You will be presented with the opening dialog box that allows you to create a new database, use the Database Wizard, or open an existing database. Select the Blank Database option and click OK.

6. Navigate to the root folder of the site you created in Dreamweaver MX. Name your file **eFlea** and click Create.

7. You will be presented with a blank database container.

8. From the Tables tab, click New to create a new table. Select Design View from the list box and click OK.

9. The Table Design view will appear. The basic use of this view is to enter the names of your fields in the left column, their data type in the middle column, and any description you would like in the right column. The list of properties at the bottom of the screen represents

(continued)

other properties you can set, and they change depending on what data types you select for your fields.

10. Create the fields that you listed in the previous steps for the User table. For each of the text fields, you can set their length to 50 for now in the Properties section, except for the state, which should be a length of 2, and the username and password, which should be 10 each.

Click the gray square to the left of the ID field and then click the key icon in the toolbar. This sets the ID field to the primary key for this table.

```
Microsoft Access                                            _ □ ×
 File  Edit  View  Insert  Tools  Window  Help

 users : Table                                             _ □ ×
     Field Name          Data Type              Description
   efleaID            AutoNumber
 ▶ Name                Text
   City                Text
   State               Text
   email               Text
   username            Text
   password            Text
   group               Text


                              Field Properties

   General | Lookup |
   Field Size          50
   Format
   Input Mask
   Caption                                  A field name can be up to 64 characters
   Default Value                            long, including spaces. Press F1 for help on
   Validation Rule                                      field names.
   Validation Text
   Required            No
   Allow Zero Length   No
   Indexed             No


 Design view.  F6 = Switch panes.  F1 = Help.                      NUM
```

11. When you close the table or click the Save icon, you will be prompted to save your table. Give it the name **Users** and click OK.

(continued)

12. Do the same for the Items table. The one thing to keep in mind with the Items table is that you always want the current date to be entered in the DateEntered field. In the Default Value property at the bottom of the screen, place the Date() function so that the database inserts this date value for you.

13. Save the table as **Items**.

You can see from this exercise that even simple applications deserve to be properly designed. These principles are as applicable here as in any larger application. As you complete these steps, you will gain a better understanding of your site and exactly what you expect it to do. You will be able to more easily spot holes in your design and plug them before your site goes live, which is always best.

Project Summary

Once you have created your tables and closed Access, your database is ready to use. In Module 11, you will connect to your database and learn to insert data into it and search what is already there.

What to Take Away from This Module

You are probably very excited about getting your Web site up and running, but it is important that you understand the impact that good database design has on your project. You must determine the use, scope, and layout of your database before you can hope to build it, and you must build it before you can connect to it and launch your site.

Following the Relational Database Design Model, properly identifying and normalizing your data, and managing your data relationships will help to ensure a stable and robust design that will allow your application to scale as your site grows. There is much more information available on the topic of relational database design, and you are encouraged to learn all you can about this very important topic.

✓

Module 8 Mastery Check

1. What is the autonumber data type designed to do?

2. Which data type forces all numbers to a two-decimal-place representation?

3. Which normal form holds that no duplicate information is allowed in the database?

4. What types of table relationships are there?

5. What is special about a primary key?

6. What data type is used to provide a unique ID for a record in Microsoft Access?

7. You can have the database enter a value for you using what property?

8. To keep from overwriting data while updating the features of an Access database, it is best to _____.

9. True or False: It is wise to store as much information as possible in a field, separating the data by commas if necessary.

10. How would you define a one-to-many relationship?

11. What number on currency would be equivalent to a primary key—the denomination or the serial number—and why?

12. How does a many-to-many relationship work in a typical database?

13. What type of form field is typically used to display yes/no answers?

Module 9

Choosing Your Database and Connecting to It

Dreamweaver MX is designed to work with many configurations of server languages, Web servers, and databases. One of the primary reasons for choosing to use a dynamic environment such as this is to connect to a database. Dreamweaver MX is capable of connecting to your database in a variety of ways, depending on the configuration on your machine and on the server that you are deploying your site from.

CRITICAL SKILL
9.1

Learn Background Information on Available Databases

Each of the server models you can work with in Dreamweaver MX—ASP, JSP, PHP, ASP.NET, and ColdFusion—has specific databases that it works well with. Although you may be fully committed to one database or another in your day-to-day workflow, putting that same data up on the Web is another matter entirely. Many database programs that you use on the desktop are not suited for Web use. Most databases have an export facility of some sort, so changing databases in many cases may be a viable option. We go over some of the pluses and minuses of the different databases that are available.

Microsoft Access

Access is one of the cornerstones of Web development because of its ease of use and universal appeal. Databases can be designed easily on Access and integrated into your Web site easily as well. It is almost certainly the best database for the job of a design-time connection, because it will run on Windows and exist even without having Access installed on the system. All you need is the MDB file that contains the data, and you will be able to connect to it via ODBC or an ADO connection string, or even through the Sun ODBC:JDBC driver if you are using JSP.

Access comes as part of Microsoft Office Professional or Premium versions, and is also available as a stand-alone product. You can get a special competitive upgrade price on Access from a variety of different databases. Having Access installed on your system is considered a must for the Windows-based Web developer, because it allows easy manipulation of tables and queries in the design environment, before actually deploying your data to the server. Access can be used on a Macintosh also, if you have SoftWindows or Virtual PC installed on the system. For a Macintosh user, it's a much more suitable alternative to the various Macintosh-only databases, because you will eventually be getting your live data from a Windows server. Keep in mind, however, that you can't use the Access database within Dreamweaver MX from the Virtual PC environment. The database has to reside on a Windows server to be able to access it from Dreamweaver MX.

In addition, Access contains a query builder that allows you to test your queries in a controlled environment before deploying them from your Web page. An Access query can be copied/pasted into the Dreamweaver MX environment with minor changes. Access databases also contain a Compact command that decreases the size of the data, and also optimizes the data for quicker access. The Compact command can be accessed right from the ODBC administrator as well.

If it sounds too good to be true, it is. Although we wholeheartedly recommend Access for use in the design environment, we can't recommend its use on a live Web server, unless you expect that your Web site will never have more than a handful of simultaneous users. Although the specifications of Access claim many more, many users have found that slow access and data corruption can result in a real-world environment. Also, if the machine that hosts your Web site isn't a Windows machine, Access might not even be an option.

TIP

Microsoft Access 2000 and above can be used as a front end to Microsoft SQL Server and to a SQL Server–like database using the Microsoft Data Engine (MSDE). The MSDE is an actual client/server data engine, which makes it much more scalable than the Jet engine of a typical file-based Access database. The MSDE is included with Access 2000.

Microsoft SQL Server

If you plan to deploy your Web site from a Windows-based server, Microsoft SQL Server would have to be the number one choice for the database. Beginning with SQL Server 7.0, Microsoft began implementing some of the ease-of-use features of Access. The Enterprise Manager (see Figure 9-1) allows quick access to tables, views, and stored procedures that make using SQL Server a snap. In addition, upsizing from Microsoft Access is a simple process as well.

Whereas Microsoft Access is a file-based database, SQL Server is a full-fledged server. Making simultaneous connections in SQL Server is no problem, and SQL Server can maintain hundreds or thousands of connections without corruption of data. In addition, SQL Server has more security than the file-based Access.

SQL Server also offers the use of stored procedures, which not only speed up the data access, but allow the use of *transactions*, which can give you the ability to execute several queries at once, thereby making it possible to do batch updates or deletes from your Web site.

NOTE

One possible scenario for stored procedures and transactions is a bank transfer. In that scenario, the first account is debited and the second account credited. When using a transaction, the two actions will always occur together. If you were to execute them as separate queries, there is always the possibility that one would execute and the other one would have some sort of error, which would have serious consequences.

Figure 9-1 The Microsoft SQL Server Enterprise Manager allows you to easily create tables, views, and stored procedures and also administer your database.

In addition, stored procedures give you the ability to retrieve return values from your database. Let's say you are adding a new customer to an e-store, and the user has entered all of his or her personal information. There would have to be a *primary key* in the database table to allow you to access that particular user in the future. When the data is being inserted, the primary key could be returned via the stored procedure to allow you to continue to access the database from within the Web application.

Microsoft SQL Server is an expensive proposition if you are deploying your site from a dedicated server. On the other hand, if you are deploying your Web application from a Web hosting company, it's certainly a viable option. Most Web hosts charge a small surcharge of $20–40 a month for the use of SQL Server, but it's well worth it if you plan to run a professional Web site.

If you have a Windows server, trial versions of SQL Server are available from Microsoft that will give you an opportunity to try out the advanced features of this database. If you are going to use a Web hosting company for deployment, you can run the SQL Server Enterprise Manager on your local machine to administer the database more easily.

Oracle

Oracle is an option for Windows-based servers, and is also available for most other servers, making it the best choice for a Web site deployed from a non-Windows-based server. Many would argue that it is the best choice for a Windows-based server as well. Oracle has all of the advanced features of Microsoft SQL Server and many more. It will run on a Linux or Sun Solaris server as well.

Oracle has advanced security and encryption features for maintaining secure access to sensitive data. Auditing features allow the tracking of users and the way that the data is accessed for even greater security.

Oracle has a tight integration with JSP servers, and has drivers available for OLE DB using ASP. ColdFusion enterprise edition also allows native connections to the Oracle server, making the connection faster and more reliable than an ODBC connection.

Disadvantages of Oracle are its high cost and relative lack of availability in a shared server environment.

MySQL

MySQL has become immensely popular in this day of open-source software. In spite of being lightweight, it is a sophisticated, efficient, and powerful database application. On top of that, the price can't be beat—it can be downloaded from various sources for free or for small licensing fees. MySQL has built up a lot of momentum over the last few years and is now a viable choice for a professional Web application.

MySQL is available in many shapes and sizes and for most configurations of servers. Whether you decide on a JSP, ASP, or ColdFusion site, you can probably find a MySQL implementation to meet your needs. The latest builds can usually be found on the MySQL Web site at http://www.mysql.com/. In addition, ODBC drivers are generally available to make quick and painless MySQL connections in the design-time environment. The MyODBC driver is available from the MySQL Web site as well. For JSP, there are several JDBC drivers available for MySQL.

One of the disadvantages of the open source databases is that they lack an "administrator" or GUI, thus making the design and implementation of the database a little tricky for beginners. An option here is to design your database in Microsoft Access and then convert your data to

MySQL format using one of the utilities that's freely available from the Web. Also, front ends for MySQL are becoming more commonplace. One of the best of the GUIs for MySQL is the urSQL utility, available at http://www.urbanresearch.com/software/utils/urbsql/.

MySQL is highly optimized for Web applications, and it's one of the fastest and most lightweight databases around. Reading from the database is very fast with MySQL, although it's slower with insert, modify, and delete tasks. It also doesn't offer some of the advanced features of its rivals, such as stored procedures and nested select statements.

DB2

DB2 is IBM's answer to Oracle and SQL Server. It is an enterprise-level database much like those two and is very well integrated with IBM's WebSphere JSP server. If you plan to implement a JSP site on a WebSphere server, DB2 would certainly be a good choice for the database. It also has ODBC drivers for simple connections, and it even has a native OLE DB driver (if you happen to be using ASP). ColdFusion Enterprise Server contains native database drivers for DB2 as well. DB2 will run on a variety of systems, such as Windows, OS/2, Linux, Sun Solaris, and HP-UX.

The DB2 Control Center (shown in Figure 9-2) is reminiscent of the SQL Server Enterprise Manager. Databases can be created easily here from scratch or from built-in templates. Views and stored procedures can also be created easily in the Control Center.

In addition, DB2 has a highly optimized in-memory search engine, making text searching one of its strong points. It was designed from the ground up with the Internet in mind, according to in-house blurbs.

IBM usually has free downloads of this enterprise-level database for developers available from their Web site, but the commercial version is pricey. Still, in terms of functionality it's right up there with Oracle and SQL Server.

Disadvantages of DB2 are its high cost and relative lack of availability in a shared server environment.

PostgreSQL

PostgreSQL is one of the best open-source databases around, and much more powerful and feature-rich than MySQL. It is starting to rise in popularity as an alternative to MySQL for PHP-based Web sites. PostgreSQL can be run easily in a Linux environment, and even comes preinstalled with some flavors of Linux, like Red Hat. Dreamweaver MX supports only MySQL as a database, but third-party add-ons allow the use of other databases.

PostgreSQL is also available for Macintosh OS X, making it one of the most attractive database servers to run on the Mac platform. The Macintosh had not been a popular platform

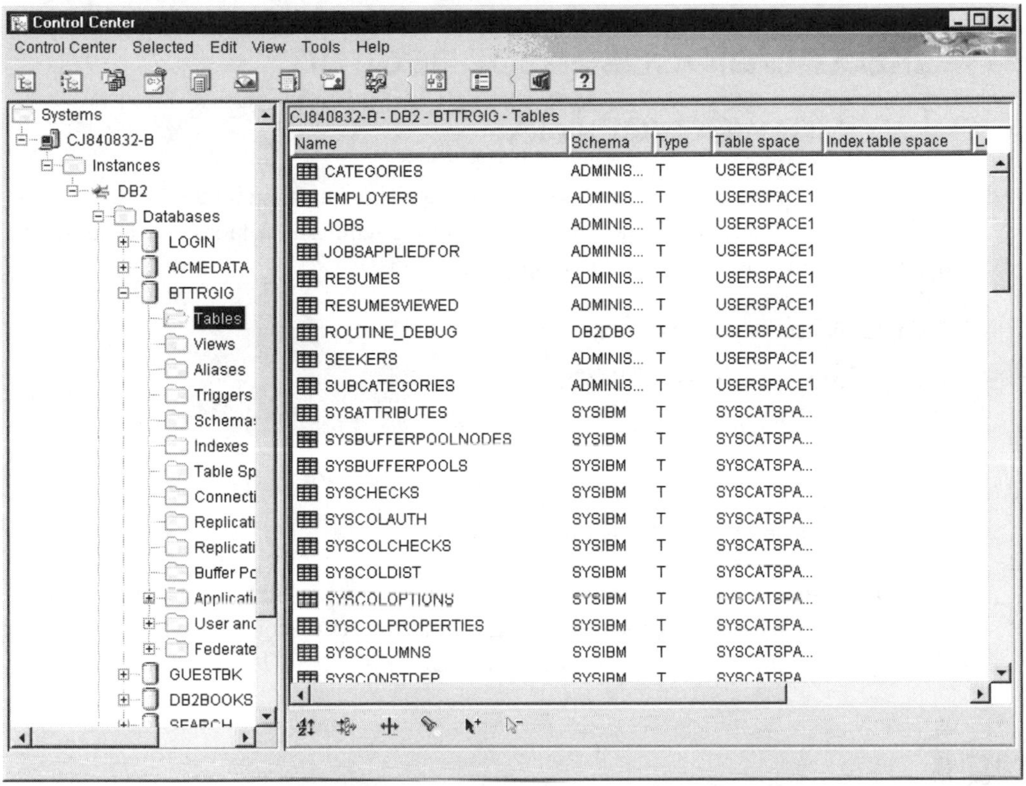

Figure 9-2 The IBM DB2 Control Center in version 7.1 of DB2 for Windows

for applications that utilize database servers until OS X came out. Now there are several good candidates for a Mac application server and database server solution.

Other Databases

Although this module has covered the major databases, several others are available that you might be tempted to use. Filemaker Pro, for example, is a popular Macintosh database, but it's not a popular option for a Dreamweaver MX Web site. Other possibilities include dBASE, FoxPro, and Paradox, but these databases don't offer the robust environment of Microsoft SQL Server, Oracle, or IBM's DB2. Above all, real-world testing will give you the best indication of whether one of these other databases will do the job for you and your planned site. You can even use a text or CSV (comma-separated values) file for a database, using Microsoft's text ODBC driver, as long as you are aware of the limitations.

CRITICAL SKILL
9.2 # Make a Database Connection in Dreamweaver MX

Database connections in Dreamweaver MX are a snap. There are visual interfaces that can assist you no matter what configuration you are working with. The database connections are defined for Windows users as one of two options:

- Using a connection on the local machine
- Using a connection on the Testing server

NOTE

Macintosh users connect through the Testing server only.

The connection information is saved in an include file that resides in the Connections folder of your site. By changing the connection information in this one file, all pages in your site that depend on the connection will reflect the changes.

NOTE

The new ColdFusion server model doesn't use a connection include file, but supports its use by allowing you to declare a variable to use as a data source. This is a very flexible strategy that leaves the decision to the developer as to how to implement the connection.

Using a local machine connection allows you to develop your sites with a local version of the database. When you are ready to deploy, you can change the connection information to point to your application server in this connection file. For example, you can name your connection as connEflea and use an Access database on your local machine, then later change the data source to point to a SQL Server database on the Web server.

Dreamweaver MX gives Macintosh users the same methods for connecting to databases that Windows users can enjoy. All of the following sections apply to Macintosh machines as well as Windows machines. The only limitations for Macintosh users are that you have to connect to your application server to get the design-time database connections. Considering that you need an application server to be able to implement a data-driven site, this is hardly a limitation.

Dreamweaver MX connects to your database on the application server through an HTTP request. This is a lot like what happens when a browser requests a page from the Web server.

The server receives the request and sends the page back to the browser. In this case, Dreamweaver MX requests the database information from the application server, and the database information is sent back to Dreamweaver MX. There is a special file that Dreamweaver MX writes to the server that takes care of the connection and communication with the program during the design phase. On an ASP server, this is an ASP file; on a JSP server, it's a JSP file; and so on. The file contains code that connects to the database on the server as it is called, reads the table and column information, and sends the information back to Dreamweaver MX. All of this is invisible to the user.

CRITICAL SKILL
9.3 Make a Database Connection with ASP and ASP.NET

In this section, we go through a few of the more popular methods for connecting Dreamweaver MX to a database using ASP and ASP.NET.

ADO Connection Using ODBC

ADO (ActiveX Data Objects) is the primary connection method for the ASP developer. The ADO provides a standard interface to the database and exposes everything that the underlying data provider can do, while still allowing shortcuts for common operations. ODBC (Open Database Connectivity) is probably the most widely used connection method with ADO. ODBC drivers come preinstalled with Windows and provide a standard way to connect to most databases. The vast majority of databases that run on Windows are ODBC-compliant.

ODBC was developed as an answer to the ever-present problem of compatibility between different machines, different operating systems, and different software. When you connect to an ODBC data source, you are connecting to the ODBC driver for that database, not the actual database. The driver does the job of translating your commands into something the database can understand—like speaking through an interpreter. You communicate to the driver with a SQL statement that complies with a limited generic subset of the SQL language. By translating the statements through ODBC there is a small performance penalty, but nothing significant in the grand scheme of things in "Web" time.

NOTE

Dreamweaver MX needs the Microsoft Data Access Components (MDAC) version 2.5 at the very minimum, so if you have version 1.5 or 2.1 installed, you need to upgrade. Version 2.6, however, doesn't contain drivers for Jet databases like Access unless you download additional components, so version 2.5 is the recommended MDAC. ASP.NET users should have 2.7 or above. The MDAC can be downloaded from http://www .microsoft.com/data.

When using ODBC, the Web page doesn't need to know where the database is located on the machine. In fact, it doesn't even have to be on the same machine, and is often located on a machine that is specifically set up as a database server and accessed through a network. You give the connection to the database a *data source name* (DSN) that allows you to refer to the connection by name in your program (or Web application). As long as the DSN points to the database in the ODBC Data Source Administrator, the Web page will be able to communicate with the database.

If you are developing ASP, JSP, or ColdFusion pages, you can connect to the database through ODBC. In JSP, there are JDBC:ODBC bridge drivers that can be used to connect via JDBC to an ODBC data source, making it necessary to define your data sources in the ODBC Data Source Administrator, as well as in the JSP administration page. In ColdFusion, all of the system DSNs that were available when ColdFusion was installed will appear in the ColdFusion Administrator and are accessible by all ColdFusion pages.

NOTE

Depending on which database you are using, the drivers may or may not be preinstalled with the MDAC. If you are running Microsoft Access, FoxPro, or SQL Server, the drivers are preinstalled and ready to run. Other preinstalled drivers include dBase, Oracle, Paradox, and Visual FoxPro. Drivers for MySQL and other databases are available on the Web or from the database manufacturer.

The ODBC Data Source Administrator is located in the Control Panel folder of Windows 95, 98, and Windows NT. In Windows 2000, this was moved to the Administrative Tools folder under Programs in the Start menu. Each ODBC driver interface is a little different, but the principles of each are the same. We step through an example with an Access database. Dreamweaver MX requires a system DSN to recognize the database. A system DSN is available to all users and all services (on Windows NT and 2000), as opposed to a user DSN, which is available only to the current user, or a file DSN, which has the DSN stored in a file (independent of users).

The first thing you need to do is define an ODBC connection in the ODBC Data Source Administrator.

ODBC Data Source Administrator

User DSN | System DSN | File DSN | Drivers | Tracing | Connection Pooling | About |

User Data Sources:

Name	Driver
dBASE Files	Microsoft dBase Driver (*.dbf)
dBase Files - Word	Microsoft dBase VFP Driver (*.dbf)
DeluxeCD	Microsoft Access Driver (*.mdb)
Excel Files	Microsoft Excel Driver (*.xls)
FoxPro Files - Word	Microsoft FoxPro VFP Driver (*.dbf)
MQIS	SQL Server
MS Access Database	Microsoft Access Driver (*.mdb)
sample-MySQL	MySQL
Visual FoxPro Database	Microsoft Visual FoxPro Driver
Visual FoxPro Tables	Microsoft Visual FoxPro Driver

Add...

Remove

Configure...

An ODBC User data source stores information about how to connect to the indicated data provider. A User data source is only visible to you, and can only be used on the current machine.

OK   Cancel   Apply   Help

Click the System DSN tab and then click Add. This will bring up the following dialog box, which will allow you to Create New Data Source.

Create New Data Source

Select a driver for which you want to set up a data source.

Name	Ve
Driver da Microsoft para arquivos texto (*.txt; *.csv)	4.I
Driver do Microsoft Access (*.mdb)	4.I
Driver do Microsoft dBase (*.dbf)	4.I
Driver do Microsoft Excel(*.xls)	4.I
Driver do Microsoft Paradox (*.db)	4.I
Driver para o Microsoft Visual FoxPro	6.I
IBM DB2 ODBC DRIVER	7.I
Microsoft Access Driver (*.mdb)	4.I
Microsoft Access-Treiber (*.mdb)	4.I
Microsoft dBase Driver (*.dbf)	4.I

< Back   Finish   Cancel

After choosing the appropriate driver for your database, click Finish. This takes you directly to the ODBC setup for the particular driver you are adding. Again, each driver has its own unique interface, but the result is the same. Following is the Microsoft Access Setup screen:

Insert a data source name and a description (if you like, although the description is not mandatory), and then select the database. By going into the Advanced tab, you can also set a login name and password. Some databases might have all of their options on one screen, like MySQL, and others might use the wizard metaphor, like Microsoft SQL Server. The bottom line is that you are assigning a data source name to a database, enabling you to refer to that database by name from this point forward.

TIP

The ODBC Microsoft Access Setup screen also offers options for repairing and compacting databases. These come in handy if you don't have a copy of MS Access on that particular machine. One of the benefits of Access is that the MDB file can be deployed anywhere, and the machine that houses the database doesn't need to have Access installed.

Progress Check

1. What is the recommended MDAC version number that you should use with Dreamweaver MX?

2. What does ODBC stand for?

3. Do you use a file DSN, system DSN, or user DSN with Dreamweaver MX?

Connecting to DSNs with Dreamweaver MX

Connecting through ODBC is a simple process, and connecting with Dreamweaver MX is even simpler. You can define a connection by going to the Bindings panel and choosing Recordset, which brings up the Recordset dialog box, and then clicking Define. You can also define a connection by going to the Databases panel and clicking the connections icon (+).

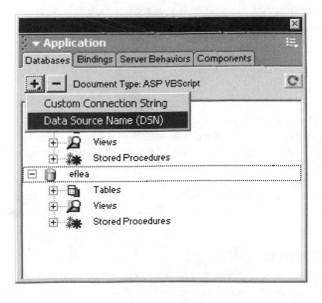

1. 2.5

2. Open DataBase Connectivity

3. System DSN

That brings up the connection dialog box, where you can choose your connection and name it. In the following illustration, you can see two radio buttons—one for a Testing server and one for a local server connection (the Macintosh doesn't have this option):

You can also fill in the username and password in this dialog box, if you've implemented them in your database. It's always a good idea to set a username and password on any database that might be accessible to others. Even if you are not worried about malicious attack, it's good to keep the database secured, if only to prevent possible corruption of data from somebody accessing the database by mistake.

NOTE

If you are using a Web hosting company, some companies will set up the data source for you. You simply need to upload the database to the Web site to a folder on the server (preferably a cgi-bin or a similarly secured directory for safety) and give the Web hosting company the information about the directory, database name, and data source name they should use. An administrator from your ISP can then set up the connection on the computer that your database resides on. Also, many hosting companies allow the user to interact with the DSN administrator through a Web-based user interface.

ADO Connection String

If you are using ASP or ASP.NET, there is another method at your disposal to connect to a database. Dreamweaver MX gives the option to use a connection string, if you choose Custom Connection String as your connection type. Using this option, you can define OLE DB (or DSNless in ASP) connections. Connection strings are also varied, but we discuss some of the more popular types.

OLE DB

OLE DB (Object Linking and Embedding) is the preferred method for connecting to a database in Windows. When you define an ODBC connection, you are putting a wrapper around an OLE DB connection to the database, and adding another step to the connection process. By connecting directly to OLE DB, you eliminate the middleman, so to speak, and create a connection that is a little speedier and a little more stable. OLE DB connections are not as universally compatible as ODBC connections, but their use has become fairly widespread. Also, many Web hosting companies require a DSNless connection or an OLE DB connection, because it requires no intervention on their part.

Instead of using the ODBC data source name, as in the preceding examples, you use the *provider*, which is specific to the database you are working with. When you install the MDAC, several OLE DB providers are installed, including an ODBC provider, which allows you to access any ODBC-compliant database through an OLE DB connection. You have the option to access the database through the native provider or through the ODBC provider, which is not the same as accessing the database through the ODBC DSN connection. Following is a typical Microsoft Access connection string using the native provider:

```
Provider=Microsoft.Jet.OLEDB.4.0;
Data Source=C:\inetpub\wwwroot\cgi-bin\eflea.mdb;
User ID=;Password=;
```

Here, you will also note that you are connecting directly to the database by using a path to that database. This speeds up the connection because your system doesn't have to access the registry to look up the data source name—it goes directly to the database. This method is not to be confused with a *DSNless* connection, which we outline next.

You enter the OLE DB connection string into Dreamweaver MX by clicking the connections icon in the Databases panel to create a new connection. This time, instead of choosing Data Source Name, you choose Custom Connection String. You are presented with the following dialog box, or something similar:

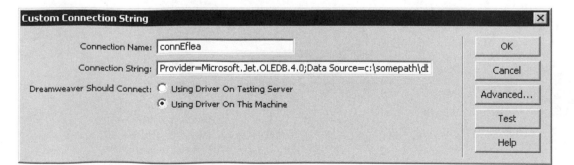

In the empty box for Connection String, you can put the Access connection string just shown, if you are using the Access database, or you can use the following string for SQL Server:

```
Provider=SQLOLEDB;Data Source=myMachineName;
Initial Catalog=eflea;User ID=sa;Password=;
```

Note that Initial Catalog refers to the actual database name in the SQL Server, and Data Source refers to the actual machine name the SQL Server resides on. Keep in mind that you must substitute your own username and password, as well as the server name, the database path for Access databases, and the initial catalog (database name) for SQL Server. ASP.NET users have an interface that actually allows you to build the connection string visually:

After you have entered the correct connection string, you can click the Test Connection button. You should see the following dialog box:

ODBC DSNless Connections

Another form of connection is available to the ASP developer: a *DSNless* connection. This connection is often preferable to the ODBC connection, because it's not mandatory that you have a system DSN set up to use it. The DSNless connection is available for most of the databases that are ODBC-compliant, and it uses the ODBC driver to connect to the database. The following string is in the format for an Access database:

```
Provider=MSDASQL; Driver={Microsoft Access Driver (*.mdb)};
Dbq=c:\inetpub\wwwroot\cgi-bin\eflea.mdb;UID=;PWD=;
```

TIP

The driver name inside the curly braces { ... } is the exact driver name as it appears in the ODBC Data Source Administrator. You can look at the Drivers tab of the Administrator to see which drivers are available and what the correct syntax is.

The Provider attribute is the default ODBC provider and is sometimes omitted from the string. ADO will assume that you are using the MSDASQL provider (the default ODBC provider) if you don't specify otherwise. It's a good idea to specify the provider directly.

The steps for connecting to the database through an ODBC DSNless connection are identical to the steps used for the OLE DB connection.

Using the Microsoft Text Driver

One of the little-known features of ADO is the ability to define a connection to a text file. The text file can have an extension of .txt, .csv, .asc, or .tab. You can set up an ODBC data source name for a text driver connection, use an OLE DB connection, or you can use a DSNless connection. Using the DSNless connection, you must fill in the ADO connection string as follows:

```
Driver={Microsoft Text Driver (*.txt; *.csv)};
Dbq=c:\yourfolder\;Extensions=asc,csv,tab,txt;
Persist Security Info=False;
```

Using the OLE DB connection type, a text driver connection string will look something like this (with quotes intact):

```
"Provider=Microsoft.Jet.OLEDB.4.0;Data Source=C:\yourfolder;
Extended Properties='text;FMT=Delimited'"
```

Of course, all of this should be placed on one line in the connection dialog box. The driver works a little differently than the standard database drivers in that you define a *directory* instead of a path to a physical database or a physical file. The first row in the text file consists of the column names. After defining the connection, you should be able to click the Test button and make a successful connection. When defining the recordset, you'll see a list of text files in the directory specified by the connection string, instead of a list of tables. When you define your SQL statement, you'll use the filename of the text file instead of a column name. A typical SQL statement using the text driver might look like this:

```
SELECT * FROM C:\inetpub\wwwroot\cgi-bin\addresses.txt
```

Make sure that the backslashes are all in the proper place in the file path. There may be some limitations when using the text driver, but there are many benefits to being able to display data in an organized fashion directly from a text file.

Project 9-1   eflea.mdb

We've covered several databases in this module, but the most widely used database by beginners is Microsoft Access. In this project, we will deploy a Microsoft Access database for the eFlea site to the local Web server and set up a local DSN.

NOTE

You will have to be on a Windows machine to follow along with this project.

Step by Step

1. Use the eFlea database that was set up in Module 8 or download the eFlea Access database from www.osborne.com.

2. Place the database into a folder named cgi-bin outside of the eFlea site. In other words, if your eFlea site is located at c:\inetpub\wwwroot\eflea, you could put your database in c:\inetpub\cgi-bin.

3. If you are on Windows NT or Windows 2000, make sure the file and the folder have IUSR_machinename permissions set up. This can be done by right-clicking on the MDB

file and then choosing the Security tab (Windows 2000). If IUSR_machinename isn't listed as a user, add the account to the list of valid users both for the folder and the actual Access database file. IUSR should have the permission level set to Full Control.

4. If you are on Windows NT or Windows 2000, go into the Internet Information Server interface and choose Properties for the folder in which the database is located. Turn off the read permission from there. This allows Web pages to read the database, but outside users will be unable to download the database.

5. Open Settings | Control Panel | ODBC Drivers (in Windows NT or 98) or Programs | Administrative Tools | Data Sources from the Start menu in Windows 2000 Server.

6. Click the System DSN tab.

7. Click Add to add the new data source.

8. Find the Microsoft Access driver on the list and choose it.

9. Type in a DSN name of **eflea**.

10. Add a description of **Database for the eFlea Web site**.

11. Click Select and browse to the database on your machine.

12. Click OK and then click OK again when presented with the next screen. You now have a system DSN that points to the eFlea database.

Project Summary

In this project, you learned how to set up an ODBC DSN. These types of connections will allow you to create connections to almost any type of database on your local Windows machine. Using the eflea connection, you will be able to follow along with the other projects in the book.

CRITICAL SKILL

9.4 Make a Database Connection with Other Server Models

Although the majority of Dreamweaver MX users will be using an ASP server, there are several other server models that you might be working with. The following sections detail the various connection methods for ColdFusion, PHP, and JSP.

ColdFusion MX

ColdFusion MX is Macromedia's latest generation of ColdFusion server. With this version, ColdFusion is now written entirely in Java, thereby changing the way that database connections are made. All connections are made through JDBC drivers that are preinstalled with the ColdFusion server, or you can use your own. The switch from ODBC to JDBC drivers, however, has not changed much the way in which your ColdFusion page uses the connection. The major change is how ColdFusion connects to the database internally.

If you are upgrading from ColdFusion 5 to ColdFusion MX, all of the ODBC and OLE DB connections were migrated to the new JDBC connection type. Databases such as Access, SQL Server, and DB2 have new JDBC drivers that are specifically designed for that database. There is also a JDBC bridge connection to ODBC (called the ODBC socket) that can be used for other databases that may not have a specific connection available.

The ColdFusion server model in Dreamweaver MX is the only server model without the plus sign (+) in the Databases tab. Instead, there is a little connection icon:

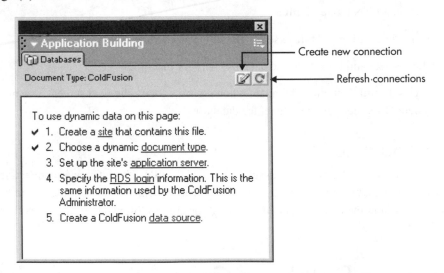

The connection icon is tied to the ColdFusion Administrator Web interface, so by clicking the icon you'll have to log in to the Administrator. If you don't have rights to the Administrator, you won't be able to connect to the database during your design phase. If this is the case, your best option is to keep a local copy of your database and a local copy of ColdFusion server running as well.

The Databases tab lists a five-step procedure to set up a data source:

1. Create a site that contains the file.

2. Choose a dynamic document type.

3. Set up the site's Testing server.

4. Specify the RDS information.

5. Create a ColdFusion data source.

The key to making the datasource work, as in the other server models, is making sure your Testing server is set up properly with the URL prefix. This prefix should be the same URL that you use to browse the pages, such as http://localhost/myfolder. If you can preview the page by pressing F12, chances are your URL prefix is correct. If you have a Web host that doesn't allow RDS connections, you'll have to use a local server and a local RDS connection.

NOTE

RDS, as used in this module, is Macromedia's own Remote Development Service technology, not Microsoft's Remote Data Service. Using RDS allows the developer to connect to a remote server as if it were his or her own machine. The file system and data sources are available to the remote development environment. Clicking the icon will bring up the Administrator. After logging in, you can click the Data Sources link to take you to the Data Sources page:

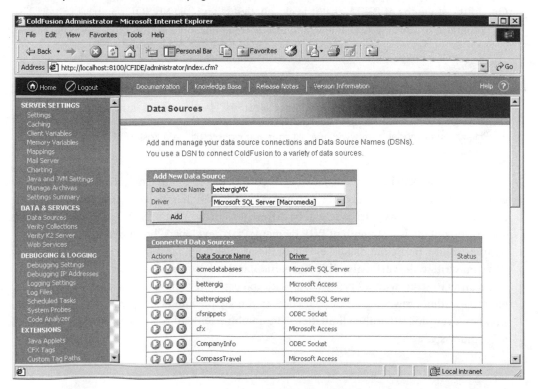

Here you'll find all of the available data sources on your server. Each data source has buttons available to allow you to edit the connection or delete it. If you upgraded from a ColdFusion 4 or 5 server, the ODBC and OLE DB connections that were migrated should be showing up in this list as well.

If you create a new data source, or edit an existing data source, there are many available options, including permission levels for most typical database operations. You can, for example, set the database to accept only SQL SELECT operations from the Web application for added security. These permission levels are in addition to any permission levels you set at the database level. These are ColdFusion-specific permissions that enhance the level of security.

After you create the data source, it will appear in the Dreamweaver MX Databases panel. The panel will show all available ColdFusion MX database connections.

The connections are also available from all of the Dreamweaver MX data sources and server behaviors that require connections, such as the Recordset, Stored Procedure, Insert, Update, and Delete server behaviors.

PHP

One of the strengths of PHP is that it is closely tied in with the MySQL database server. The two programs are almost inseparable, and most PHP applications connect to a MySQL database.

NOTE

After MySQL, the second most popular database for PHP development is PostgreSQL. Dreamweaver MX doesn't support PostgreSQL out of the box, however. You can use the PHAkt server model from www.interakt.ro if you want to utilize a PostgreSQL database server.

Connection is made through native PHP code. Unlike ASP or ColdFusion, which have a generic method of communicating with any database, PHP has native code that is different for each database. The MySQL code will be different from the PostgreSQL code, and vice versa. This is looked on as a strength of PHP by many PHP developers, because the code has been optimized for a particular database. One of the problems with this approach is that the code that you write will work only with that particular database. In other words, if you code an application to work with a MySQL database, you can't go back later and upgrade to a DB2 database without rewriting all of your code. If you are planning to implement a PHP/MySQL site, however, this is hardly a limitation. The combination will serve you well for most small- to medium-scale sites.

To make the connection, click the plus sign (+) in the Databases panel and click MySQL Connection, or click Define in the Recordset dialog box. That will bring up this dialog box:

There are five parameters to fill in, and a successful connection depends on your MySQL server being set up with the proper permission levels to be able to access it from the Web application.

- **Connection Name**   Give a name to your connection. A good habit is to put *conn* before the database name, as in *connDatabaseName*.

- **MySQL Server**   This is the name of your server, or the IP address.

- **User Name**   You should have a user set up in MySQL to work with the database. Never use the Root user, because you can run into security problems.

- **Password**   The user's password.

- **Database**   The database that you want to connect to. Click Select to pull up the dialog box shown in the following illustration. All of the available databases are shown.

After setting up a successful connection, the connection will appear in the Databases panel, along with a list of all of the tables available in the MySQL. Views and stored procedures aren't supported by MySQL as of this writing, so those trees will be empty in the Databases panel. Future versions of MySQL promise to support these standard database features.

JDBC Connections

JDBC (Java Database Connectivity) is the standard for connecting a Java application or Web page to a database, much like ODBC is the standard for ADO. The JDBC technology is central to the Java platform, and is the primary method to connect a JSP page to a database. The JDBC classes are located in the java.sql package. As with the ASP and ColdFusion connections, the Dreamweaver MX JSP connection requires the data source to be specified in a connection string. Those familiar with JSP will note that you need to provide only the driver, username, password, and the URL string in the connection definition dialog box. Dreamweaver MX takes care of writing the code to actually connect to the database, manipulate the recordset, and then disconnect with a *recordset.close()* method and a *connection.close()* method.

JDBC, like ODBC, uses a generic SQL implementation rather than trying to cater to one specific database. Java was designed as a cross-platform language, and JDBC was designed as a cross-database connection to allow a Java application to talk independently to a database.

There are four basic classifications of JDBC drivers for JSP and Java, which are characterized in Table 9-1.

JDBC Type	Description
Type 1	The beginnings of JDBC provided bridges to ODBC. Because they had to "bridge the gap" to the ODBC driver, they weren't pure Java. Drivers such as the Sun JDBC:ODBC bridge are Type 1 drivers.
Type 2	These are the first attempts to connect to native database drivers without relying on the ODBC interface. Again, these aren't 100 percent Java and require binary code on the client machine.
Type 3	These are generally 100 percent Java implementations that still require server middleware to connect to the database.
Type 4	These are true Java implementations that connect to the database directly through native network protocol. These are the latest and best type of driver to use for your database connection, and are generally proprietary for each individual database.

Table 9-1 The Four Basic Classifications of JDBC Driver Available for JSP Pages

Dreamweaver MX is ready to run with the Sun JDBC:ODBC bridge, provided you are accessing a server with ODBC data source availability. To use the bridge connection, you need to do the following:

1. Bring up the Define Connection dialog box by clicking the plus sign (+) in the Databases panel. A drop-down list of available drivers will appear.

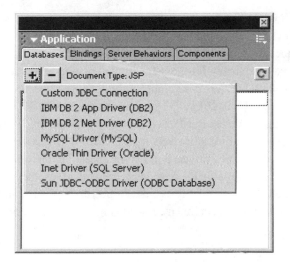

2. Choose Sun JDBC-ODBC Driver (ODBC Database) from the drop-down box, or choose Custom JDBC Connection to type it in by hand.

3. Give the data source a name (such as connEflea).

4. Choose a username and password, if you've defined them for your database.

5. Fill in the URL field, or substitute your own database information for the variable that might be in a preformatted URL field, such as [odbc dsn]. This, again, is specific to the driver you use. In the case of the Sun driver, you fill in the following:

```
jdbc:odbc:yourdsnName (replacing the jdbc:odbc:[odbc dsn])
```

6. Choose either Use Driver On This Machine or Use Driver On Testing Server.

The Sun JDBC:ODBC bridge driver, although fairly easy to use, isn't recommended for anything other than testing. It's unreliable on certain JSP servers, such as the JRun Server from Macromedia, as documented on the Macromedia Web site. We recommend a Type 4 JDBC driver that's tailored specifically for the database you plan to implement. A comprehensive list of the available JDBC drivers is available at the Sun Web site, at http://java.sun.com/ products/jdbc/driverdesc.html. IBM DB2 comes with its own JDBC drivers, as does Oracle. If you are implementing an Access or MS SQL Server database, you'll have to find a third-party driver. Macromedia's JRun Enterprise Server ships with JDBC drivers for SQL Server.

Generally, third-party JDBC drivers don't come cheap, but there are often trial or developer versions of these drivers available for download. In many cases, the software vendors will allow you to use the driver indefinitely as a developer, and only prohibit you from using the driver in a production environment. In any case, it is wise to test the driver fully before deciding to purchase one.

Progress Check

1. What does JDBC stand for?

2. What does the Sun JDBC:ODBC driver accomplish?

Macintosh Database Connections

The Apple Macintosh has long been a favorite among graphic artists and Web designers. With the advent of the iMacs and the newer G4 Macintoshes, Apple is once again a viable alternative to Windows as a tool for professional Web developers. Until now, however, Macintosh Web developers didn't have access to the same types of dynamic Web page creation using database connections to ADO, JSP, and ColdFusion. Dreamweaver MX hopes

---

1. Java Database Connectivity
2. Allows a JDBC connection to an ODBC datasource

to bridge that gap by providing a *design-time* connection to a live database that resides on the Testing server.

Connecting to the Database Server from a Macintosh

The key to a successful database connection from a Macintosh to a remote server is the Site Definition dialog box. Beginning with UltraDev 4, all database connections are achieved through HTTP, allowing Macintosh and PC users to enjoy the same types of connections. To set up a connection, you must be connected to the Internet and have access to your Testing server.

When defining your site, the Testing Server dialog box has to be filled out properly to connect to your server. If you have defined your site correctly and are able to view your pages by previewing (using F12), the database connections should work as well. The URL prefix will be the determining factor in getting the connection to work. If your site is located at http://192.168.0.4/mysite/, that's exactly where the URL prefix should be pointing.

TIP

If you can access your site through a Web browser, the address used to access the site root is the address you should type into the URL Prefix field. If you can't access the site from a browser, Dreamweaver MX can't access it either.

Summing Up: The Dreamweaver MX Databases

We've gone over a few of the connection methods available to the Web developer in Dreamweaver MX. After the connection is made, the next step is to retrieve the data from the database that you want to display on the page.

Project 9-2 Connecting to the Database

Building upon the last project, we now attempt to connect Dreamweaver MX to the system DSN that was set up in Project 9-1.

Step by Step

1. Start up Dreamweaver MX in the eFlea site that you set up earlier.

2. Go to the Databases panel and click the plus sign (+) to create a new connection.

(continued)

3. Click Data Source Name (DSN) Connection.

4. Name the connection **eflea**.

5. Choose the eflea connection from the drop-down list of DSNs. The eflea connection should be there if you finished Project 9-1.

6. Type in a username and password if you have one set up for the database.

7. Click the radio button for Use Local DSN if you are using a local connection on your machine, or click Using DSN On The Testing server if the DSN is set up for the remote Web server.

8. Click Test, and if the connection was successful, a dialog box will pop up telling you that you made a successful connection.

9. If you were successful, click OK. If not, retrace your steps and try to determine the problem. One common problem when using Testing server is that you don't have the URL prefix set up properly in your site definitions.

10. Click Done. Your connection is now ready for use by Dreamweaver MX.

Project Summary

In this project, you learned how to use the ODBC DSN connection you created in the last project to actually connect inside of the Dreamweaver MX environment. Using this connection, you will be able to complete the other projects in the book.

Progress Check

1. You can set up a connection from the Databases panel. What is another method to accomplish this?

2. Name the three primary connection methods for ADO (the connection method for ASP).

---

1. Click the Define button on the Recordset dialog box.
2. ODBC, OLEDB, and DSNless

What to Take Away from This Module

A Web application has many options for databases and methods of connecting to them. We have shown a few of the different databases available to help you determine what is the best database for your application. Also, depending on which server model you use, there are a variety of ways you can connect to the database. After reading this module, you should have a basic understanding of the methods that Dreamweaver MX uses to connect to the database.

✓

Module 9 Mastery Check

1. What is meant by a local database connection?

2. What do the letters ADO stand for, and what is the significance of ADO for ASP developers?

3. What do the letters ODBC stand for, and what is ODBC's purpose?

4. Where is the connection information for your site located in the Dreamweaver MX environment?

5. How does Dreamweaver MX communicate with the database?

6. What database does Dreamweaver MX allow you to use for PHP development?

7. True or false: Microsoft Access will handle thousands of simultaneous users.

8. Which of the following database server are available for free: Oracle, PostgreSQL, DB2, MySQL?

9. True or false: The databases panel in Dreamweaver MX allows you to create databases.

10. How does Dreamweaver MX make a connection to a database?

11. True or false: ColdFusion MX uses ODBC drivers natively.

Module 10

A SQL Primer

Once you have a database set up for your site, you will need to turn your attention to
getting data in and out of it. The kind of site you are planning to build will, in some ways,
dictate how familiar you will need to be with the language of data access. If you just need to
provide your users with access to existing data, allowing them to search and view what is
already there, you may be able to get by with just a small portion of the capabilities of your
database system. If, however, you will be collecting and deploying information in a true
dynamic environment, you will want to become very familiar with the subject of this module.

You will be surprised to see exactly how much of this Dreamweaver can do for you without
your needing to know a lot of SQL. We look at those capabilities starting in Module 11. But
it will not take long before you will want to do more sophisticated data manipulation. This
module is here as a reference for when that happens. You may want to read it now, or you may
want to skip ahead and come back to it when you need it, but you will, as they say, be back.

In this module, we cover the language of the modern database. Structured Query Language
(SQL, pronounced "sequel") began life in the IBM labs of the late 1970s. As the relational
model of database design was taking hold, there was a need for a structured way to interact
with the individual tables that make them up. Utilizing fewer than 30 keywords, SQL is a
simple, yet powerful, means of performing a variety of operations on your chosen database.

NOTE

There are at least two SQL standards proffered by ISO and ANSI, plus the variants that
are implemented by the manufacturers of the different database programs. This module
attempts to adhere to the ANSI standard. When you select the database application
you will use for your site, you will do well to obtain a SQL reference specific to the
brand and version you have chosen.

The individual commands that you construct using the SQL language are known as
statements. SQL statements range from very simple, with as few as four words, to very
complex with intricate joins and subqueries. There are entire books written on the topic, and
this module cannot hope to adequately cover everything you might want to know about it.
However, an overview will be very helpful as you get started with Dreamweaver and will
serve as an excellent jumping-off point for further study as your needs develop.

CRITICAL SKILL
10.1 Understand Basic SQL

A vault full of money is no good if you don't have the combination. A book full of knowledge
is no good if you can't read. And a database full of information is no good if you don't have a
way to get it out. SQL provides a means of getting information out of your database through

the use of a query. Although they are not written like questions, the purpose of SQL queries is to ask for information from your tables.

NOTE

The name Structured Query Language can be misleading. SQL can actually do much more than just ask for information from your database. It can create tables and modify their structure. It can insert, update, and delete data. The term "query" is simplistic compared to the actual power of the language.

The questions you can ask are limited only by the data you have chosen to store in your tables. For instance, your database may have a table that holds information about architects. You could write a SQL query to ask that table for a listing of all of the left-handed, commercial architects that live in Orlando. As long as you store the city where each architect lives, their specialty, and whether they are right-handed or left-handed, your database will respond with a list of architects that meet the criteria you have specified. If, on the other hand, you have never established dexterity as a field of data to be collected, your database will not know how to handle a query that uses it as criteria.

So it is very important that you consider the kinds of questions you will need to ask your tables when you are setting them up. You don't want to collect a bunch of data only to find out that you missed an important component that makes it useless for your intended purpose. So that you can see how this works in a different context than the eFlea database, let's create a new table to work with that tracks the receipt of payments.

Consider the things you need to know about a payment you have received in order to store it in a meaningful way. You would need to know what account to credit the payment to, the date it was received, the check number, and the amount. You might also want to set up a field to serve as a unique identifier for a particular transaction. This field would be a numeric field that automatically increments each time a new record is added to the table.

NOTE

The concept of a unique identifier for each record is an important one to grasp. Most databases offer some means of automatically creating an incremented counter for each record as it is added to the table. In Access, it is called an autonumber data type. The database structure for the Payments table is shown here:

Field Name	Data Type	Width
Transaction	Autonumber	4
Account	Text	5

Field Name	Data Type	Width
CheckNumber	Text	10
Amount	Money	8
DateReceived	Date	8

Next, this table needs some data you can work with:

Transaction	Account	CheckNumber	Amount	DateReceived
1	12345	301	200.53	10/25/00
2	47638	1245	100.00	10/26/00
3	75892	746	503.42	10/30/00
4	12345	321	150.04	11/03/00
5	75892	803	400.00	11/05/00
6	12345	340	623.00	11/10/00

The *Select* Statement

The foundation on which the SQL language is built is the *Select* statement. Just as its name implies, the *Select* statement is a statement used to select a row or rows of data from a table or tables that meet the set of criteria that you provide. Although a *Select* statement can be very complex, the simplest form provides two pieces of information for the database to act upon: what you want to see and where it comes from. For instance, the following *Select* statement retrieves all of the fields from all of the records in the Payments table:

```
Select * From Payments
```

The asterisk is shorthand for "show me all of the fields," so the above statement produces identical results to the following statement:

```
Select Transaction, Account, CheckNumber, Amount, DateReceived From Payments
```

This simple query is actually providing a number of pieces of information to the database:

- **Select**   The *Select* keyword is used to identify the following statement as a query to the database for information. Other keywords such as *Update* or *Insert* or *Delete* might be used in this position to implement other actions, which are covered later.

- *** or field names**   The asterisk or list of field names tells the database what fields you want to see and in what order.

- **From**   The *From* keyword is required for all *Select* statements. It identifies which table or tables the requested data is found in.

● **Table names** The listed table or tables are used to fulfill the request.

There is another piece of information provided because this SQL statement ends where it does. The lack of any additional information beyond the table name indicates that you want to see all of the records in the specified table. You can, of course, filter your results by any number of criteria, which will be covered shortly.

Returning to the original query, it becomes clear what data will be returned:

```
Select * From Payments
```

or

```
Select Transaction, Account, CheckNumber, Amount, DateReceived From Payments
```

returns the following resultset:

Transaction	Account	CheckNumber	Amount	DateReceived
1	12345	301	200.53	10/25/00
2	47638	1245	100.00	10/26/00
3	75892	746	503.42	10/30/00
4	12345	321	150.04	11/03/00
5	75892	803	400.00	11/05/00
6	12345	340	623.00	11/10/00

Selecting Specific Fields

You can select only specific fields from the table by identifying them in your query, as shown here:

```
Select Account, Amount From Payments
```

which returns the following:

Account	Amount
12345	200.53
47638	100.00
75892	503.42
12345	150.04
75892	400.00
12345	623.00

Changing the Order of the Returned Fields

You can also change the order in which fields are returned by specifying the order you want in your statement:

```
Select Transaction, Account, DateReceived, Amount, CheckNumber From Payments
```

This returns:

Transaction	Account	DateReceived	Amount	CheckNumber
1	12345	10/25/00	200.53	301
2	47638	10/26/00	100.00	1245
3	75892	10/30/00	503.42	746
4	12345	11/03/00	150.04	321
5	75892	11/05/00	400.00	803
6	12345	11/10/00	623.00	340

Selecting Only Unique Records

Suppose that you need to find out what accounts are represented in your Payments table. You might execute a SQL query like this:

```
Select Account From Payments
```

which would, of course, return:

Account
12345
47638
75892
12345
75892
12345

This result does show you all of the accounts that are represented on your Payments table, but it gives every instance of each account number, which could be unwieldy in a larger table. SQL provides a means of identifying and displaying only unique values in your table. You still get a resultset that contains all of the individual account values that are represented in your database, but you get each value only once. This is accomplished with the *Distinct* keyword, as follows:

```
Select Distinct Account From Payments
```

which returns:

Account

Account
12345
47638
75892

Project 10-1 Querying the eFlea Database

Now let's apply this to the project at hand: the eFlea database. Even though Dreamweaver can do a lot of this for you, we are going to jump into a more advanced mode so you can have a clear understanding of what is happening.

Project Goals

By the end of this project, you will

- Understand how to use Dreamweaver's Bindings panel to begin the process of creating a recordset

- Learn to write and test a *Select* statement in Dreamweaver

Step by Step

1. With your eFlea project open in Dreamweaver, create a new document that you can test in. Call it whatever you like, but give it the extension of the platform you are working in (.asp, .aspx, .jsp, .cfm, or .php).

2. On the Bindings panel, click the plus (+) button and select Recordset (Query).

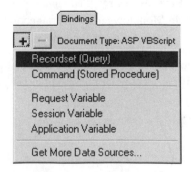

(continued)

3. The Recordset window will open. Click Advanced to get to where you can enter your own SQL statement.

```
┌─────────────────────────────────────────────────────────────────────┐
│ Recordset                                                      [×]    │
│                                                                       │
│       Name: [Recordset1          ]                      [   OK   ]    │
│                                                                       │
│ Connection: [eflea          ▼]  [Define...]            [ Cancel  ]    │
│                                                                       │
│                                                        [  Test   ]    │
│        SQL: ┌───────────────────────────────┐▲                       │
│             │                               │         [ Simple... ]   │
│             │                               │                         │
│             │                               │         [  Help  ]      │
│             │                               │▼                        │
│             └───────────────────────────────┘                        │
│                                                                       │
│  Variables: [+][−]                                                    │
│             ┌──────────┬───────────────┬──────────────────┐          │
│             │ Name     │ Default Value │ Run-time Value   │          │
│             ├──────────┴───────────────┴──────────────────┤          │
│             │                                              │          │
│             │                                              │          │
│             └──────────────────────────────────────────────┘         │
│                                                                       │
│  Database ┌──┬────────────────────────────┐   Add to SQL:            │
│    Items: │⊞ 🗐  Tables                    │   [   SELECT   ]         │
│           │⊞ 🔍  Views                     │                          │
│           │⊞ ☀  Stored Procedures          │   [   WHERE    ]         │
│           │                                │                          │
│           │                                │   [  ORDER BY  ]         │
│           └────────────────────────────────┘                         │
└─────────────────────────────────────────────────────────────────────┘
```

4. In the Advanced window, you will see a place to name your recordset and choose a connection. Creating recordsets will be covered in more detail in Module 11. For now, you can leave the default Recordset1 or you can name it whatever you like. You should have created a connection in Module 9, and that connection should be available to you in the Connection drop-down list. Select that connection.

5. The next box in the window is the SQL box. You can use this box to enter your own SQL statements. As a matter of fact, a popular method of constructing SQL statements is to use the Query designer in Access, switch to SQL view and copy the SQL statement text, and then come to this window and paste it in. You need only delete the semicolon that Access places at the end of the query for it to work in Dreamweaver. This is a quick and easy way to get a statement that is virtually guaranteed to work properly when using an Access database.

6. Because you know you have a table called Users in the eFlea database, write a SQL statement to return all of the records from that table. In the SQL box, type the following:

```
Select * from users
```

7. Click Test. Access will test your query against the eFlea database defined in the connection you chose. If you wrote the query correctly, and there is data in your database, you will get

(continued)

a sample (up to 25 records) of your data. You have successfully written and tested your first SQL statement.

Record	efleaID	Name	City	State	email	username	password	group
1	1	Ray West	Orlando	FL	ray@wor...	ray	west	admin
2	2	Tom Muck	Dale City	VA	tommuck...	tom	muck	user
3	3	Joel Marti...	Orlando	FL	joel@wor...	joel	martinez	user
4	4	Jim Feed	Los Ange...	CA	jim@som...	jim	freed	user

Test SQL Statement

Previous 25   Next 25   OK

8. Click OK to return to the SQL window. Now change your query to only select some of the fields from the Users table. Type the following statement into the SQL box:

```
Select Name, City, State From Users
```

Recordset

Name:	Recordset1
Connection:	eflea ▼ Define...
SQL:	Select Name, City, State From Users

OK
Cancel
Test
Simple...
Help

Variables: **+** **−**

Name	Default Value	Run-time Value

Database Items:
☐ 🗐 Tables
☐ 🔍 Views
☐ ✳ Stored Procedures

Add to SQL:
SELECT
WHERE
ORDER BY

9. Click Test again and you will be shown only the fields that you asked for.

Test SQL Statement

Record	Name	City	State
1	Ray West	Orlando	FL
2	Tom Muck	Dale City	VA
3	Joel Martinez	Orlando	FL
4	Jim Feed	Los Angeles	CA

Previous 25   Next 25   OK

(continued)

Project Summary

It is not difficult to get data out of a database if you know the right way to ask for it. Dreamweaver will do these things and much more for you, but it will be more meaningful to you and you will be better able to determine exactly what information you need when you are aware of what is taking place behind the scenes.

Progress Check

1. What does SQL stand for?

2. What kind of statement is used to request data from a database in SQL?

3. What keyword can you use to avoid duplicate data in your query?

CRITICAL SKILL
10.2 Learn to Use SQL Expressions and Conditions

As stated earlier, a SQL statement can do much more than just ask for a listing of all of the records in a database table. This section covers the manipulation of data with expressions and the filtering of data with conditions.

Expressions

You may be familiar with expressions from other programming you have done. An expression is anything that returns a value, such as 2 + 2 or variable1 + variable2. Expressions can also be used within SQL statements to perform operations on the values in your tables and return a result in your query. To help illustrate this, add a new table called Accounts that will go

---

1. Structured Query Language
2. A *Select* Statement
3. Distinct

along with the payments table from the earlier example. The following shows the structure of the table:

Field Name	Data Type	Width
Account	Text	5
FirstName	Text	20
LastName	Text	20
City	Text	25
State	Text	2
ZipCode	Text	5

This table simply holds information about the accounts that will be sending you payments. You have a first name, last name, city, state, and ZIP code for each account. These tables will help illustrate many of the powerful capabilities of expressions in SQL statements.

NOTE

You would likely want to capture much more information about an account holder than just their name and city, state, and ZIP code, but this amount of information will serve to demonstrate the point without introducing extraneous detail that will only serve to confuse.

Because there are three accounts that are making payments (as seen in the previous example), you need to make sure that those three accounts are represented in the Accounts table. Following is some sample data:

Account	FirstName	LastName	City	State	ZipCode
12345	Jim	Randolph	Orlando	FL	32886
47638	Susan	Tudor	New York	NY	10011
75892	Trevor	Patrick	El Paso	TX	79925

You could certainly get information out of this table using the same kinds of queries as earlier. For example:

```
Select * From Accounts
```

would return this:

Account	FirstName	LastName	City	State	ZipCode
12345	Jim	Randolph	Orlando	FL	32886
47638	Susan	Tudor	New York	NY	10011
75892	Trevor	Patrick	El Paso	TX	79925

But what if you needed the account holder name to display on a screen or on a letter or bill? If you have had any experience with databases, you know it is impossible to get two separate fields—such as FirstName and LastName fields—to line up together for every record. You need a way to put the FirstName and LastName fields together so that they display properly. You can use an expression for that.

The expression you will use will join two strings (pieces of text) together. This is known as concatenation. Depending on what brand of database you are using, this may be done in a slightly different way.

The idea behind concatenating two strings in a SQL query is to combine the field values together, possibly with some literal text that makes it display properly. To combine the field values, you will use either the & operator or the + operator, depending on your database version.

NOTE

The + operator is often used to concatenate strings, but you can get unpredictable results if you are not sure of your data types. When a + operator is used on two numbers, they will be added together. When it is used on two strings or one string and one number, the two values will be concatenated.

Consider the following SQL query:

```
Select Account, FirstName, LastName from Accounts
```

This statement returns:

Account	FirstName	LastName
12345	Jim	Randolph
47638	Susan	Tudor
75892	Trevor	Patrick

But you need the first name and last name together, so you might try:

```
Select Account, FirstName & LastName As Name From Accounts
```

Notice that the & operator was used. Your statement may need to read:

```
Select Account, FirstName + LastName As Name From Accounts
```

Also notice the *As* keyword. This keyword is used when an expression is entered to provide a name by which the results will be referenced. It creates a kind of virtual field name that can be referenced just like a real table field once the result set is generated. This query will return a field called Name, which is not really a field at all, just a title you have given to the results of your expression.

You might think that you are in good shape with this query. Look at the results:

Account	Name
12345	JimRandolph
47638	SusanTudor
75892	TrevorPatrick

The database has taken your instructions quite literally and has concatenated the string values next to each other. As mentioned earlier, you must often combine field values with some literal string values to get the proper display values from the query. Try this:

```
Select Account, FirstName & ' ' & LastName As Name From Accounts
```

which returns:

Account	Name
12345	Jim Randolph
47638	Susan Tudor
75892	Trevor Patrick

The preceding statement concatenates not only the two database fields but also a literal space to result in the logical display of the first name and last name. The following query takes this concept one step further:

```
Select Account, FirstName & ' ' & LastName As Name, City & ', ' &
State & ' ' & ZipCode As Address From Accounts
```

which returns:

Account	Name	Address
12345	Jim Randolph	Orlando, FL 32886
47638	Susan Tudor	New York, NY 10011
75892	Trevor Patrick	El Paso, TX 79925

This statement concatenates the City, State, and ZipCode fields together with a comma and a space between the City and State fields, and a space between the State and ZipCode fields, to result in an expected display format for the address of the account holder.

You can use expressions to do any number of additional manipulations on your data. You might find a need to multiply a unit price times a number of units ordered field to get a subtotal, or a subtotal times a sales tax figure to get the sales tax. Expressions are a powerful way to manipulate your data against itself or against external values that you introduce.

Conditions

So far, you have had practice retrieving data from your database in blocks that include everything that is available in the tables. Chances are, however, that you will need to filter the results of your data so that only certain records are retrieved. Data can be filtered by the use of conditional clauses such as the *Where* clause. The *Where* clause enables you to specify criteria against which the data in your tables will be compared. Only those records that meet your criteria will be returned in the resultset. Consider the following SQL statement:

```
Select * From Payments Where Account = '12345'
```

Depending on your brand of database, this query may need to read:

```
Select * From Payments Where Account Like '12345'
```

NOTE

In this example, the account number is enclosed in quotes because the field was defined as a text field. Had this field been identified as a numeric field, the quotes would not be necessary.

This statement returns the following records:

Transaction	Account	DateReceived	Amount	CheckNumber
1	12345	10/25/00	200.53	301
4	12345	11/03/00	150.04	321
6	12345	11/10/00	623.00	340

Notice that only records with the account number 12345 were returned because that is the criteria you specified in the query. The *Where* clause could also be used in the Accounts query used earlier:

```
Select Account, FirstName & ' ' & LastName As Name, City & ', ' &
State & ' ' & ZipCode As Address From Accounts Where LastName =
'Randolph'
```

which returns:

Account	Name	Address
12345	Jim Randolph	Orlando, FL 32886

Additional Operators

In addition to the equal (=) operator, several other operators are available to you to use as part of expressions and conditions. Table 10-1 lists many of the operators and their intended uses.

Operator	Use
*	The multiplication operator used to multiply field values by one another or by literal values that you provide.
/	The division operator used to divide field values by one another or by literal values that you provide.
–	The minus operator used to subtract field values from one another or to perform subtraction with field values and literal values that you provide.
>	The greater-than operator used in a conditional *Where* clause such as: *Select * From Payments Where Amount > 300.00.*
<	The less-than operator used in a conditional *Where* clause such as: *Select * From Payments Where Amount < 300.00.*
>=	The greater-than or equal-to operator used in a conditional *Where* clause.
<=	The less-than or equal-to operator used in a conditional *Where* clause.
<>	The not-equal-to operators used in a conditional *Where* clause.
AND	The logical *And* operator used in a conditional *Where* clause, such as: *Select * From Payments Where Account = 100.00 AND Amount >> 400.00.*
OR	The logical *Or* operator used in a conditional *Where* clause, such as: *Select * From Payments Where Amount < 100 OR Amount > 400.00.*
Like	The *Like* operator used in conditional *Where* clauses when a wildcard is necessary. For example: *Select * From Accounts Where LastName Like 'Ran%'* would return any record where the LastName started with "Ran".
Not	The Not operator used in a conditional *Where* clause, such as: *Select * From Accounts Where LastName Not Like 'Ran%'.*

Table 10-1 SQL Operators

Operator	Use
¬	The single character wildcard operator. Used when you don't know a single character, such as: *Select * From Accounts Where State Like 'C_'*. This statement would return any record where the State field contained CA, CO, CT, or C plus any other one character.
%	The multiple character wildcard operator used like the _ operator except that it allows for multiple characters.

Table 10-1 SQL Operators *(continued)*

Project 10-2 Filtering Query Results

Let's build on the last project by using a *Where* clause to filter the results of the Select query we created.

Project Goals

By the end of this project, you will

- Learn how to use a *Where* clause to filter a number field
- Learn how to use a *Where* clause to filter a text field

Step by Step

1. You are going to build on the query you wrote in Project 10-1, so return to the Advanced page of the Recordset window and enter the following SQL statement:

```
Select Name, City, State from users
```

2. Filtering against a field with a number data type is different from filtering against a text field. The only numeric field in the users table is the efleaID field. If you were trying to isolate a certain user, you might select only the records that were associated with that person's ID. Add to the query in the SQL box so that it reads like this:

```
Select Name, City, State from users where efleaID = 2
```

Recordset

Name:	Recordset1
Connection:	eflea ▼ Define...
SQL:	Select Name, City, State From Users where efleaID = 2

OK
Cancel
Test
Simple...
Help

Variables: **+** **−**

Name	Default Value	Run-time Value

Database Items:
⊞ 📇 Tables
⊞ 🔍 Views
⊞ 🌟 Stored Procedures

Add to SQL:
SELECT
WHERE
ORDER BY

3. Click Test. Only one record will be returned: The record whose ID is 2. Notice that it is not necessary to ask the database for the field against which you are filtering. You asked only for the Name, City, and State fields, but you filtered against the efleaID field. Note that the number to the left of your test result is a record counter for Dreamweaver resultset. It is not data from the database.

Test SQL Statement

Record	Name	City	State
1	Tom Muck	Dale City	VA

Previous 25   Next 25   OK

Project
10-2

Filtering Query Results

(continued)

4. Now suppose that you wanted to see everyone who lived in a certain city. Filtering against a text field is a little different. You cannot use the = operator against text. In Access, you use the *Like* operator. Type the following query into the SQL box:

```
Select Name, City, State from users where City Like 'Orlando'
```

5. Click Test, and only records where the city is Orlando will be returned to you.

6. Using the *Like* operator also allows you to use a wildcard operator when you want to match only part of a word. For instance:

```
Select Name, City, State from users where City Like 'O%'
```

with the % wildcard character returns any record where the city starts with an "O".

Project Summary

You are well on your way to understanding the basics of data access. You can now select information out of your database that contains information that is important to you, such as a particular city or ID number. With this understanding, the following discussion of more advanced SQL capabilities should make more sense to you.

Progress Check

1. What two characters can be used as wildcard characters?

2. The statement 3–2 or variable1/variable2 is known as what?

3. What does a condition allow you to do?

CRITICAL SKILL
10.3 Learn to Use SQL Functions

Although you can choose to implement certain operators within expressions that you construct to manipulate your data, there are also a selection of functions available for you to use. Functions are, in essence, prewritten snippets of code that perform an operation and return a value. The code snippets are available to you simply by calling the function and providing the value or values on which it will operate. This section covers common SQL functions and their uses.

NOTE

Again, you will need to reference the language guide for your brand of database to see the full range of functions that are available to you. Some of the functions discussed here may not be available, and you may have others that are specific to your implementation.

Date and Time Functions

Data and time functions enable you to perform manipulations on dates and times that you have stored in your database. Much like expressions, these functions are called within the *Select* statement. You can use the *As* clause to give the resulting value a unique name that you can use to refer to the results.

Because there is a Date field in the Payments table, try the following examples using that data:

```
Select * From Payments Where DateReceived Like '10/25/00'
```

1. _ and %
2. An expression
3. Filter the data that is returned by a query

would return:

Transaction	Account	DateReceived	Amount	CheckNumber
1	12345	10/25/00	200.53	301

But suppose you wanted to find all the accounts for which you have received a payment in the last 30 days:

```
Select * From Payments Where DateReceived >> DateAdd(m,-1,Date())
```

The results that this query returns depends on the date that you run it. If the date is 12/1/2000 when the query is run, it will return:

Transaction	Account	DateReceived	Amount	CheckNumber
4	12345	11/03/00	150.04	321
5	75892	11/05/00	400.00	803
6	12345	11/10/00	623.00	340

This query makes use of two functions (both of which are Microsoft database functions, but there will be equivalents for the product you are using). The *Date()* function gets today's date. The *DateAdd* function adds a variety of date parts to a supplied date to get a result. This query uses *DateAdd* and passes in three values:

- The unit of time that will be added to the supplied date (*m* for month in this case; it could also be *d* for day, *w* for week, or other available values)

- The number of units to add (in this case a −1, so one month will be subtracted)

- The supplied date (in this case, the result of the *Date()* function, or 12/01/2000 if that is the current date)

So the result of the *DateAdd* function (if the date is 12/01/2000) is 11/01/2000. To the database, this query looks like:

```
Select * from Payments Where DateReceived >> '11/01/2000'
```

which returns the records in which the DateReceived field is greater than 11/1/2000.

CAUTION

The *Date()* function gets the system date on the machine where the code is being run. If the database resides on your local machine, its system date will be used. If the database is on a Web server or its own database server machine, that computer's system date and time will be used for these functions. Make sure that your remote computers are synchronized with your development machine in order to get the most predictable results. This can cause some concern if your ISP's server is in a different time zone or even a different country. You may have to make systematic adjustments for the time difference between your local site and your ISP's location.

Other date and time functions are available for your use, depending on the database you choose to use. If you can define in prose the end result you need to obtain, there is most likely a function or combination of functions that will allow you to manipulate your dates and times to return the proper set of records.

Aggregate Functions

Aggregate functions allow you to retrieve results that are based on the combined data of records in your table. For instance, you might need to determine the amount of the largest payment you have ever received, or the average of the payments made during a particular period of time. Aggregate functions allow you to do this.

Five aggregate functions are covered in this section:

- *Count*

- *Sum*

- *Avg*

- *Min*

- *Max*

You may have others available to you.

The *Count* Function

The *Count* function is used, strangely enough, when you need to count something, such as the number of account holders who live in Wyoming or the number of payments received during any specific period of time. Suppose you need to determine the number of payments received during the month of November 2000. There may be a couple of ways to do this, but here is one way using the *Count* function:

```
Select Count(Transaction) As Payments From Payments Where DateReceived
>= '11/01/00' and DateReceived < '11/30/00'
```

This query returns:

Payments

3

In the query, a unique identifier (the transaction number) was selected as the field value to count. The database then selected all of the records where the payment was received in November and counted the number of unique transaction numbers, returning 3. You can use the *Count* function to count any unique set of values in your tables.

The *Sum* Function

The *Sum* function returns a sum of a collection of fields. Suppose, in addition to the number of payments received in November, you also needed to know the sum of those payments. The *Sum* function will select the records that match the criteria in your *Where* clause, add them up, and return the value to you:

```
Select Sum(Amount) As Total From Payments Where DateReceived >>= '11/01/00'
 and DateReceived < '11/30/00'
```

which returns:

Total

1033.01

The *Avg* Function

The *Avg* function returns the average of the values in the field that you select for the records that meet your criteria. If you needed to know the average payment received in the month of November, you could just run the preceding two queries and then divide the total by the Payments result. Or you could do this:

```
Select Avg(Amount) As Average From Payments Where DateReceived >>= '11/01/00'
and DateReceived < '11/30/00'<
```

which returns:

Average
344.34666

The *Min* and *Max* Functions

Keeping with the November payments theme, you may also want to know the amount of the smallest and largest payments received during November.

```
Select Min(Amount) As Minimum From Payments Where DateReceived >>= '11/01/00'
    and DateReceived < '11/30/00'<
```

returns:

Minimum
150.04

```
Select Max(Amount) As Maximum From Payments Where DateReceived >>= '11/01/00'
    and DateReceived < '11/30/00'<
```

returns:

Maximum
623.00

Arithmetic Functions

A number of arithmetic functions are available. Their use is similar to the other functions. Table 10-2 lists some common arithmetic functions and their uses.

Function	Use
ABS	Returns the absolute value of the value operated on
CEIL	Returns the smallest integer greater than or equal to the value operated on
FLOOR	Returns the largest integer less than or equal to the value operated on
COS	Returns the cosine of the value where the value is the radians (not degrees)
COSH	Returns the hyperbolic cosine of the value where the value is the radians
SIN	Returns the sine of the value where the value is the radians (not degrees)

Table 10-2 SQL Arithmetic Functions

Function	Use
SINH	Returns the hyperbolic sine of the value where the value is the radian
TAN	Returns the tangent of the value where the value is the radians (not degrees)
TANH	Returns the hyperbolic tangent of the value where the value is the radian
EXP	Raises the mathematical constant e by the provided value
MOD	Returns the modulus (remainder) of two provided values
SIGN	Returns a −1 if the value provided is less than 0, a 1 if it is greater than 0, and a 0 if the value is 0
SQRT	Returns the square root of the value provided
POWER	Raises one value to the power of a second value
LN	Returns the natural logarithm of the value
LOG	Returns the logarithm of one value in the base of a second value

Table 10-2 SQL Arithmetic Functions *(continued)*

String Functions

String functions are functions that are available to operate on text values. They work in similar fashion to other functions, with a value or values (either literals or field references) being provided. Table 10-3 lists common string functions and their uses.

String Function	Use
CHR	Converts an ASCII value to its string equivalent
CONCAT	Concatenates (splices together) two values
INITCAP	Capitalizes the first character of each word and makes all of the remaining characters lowercase
UPPER	Capitalizes all of the characters in the string
LOWER	Makes all of the characters in the string lowercase
LPAD	Pads the left of a provided string with a character that you also provide for as many spaces as you indicate
RPAD	Pads the right of a provided string with a character that you also provide for as many spaces as you indicate
LTRIM	Trims all spaces from the left of a string value
RTRIM	Trims all spaces from the right of a string value
REPLACE	The REPLACE function takes three values: the string to be searched, the string you are looking for within the searched string, and what you want each occurrence of the string you are looking for replaced with. If the third value is omitted, the found characters are deleted and replaced with NULL.

Table 10-3 Common String Functions

String Function	Use
SUBSTR	Returns a piece of a string value starting at the character position you provide and continuing for as many characters as you specify
LENGTH	Returns the length of a provided string value

Table 10-3 Common String Functions *(continued)*

You will likely have additional string functions available to you in your database application.

CRITICAL SKILL

10.4 Learn to Use SQL Clauses

Clauses are optional parts of a SQL statement that specify additional criteria for the query or additional work that needs to be done before the results are returned. The *Where* clause was already covered earlier in this module. There are two other clauses you need to be aware of:

- *Order By*
- *Group By*

The *Order By* Clause

The *Order By* clause provides a means by which you can sort your data in either ascending or descending order based on what field you choose. Depending on the type of application you are developing and the specific use of the query you are working on, you may want to sort account holders by their last names or payments by the dates they were received. The *Order By* clause lets you specify which field or fields are used to sort your data.

NOTE

One of the premises of the relational database is that physical storage is of little importance. Depending on how data is entered and what indexes operate on it, you may find that the most recently entered records in a particular table do not appear at or near the end of the table. It is wise to specify how you want data ordered if it is at all possible that the sorting will matter when the data is used or displayed.

An unordered query on the Accounts table like this:

```
Select * From Accounts
```

returns this:

Account	FirstName	LastName	City	State	ZipCode
12345	Jim	Randolph	Orlando	FL	32886
47638	Susan	Tudor	New York	NY	10011
75892	Trevor	Patrick	El Paso	TX	79925

But it may be important for you to have the data sorted by the account holder's last name. You could add an *Order By* clause like so:

```
Select * From Account Order By LastName
```

which would return:

Account	FirstName	LastName	City	State	ZipCode
75892	Trevor	Patrick	El Paso	TX	79925
12345	Jim	Randolph	Orlando	FL	32886
47638	Susan	Tudor	New York	NY	10011

You could also add the ASC designation for ascending, making the records sort from *A* to *Z*. This is the default option, though, so it is not necessary. If you want them in *Z* to *A* order, however, you would need to specify the descending option:

```
Select * From Account Order By LastName DESC
```

which would return:

Account	FirstName	LastName	City	State	ZipCode
47638	Susan	Tudor	New York	NY	10011
12345	Jim	Randolph	Orlando	FL	32886
75892	Trevor	Patrick	El Paso	TX	79925

Ordering by More Than One Column

You can also order by more than one column at a time. Say, for instance, that you wanted to order by account number in the Payments table and then by the amount so that you would get a result ordered by the account number, and then within each account number the payment amounts would be ordered from smallest to largest.

```
Select * From Payments Order By Account, Amount
```

would return:

Transaction	Account	DateReceived	Amount	CheckNumber
4	12345	11/03/00	150.04	321
1	12345	10/25/00	200.53	301
6	12345	11/10/00	623.00	340
2	47638	10/26/00	100.00	1245
5	75892	11/05/00	400.00	803
3	75892	10/30/00	503.42	746

The *Group By* Clause

The *Group By* clause enables you to perform aggregate functions on groups of records and display them by group rather than operating on the entire table. For instance, if you wanted to find out how many payments had been received into the Payments table, you could run the following query:

```
Select Count(Transaction) As NumberOfPayments From Payments
```

which would return:

Number Of Payments
6

But you may need to see how many payments each account has made. You want to count transactions, but you want to group them by the account number so that you get a listing of each account and the number of payments made to that account. The *Group By* clause lets you do this:

```
Select Account, Count(Transaction) As NumberOfPayments From Payments
Group By Account
```

returns:

Account	NumberOfPayments
12345	3
75892	2
47638	1

The *Having* Clause

Closely related to the *Group By* clause and other aggregate functions is the *Having* clause. If you are using the *Group By* clause and need to set criteria to be applied to the date, you cannot use a *Where* clause because of the order in which the various parts of the statement are processed. In this case, you need to use the *Having* clause:

```
Select Account, Count(Transaction) As NumberOfPayments From Payments
Group By Account Having Account Like '12345'
```

which would return:

Account	NumberOfPayments
12345	3

You can also apply an aggregate function in the *Having* clause:

```
Select Account, Avg(Amount) AS AveragePayment From Payments Having
Avg(Amount)
  >> 400.00
```

which would return:

Account	AveragePayment
75892	451.71

Progress Check

1. A snippet of code that performs an operation and returns a value is known as what?

2. What function might you use to determine how many customers you had from a particular state?

3. Functions that allow you to retrieve results based on the combined data of records in your table are known as what?

4. What would you add to a query so that your results were returned alphabetically?

---

1. A function
2. The *Count* function
3. Aggregate functions
4. An *Order By* clause

Ask the Expert

Q: Why do I have to know all of the SQL stuff if I am using Dreamweaver?

A: There is a lot that you can do in Dreamweaver without knowing a lot of SQL. There will come a time though (there always does) when you will want to do something that the tools in Dreamweaver don't allow for. The beautiful thing about this program is that it always allows you a way to get at the details, whether it is the code in your page or the SQL in your recordset. The more you know about the underlying technology, the more sense the whole thing will make. You will be able to better plan and implement your sites.

Q: Can I use the information in this module with any database?

A: Pretty much. We have tried to adhere to the standard SQL language so you should be safe with most of it. Most commercial databases use their own dialect of the language, but it is most often a factor with programming advanced features like stored procedures and triggers. Also, some advanced features such as subqueries and stored procedures are not available in all database programs. Consult the documentation that came with your program if you are unsure of its support for a particular command or statement.

CRITICAL SKILL

10.5 Learn to Use SQL Joins

So far, all of these examples have pulled data from only one table at a time. It is very likely, however, that you will spend a great deal of your time mixing the data from more than one table into your results. To do so, you will need to use joins to identify the ways in which tables relate to one another. There are several kinds of joins; two basic types will be covered here:

● Inner joins

● Outer joins (left and right)

 NOTE

There is also a type of full join known as a Cartesian product, where all records from both tables are returned regardless of whether they relate to records in the other table. Although there is some limited use for these, they will not be covered here.

Inner Joins

Inner joins are the most common type of join. They are used when you want to see all of the records in two tables that have a direct relation to each other. For instance, review the records in the Accounts and Payments tables used in the prior examples. You will notice that each record in the Accounts table (identified by the account number) has related records in the Payments table. In other words, every account in the Accounts table has made at least one payment.

When you want to see the records, and only the records, that are related in the two tables, you can use an inner join. Each time a query was run in the previous sections, it was run on only one table. Suppose that you wanted to return information that spanned both tables. Maybe you need to see not only the account numbers and payment amounts, but also the names of the account holders who made those payments.

```
Select Acccounts.Account, Accounts.FirstName, Accounts.LastName,
Payments.Amount From Accounts Inner Join Payments on Accounts.Account
= Payments.Account
```

returns:

Account	FirstName	LastName	Amount
12345	Jim	Randolph	150.04
12345	Jim	Randolph	200.53
12345	Jim	Randolph	623.00
47638	Susan	Tudor	100.00
47638	Susan	Tudor	400.00
75892	Trevor	Patrick	503.42

Outer Joins

There will likely be times when you need to query data from a table where you know or suspect that unrelated records exist. For instance, it is entirely possible that you have an account holder set up in the Accounts table who has not made any payments yet. To help illustrate, add a fourth account holder to the Accounts table:

Account	FirstName	LastName	City	State	ZipCode
12345	Jim	Randolph	Orlando	FL	32886
47638	Susan	Tudor	New York	NY	10011
75892	Trevor	Patrick	El Paso	TX	79925
98734	Victor	Patitucci	Atlanta	GA	30305

If you were to run the same inner join query on the two tables now that this new record exists, you might be surprised to receive the exact same results as you did before you added your new account holder. Because there are no related records in the Payments table, this account is ignored by an inner join query. To see it in the results, you must use an outer join.

There are three types of outer joins: left, right, and full. The names relate to which tables are given the special attention that an outer join provides. If you think about the tables that you join being next to one another on a board or a data environment display, the first one referenced in the join expression is on the left and the second is on the right. The full outer join (or Cartesian product) is of dubious use and will not be covered here.

So, in the example being used here, you want to make sure that you see all of your account holders listed, whether or not they have made a payment. The Accounts table will be on the left, so you will get a listing of all accounts and their related payments in addition to a listing of the accounts that have no payments:

```
Select Acccounts.Account, Accounts.FirstName, Accounts.LastName,
Payments.Amount From Accounts Left Outer Join Payments on
Accounts.Account = Payments.Account
```

which returns:

Account	FirstName	LastName	Amount
12345	Jim	Randolph	150.04
12345	Jim	Randolph	200.53
12345	Jim	Randolph	623.00
47638	Susan	Tudor	100.00
47638	Susan	Tudor	400.00
75892	Trevor	Patrick	503.42
98734	Victor	Patitucci	

The right outer join is used when you suspect that there are records in the right (payments) table that have no account holder. The need for right outer joins can indicate a data integrity problem in your tables. Although it is perfectly acceptable to have an account holder who has made no payments (acceptable to your database, that is, if not to your accounting department), it is problematic to have payments that have no account holder. Nonetheless, right outer joins can be used to display records in your related table that have no corresponding records in the main table.

NOTE

Notice the "dot notation" in the query. When you are using tables that have the same field name in each of them, you must identify from which table you intend the data to come. Use the format table_name.field _name to clearly identify your intentions to the database. There is also a method in which each table is given an alias within the query, making it simpler to reference.

CRITICAL SKILL

10.6 # Learn to Use SQL Subqueries

Subqueries are queries within another query. Sometimes it is not possible to construct a result set directly from the data in your raw tables. It may be necessary to do some "pre-processing" to develop a subset of data that you want to query. If you are familiar with Access queries, you may have queried a query before, and you have a good idea of the concept. In some other languages, such as FoxPro, you can actually select data into a cursor and then query that cursor directly. SQL itself does not really have a way to do that, but you can include queries within your queries to simulate the same thing.

NOTE

Some databases do not support subqueries, and there are often ways to get around their use with complex *Where* clauses. They are handy to use, however, if you have access to them.

There are two types of subqueries covered in this section:

- The *In* statement
- The embedded *Select* statement

The *In* Statement

The *In* statement is used with the *Where* clause of a SQL query to identify a list of values to be used as criteria for the primary query. For a simple example, suppose you wanted to select all of your account holders who live in New York or Florida. Using the *In* statement, you could create the following query:

```
Select * From Accounts Where state In ("NY", "FL")
```

The *In* statement allows you to specify a list of criteria against which the primary query will be tested. Any record in which the state is NY or FL will be pulled in the above query. You can also use an embedded *Select* statement within the *In* statement.

The *Embedded Select* Statement

An *embedded Select* statement is a complete query, including any legal portion of a *Select* statement, contained within the *Where* clause of the primary query used along with the *In* statement. Suppose you wanted to see a list of account holders who had made payments on their accounts. Consider this statement:

```
Select * From Accounts Where Account In (Select Distinct Account From Payments)
```

Notice how the various elements of the SQL statement begin to come together as the queries get more complex. In this statement, a distinct (or unique) list of account numbers that appear in the Payments table is created. Then the primary query pulls the records from the Accounts table that have account numbers that appear in the subquery list. Also, if you wanted to see the opposite—those account holders who had not made payments—you could insert the *Not* operator as follows:

```
Select * From Accounts Where Account Not In (Select Distinct Account
From Payments)
```

NOTE

You may find it interesting to know that an embedded *Select* statement can also be used within the *From* clause of the primary query. Queries this complex are beyond the scope of this module, but as you become more proficient with the SQL language, you will likely find a use for the capabilities that this structure provides.

CRITICAL SKILL
10.7 Learn to Use SQL Action Queries

In addition to *Select* queries, there are also queries that perform some action on your database. This section covers three types of action queries:

- *Insert* queries
- *Update* queries
- *Delete* queries

Insert Statement

If you are planning on collecting information from your users, the time will quickly come when you need to insert information into a table. The *Insert* statement lets you do just that. There are two ways to use the *Insert* statement.

The first way to use the *Insert* statement is the direct insertion of values into the fields of the database. Used this way, the *Insert* statement enables you to identify the fields that you want to populate and the values you want to place in those fields. Suppose that you need to add an account holder to the Accounts table:

```
Insert Into Accounts (Account, FirstName, LastName, City, State, ZipCode)
Values ('73647', 'Theresa', 'Andrews', 'Chicago', 'IL', '60606')
```

Running this statement causes a new record to be added with the specified values.

It is also possible to use a *Select* statement to provide the insertion values for your *Insert* statement. Suppose you had a backup Accounts table with the same structure as the Accounts table, and you wanted to copy the Accounts table data into it:

```
Insert Into BackupAccounts (Account, FirstName, LastName, City, State,
ZipCode) Select * From Accounts.
```

The *Select* statement used in place of the *Values* clause provides the insertion values. This statement can be any legal SQL statement that provides the correct number of fields in the correct order with the correct data types to insert data into the indicated table.

Update Statement

If data never changed, you would not need the *Update* statement. The *Update* statement enables you to change data in your tables. For instance, suppose that one of your account holders got married and changed her last name:

```
Update Accounts Set LastName = "Thomas" Where Account = '73647'
```

This query locates the record for account number 73547 and changes the LastName field to "Thomas".

Delete Queries

Delete queries delete records from your tables when provided criteria are met. If you wanted to delete all records (much like selecting all records), no criteria are supplied:

```
Delete From Accounts
```

This query deletes all records from the Accounts table, ruining your data and probably your job. To be selective in what is deleted, provide criteria that uniquely identifies the record or records you want to delete:

```
Delete From Accounts Where Account = '73647'
```

This statement deletes only the record for Theresa Andrews that was created and altered in earlier sections.

You can also delete multiple records at once. Suppose you needed to purge all payments received before a certain date from the Payments table:

```
Delete From Payments Where DateReceived < '01/01/1990'
```

The version deletes all records that contain payments received before 1990.

CRITICAL SKILL
10.8 Learn to Use SQL Variables

Within your use of Dreamweaver, you will likely need to use variables in your SQL statements to dynamically filter data. Although the specifics of this operation are covered in a later module, it is important that you understand the concept here.

Each of the queries performed in this module so far have been based on hard-coded criteria, where you specified a date or series of dates to search for, or specified the last name of the account holder you wanted to find. In most real-life cases, you will not know this information until your users begin to interact with your application and tell you the things they need to find. Within your ASP, JSP, PHP, or CF code, you will allow for the capture of this data into variables that you can insert into your SQL statements, thus dynamically creating a query that is customized to the visitor's needs.

Remember that a SQL statement is really just a line of text. It does not get parsed out and take on meaning until it arrives at the database as a query. Until the statement is sent to the database, you can perform a number of common programming techniques on it to construct it as you see fit. One of the most common procedures is to use variables in the *Where* or *Having* clause.

Suppose you know that a certain portion of your application will need to pull payments for a particular account number. Maybe account holders can sign in and view the payments posted to their accounts. But you won't know which account holder's information to pull until account holders log in and tell you they want to see their payment history. By capturing their account numbers at login, you can be prepared to show them their payments by setting up your SQL statement as follows.

You can begin by writing your SQL statement as if you knew the account number you wanted to view, like so:

```
Select * From Payments Where Account Like '12345'
```

Then go back and take the hard-coded value out and prepare the statement to accept a variable. In this case, the variable name will be *acct*:

```
Select * From Payments Where Account Like & acct
```

NOTE

Depending on your database implementation, you may need to use the + operator instead of the & operator.

This code will actually be processed by the code in your page, and Dreamweaver helps you set this up without having to code it by hand. By the time the query gets to the database, it is fully formed and in a format the database expects to see. If the visitor logged in with a username that indicated his account number was 12345, the SQL statement with the variable would look exactly like the one preceding it to the database. This method simply allows you to put off the designation of the account number until run time when it can be determined by the user's information.

What to Take Away from This Module

Structured Query Language (and its various permutations) is a powerful programming language. Part of its power lies in its capability to use a relatively simple set of commands and keywords in a variety of combinations that build on one another and provide a means of manipulating data in almost any way you can imagine. Using SQL in a programming environment increases the kinds of manipulations you can perform on your data to query, display, and use it any way your application might require.

This module has introduced you to the language, functions, and use of SQL in a general fashion. It is intended to help you get started with Dreamweaver's data access capabilities and provide you with an idea about SQL's structure so you will be able to determine your needs and know in what direction you are likely to find help for the problems you face. Using this information, you should be able to successfully build a number of different kind of sites, because Dreamweaver is so helpful in constructing, implementing, and manipulating your SQL statements.

✓

Module 10 Mastery Check

1. Name the four essential parts of a basic *Select* statement.

2. What is the definition of an expression in the context of SQL?

3. What are the three types of action queries discussed in this module?

4. What function would you use to return the total of all of the payments made by a certain customer?

5. What type of join returns only those records that have matching data in two tables?

6. When you will need to filter your data by a value provided by the user of the application at run time, what will you use in your SQL statement?

7. Name two types of subqueries discussed in this module.

8. +, *, and / are examples of _____.

9. What does the acronym SQL stand for?

10. Sum and Avg are examples of _____.

Part III

Working with Your Data

Module 11

Displaying Your Data

I f you have just come from Module 10, your head may be spinning a bit, and you may be wondering how you are going to get a handle on this enough to get any work done. Well, now it's time to see the real power of Dreamweaver. Whether you have ever coded a dynamic site before or not, you are going to be amazed at the ease with which you can get data from a database and place it on your pages.

Create Recordsets

A database can be a big thing with a lot of data in it. Although it is a convenient and organized place to store information, that information is really useful only if you can drill down to the specific bit you need and pull it out so you can work with it. Doing that is called creating a recordset.

A *recordset* is a set of results that are given to you by the database in response to a query you have built. It is kind of like asking someone to go through the filing cabinet and pull all of the applications from people who live in Utah sorted alphabetically, put them in a file folder, and bring it to you. Once you get the folder, you can flip through it, spread it out in front of you, pull some applications out and throw them away, or make some changes on the forms. A recordset is all of the computerized information that matches that same request delivered to you as a package you can do something productive with.

Project 11-1 Creating a Recordset

Before you can do anything with the data in your database, you must first create a recordset. The exact form this takes depends on what server model you are using. It might be an ADO recordset in ASP or a CFQuery in ColdFusion. But when using the Recordset server behaviors in Dreamweaver, it will not matter which server model you use. Dreamweaver can create the recordset for you with just a little help.

Project Goals

By the end of this project, you will

- Understand the Recordset server behavior
- Learn to create a simple recordset in Dreamweaver

Step by Step

1. With the eFlea project open in Dreamweaver, create a new document called **users.asp**. You will use this page throughout this module.

2. Click the plus (+) button on the Bindings panel and select Recordset (Query) from the drop-down list.

3. The Recordset window will appear. In the Name box, name this recordset **rsUsers**. The *rs* at the beginning identifies this as a recordset.

4. Choose the connection that you established for the eFlea database in the Connection drop-down list.

5. After a moment, the tables from the eFlea database will populate the Table drop-down list. Select the Users table.

6. Leave the Columns radio button set to All. This will retrieve all of the records in the Users table into your recordset.

(continued)

7. Click Test. Your results will appear.

Re...	efleaID	Name	City	State	email	username	password	group
1	1	Ray West	Orlando	FL	ray@work...	ray	west	admin
2	2	Tom Muck	Dale City	VA	tommuck...	tom	muck	user
3	3	Joel Marti...	Orlando	FL	joel@wor...	joel	martinez	user
4	4	Jim Feed	Los Angeles	CA	jim@some...	jim	freed	user

Test SQL Statement

Previous 25   Next 25   OK

NOTE

This set of results will look very similar to the SQL query you wrote in Module 10. As a matter of fact, click Advanced in the Recordset window. On the Advanced page, you will see the SQL query that was created when you made your selection on the Simple page. It is the same query that you typed in by hand in Module 10. Seeing this from both sides will give you a greater appreciation of what is happening as you use Dreamweaver.

8. Click OK to return to the Recordset window.

9. You can also select only certain fields from the table by changing the Columns radio button to Selected and highlighting the columns you want to see.

10. The Filter section lets you pick four items: the field to use in the filter, the operator to use in the filter, what source of the condition you want to use as the filter, and what exactly that condition is. So you might pick City as the field, Begins With as the operator, Entered Value as the source, and the letter *O* as the condition. This would return all records where the city name begins with an *O*.

11. The Sort section allows you to select a field to sort on and whether you want the sort ascending or descending. Select the Name field and Ascending.

12. Click Test and a resultset will appear that shows only records of people from cities beginning with an *O*, sorted by their names in ascending order (A to Z).

(continued)

13. Because you will want more records to work with, click OK and remove the filter by setting the Filter field to None. Click OK again.

14. When Dreamweaver returns you to the Bindings panel, you will now have a recordset called rsUsers displayed. Click the plus (+) button next to the recordset name and a list of the available fields will appear.

Project Summary

Creating a recordset on your page involves several steps: defining a connection, building a basic SQL statement, and then filtering or ordering it by some parameter in order to get back the records that you need. Dreamweaver simplifies much of this process by providing simple, visual tools to allow the quick construction of recordsets. Once your recordset is built, adding that data to your pages is also made easy through Dreamweaver's data binding capabilities.

Progress Check

1. A set of results that is given to you by a database in response to a query you have built is known as a _____.

2. A list of the fields that your query returns can be found in which Dreamweaver panel?

3. What must first be established before a recordset can be created?

CRITICAL SKILL
11.2 Display Data on Your Page

Look again at the recordset that was created in Project 11-1. It contains the following fields:

- EfleaID
- Name
- City
- State
- Email
- Username
- Password
- Group
- First record index
- Last record index
- Total records

Most of these you should recognize as the fields that you built into the Users table of the eFlea database. But the last three can be a little confusing. They aren't really fields in your database, and they just appear there at the end of your recordset.

---

1. Recordset
2. The Bindings panel
3. A data connection

The First Record Index, Last Record Index, and Total Records "fields" in your recordset are position markers. They indicate to you which records appear on the current page and what the total number of records is. If you were showing 5 records on each page out a total of 25 records, you could use these fields to show that on your page. They keep track of where you are in your recordset and can tell the user that he or she is currently viewing records 1 through 5 of 25, for example.

How you use these fields is up to you. You can show only the total, or maybe you will be showing just one record per page, so you will use just the First Record Index and the Total Records to say "1 of 25" or, as users page through the records, "16 of 25." You have likely seen this feature when you have searched any number of Internet sites. Dreamweaver makes it incredibly simple to implement. Look just how simple it is.

Drag and Drop Data

For now, don't worry about making it pretty. Just get some data on the page so you can get a handle on how Dreamweaver allows you to manipulate your recordset fields. With the users.asp page open, simply drag and drop fields from the Bindings panel onto the page. They will snap to the upper left of the page, as simple HTML always does.

Drag the first few fields onto your page (down to the Username field). Press ENTER in between so that you end up with one field per line down the left of your page. After the Email field, drag the First Record Index field, then place a space, type **of**, another space, and then drag the Total Records field. Your page should look something like Figure 11-1.

Save your page. Make sure you have an application server (such as IIS or ColdFusion Server) running on your computer, and press F12 to preview the page. When your browser loads, you should get the first record from your database displayed on the page along with 1 of [number] (depending on how many records are in your database) at the bottom. That could not have been easier. It doesn't look like much, but doing this on a page that has a graphic design already on it is no more difficult.

Now, you may be thinking that this is great, but how do you get to the next record, or the one after that? How useful is it to tease your users with the fact that more records exist if they can't get to them? Adding the capability to page through records is just as simple. You will use another server behavior (actually a set of them) called Move To Record.

Move To Record

In the same panel as your data binding is the list of available server behaviors. *Server behaviors* are Dreamweaver extensions that insert server-side code (such as ASP or

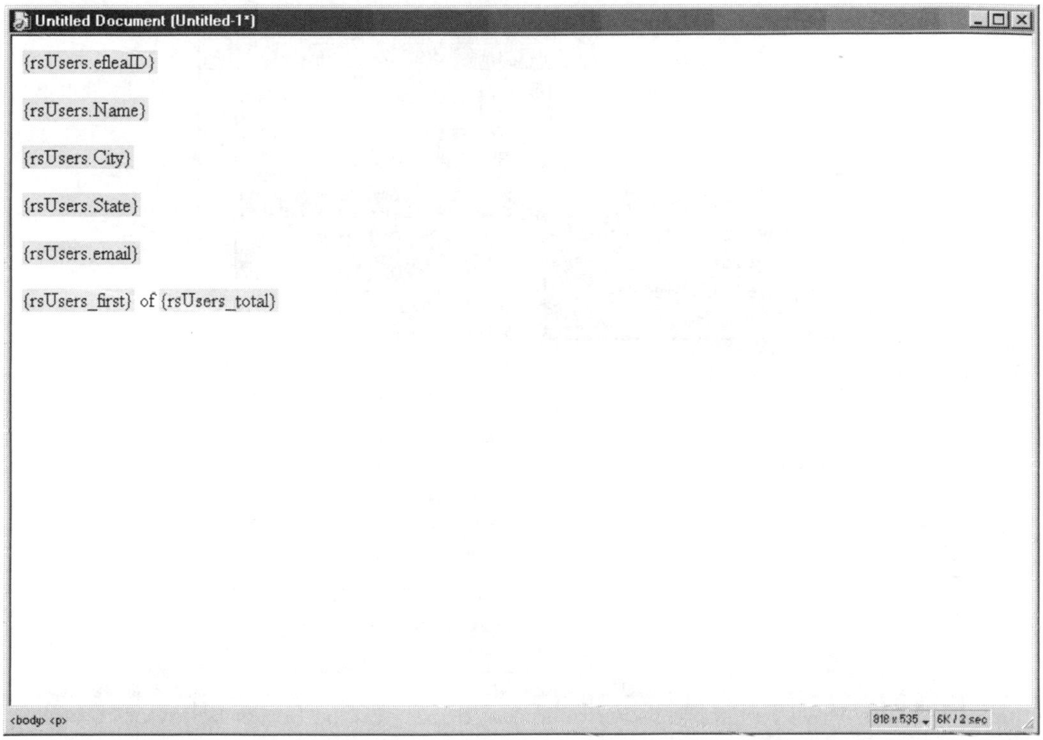

```
Untitled Document (Untitled-1*)                                    _ □ ×

{rsUsers.efleaID}

{rsUsers.Name}

{rsUsers.City}

{rsUsers.State}

{rsUsers.email}

{rsUsers_first} of {rsUsers_total}




<body> <p>                                      818 x 535 ▾  6K / 2 sec
```

Figure 11-1 Drag and drop fields to create a simple page.

ColdFusion) into your pages. Position your mouse on the next blank line of the page. Then click the plus (+) button on the Server Behaviors panel. A list of server behaviors will appear that you can pick from, as shown in Figure 11-2.

Select the Move To Record option and choose Move To Next Record from the choices there. You will be presented with the Move To Next Record dialog box. Because you have no other links on the page and only one recordset exists, these two choices are made for you. Click OK to continue, and a new link will appear with the text "Next." Save your page and

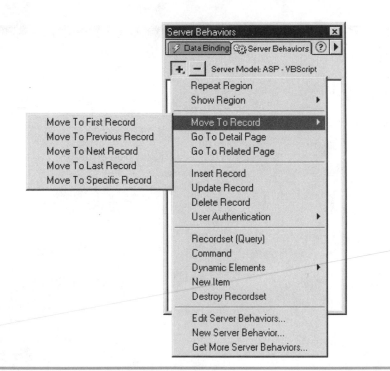

Figure 11-2 The Move To Record server behaviors appear on the Server Behaviors panel.

preview it in your browser. You now have the ability to scroll through all of the records in your database by clicking this Next link.

Adding additional navigational links works the same way. You can add Move To Record server behaviors to create links that move the user to the previous record, the first record, the last record, or a specific record in the recordset.

CRITICAL SKILL

11.3 Display Multiple Records with Repeat Region

Suppose, though, that you want to display five, ten, or even more records on a page at the same time. It can be cumbersome to page through records one at a time, especially when there is relatively little information in each one. You can do this quite nicely using another server behavior called Repeat Region.

Project 11-2 Displaying More Than One Record at a Time

You will often have more than one record to display on a page, or even a list of records to display across several pages. Dreamweaver's Repeat Region allows you to easily loop through recordsets and select how many records to show per page.

Project Goals

By the end of this project, you will

- Learn to position data on your page
- Learn to use the Repeat Region server behavior to display multiple records at once

Step by Step

1. The Repeat Region server behavior that you will be using in this project does exactly what it sounds like—it allows you to repeat a region of your page that has some data in it. So to start with, you will need a region. You will build it by using a table. Clear off the users.asp page and insert a table from the Insertbar. Give it 2 rows and 4 columns and set it to fill 75 percent of the page width.

NOTE

If you look at the Server Behaviors panel, you will notice that each field that you dragged onto the page is listed as dynamic text. To properly and completely remove these from your page, highlight each one and click the minus (–) button on the panel. Just deleting them on the page can leave code behind that can interfere with other items you may subsequently add to the page.

(continued)

2. In the first row of the table, type your column headers. From left to right, they should be ID, Name, City, and State. These are the fields that you will use to fill the columns. You can format this text however you like.

3. Now, use the same drag and drop technique you used earlier to drag these four fields into the table. Place each field from the Bindings panel into the appropriate cell in the second row of the table.

4. So that you can see that it is working so far, save the page and press F12 to preview it in a browser. You should see the first record from your recordset displayed in four columns with a header row.

5. Now comes the repeat part. When you hover your mouse over the left border of the table, it should turn into a little arrow pointing directly to the right. This indicates that you are selecting the entire table row. Click to actually select the second row of the table and a dark border will appear.

ID	Name	City	State
{rsUsers.efleaID}	{rsUsers.Name}	{rsUsers.City}	{rsUsers.State}

`<body> <table> <tr>`

6. In the Server Behaviors panel, click the plus (+) button and choose Repeat Region from the list of Server Behaviors that appears. The following dialog box will appear:

Repeat Region

Recordset: rsUsers

Show: ● 10 Records at a Time

○ All Records

OK   Cancel   Help

7. In this dialog box, you can choose which recordset to pull the data from and how many records to display on each page. You may not have a lot of data in your recordset, and you will want to see this actually work, so set this number to 2. You will see multiple records on each page and how the Repeat Region server behavior handles navigation to the remaining records.

(continued)

8. This row of the table will now have a tab on it labeled "repeat" that indicates it is part of a repeat region. Notice that you applied the server behavior to only the second row. This isolated the first row as a header row, which need not be repeated.

9. Below the table, use the Move To Record server behaviors to add Previous and Next links so that the recordset can be navigated.

10. Use the record index fields to display the recordset position to your user. This time, you will want to use both the First Record Index and the Last Record Index because you are displaying more than one record on the page. Drag the First Record Index field onto the page. Type a space and then **to** or **through** or whatever you would like it to say. Drag the Last Record Index, type **of**, and then drag the Total Records field.

11. Save your page and preview it in a browser. You have created an easy way to navigate the records in your database. How you format this is up to you. You can create any design and drag and drop your fields into it. Dreamweaver's method of adding data to your pages keeps the design elements separate so that the design and the data are independent of one another. This makes Dreamweaver particularly suited for team development.

Project Summary

If you were expecting Dreamweaver to make data access easy, you should not be disappointed. You were able to accomplish in just a few steps what would take many lines of code to accomplish by hand. You can experiment with recordsets of different sizes and determine what Repeat Region settings are best for you.

CRITICAL SKILL

11.4 Use Live Data View

Before you leave the users.asp page that was used in the last project, use it to take a look at one of the truly ingenious parts of Dreamweaver: the Live Data view. Live Data view allows you to "bounce" your pages off your development server while remaining in edit mode. This means that you can see real data from your database (rather than placeholders) on your page while retaining the ability to edit the layout. This is especially useful when you are trying to determine how much space is needed for a particular field of data. If you were hand-coding, you would need to change your page layout, save the page, upload the page, and if it wasn't right, do it all over again. In Dreamweaver, you can skip all that hassle and edit as you view data right from the database.

Ask the Expert

Q: I like these server behaviors. Are there others available other than the ones that come with Dreamweaver?

A: Yes. Additional objects, behaviors, commands, server behaviors, and other items (known as extensions) can be downloaded from the Macromedia Exchange (www.macromedia.com/exchange) and from other places around the Web. Check Appendix B for some suggestions.

Q: What if what I need is not available?

A: You have a couple of options. You can ask someone very nicely to make one for you, or you can learn to do it yourself. Dreamweaver MX includes the Server Behavior Builder, which makes building new server behaviors extremely easy. You can learn more about the Server Behavior Builder and extensions in general in *Dreamweaver MX: The Complete Reference* and in *Building Dreamweaver and UltraDev 4 Extensions*.

Before you use Live Data mode, you need to make sure that it is set up properly in your site definition. On the Application Server tab of your site definition, there is a URL prefix setting that tells Dreamweaver the local path to your site using either localhost, your computer's name, or the reserved IP address 127.0.0.1 to resolve to your local application server.

Once you are set up, turning on Live Data view is easy. There is a button on the toolbar to the immediate left of the Page Name text box. Clicking it places you in Live Data mode.

Alter the layout of the page and you will get a taste of how useful a tool this is. If your data does not fit in a particular cell, you can drag the cell to make it larger. If a cell is too big, you can drag it smaller. Whatever alterations need to be made to accommodate your data can be made while you are looking at actual data from the database.

Take a look at the Live Data toolbar that appears when you enter Live Data view. You can stop the loading of a page with the Stop button. You can refresh the page after making changes with the Refresh button. You can also set the page to auto-refresh when changes are made, but this can slow you down, so use it carefully.

There is an address that looks suspiciously like a Web address, but it ends with a *?* and an empty box. Use this if your page depends on URL parameters that come from another page. Live Data view is an isolated page view. You cannot navigate your site or post into Live Data view from another page, so there needs to be some facility to set up input parameters if a page expects to see them. If those parameters come in the URL string, you can use this text box to supply them. If your page needs data that comes from a form post or from a session variable, you can use the Settings button to the right of the toolbar to enter that information. It will be processed by the server to complete the loading of this page.

What to Take Away from This Module

You should, by now, be seeing the power of this application. Dreamweaver is truly unlike any other Web development software. It allows the inclusion of data-driven content in several language platforms without programming. But you can do more than just display simple data. You can search, insert new records, and update existing records. You will learn to do all of these with the same ease in coming modules.

✓ *Module 11 Mastery Check*

1. What feature of Dreamweaver MX allows you to edit your pages while viewing real data from your database?

2. What server behavior can be used to display more than one record at a time on your page?

3. What feature of Dreamweaver makes it particularly suited for team development?

4. Additional server behaviors are available where?

5. How can you tell that a portion of your page is included in a Repeat Region?

6. List three steps to getting a recordset on your page.

7. What are the three position indicators supplied by Dreamweaver for your recordsets?

8. You can quickly preview a page in a browser by pressing what hotkey?

9. Dreamweaver makes it easy to scroll through your recordset with which set of Server Behaviors?

10. A set of results sent by a database in response to a query is known as a _____.

Module 12

Searching Your Data

One of the prime reasons to have a database is to organize your data so it can be accessed and presented in a meaningful or useful way. Search engines such as Yahoo!, Google, and HotBot all use highly optimized search algorithms and indexed tables. Although your Web site probably won't require the industrial-strength engines of these search sites, a search page will likely be a desirable addition to your site.

CRITICAL SKILL
12.1 Learn the Principles Behind Searching a Database

The key to a successful data-driven Web site is being able to retrieve the information you need from a well-organized database. Furthermore, the key to programming a data-driven site is being able to write the SQL statements needed to retrieve the desired information. SQL is the language you'll need to use to retrieve your data. You'll also need to become proficient in SQL if you want to build a more advanced site, whether you are working in ASP, JSP, PHP, ASP.NET, or ColdFusion.

NOTE

The SQL that you write in the Dreamweaver MX environment will be specific to whichever database you choose to work with. We are building this sample site using MS Access, so the SQL we'll be using will be specific to Access. It can be easily adapted—and, in most cases, used verbatim—to whichever database you happen to be using.

To recap the basics of SQL: the simplest form of SQL is in the form of the following statement, which will return all rows to the page:

```
Select * from myTable
```

To take this one step closer to an effective search statement, we add a parameter, like this:

```
Select * from myTable where firstname = 'Tom'
```

A statement like that works well if you know in advance what you are searching for. When it's just you and the database, you can write SQL statements like this all day and get the results you want. But when you're writing SQL for the Web, and you're getting your search criteria from the user, that's a little more difficult.

Form Fields and Forms

Typically, you'll ask the user to fill out one or more fields, and you'll use the resulting input to drive your query to the database. The fields could be almost any type of form field:

- Text field

- Checkbox

- List/menu

- Radio button

- Text area

The form fields have to reside inside a *form*. The easiest way to understand a form is by pretending the form is an envelope. Inside the envelope, you place the items you want to send. You seal the envelope and send it off to someone. When the person at the other end receives the envelope, he or she will open it and perform some action on the contents of the envelope. In HTML terms, the address you are sending the envelope to is the *action* page. When you create a form, you specify the action page. This is just like addressing an envelope so that the postman knows where to deliver it. A form tag can look like this in HTML:

```
<form name="myform" method="post" action="results.asp">
</form>
```

The *method* attribute is the type of form submission you are performing. The two primary methods are *get* and *post*. Using our envelope analogy, a *post* would be like a sealed envelope. You are placing the contents of the form submission inside the envelope so that others can't see what's in it. The *get* method will allow others to see what is inside, and would be like taping the contents to the outside of the envelope or sending a postcard. When you submit a form using the *get* method, the form field contents are displayed on the URL string of the client. When you insert a form in Dreamweaver MX, you will have to concern yourself with the details of the method and the action of the form and insert these attributes by hand.

NOTE

The URL variables, also known as the *query string* variables, can pass only a limited amount of information in addition to the security concerns. In a search form, however, they offer the search page the ability to be saved as a favorite or sent as a link, because the search criteria becomes part of the link. Search engines such as Google operate like this.

There are a couple of ways to get the form on the page. You can click Insert | Form and the empty form will be inserted, as the previous code illustrates. The form tag in Dreamweaver MX is a Dreamweaver MX *object*, located on the Insert bar. You can also insert a form field from the Forms tab on the Insert bar.

There is another method that combines two steps in one and makes it a little easier. First, place a text field on the page by clicking Insert | Form Objects | Text Field.

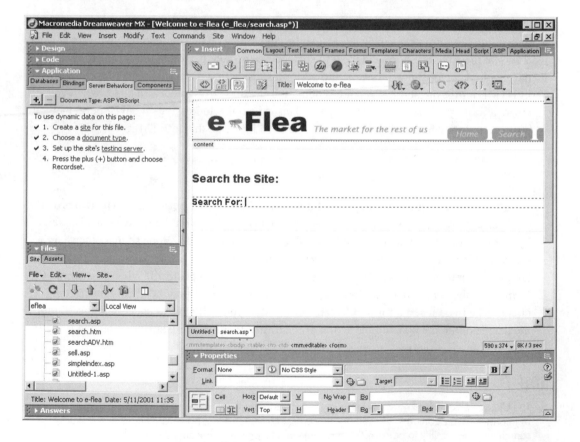

In Dreamweaver MX, when you place any form field on the page for the first time, the program will ask you if you want to place it inside a form.

If you click Yes, the form field will be inserted, and the form tag will be placed around it as well. The form tag shows up as a light outline boxed around the form fields in the design environment.

When you first insert the form field and the form on the page, they are inserted with default values you will have to change. It is a good idea to get in the habit of changing the names and attributes of the tags as you insert them on the page. There are several ways to edit the tags. The Property Inspector is one of the easiest methods.

The Property Inspector lists the Form Name, Action, and Method attributes. The Action attribute is even supplied with a browse folder button, so you can choose the file that is going to be your action page.

Another method of changing the attributes of the tag is to choose Edit Tag <form> from the contextual menu (or press CTRL-F5). That brings up the tag editor:

Also on the contextual menu is the *Quick Tag Editor*, which can be accessed with the menu item Edit Tag Code *<tagname>*. The Quick Tag Editor is available for any tag that you want to isolate and edit by hand as well. It will prompt you with a drop-down list of possible items for the selected tag.

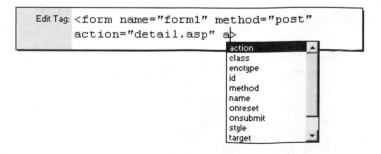

The Quick Tag Editor is especially handy for forms and form objects, where you will always want to insert your own values and not rely on the defaults. For a form element, you'll want to replace the name with a meaningful representation of what the form field will contain, such as first name or address. Some Web developers like to add a prefix to their form elements with a meaningful three-letter abbreviation such as *txt* for a text field, *chk* for a check box, or *rdo* for a radio button.

Project 12-1 search.htm

Most Web sites are going to need a search form of some sort. The eFlea site is a data-driven site that allows users to search items that are available for sale. This project will allow you to create a simple search form in Dreamweaver MX that will allow searching of the eFlea database. The goals of this project include

- Creating a form and setting the method and action

- Adding a form element to accept the user input

- Adding a submit button to allow the form to be submitted

Step by Step

1. Create a new blank page in Dreamweaver MX and save it as scarch.htm. This page won't have any server-side code on it, so you can save it as an HTML file.

2. Attach the page to the eFlea template by clicking Modify | Templates | Apply Template To Page. This will bring up the Select Template dialog box in which you can choose the site (eFlea) and the template (eflea_template).

3. In the title bar of the page, place a document title, **Search eFlea**. This title will be the actual HTML <title> that will be inserted into the page.

4. Put a title heading on the page in the content area with the following text: **Search the eFlea site**.

5. Press ENTER and insert a form below the title by clicking Insert | Form.

6. Without moving the cursor out of the form, go back to the Insert menu and click Insert | Table. The table should have one row and three columns with a width of 75 percent and a border of 0. If you switch to Code view, the table should be inside the form. If it isn't, you can either manually change the code so that the table is in the form, or you can undo the steps you've performed and try again. It is important that you don't move the cursor out of the form after you insert it if you want the table to be placed in the form. Later, when you

(continued)

become more comfortable with the program, you'll find that you can drag and drop objects on the page and place them where you want them, or even drag and drop sections of code while in Code view.

7. Place some text, **Search on**, in the first column of the table.

8. In the second column of the table, insert a text field by clicking Insert | Form Objects | Text Field.

9. If your Property Inspector isn't showing, click Window | Properties to show the Inspector. Change the name of the field to **txtSearch** and change the Char Width to **40**. This will make the text field wider. You can leave the other settings set to the default values: Single Line, Max Chars empty, and Initial Value empty:

10. In the third column of the table, you are going to put a submit button. Click Insert | Form Objects | Button.

11. If all of your default values are correct, the Property Inspector should display a button name of Submit, a label of Submit, and an action of Submit Form. If any of these are different, put the correct values in now.

12. If you have your invisible elements turned on, you should see a border around the table that represents the form. Click on this and the form Inspector should pop up in place of the button Inspector. If your invisible elements are off, you can turn them on by clicking View | Visual Aids | Invisible Elements. The form Inspector will show up with invisible elements off if you have your cursor positioned inside the form, but while you are beginning, you should leave these elements on.

13. Change the Method attribute of the form in the Inspector to *get* if it isn't set that way already. Using the get method allows the user to save the URL as a favorite or copy/paste the link in a document or email. The search criteria then becomes part of the link.

14. Give the Action attribute a value of **Results.asp** (or Results.jsp, Results.php, Results.aspx, or Results.cfm, depending on your server model). You can leave the Name attribute set to the default of form1. Form names are generally more important later when you have more than one form on a page.

15. Save the file again. You've completed the search form.

Project Summary

In this project, you learned how to create a basic search form. We showed that you can use the get method in a search form to allow the user the ability to copy/paste the URL as a link with the full search criteria. In the next project, you'll create a results page to go along with this search form.

CRITICAL SKILL
12.2 Create a Simple Search Page

The easiest form of search will take a predefined string and try to make a match on it. You can do that by using a drop-down box with values in it (which you define) that you know are valid values of a database column. For example, let's say you wanted to find all items in one of five predefined categories: art, music, books, magazines, and miscellaneous. You could load up a list/menu, and the user would have to pick one of the five choices. You could then use a SQL *select* statement to address your database and find every row in the database that matches the item the user selected. To do that, set a variable to the incoming form data and use scripting to attach it to the SQL statement. First, you would set a variable equal to the incoming form data (a *Request* variable) in the server-side script (note that the following is for ASP VBScript):

```
myformvariable = Request("myformelement")
```

Then you would use this variable in the SQL statement. Typically, the statement will look something like this:

```
"Select * from myTable where categories = " + myformvariable
```

This can get more complex when you have more form fields and more matches using fuzzy logic (partial matches). Luckily, Dreamweaver MX makes it a little easier with a visual interface that will help write the appropriate SQL for you and insert the code necessary to connect to the database and return the rows that you want to return.

You created recordsets in Module 11, but when you allow the user to search, you will create recordsets based on values the user defines. The Recordset dialog box has two modes, which were discussed earlier. The simple Recordset dialog box looks like this:

The dialog box allows you to place filters into the query based on form variables, session variables, and other types of input. The simple dialog box writes all of the SQL for you. This might seem like the way to go, especially if you are a beginner, but we have to advise against using this dialog box. The simple dialog box hides the details of the SQL, but it's the SQL that you are going to need to be able to do any sort of data manipulation with your Web page. After getting your feet wet with the program, you can switch back and forth between the simple and advanced dialog boxes to see the SQL that is being generated and also see how the variables are used. When you feel comfortable with the SQL creation of the simple Recordset dialog box, you can begin using the advanced version of the Recordset dialog box, shown next.

```
Recordset                                                          [X]

    Name:  rsSearch                                                      OK

Connection:  eflea                    ▼    Define...              Cancel

     SQL:  SELECT efleaID, Item, Description, AskingPrice    ▲      Test
           FROM Items
           WHERE Description LIKE '%rqSearch%'                     Simple...
           ORDER BY DateEntered DESC
                                                             ▼     Help

Variables:  [+] [−]

           Name          Default Value    Run-time Value
           rqSearch      %                Request("txtSearch")




Database        ┌──────────────────────────┐ ▲   Add to SQL:
   Items:       │      ▦  Item             │
                │      ▦  Description      │         SELECT
                │      ▦  DateEntered      │
                │      ▦  AskingPrice      │         WHERE
                │      ▦  Keywords         │
                │  ⊞ ▦  ratings           │        ORDER BY
                │  ⊞ ▦  users             │ ▼
                └──────────────────────────┘
```

The advanced version of the Recordset dialog box allows you to use some drag-and-drop functionality, but also allows for hand-coding the SQL statement, which is what you'll need to do in most cases. It also has several other advantages:

- It allows you to specify the type of *Request* variable you are using, whether a form variable or URL variable, but gives you the flexibility of choosing a generic *Request* that is used by some of the recordset navigation server behaviors.

- It allows you to specify the default value. Typically, in a search situation you can use the wildcard character % as a default value. Wildcards allow matches on anything, so a match on just a wildcard with no other text will return all records.

- It allows you to pull data from more than one database table at a time.

- It shows you the SQL code, furthering your knowledge of the language and allowing you to make manual changes in the SQL statement.

- It allows you to name your own variables instead of relying on the generic *MMColParam* name that Dreamweaver MX automatically inserts when using the simple Recordset dialog box, and it also allows more than one variable.

Most databases contain advanced query builders that make it easier to work within the RDBMS. You can use the query builder of your RDBMS to create the SQL and paste it directly into the advanced box.

Progress Check

1. What language is used for conducting a search on a database?

2. What is a "wildcard" character?

3. What is an *action* page?

Project 12-2 Results.asp

The search form that you created in Project 12-1 is the first part of the two-part process of searching the database. The user enters the search word and then clicks Submit. The page that will process the search needs to be created, and you'll do that in this project.

Step by Step

1. Create a new blank page in Dreamweaver MX and save it as **Results.asp**. If you are working in ColdFusion, you should save it as Results.cfm; in JSP, you should save it as Results.jsp; etc. In the title bar of the page, make the page title **Search Results**.

---

1. SQL, or Structured Query Language
2. A character that matches anything, like a wild card in a card game
3. The page that a Web form is submitted to

2. Attach the page to the eFlea template by clicking Modify | Templates | Apply Template To Page. This will bring up the Select Template dialog box in which you can choose the site (eFlea) and the template (eflea_template).

3. Add a recordset to the page. If your Bindings panel isn't showing, click Window | Bindings to bring the Bindings panel to the front. Then click the plus sign (+) on the palette and click Recordset. This will show the Recordset dialog box.

4. There are several things you need to do in this dialog box. First, give the recordset a name. Recordsets should always have a meaningful name so that when you have several on a page you'll be able to follow your code logic more easily. Name this one **rsSearch**; the *rs* prefix denotes it as a recordset object.

5. Set the Connection drop-down box to the eFlea connection that you created in Module 9.

6. Add a variable to the Variables box by clicking the plus sign, shown in the next illustration. The variable should be set up as in the following table, depending on your server model:

	Name	Default Value	Run-Time Value
ASP	*rqSearch*	%	*Request("txtSearch")*
JSP	*rqSearch*	%	*request.getParameter("txtSearch")*
CF	*rqSearch*	%	*#url.txtSearch#*
PHP	*rqSearch*	%	*$_GET["txtSearch"]*
ASP.NET	*rqSearch*	%	*Request.QueryString ("txtSearch")*

- **Name** A name you give the variable that will be used in the SQL statement.
- **Default value** A special variable that Dreamweaver MX uses when no data is sent to the page.

(continued)

●   **Run-time value**   A value used when the page is browsed. It will be dynamically inserted into the SQL statement using the variable that you set up.

7. Next, you'll write the SQL statement. This can be written directly by hand, or you can use the point-and-click method for most of it and fill in the details not available to the wizard by hand. Simply highlight each of the following columns in the Items table in turn and click Select:

●   FleaID

●   Item

●   Description

●   AskingPrice

8. Next, click the Description field in the Database items box and then click the Where box. By now, your SQL should look like this:

```
SELECT FleaID, Item, Description, AskingPrice
FROM Items
WHERE Description
```

9. You'll have to code the variable into the SQL statement by hand. You'll put wildcard characters around this variable and then enclose the whole thing in single quotes.

Dreamweaver MX will take care of replacing this variable with the correct values in the script on the page. At the end of the SQL, you'll add the following:

```
LIKE '%rqSearch%'
```

10. Go back to the wizard approach to add an "order by" clause to the SQL statement. Click on the DateEntered field in the Database items box and then click the Order By button. This will insert the clause in the appropriate place in the SQL statement.

11. One final addition to the SQL that you'll make by hand—you want the Order By to be in descending order with the most recent at the top. You can do that with the *DESC* keyword in the SQL statement. Put it at the very end of the statement. By now, your finished SQL statement should look like this:

```
SELECT efleaID, Item, Description, AskingPrice
FROM Items
WHERE Description
LIKE '%rqSearch%'
ORDER BY DateEntered DESC
```

12. Click OK on the Recordset dialog box. The recordset code is automatically inserted into the page, and it also shows up in the Bindings panel.

13. Next, you'll have to put some HTML elements on the page to allow the data to be displayed. Add some title text to the page, with a trailing colon (**Search Results:**).

14. Open the Bindings panel again and click the plus sign to add a new data element to the page. This time it's going to be a simple *Request* element. Click Request Variable and pick *Request* from the drop-down list. Give it the name of the incoming Request variable, **txtSearch**. After creating the *Request* element in the Bindings panel, you can drag the field to the page and place it next to the Search Results heading. When a user comes to the page after making a search, he or she will see "Search Results:" followed by his or her search text.

15. Press ENTER and then click Insert | Table to insert a table onto the page. The table should be two rows and three columns so you can have a heading and a result, with a width of 75 percent and a border of 0. In the first row of the table, place the column headings **Item**, **Description**, and **Asking Price**.

16. Expand the Recordset item in the Bindings panel and then drag the database columns to the second row of the table, corresponding to the headings.

17. Select the second row of the table by clicking the <tr> tag in the tag selector on the bottom of the design screen, or by CTRL-clicking each table cell until they are all selected, or by simply dragging your mouse across the three table cells.

Project
12-2

Results.asp

(continued)

18. Open the Server Behaviors palette and click the plus (+) sign. Choose Repeat Region from the list and click All Records in the dialog box.

19. Close the page and then open up search.htm again. Browse that page and enter some search criteria that you know will show up in the description, such as **book**. If you click Submit, the Results page should show up with all matches for the word you are searching for. If you don't enter any text, all records should be displayed. If you've come this far and everything is working, congratulations—you've just created a search results page for the eFlea site.

Project Summary

In this project, you learned how to create a recordset using the Advanced recordset dialog box. The advanced box allowed you to create the SQL statement and specify the search parameter that will be entered by the user. You then built a results table using a table and a Repeat Region server behavior.

CRITICAL SKILL
12.3 Validate Form Data

When a user enters something in a form, you have to provide a method of validating the data to make sure it is in an acceptable format. For example, if you want the user to input a phone number, you should make sure that it's a valid phone number. The reasons for this are many, but here are a few of the most important:

● You want to prevent database errors from occurring. If a user enters text when the field requires a number, there will be a database error.

● You want your database to contain only valid data. If your database contains invalid data, it can only slow things down in the long run and even cause possible errors down the road when you have to use the data in a meaningful way, such as in a report.

● You don't want a user entering HTML or JavaScript code that could later be displayed and/or executed, causing problems or embarrassment.

● A more malicious user might enter server-side code or even SQL in the form fields to try to hack your site. A successful hack could destroy your database or deface your site.

JavaScript Validation

The most basic form of validation uses client-side JavaScript. You can place validation on any or all fields that the user can fill out and check the data against predetermined criteria without ever accessing the server. This can be considered a front-line defense against potential bad data.

To demonstrate this, open your search.htm page and browse to it. Place this code in the search field and then click Submit:

```
<script>alert("I'm a hacker")</script>
```

You should see an alert box when the Results page comes up—the script actually executed on the client because the server wrote it out to the page. Even though you were only trying to display the search field that the user entered, something else happened. The server didn't know that it wasn't supposed to send JavaScript to the browser.

Dreamweaver MX comes with a very basic client-side JavaScript validation behavior. The behavior checks for a valid numerical input, and it checks for a required field as well. Other validation routines can be found on the Web in numerous places. If you plan to do substantial work with the Web, you should have a stock supply of JavaScript validation routines that you can use when you need them. Also, many JavaScript validation routines exist as Dreamweaver behaviors that can be downloaded from the Macromedia Exchange and other sites around the Web. Extensions are covered in Module 17.

Client-side logic will probably catch 95 percent of the bad data that might come into your site. By using client-side validation, you prevent trips to the server for simple validation, keeping your site running faster by not wasting resources on it, and also giving the user immediate response to the form submission without having to wait for a round trip to the server.

If it sounds too good to be true, it is. Although these are all good reasons to use JavaScript to validate your data, it is not infallible. Users can turn off JavaScript in their browsers, or they can post from their own forms. Other lines of defense are needed to supplement the client-side test of the data.

Server-Side Validation Code

The next line of defense against bad data can be performed on the server. You can write server-side code to handle validation of all incoming data. This must be done in the language of the server, so if you are doing validation on an ASP VBScript site, for example, you could have code like this to check your incoming *Request* variable for numeric input:

```
<%
If Not IsNumeric(Request("myFormField")) Then
      Response.Write("Please go back and enter a number")
      Response.End
End If
%>
```

Also, server behaviors that handle server-side validation can be downloaded as extensions to Dreamweaver MX from various places on the Web.

The server can also implement other defense mechanisms against invalid or forged data. For example, for strictly displaying data that was entered in a form field on the previous page, you can *HTML encode* or *URL encode* the incoming data. This doesn't validate the data in any way, but it does provide a way to guard against malicious scripts and other possible hacker attacks. To HTML encode the data in Dreamweaver MX, select the data source on the page and click the corresponding data source in the Bindings panel on the far right to display the drop-down list of data formats. These special formats allow you to change the display of the data on the page. You'll notice that one of them is for HTML encoding the data.

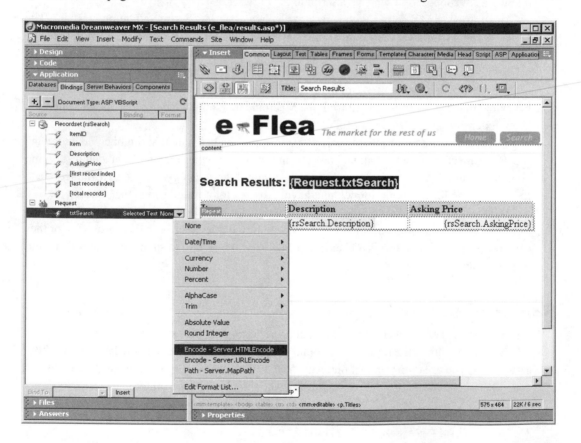

After applying an HTML encoding format to the *Request* variable on the Results page, the hacker script described in the previous section will be displayed as the encoded version of the script, with special characters translated to their HTML encoded counterparts. The less-than and greater-than signs in the tags show up as *< >* and the script functionality is dismantled completely.

Validating Using Your Database

Validation inside the database can often be the most efficient solution. Databases are highly efficient at doing checks on the data. Any invalid data coming to the database can trip an error and return an error condition to your Web page that can be handled by a global error-handler page. It's beyond the scope of this book to demonstrate this technique. The methods used would be different for every server model and every RDBMS. In an enterprise-level application, data validation is essential every step of the way. For a small- to medium-size site, you can apply client- and server-side validation and be perfectly safe from invalid data.

Progress Check

1. What are the three primary methods of validating data for a data-driven Web site?

2. What are two advantages that make JavaScript a good choice for validating data?

3. What is a disadvantage of client-side JavaScript?

CRITICAL SKILL
12.4 Search a Database with Multiple Search Criteria

You can't go very far with a search page if you can input only one word for a database search. Many of the top search engines allow all kinds of searches using operators such as AND, OR, NOT, and allowing quotes for exact phrase matches and optional commas for multiple-word matches. Most of the search engines are smart enough to know that when you type **Search For: web asp vbscript** you don't mean you are looking for the phrase "web asp vbscript." The search engine will break it down into the single words and search for each word individually and match only the content that matches all the words. In fact, in some advanced searches the engine will allow the user to specify whether to use all the words, any of the words, or the exact phrase.

---

1. Client-side scripting, server-side scripting, and database-level validation

2. JavaScript runs on the client so the server doesn't need to be called, lessening the strain on the server. The user gets a more immediate response because the server doesn't need to be called.

3. JavaScript can be turned off or bypassed by malicious users.

Sophisticated search engines allow you to enter many different combinations of search criteria. Although it's beyond the scope of this book to go into detail about the different methods, you should be aware of what you might need and possible approaches to the problem.

Obviously, the most basic requirement is to allow for multiple words in the search. It is impossible to predict how the user will enter the data, however. You can specify the requirements on the page, such as "Enter your search words separated by commas—phrases can be enclosed in quotes." As you can imagine, these two simple requirements can drastically increase the complexity of the code contained in the page.

There are basically two ways to approach the problem:

- Add server-side code to the page to handle the different situations. This requires a thorough knowledge of the language you are using in your site. The words can be broken down and the SQL statement can be generated dynamically based on the words and/or phrases entered.

- Build a stored procedure within the database to handle the tasks. Again, this requires a thorough knowledge of the database and stored procedure creation. Some databases, such as Access, don't have stored procedures available to them.

Another consideration for an advanced search page is that you may want to allow searches of multiple columns in the database. Again, the same problems arise. The code has to be dynamic to allow for the multiple words and phrases, but now it also has to work across several columns. The next project will attempt to address a couple of these issues in a way that can be applied easily in the Dreamweaver MX environment using the point-and-click and drag-and-drop functionality of the program.

Project 12-3   search.htm and results.asp Revisited

The search form that you created in Project 12-1 contained one field for a database search. The results page created in Project 12-2 conducted a database search based on that one field that was entered by the user. This project expands on that to allow a search based on two fields and a search across three different database columns.

Step by Step

1. Open the search.htm page and position your cursor to the right of the Submit button and inside the table cell. If you press the TAB key, this should create a new blank row in the table for a second form field.

2. In the first field of the second row, type the text **Listed After (mm/dd/yy)**.

3. In the second field of the second row, insert a text field by clicking Insert | Form Objects | Text Field.

4. Open the Property Inspector (if it isn't already open) by clicking Window | Properties. Change the name of the new form field to **txtDate** and give it a Char Width of **40** to match the other form field.

5. Close this page and open the Results.asp page. You are going to have to change the SQL statement so that it retrieves data based on the values of both form elements.

6. Open the recordset again by double-clicking on the recordset in the Bindings panel.

7. Add another variable to the recordset by clicking the plus (+) sign. The variable should read as follows:

	Name	Default Value	Run-Time Value
ASP	rqDate	01/01/2001	Request("txtDate")
JSP	rqDate	01/01/2001	request.getParameter("txtDate")
CF	rqDate	01/01/2001	#url.txtDate#
PHP	rqDate	01/01/2001	$_GET["txtDate"]
ASP.NET	rqDate	01/01/2001	Request.QueryString("txtDate")

8. Change the SQL to reflect the new variable. You'll also have to add the Keywords column to the SQL so that the search can be made on Keywords as well as Description. The new SQL statement will read like this:

```
SELECT efleaID, Item, Description, AskingPrice
FROM Items
WHERE Description LIKE '%rqSearch%'
AND Keywords LIKE '%rqSearch%'
AND DateEntered > #rqDate#
ORDER BY DateEntered DESC
```

9. Save the page and open the search.htm page again. You should be able to browse the page and conduct a new search. If you leave the Date field blank, all records that match the first search criteria will be returned. If you fill in both fields, you will be able to refine your search by the date entered in the *txtDate* field.

Project Summary

In this project, you built upon the previous projects and created a more advanced search and results page that allowed a user to type in a date as well as a search word for the search. The date field allows the user to display only the set of records that were entered after that particular date.

Ask the Expert

Q: Can a more advanced search be accomplished with Dreamweaver MX that allows for more options or more search criteria?

A: The answer is yes and no. There are no built-in wizards or server behaviors that allow you to conduct advanced searches in the core Dreamweaver MX program. To build a dynamic search page would require a complex script to be hand-coded or a stored procedure within your RDBMS. If you are interested in more advanced searches, you should become proficient with the language of your choice and implement it with code. The entire concept of coding for advanced searching boils down to string manipulation— the words are coming into the action page, and the action page has to deal with the words in some way. After separating the words, or leaving them whole if you are dealing with a phrase, a dynamic SQL statement needs to be written. This can be done on the page or in the SQL in a stored procedure. When we talk about a "dynamic" SQL statement, it simply means that it is tailored to the specific search being conducted. For example, a user might enter the following:

```
book, asp, dreamweaver, "Ray West", "Tom Muck"
```

The SQL has to be written dynamically to allow the phrases "Ray West" and "Tom Muck" to be matched, rather than the individual words "Tom", "Muck", "Ray", "West". It also has to match the individual words "book", "asp", "Dreamweaver". The script would have to look for quotation marks and treat the words inside the quotation marks as a phrase, and it would also have to treat words separated by commas as individual words. The component parts of the script would not be very hard to code, but the complete script would be quite complex and require a lot of thought to take into account the different situations.

What to Take Away from This Module

In this module, we've given a brief overview of a typical search mechanism in a data-driven Web site. We've also shown you how to build a simple search form and a simple search results page using Dreamweaver MX. Form validation was discussed, as well as several different methods for performing validation. Finally, we showed you how to create a more sophisticated search page and results page by modifying the original pages that you created.

✓

Module 12 Mastery Check

1. What is the purpose of a form on a Web page?

2. What are the two primary attributes of the <form> tag that you need to change to adapt a Web form to your own application, and what settings do these two attributes reflect?

3. Can you enter SQL in the simple recordset dialog box?

4. What is the default value used for in the Recordset dialog box when you add a variable to the SQL statement?

5. What is the reason to HTML encode or URL encode a string of data entered by a user when displaying it on a Web page?

6. Which method allows for more data to be passed: GET or POST?

7. Which method works better for search forms and why?

8. What are two advantages to using the Advanced recordset dialog box in Dreamweaver MX?

9. What is the wildcard character in SQL?

10. Which SQL keyword(s) is used to sort a recordset?

11. True or False: Client-side form validation is foolproof.

12. The Repeat Region is applied to which element on the page to create a typical search results page?

Module 13

Recordset Navigation

In Module 12, you created a search page with a results page. The results page simply listed all of the records that were returned from a search. If the search returns a lot of matches, however, you don't want to display them all on one page. You have to create scripts that handle the recordset navigation—paging through a resultset. Luckily, Dreamweaver MX has built-in server behaviors that handle all the details of these scripts and hide the complexity from you.

CRITICAL SKILL
13.1
Create Pages with Repeat Region and Recordset Paging Server Behaviors

The repeat region server behavior that you used in the last module returned all rows from the query. There is also an option on the server behavior to return a predefined number of rows from the database.

A typical results page will display 10 results at a time, so 10 is the default value in the dialog box. You can change this value to whatever you want, however. The number you place in the box will be used by the server-side script that Dreamweaver MX automatically creates to determine how many rows to display.

When you set a repeat region to 10 records, your page also needs a way to determine which page it should show. If you have 80 matches in the database, and you are displaying 10 records per page, you'll have to display 8 different pages of results, and there needs to be a way to keep track of where you are in the sequence. Dreamweaver MX includes server behaviors that will do all of this for you as well.

The Recordset Paging Behaviors

If you open Dreamweaver MX and open the Server Behaviors panel, you'll see a submenu in the panel named Recordset Paging (formerly called Move To Record in UltraDev 4).

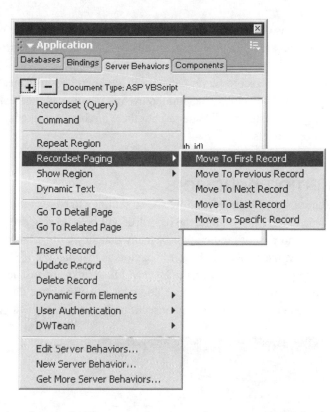

This menu has four or five items, each representing a server behavior you can apply to a page that has a repeat region applied to it. These server behaviors don't work on their own—the Repeat Region is a requirement. The five possible server behaviors are

- Move To First Record
- Move To Previous Record
- Move To Next Record
- Move To Last Record
- Move To Specific Record*

* Not available in all server models

These server behaviors can be applied to text items or images by making a selection on the page that you want the link assigned to, or they can be applied individually by placing your cursor on the page where you want the link to appear. Then you can just assign some new text by filling in the dialog box when you apply the server behavior. The server behaviors are associated with specific tasks, but they are generally applied as a set of four—first, previous, next, and last.

The Move To Specific Record server behavior is odd man out this time. It's not needed for the paging functionality, and actually has limited use in Dreamweaver MX. It can be used to create a detail page in a master-detail page set, but there are better methods. It is also not available in all server models.

The Show Region Behaviors

The Move To Record server behaviors allow you to set links to pages returned by your recordset. Because the page is dynamic, the recordset will be returning different matches all the time, and there is no way of predicting how many matches will be returned. One thing you will notice about the Move To Record server behaviors is that the link is always active. When you are at the last record in the resultset, the Next and Last links are still active, even though they no longer have any purpose on the page. You may as well remove them if you are already on the last record. You do this by using another set of built-in server behaviors—Show Region.

Each of the Show Region server behaviors has a specific use that applies to the state of the recordset. For example, there is a Show Region If Recordset Is Empty behavior. This is handy to show alternate text if there are no results in a recordset. There are a couple of specific Show Region server behaviors that work well with the Move To Record server behaviors: Show If

Not Last Record and Show If Not First Record. You apply these behaviors to the area on the page that you don't want to show up. The First and Previous links shouldn't be displayed when you are on the first record because there is nowhere to link to. You can apply the Show If Not First Record to the First and Previous links and they will be hidden when the user is on the first record.

Project 13-1   results.asp

The Move To Record server behaviors allow you to add recordset paging to the results obtained from a search, or any recordset results, so this project allows you to add the server behaviors to the Results page that you created in the projects for Module 12.

Step by Step

1. Open the results.asp file (or your own particular results page).

2. Open the Server Behavior panel by clicking the Server Behaviors tab in the Application panel group or by clicking Window | Server Behaviors:

Window Help	
✓ Insert	Ctrl+F2
✓ Properties	Ctrl+F3
Answers	Alt+F1
CSS Styles	Shift+F11
HTML Styles	Ctrl+F11
Behaviors	Shift+F3
Tag Inspector	F9
Snippets	Shift+F9
Reference	Shift+F1
Databases	Ctrl+Shift+F10
Bindings	Ctrl+F10
✓ Server Behaviors	Ctrl+F9
Components	Ctrl+F7
Site	F8
Assets	F11
Results	▶
Others	▶
Arrange Panels	
Hide Panels	F4
Cascade	
Tile Horizontally	
Tile Vertically	
index.asp	
results.asp	
Translated Source Viewer	

Project
13-1

results.asp

(continued)

3. Double-click the Repeat Region item that is in the panel (already applied to the page). This will bring up the Repeat Region dialog box again. At this point, you are editing the existing Repeat Region on the page—don't create a new one.

4. Change the radio button from Show All Records to Show __ Records. Fill in the box with the number 10, to show 10 records.

5. Click OK to apply the server behavior to the page.

6. Position your cursor below the table on the page and type in the following text:

```
First | Previous | Next | Last
```

7. Highlight the text "First" on the page and open the Server Behavior panel again. This time choose the Recordset Paging submenu and apply the server behavior Move To First Record. When the box pops up, it will already have the selected text "First" listed in the dialog box, as well as the recordset name, because there is only one recordset on the page. Click OK to apply the server behavior.

8. Do the same thing for each of the words in the navigation bar in turn. Select the text, apply the appropriate server behavior (Move To First, Previous, Next, or Last Record), and click OK. When you are done, you should have four links that allow you to page through your recordset.

9. Save the page again and then browse it to try out the new navigation. Because you are browsing the results page using the default values in the search criteria, all records will be returned, allowing you to test out the paging by clicking Next or Last until you get to the end of the resultset, and clicking the First or Previous link to get back to the beginning.

10. Next, you'll add the Show Region server behaviors to the page by selecting the First link and applying the server behavior Show Region If Not First Record. Do the same for the Previous link. For the Next link, apply the server behavior Show Region If Not Last Record. Do the same for the Last link.

11. Save the page and then browse it again. Now the First and Previous link shouldn't be showing when you are on the first page. Also, when you page forward and get to the last record, the Next and Last links should be hidden. If everything is working okay, exit Dreamweaver MX and take a break! You deserve it.

Project Summary

In this project, you learned how to apply recordset navigation to a page that contains a recordset, table, and repeat region. You learned how to add links that allowed navigating to the first set of records, previous set of records, next set of records, and last set of records.

CRITICAL SKILL
13.2 Add Recordset Status Information

Moving through the recordset is only one part of the picture when you're dealing with recordset navigation. You'll also want a way to show users exactly where they are in the recordset—which page they are on or which record they are on. In addition, you'll want a way to show how many records are returned. When there are only First, Previous, Next, and Last links on the page, there is no indication of how many pages there may be or which particular page users are on.

That's where the built-in variables of the Dreamweaver MX recordset come in handy. After declaring a recordset, you can see the columns your recordset uses in the Bindings panel. Three additional items show up by default as well:

- First record index
- Last record index
- Total records

These elements can be dragged to the page just like the recordset fields and placed near your recordset navigation links so users can know where exactly they are. These items are shown below your database fields in the Bindings panel:

These special variables will show up as text, and they can be treated as text when you are editing the page. Typically, you may want to insert some text such as this:

```
Showing records 1 through 10 of 98 total records
```

The easiest way to do this is to create your text on the page using the numbers as temporary placeholders. You can then highlight each placeholder in turn and drag the corresponding recordset status variable to the page to take the place of the placeholder. CSS styles and HTML styles can be applied easily to the entire line of text rather than the individual elements that make up the line.

Progress Check

1. After applying a recordset to the page, which server behavior is a prerequisite to applying a Recordset Paging server behavior?

2. Where do the recordset status variables appear in the Dreamweaver MX environment?

3. Which Show Region server behavior is needed to hide a First and Previous link when you first view the page?

CRITICAL SKILL
13.3 Use the Show Region Server Behaviors on Search Results

You've built a successful search page now, complete with a matching results page. The results page can display 10 records at a time, which can be paged through. What happens when the search doesn't return any records? Usually, one of two things: either an error, or a page that looks like something is missing.

---

1. Repeat Region
2. In the recordset tree of the Bindings panel after declaring a recordset
3. Show Region If Not First Record

Errors can be prevented by applying the Show Region server behaviors to the page. Simply follow these steps:

1. Select the entire contents of the recordset results, including the table, repeat region, paging links, and the recordset navigation variables.

2. Apply the Show Region If Recordset Is Not Empty server behavior to the area.

Now when you search for a word or phrase and there are no matches, you don't have to worry about database errors.

The other problem is that the page still looks like there is something missing. In fact, there *is* something missing: alternate text. Whenever you have a recordset on a page that might not return a value, you should include some alternate text to be displayed, such as, "Your search returned no matches." You can enter this text right into the design environment as well:

1. Add some alternate text to the page in an area below the dynamic table.

2. Apply a Show Region If Recordset Is Empty server behavior to the region.

Now when you browse the page and there are no matches, the alternate text is displayed, allowing for a more pleasant user experience. If you were to look at the underlying code, you would see something like this:

```
<% If rsSearch.EOF And rsSearch.BOF Then %>
    <p>There were no records that matched</p>
<% End If ' end rsSearch.EOF And rsSearch.BOF %>
```

The code is saying "if the recordset is at the beginning AND the recordset is at the end, there are no records—show the code up to the End If statement." Dreamweaver MX allows you to create code like this through the simple point-and-click interface of the server behaviors.

CRITICAL SKILL
13.4 Create a Master-Detail Page Set

When you visit a search page for an e-store and are shown a list of matches for your search, you are viewing what is commonly known as a *master* resultset page. Typically, you are shown only a few details of the matched records and a link that will allow you to drill down to a page with more details. This would be the *detail* page of the master-detail page set.

The concept is used quite often in e-stores, where a Web user can browse a catalog of products, or search for a product and be shown a list of matches to the search. The detail page will typically display a picture and every bit of information that is available for a product.

The results page that you built in Projects 2 and 3 in Module 12 would be considered a master page. Only a small bit of information was returned. The detail page can be linked from that master page by providing a link on one of the fields on the page and then adding a *URL parameter* or *query string variable* to the link (it can be referred to by either name). A URL parameter is nothing more than a variable that is appended to a URL. A link with a URL variable added to it looks like this:

```
<a href="details.asp?id=2373">Hedge Clippers</a>
```

In this case, the text is "Hedge Clippers." The actual link behind the text is a relative link to the details.asp page, with a URL parameter named "ID" with a value of 2373. Links like these are generally hidden from the end user behind some descriptive text. The URL variable for a detail page typically contains the primary key for the item that the detail page is going to supply the details for. By passing a value of the primary key of the database table to the detail page, a recordset can be created that will pick out the one item in the database table that the URL variable matches.

The key to the detail page is returning the correct record. This is done through the SQL that you write on the detail page. If you are filtering the recordset by a URL variable, the pseudo-code version of the SQL statement might look like this:

```
"Select * from myTable WHERE ProductID = " + Request.URL("id")
```

Once again, Dreamweaver MX hides the details of this. In the Dreamweaver MX recordset creation dialog box, you will declare a variable based on an incoming URL variable, using the syntax of your language. We assume that the ProductID field in the database is a numeric column:

	Name	Default Value	Run-Time Value
ASP	*rqID*	0	*Request.QueryString("ID")*
JSP	*rqID*	0	*request.getParameter("ID")*
CF	*rqID*	0	*#URL.ID#*
PHP	*rqID*	0	*$HTTP_GET_VARS["ID"]*
ASP.NET	*rqID*	0	*Request.QueryString["id"]*

In the SQL creation dialog box shown here, you can insert the SQL using the variable that you defined as a placeholder for the actual *Request* element:

```
Select * from myTable WHERE ProductID = rqID
```

Unlike the search results page, the request element that is used to find a database column is a numeric type, so single quotes aren't needed in the SQL statement. Also, you'll notice that the default value is 0 this time, and not % like on the results page. Once again, because the ID field in this case is a numeric field, the default value of % would cause an error. You can use 0 because there shouldn't be any records in your table with a primary key value of 0. Unlike the search page, there is no fuzzy logic when you are accessing a detail page—you know exactly which record you want.

Project 13-2 details.asp

You already have a master resultset page—the results page from the search in Module 12. Now it's time to turn that results page into the master page in a master-detail page set. You'll make a simple modification on that page before creating the entire detail page step by step.

Step by Step

1. Open the results.asp file (or your own particular results page).

2. Select the rsSearch.Item text in column 1 of the table in the design environment. This will cause the column to be selected in the Bindings panel and the Server Behaviors panel as well.

3. Open the Server Behaviors panel.

4. Click the plus sign (+) to add a new server behavior, Go To Detail Page.

5. In the Go To Detail Page dialog box, there will be several items to set, as shown next. The illustration shows all parameters filled in for this project.

- **Link**   Should be already set to the selection of the item
- **Detail Page**   details.asp (or details.jsp, details.php, details.aspx, or details.cfm)
- **Pass URL Parameter**   ItemID
- **Recordset**   rsSearch
- **Column**   ItemID
- **URL Parameters**   Checked
- **Form Parameters**   Checked

6. Click OK and save the page.

7. Open a new page. Name it details.asp and save it in the eFlea folder.

8. Attach the page to the eFlea template by clicking Modify | Templates | Apply Template To Page. This will bring up the Select Template dialog box in which you can choose the site (eFlea) and the template (eflea_template).

9. Create a new recordset by clicking the plus sign in the Bindings panel and clicking Recordset.

10. The new recordset should be named rsDetails. Several things need to happen in this recordset. You need to bring in all of the data available for one particular record based on the ItemID. Some of this information is stored in the Users table. The SQL for the recordset will look like this:

```
SELECT Items.ItemID, Items.efleaID, users.Name, users.City,
users.State, users.email, Items.Item, Items.Description,
Items.DateEntered, Items.AskingPrice
FROM Items
INNER JOIN users
ON Items.efleaID = users.efleaID
WHERE ItemID = rqItemID
```

11. The variable needs to be set up in the Recordset dialog box as well. You can see from this statement that the variable name is *rqItemID*. Fill in the other values as listed in this table and then click OK to save the recordset.

	Name	**Default Value**	**Run-Time Value**
ASP	rqItemID	0	Request.QueryString("ItemID")
JSP	rqItemID	0	request.getParameter("ItemID")
CF	rqItemID	0	#URL.ItemID#
PHP	rqItemID	0	$HTTP_GET_VARS["ItemID"]
ASP.NET	rqItemID	0	Request.QueryString["ItemID"]

12. Insert a table on the page by clicking Insert | Table and set it to 5 rows, 3 columns, at 80 percent width and no border. This will form the layout structure of the item detail display on the page.

13. Set up the HTML table that you just added to the page with the captions and recordset columns exactly as follows:

- **Row 1, cell 1**   eFlea Item: {rsDetails.ItemID}
- **Row 1, cell 2**   Posted By:

(continued)

- **Row 1, cell 3** Insert a four-row, one-column table and add the following: {rsDetails.Name} {rsDetails.City}, {rsDetails.State} {rsDetails.email}

- **Row 2** (nothing)

- **Row 3, cell 1** Item: {rsDetails.Item}

- **Row 3, cell 3** Asking Price: {rsDetails.AskingPrice}

- **Row 4** (nothing)

- **Row 5** Merge the three cells in this row by selecting all three cells and right-clicking Merge Cells.

- **Row 5** Description: {rsDetails.Description}

14. Save the page. Try to access it by using the Results page and then clicking on the newly created links. Each link should take you to a different record on the detail page. The detail page in the Dreamweaver environment should look like the image shown next.

Project Summary

In this project, you created a details page that listed details for a record listed on the master page. You also learned how to link to that details page from the master page using a Go To Detail Page server behavior.

CRITICAL SKILL

13.5 Use Application Objects

Now that you know how to insert recordset navigation using server behaviors, we show you a faster way to do it with an Application Object.

Application Objects were called Live Objects in UltraDev 4. The objects reside in the Insert panel (DW workspace) or on the Insert bar (DW/Coder style workspace) and can also be found in the Insert menu under the Application Objects menu item, as shown next.

An Application Object is simply an object that contains server-side code, usually in the form of a server behavior. Most Application Objects will automatically insert the code necessary to replicate one or more server behaviors. For example, the Recordset Navigation Bar will insert First, Previous, Next, and Last links on the page. It will also automatically insert the Move To First, Move To Previous, Move To Next, and Move To Last server behaviors, as well as the Show Region server behaviors to show each link depending on recordset status. This one object effectively adds a table, four hyperlinks, and eight server behaviors to the page with one click.

Once the Application Object is on the page, however, any editing has to be done using the individual server behaviors or HTML objects that were inserted. That's why it is necessary to know the individual components that make up the Application Objects.

Recordset Navigation Bar Application Object

To replicate Project 13-1 using an Application Object, you need only click Insert | Application Objects | Recordset Navigation Bar and then choose Text or Images in the dialog box. The Application Object does the rest and inserts all of the individual server behaviors and code to the page. The effect is similar to the project you just completed, but there are no text delimiters between the links—each link is contained in a separate cell in a table. Whichever method you ultimately decide to use for your site, it's good to have the flexibility to do it either way.

Recordset Navigation Status Application Object

The Record Navigation Status Application Object is similar to the recordset status variables that were described earlier in "Add Recordset Status Information." By inserting this object on the page, you are effectively inserting all three of the status variables on the page. The resulting text in the design environment will look like this:

```
Records {rsSearch_first} to {rsSearch_last} of {rsSearch_total}
```

Just like the status variables you inserted manually, you can go back and edit the text from this Application Object. Once the Application Object is inserted, the various parts of the object can be edited individually, but the whole object can't be edited as a unit any more. In this case, the object consists of the three recordset status variables (first record index, last record index, and total records) and some text.

Master-Detail Page Set Application Object

This is the king of all Application Objects. The requirement for adding it to the page is to have a recordset declared that will return all records needed for the detail page. What this Application Object enables you to do is to insert the following into your site:

- A master page, like the results page built in Module 12, with a Repeat Region server behavior already applied

- Recordset navigation using First, Previous, Next, and Last links on the master page

- Recordset status variables on the master page

- A detail page like the page built in Project 13-1

As you can see, this object can save you a lot of time and a lot of steps. However, without knowing what the various parts of this object do, you will soon be lost. Module 12 and the first part of this module have prepared you for using this Application Object. Just as you wouldn't want to be thrown into a boxing ring with a championship fighter without being first taught the right cross, left jab, uppercut, and overhand right, at the bare minimum you need to know the individual server behaviors that make up this Application Object.

The Master-Detail Page Set Application Object looks like this:

The recordset has to be created already before you can apply this Application Object. You can then apply it and choose which database columns you want to appear on the master page by clicking the plus (+) and minus (−) buttons on the interface. You can also change the order in which they will appear by clicking the up and down arrows on the interface. The finished master page looks like this:

The control for the detail page is the same. Choose your database columns and then choose the order in which you want them displayed. Dreamweaver MX will create the detail page based on a simple table using the database columns as labels and having each database column on a separate row of the table. The finished detail page looks like the image shown next.

The layout of the pages leaves something to be desired, but you can adjust this later using the Dreamweaver MX design tools. The timesavings of having all of the application logic automatically written to the page are enormous.

Whether you choose to build your pages manually using the built-in server behaviors or by using the shortcut methods of Application Objects, Dreamweaver MX provides the tools needed to speed up your development time.

Ask the Expert

Q: **I've applied the Move To Record server behaviors to the page, and Dreamweaver MX seems to have generated an awful lot of code. Isn't there a more efficient way of simply moving through a recordset?**

A: Again, there is no yes or no answer. There are certainly cleaner ways to do certain things as compared to using the built-in server behaviors, but you also have to consider that the server behaviors are taking a lot into account and also are able to handle a lot of different situations. For example, the server behaviors will work for client-side and server-side recordset cursors. There is extra code to take both situations into account. In addition, the code will capture the URL and Form variables and make sure they always get added to any link that is generated by the program, such as the Go To Detail Page server behavior. Lastly, the code will keep track of all of the recordset paging. To do this, the page will retrieve a URL variable, compute the current recordset position, add an offset to it (or not, depending on the current position), and then display the appropriate records.

Another point to consider is that a lot of the code is contained in IF statements. Technically speaking, if the IF statement fails, any code within that statement will never be executed, so it doesn't add much to the overall execution time of the page.

What to Take Away from This Module

In this module, you were introduced to recordset paging using Dreamweaver MX's built-in server behaviors and Application Objects. How to show and hide sections of the page based on the state of the recordset using Dreamweaver MX's built-in Show Region server behaviors was demonstrated. The master-detail page set concept was explained and the built-in server behaviors were used to build a detail page. Finally, Application Objects were introduced as a shortcut method of building pages.

✓

Module 13 Mastery Check

1. What is the difference between a server behavior and an Application Object?

2. What is the purpose of the master-detail page set?

3. What is required before you can apply a Master-Detail Page Set Application Object?

4. What are two reasons for using a Show Region server behavior?

5. Can you edit an Application Object after you apply it?

6. What is the purpose of the query string (URL) variable in the link to the details page from the results page?

7. What does the Recordset Navigation Status Application Object do?

8. Can you create Master-Detail page sets manually?

9. How do you manually create a link to a detail page from a master page?

10. What does the Recordset Navigation Bar application object do?

11. How can you create the same effect manually using Server Behaviors?

12. How do you show alternative text if there are no results on a result page using Dreamweaver MX?

Module 14

Creating Dynamic Form Objects

389

Module 15 deals with inserting, updating, and deleting data in your database. To perform these tasks, you need to be able to properly use forms to post new or updated information to your recordsets. This depends on your ability to bind data to the variety of form elements that are available, creating dynamic forms. This is a short module, but it provides a critical education in the basics that will be required in upcoming projects.

CRITICAL SKILL
14.1 # Bind Data to Text Boxes

When you place a form on your page that is intended to collect information, it is generally an unbound form. This means that its elements—the text boxes and list boxes that make it up—are not tied directly to any data source. Information is entered into the form, the form is then posted, and the information is passed off to a recordset or an e-mail process or some other function that the data was needed to complete.

When you bind form elements, you tie them directly to fields in a recordset. Each time the page loads, those form fields will contain data from the database. They may not always contain the same record (the results of a search may dictate that), but their purpose is to display data from the database in form objects. This facilitates the reposting of that information.

For instance, if you want a user to be able to update a record, it is unlikely that you will know exactly which field he or she will need to edit at any given time. It could be an address change or a mistyped phone number. The process of updating a record, as you will see in Module 15, involves posting a form of data to a server behavior that completes the operation. Binding all of the recordset information to form fields allows the end user to edit whichever piece of data needs to be changed and then post the entire form back to the database, updating the record.

Text Fields

To get started, create a simple recordset and bind some data to a couple of text boxes. You can use any page, but start fresh in order to see the whole process. Create a new page and call it bindtest.asp. Create a new recordset that includes all of the users from the Users table.

Next, insert two text fields from the Form tab of the Insert bar.

Now drag fields from the Bindings panel onto these two text boxes. Simply double-click and hold on the Name field, drag it on top of the first text box, and release the mouse. Do the same with the City field. The text boxes will turn blue, and the recordset name and field name will appear in each of them, indicating that they are bound to the data in those fields.

Make sure that your application server is running, and click the Live Data View button. Your page should load with the information from the Name and City fields in the first record of your recordset in each of the text boxes.

Now, if you had a Submit button on the form, you could click it, and this data (or any alterations you made to it) would be posted to update the record, e-mail the record, or whatever needed to be done. The information was fed from the database directly into the form fields from which it could be directly altered and operated on. That is the power of data-bound form objects.

Now change your query slightly so that it accepts a URL parameter as a filter. Double-click the recordset in the Bindings panel. In the Recordset dialog box, change the Filter property from None to **efleaID**. Make the filter equal to a URL Parameter called **ID**.

When you rerun Live Data view, you can enter **ID = 2** (or any other number that exists as an efleaID in the database) into the URL query string box on the Live Data toolbar (shown in the next illustration), and information from the corresponding record will appear when you click Refresh.

Refresh   Live Data   Live Data Query String box

You can start to see how useful this can be. By choosing any record and passing its ID into the page in the URL string, you can pick a record to populate your data-bound form controls. This will come in especially handy when inserting and updating records in Module 15.

NOTE

There is another way to insert bound form elements that bears mentioning. When you drag a field from the Bindings panel to a text box, you are actually creating an instance of a server behavior. You can see this when you look in the Server Behaviors panel and see all of the dynamic text fields listed. You can also make a form element dynamic by clicking the Server Behavior plus (+) button under the Dynamic Elements menu. You will be asked to choose which of the elements on your page to apply the behavior to and which of the database fields should be bound to it.

```
Recordset (Query)
Command

Repeat Region
Recordset Paging        ▶
Show Region             ▶
Dynamic Text

Go To Detail Page
Go To Related Page

Insert Record
Update Record
Delete Record
Dynamic Form Elements   ▶    Dynamic Text Field
User Authentication     ▶    Dynamic CheckBox
DWTeam                  ▶    Dynamic Radio Buttons
                             Dynamic List/Menu
Edit Server Behaviors...
New Server Behavior...
Get More Server Behaviors...
```

```
Dynamic Text Field                                    ☒

  Text Field:  "textfield" in form "form1"      ▼         OK

  Set Value To:  <%=(rsTest.Fields.Item("Name").Value  ☑   Cancel

                                                          Help
```

Hidden Fields

Hidden fields are a special type of form field that is not shown to the user, but it can be used to great advantage in a dynamic site. You can pass recordset fields or other variables to the next page for inserting or updating a database through a hidden field. This is great for such things as user IDs that you don't want the user to see or modify.

The hidden field is also in the Forms tab of the Insert panel. To insert it into your page, simply make sure that your cursor is located within the form on the page in Design or Code view, and click the Hidden Field button on the Insert panel. The hidden field will show up as a small shield in the design environment.

Binding data to a hidden field is just as easy as binding the data to a text field. Simply drag and drop the dynamic data to the hidden field in the design environment.

NOTE

Hidden fields don't show up in the design environment if you've turned off invisible elements from View | Visual Aids.

CRITICAL SKILL

14.2 Bind Data to Radio Buttons and Check Boxes

Radio buttons and check boxes can be used to better define the choices you want your users to make. They are used in the following situations:

- **Radio buttons**   When there are several things to pick from and you want to allow one and only one choice to be made

- **Check boxes**   When there are a series of selections to be made and more than one choice is permitted (as in a list of interests) or when a simple Yes or No response is sufficient

Radio Buttons

It is important that you understand how radio buttons work before you try to bind data to them. A series of radio buttons can be placed on your page to represent a variety of choices that can be made. For instance, when answering regarding the gender of a person, you would likely have two radio buttons: one for male and one for female. One and only one answer is appropriate, and radio buttons will allow only one selection. If you choose one option and then choose a different one, the original choice becomes unselected in favor of the new choice. Radio buttons accomplish this level of interactivity by collecting from the developer two pieces of information: the name of the radio button group and the value when each button is checked.

NOTE

Naming radio buttons is different from naming other form elements such as text fields. Although no two text fields should have the same name, a group of radio buttons all share the same name. That is how they are identified as a group.

Insert two radio buttons into the form on the bindtest.asp page. Name them both **radGroup** in the Property Inspector. Set the value of the first to **admin** and the value of the second to **user**.

These radio buttons will correspond to the Group field of the Users table in the eFlea database. The Group field identifies an individual as a regular user or as an administrator. In the database, the Group field contains administrators (admin) and users (user). These descriptions are stored in the Users table. Because there is a choice of a defined, small number of options, and because only one of them may be chosen for each user, a set of radio buttons will work nicely for this.

NOTE

Radio buttons can be added as a group easily in Dreamweaver MX by choosing Radio Group from the Insert bar.

It is this group of radio buttons, rather than each individual button, that will be bound to the database. The data that exists there needs to check the proper button in the group based on the value found in the field.

In the Server Behaviors panel, click the plus (+) button and select the Dynamic Elements menu. Then select Dynamic Radio Buttons. You will be prompted to select the group of radio buttons that you want data bound to from the Dynamic Radio Buttons dialog box. Select the radGroup group. Next, click the lightning bolt next to the Select Value Equal To text box and select the Group field from the list of recordset fields that appears. You have bound the data from the Group field to the radGroup radio button set.

Dynamic Radio Buttons		✕
Radio Button Group:	radio "radGroup" ▾	OK
Radio Button Values:	admin user	Cancel
		Help
Value:	admin	
Select Value Equal To:	<%= (rsTest.Fields.Item("group").Valu ⚡	

Make sure your application server is running and turn on Live Data view. As you look at different records (by setting their IDs in the URL string), you will see the radio buttons in this group change according to the value that is in the Group field. When the user has an "admin" in the field, the radio button with the value of "admin" is checked, and when the user has a value of "user" in this field, the radio button with the value of "user" is checked.

Check Boxes

Check boxes are used when the questions you are asking all have Yes or No answers, such as, "Is this person active in the system?" or "Do you like broccoli?" There can be a series of questions that each has its own Yes or No answer. If a page directs a user to check all of the boxes next to the hobbies they are interested in, the user is essentially answering Yes or No to a series of questions that ask "Do you like golf?" and "Do you like chess?" even though the list may just say "Golf" and "Chess." If they check the box, they are answering Yes; if not, they are answering No by default.

NOTE

Technically, a check box can be used for any question to which there are exactly two answers—one answer being represented by a checked box, the other by an unchecked box. This is a somewhat impractical way to retrieve information, and check boxes are best kept for Yes/No types of queries. If there are two static answers to a question, such as male and female for a gender question, use radio buttons to collect more meaningful data regarding the selection. In this sense, check boxes do not allow a degree of response the way that radio buttons do. In our example, you either like golf or you don't. With radio buttons, a group could be defined called golf, and ten radio buttons in that group could have the values 1 to 10. A selection in this range would give a degree of interest in the game of golf. Carefully consider your needs when deciding which form elements to use.

You can place a check box on your page and drag a field on top of it just as you did with a text field, but don't do it—it doesn't work. You'll need to use the Server Behaviors menu to properly insert and set the properties for a dynamic check box. From the Dynamic Elements menu on the Server Behavior panel, select the Dynamic check box. A dialog box will appear asking you to choose the check box you want the behavior applied to. Click the lightning bolt to choose the recordset field that you want the box bound to. Navigate to the active field in the recordset and choose it.

The next field is very important, and it is what you miss out on if you try a shortcut way to apply this server behavior. In this server behavior, you are causing a box to be checked if a recordset field equals a certain value. Now, as a technical matter, that value can be anything, but most often it is a True/False, Yes/No, 1/0 type of value. In this case, you want to check the box if the active field is True, so enter True in the text box labeled Equal To.

Make sure that your application server is running and turn on Live Data view. As you choose different records to be displayed, you will notice that the check box is either checked or not depending on the value of the active field in that record.

CRITICAL SKILL
14.3 Bind Data to List Boxes

List boxes are an extremely popular way to display data and offer choices to users. They allow the selection of one or more choices in a defined list. The list can be predefined and hard-coded into the form element, or it can be dynamically generated from a database recordset.

There are two parts to the data that populate list boxes: the item label and the value. The item label is the part that the user sees. The value is the part that is actually used to update the database. Consider the structure of the eFlea tables for a moment. Each user has an ID. That ID is the piece of information used to identify the user in the Items table. You aren't storing the user's name over and over in the Items table, you are storing the user's ID and referring back to the Users table to find out who that ID belongs to.

The dynamic list box in Dreamweaver MX also gives you an option to create a static item to display in addition to the dynamic items. The static item is great for giving your user directions at what to choose in the list box. For example, a list of U.S. states might say "**Choose State**" in the static option to show the user what to do.

That is fine for the database, which can look things like that up very quickly. But your user won't know who user 3 is. They need to see the names, but you need to store the ID. A list box is great for this.

Insert a list box into your page from the Forms section of the Insert panel. In the Server Behaviors panel, go to the Dynamic Elements menu and choose Dynamic List/Menu. A dialog box will appear asking you to make several selections to populate your list box. First is the recordset that will supply the data. Remember that you may have more than one recordset on your page, so you may need to change the default recordset that appears.

The next choice should be familiar to you by now. You must select which list menu you are intending to make dynamic. If there is only one, you have no options, but if there are several list menus on your page, be sure to pick the correct one.

The next two options list the fields that exist in the recordset that you selected at the top of the dialog box. Choose which field will supply the labels and which will supply the values. Because this example is using a recordset of users, select the Name field for the labels and the efleaID field for the values.

The last choice you need to make is to identify how the page determines the initial state of the list menu when the page loads. Click the lightning bolt, and your page's recordsets will appear so you can browse to the proper field. You could use a different recordset, but for now, just choose the efleaID field from the current recordset.

Consider how this will make your page react. Because the efleaID is passed in as a URL parameter in your test page and filters the database, the Name text field contains the name of the current efleaID. If the list menu is set to the value of efleaID, it will display the associated name, or the same name that is in the top text field on the page.

Make sure that your application server is running and turn Live Data view on. Enter different IDs in the URL parameter. If the top text field and the list menu agree each time, your list menu is working properly.

NOTE

It is important to remember that if you were to submit a form that is set up this way, the value that the list menu would submit would not be the label, it would be its associated value. So even though you would be looking at a person's name, the value that the database would receive would be that person's ID.

Progress Check

1. What two things should be supplied to a list menu to populate it?

2. To insert dynamic text into your page, recordset fields can be dragged and dropped from where?

3. True or false: You can have only one recordset on a page.

Project 14-1 Binding a Page of Data

Let's pull together all that you've learned in this module into a project that uses the Users table and the Items table to populate several form fields. This project approximates the steps you might take to bind a page in a real project. It will be helpful in Module 15 when recordset updates are discussed.

---

1. Item labels and values
2. The Bindings panel
3. False

Project Goals

By the end of this project, you will

- Learn to bind multiple recordsets to form elements to make a functional page

Step by Step

1. In the eFlea project, create a new page and call it bindproject.asp.

2. You will need two recordsets on this page. First, create the Users recordset selecting the Name field and the eFleaID field. It will be used to populate a list menu and does not need to be filtered.

3. Next, create the Items recordset. It will be a list of the items in the database. It should be filtered by the itemID that will be passed in as a URL string, just as we did earlier in this module. In the Filter section of the recordset definition page, set itemID equal to a URL parameter called itemID.

4. The base information on this page will be about an item. In the Server Behaviors panel, expand the Items recordset so that you can easily refer to the fields. There are six fields that need to be bound to the page:

- Item ID
- Item name
- Description
- Asking price
- Active indicator
- User (seller) of the item

5. From the Forms tab of the Insert bar, insert a form.

6. Insert a table from the Common tab of the Insert bar into the form. The table should have six rows and two columns.

7. Label each cell as follows:

- ID:
- Item:
- Description:

(continued)

- Price:
- Active:
- Seller:

8. From the Forms page of the Insert bar, insert text fields into the second column in the top four rows, a check box in the Active row, and a list menu in the Seller row.

9. From the Bindings panel, in the Items recordset, drag the itemID field to the ID text menu. Drag the Item field to the Item text field. Drag the Description field to the Description text field. Finally, drag the AskingPrice field to the Price text field. Your page should look something like this:

10. Use the Server Behaviors menu to select a dynamic check box. Set it so that the check box in your Active row is checked if the Active field in the Items recordset has a value of True. Refer to the "Check Boxes" section earlier in this module if you need help with this.

11. Use the Server Behaviors panel again to insert a dynamic list menu.

12. Select the list menu from your Seller row.

13. Select the Users recordset to populate the list menu. This will fill the menu with all the users in the system. The labels will come from the Name field in the Users recordset, and the values will come from the efleaID.

14. Choose a static option of 0 with a label of "**Name**".

15. In the Select Value Equal To box, click the lightning bolt and select the efleaID from the Items recordset. This setup will populate the list menu from the Users recordset and select the label to display based on the value in the current record of the Items recordset.

16. Make sure that your application server is running and turn on Live Data view. As you set different itemIDs in the URL parameter to view different items, the list box will change to reflect the seller of the current item from a list of users supplied by a totally different recordset.

Project Summary

Learning to bind data from recordsets to form elements on your pages is one of the first things you need to do in order to successfully insert and update records. This project has taught you to use the features of Dreamweaver MX's elements to make this job simple and efficient. You can now move on to performing some actual work using these techniques.

What to Take Away from This Module

One of the amazing powers of Dreamweaver MX is its capability to make the tedious parts of Web application development into simple, efficient operations. The less time you need to spend dealing with issues like data binding, the more time you can spend on the unique aspects of your site. Dreamweaver MX helps you get to the fun part by providing powerful tools to automate the repetitive, yet necessary parts. In Module 15, you will use what you learned in this module to insert and update records into your database.

✓

Module 14 Mastery Check

1. What panel allows you to bind data to a form field?

2. What form element is populated with labels and values?

3. Why should you always use the Server Behaviors panel to create dynamic check boxes?

4. A check box is designed to provide answers to questions that have how many possible responses?

5. Radio button groups are identified by what two things?

6. How should radio buttons be named?

7. If you have a list of four multiple choice questions with one possible answer, should you use radio buttons or check boxes?

8. If you have a list of four multiple choice questions with more than one possible answer, should you use radio buttons or check boxes?

9. What purpose does the static option serve in a list menu?

10. What are hidden fields used for?

Module 15

Inserting, Updating, and Deleting Data

Being able to display all of the data in your database is nice, and being able to search for the particular record you want is even nicer, but there is only so much you can do with the records that exist in your tables. Pretty soon you will need to be able to add records, and change or delete the ones that are already there. As with many applications, Dreamweaver provides more than one way to accomplish these tasks, but, because we are interested in letting Dreamweaver do most of the work for us, this module looks at two methods that get the job done quickly and efficiently using server behaviors and application objects.

CRITICAL SKILL
15.1 Insert New Record in Your Database

Inserting data is the process of putting new records into a database. Your page collects information from an end user and uses it to add a new entry to the database. You may need to add a user to your site or add an item that a person wants to sell. For any of these, the process is essentially the same.

Project 15-1   Inserting Data

There are several ways to insert records into your database using Dreamweaver. You can hand-code it all, you can use stored procedures, and you can build your forms by hand and apply server behaviors to connect the data to the database. But because this is a beginner's guide that is focused on getting the most out of Dreamweaver's built-in functionality, we will insert data using a special application object called the Record Insertion form.

The Record Insertion form is a unique object that does just about everything for you. You don't even need to create a recordset on the page.

Project Goals

By the end of this project, you will

- Learn to insert records in your database
- Learn to use the Record Insertion form
- Learn to alter the Record Insertion form to customize your page

Step by Step

1. In the eFlea project, create a new page and call it newitem.asp. You will use this page to insert a new item into the Items table of the database.

2. Although the Record Insertion object will create a recordset for you to insert into, you will need a recordset of users, as was used in the project in Module 13 to populate a list menu of users. Create that recordset and call it users.

3. On the Insert bar, select the Application tab.

4. Click Insert Record Insertion Form. The following dialog box will appear:

5. The resulting dialog box requires quite a bit of information from you. First, choose the eFlea connection from the Connection drop-down box.

6. Choose the Items table as the table you want data inserted into.

7. The next box asks for the page to which you want the user redirected after the insert takes place. Choose whichever page you prefer. It could be a thank you page or a search page. Either type in a page name or use the Browse button to find the page you want.

8. When you select a table, the Form Fields box is populated using the fields from the database table. At this point, you can choose which fields, if any, to remove from this list and format the properties of the rest of them. Because you know that ItemID is an autonumber field, you know that you cannot insert a value into it. Highlight it and click the minus (–) button to remove this field as one that will be inserted.

9. Date Entered is also populated by a default value in the database. Select it and click the minus button.

(continued)

10. Each of the remaining fields have four properties you can set for them: their label, what kind of form element will be used to represent them, what type of data the field expects, and a default value. The object does a pretty good job of guessing at these properties, but some editing does need to be done. For instance, the AskingPrice field can be named Asking Price, but you should probably put a space between "Asking" and "Price" rather than leaving it as one word as it is in the database. Correct the labels for each field however you like, but only to the label, and not the form field name, or your code may fail.

11. By default, all of the fields have been assigned a text field as their form element except for the Active field, which gets a check box. These are all fine, except for the eFleaID field, which you will want to use a list menu for. Change the Display As property for the eFleaID field to a list menu.

12. When you set the eFleaID field to a menu, a Menu Properties button appears. Click it. The following dialog box will appear:

13. Choose to populate menu items from the database, and the dialog box changes to this one:

14. Choose the Users recordset. Choose the Name field for the Labels property and the eFleaID field for values. Leave the Select Value Equal To box empty and click OK.

15. You will be returned to the main Record Insertion form. Click OK.

16. The form, fields, and Submit button necessary to insert new records will be created for you, as shown here:

17. The only thing left to do is to add a manual entry into the eFleaID list menu to tell the user to select a seller from the list. Click the list menu box so that its Property Inspector appears. Click the Dynamic button to display the interface for the list menu. This interface allows you to choose from which recordset the data for the list menu comes, but it also allows you to insert static options, like a Select Seller option that appears at the top of the list.

18. In the Item Label column, type **Select Seller**. In the Values volume, type **0**.

(continued)

19. Save your page and upload it to your server or run it locally. Fill in the fields on the form and click Insert Record. Your data will be inserted into the database, and you will be redirected to the page you chose.

Project Summary

If you have never hand-coded a Web application before, it is hard to appreciate exactly how much effort is saved using Dreamweaver. You have just created the ability to accept input from your users and insert it into a database. Next, you'll learn to update that information.

NOTE

Although we can show you all of the steps to creating the portions of your site, it is sometimes easier to grasp when you see it in a working application. You can view an example of this application at www.e-flea.us.

Ask The Expert

Q: Can I use stored procedures to perform database access in Dreamweaver?

A: Absolutely, but because the application objects actually create recordsets for you, they are not well suited to use with stored procedures. There are other ways to perform these same procedures that can take advantage of more advanced database functionality. You can learn more about these in *Dreamweaver MX: The Complete Reference* (McGraw-Hill/Osborne, 2002), which is a good place to go after you are comfortable with the material in this book.

Q: What if I am using PHP, JSP, or ColdFusion for my site? Is anything different?

A: Not really. That is part of the beauty of this built-in functionality. Once your connection is defined, and as long as you use Dreamweaver's objects and behaviors, you should be able to follow the same steps and create pages for the different supported server languages. Do be aware, though, that there has been some divergence in the ways that the server models work since earlier versions. You will find different functionality for some of the newer server languages such as ASP.NET and PHP and may not have access to all of the application objects that come with the ASP server model.

Project 15-2 Inserting Data with More Control

The Record Insertion Form takes most of the pain out of generating a page that inserts data into your database. But that ease of use comes with the loss of some of the control that you might need when you try to perform more complex procedures. To prepare you to handle the widest variety of instances, this project shows you a second way to accomplish the insertion of a record and also a method of sending an e-mail from your site once the insertion is complete.

Project Goals

By the end of this project, you will

● Learn an additional method of inserting records into your database

● Learn to add code to your page to facilitate the sending of an e-mail after the insertion is complete

Step by Step

1. The insert page you will be creating is the page that users are directed to when they click the Sell Stuff link on the home page. Create a new page called sell.asp in your Site Manager for the eFlea site.

2. This insert page will be a little different in that you want users to enter items for themselves and not for other users. So you won't put a list box with all of the users' names. The user will either need to know his eFlea ID or you will have to develop some way to collect it through a user login. Registration and login are covered in Module 16.

3. You will need five text boxes on your page and a Submit button. The text boxes should be labeled and named as follows:

Text Box Label	Text Box Name
EfleaID	ID
Item	Item
Description	Description
Asking Price	Price
Keywords	Keywords

(continued)

4. Select the form on your page and name it **itemform**.

5. On the Server Behaviors panel, select the Insert Record server behavior.

6. The resulting Insert Record dialog box has several choices for you to make. First, select the eFlea connection that you have been using in the project. That selection will return a list of tables from the database in the next list box. Select the Items table to insert this record into.

7. Next, select a page that the user will be directed to when the insert is complete. This might be a thank you page that you create, or it may simply be the index page of your site. You may type in a page name or browse for an existing file.

8. The lower portion of this dialog box is where you tell Dreamweaver where the information that you want inserted comes from and into which database fields it goes. Select the itemform form (the only one on this page) as your source. The box beneath it lists all of the available input boxes from that form. You should see your five textboxes listed there.

9. Click each of the textboxes listed. As you do, the two list boxes at the bottom of the dialog box will update with two pieces of information about that form field—which database field its data will be inserted into and in what form that data will be sent. For each of the textboxes, select which database fields you want the data to go into and select whether the data is numeric, text, or any of the additional choices listed. For our purposes here, the eFleaID field should be numeric, and the rest should be text.

10. Click OK and your simple insert form is complete. Any data entered into the form on your page will be inserted into the appropriate fields in the database.

11. Now, make a couple of changes that will allow you to use the eFleaID from the database of a person who has registered and logged in to your site. The easiest way to do this using the Insert Record server behavior is with a hidden text box in your form. Delete the eFleaID text box and replace it with a hidden text box from the Insert bar.

(continued)

12. Name the hidden field ID.

13. Double-click the Insert Record server behavior in the Server Behaviors panel.

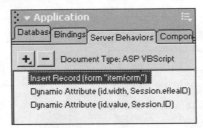

14. Make sure that the server behavior has correctly identified the hidden form field and is inserting its contents into the eFleaID database field.

15. This hidden field needs some data, because your user cannot type into it. You need to set a default value that is equal to the eFleaID of the user that has logged in. Registration and login are covered in Module 16, so refer to it and to the sample site for more information about creating a session variable called ID.

16. Once you have created the session variable ID, you can make it a data source in your Bindings panel. Click the plus (+) button and select Session Variable from the list.

17. In the resulting dialog box, type **ID** (or the name you have assigned to your session variable).

18. Your session variable will appear as a data source in the Bindings panel. To assign the session variable to the hidden form field, simply drag it from the Bindings panel onto the icon that represents the hidden form field on your page.

19. You can now save your page; the session variable value that is set at log in will be used as the ID that is inserted in the new record, saving your user from having to remember his or her ID.

20. The last piece of this project is the addition of some code to send an e-mail after the insertion is complete. You are going to need to identify the place in your code that is after the insert and right before the redirection to the results page. It looks like this.

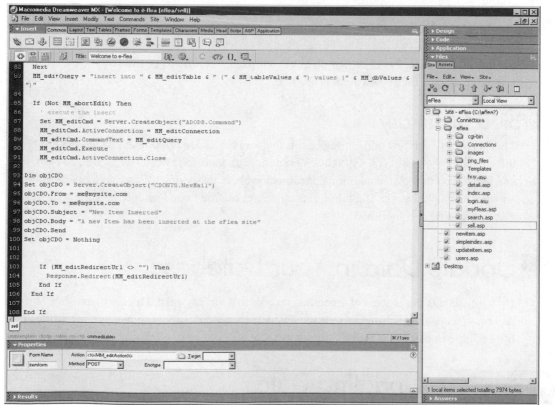

21. Change to Code view in Dreamweaver so that you can identify this spot. Notice that it is just above the <html> tag right before the *Response.Redirect* command.

(continued)

22. You will need to be running on Microsoft Internet Information Server to use this code, and you must have the CDO mail component installed, which was covered in Module 1. You will likely want to make adjustments to the e-mail addresses and the body. Just make those changes within the following code, and you should be fine. There is more information about CDO mail and other e-mailing methods in our other book, *Dreamweaver MX: The Complete Reference* (McGraw-Hill/Osborne, 2002).

```
Dim objCDO
Set objCDO = Server.CreateObject("CDONTS.NewMail")
objCDO.From = me@mysite.com
objCDO.To = me@mysite.com
objCDO.Subject = "New Item Inserted"
objCDO.Body = "A new Item has been inserted at the eFlea site"
objCDO.Send
Set objCDO = Nothing
```

23. Insert this code at the identified place in your page. Save the page and you should receive an e-mail each time a new item is inserted.

Project Summary

This is just an overview of the components that you can use to build insert pages and send information by e-mail. You will quickly want to learn more advanced techniques, and we encourage you to seek out additional information about these topics. They will be central to any database applications you build; it is important for you to understand the variety of ways that they can be accomplished.

CRITICAL SKILL
15.2 Update Data in Your Database

Updating data is the process of amending records that already exist. Once you navigate to a record, you can make changes to the data, update the record, and those changes are written to the database in place of what was originally there.

Project 15-3 Updating Data

Again, there are several ways to accomplish the updating of data in Dreamweaver. This project teaches you how to use the Record Update object to take advantage of Dreamweaver's built-in functionality. The process is very similar to inserting data, but there are a few key differences to pay attention to.

Step by Step

1. In the eFlea project, create a new page called updateitem.asp.

2. You will need two recordsets to select a record to update and to perform the update. They are the same two recordsets you used in Module 14 and earlier in this module. Create a recordset called users that contains all of the records in the Users table. Also, create a recordset called items that is filtered by the itemID equal to a URL parameter called itemID. It is from this recordset that the initial record is pulled.

3. From the Insert bar, select the Application tab and click Record Update Form.

4. Choose the eFlea connection.

5. Choose the Items table as the table to update.

6. Choose the Items table as well in the Select Record From table.

7. Select itemID as the Unique Key Column. This is the column that is guaranteed unique for every record in the items table so that the database knows when it locates a certain itemID, it is updating the proper record.

(continued)

8. Select a page to redirect to after the update is complete.

9. The bottom half of the page is just like the Insert Record project. Delete the itemID and data-entered fields, because they are not updatable. Format the labels so that they will display appropriately.

10. For the eFleaID field, change the Display As option to Menu. Click Menu Properties. Select the Name and eFleaID fields from the Users table to populate the list menu. The initial value should already be set to the eFleaID field from the items recordset.

11. Click OK to insert the object.

12. Save your page. When you run the page, you will be able to update a record and will then be redirected to the page you chose. Keep in mind that this update page requires that a record be selected, much as you learned to do when searching your database. The recordset on this page expects a URL parameter called itemID, which will be used to locate the record that you want updated.

Project Summary

Inserting and updating data have many aspects in common. One of the great things about using a program like Dreamweaver is the similarity that the different processes inherit when they are performed inside the same interface. This fact significantly accelerates the learning curve as you learn to get around inside Dreamweaver and begin to instinctively recognize how it expects you to respond.

CRITICAL SKILL
15.3 Delete Data from Your Database

There will no doubt come a time when there is data in your tables that you need to get out. It is old, incorrect, or in some other way no longer useful to you. There is not an application object for deleting a record, but there is a server behavior that acts much the same.

First, create a form on your page and populate it with at least one unique column (itemID in the case of the example used here). How much other data you choose to display is up to you. You should choose to display enough to give the user confidence that he or she is deleting the correct record, but every piece of data is not necessary. Use the appropriate form elements and bind your data to them as you learned in Module 13.

Use the same items recordset used in Project 14-3 to select the record from. Again, the recordset uses the itemID URL parameter, which must be passed in to locate the proper record.

Once your recordset is in place and the data is bound to the form elements, you can apply the Delete Record server behavior from the Server Behaviors panel.

Delete Record

Connection:	eflea	Define...
Delete From Table:	Items	
Select Record From:	users	
Unique Key Column:	ItemID	☑ Numeric
Delete By Submitting:	form1	
After Deleting, Go To:	search.asp	Browse...

OK
Cancel
Help

You should recognize all of the information that is being requested of you by this point. Select the connection and the appropriate tables in which the deletion will take place. Choose a page to redirect to and select the form that your fields exist in. This will set the proper form to be posted, causing the delete to occur.

CAUTION

Once you delete a record, it is for good. Unless you build in some functionality for capturing deleted data for warehousing in another table or database, you cannot reverse the effects of a delete. Keep this in mind when determining the level of access to these capabilities you will allow your users to have. It is often more advisable to "deactivate" a record by having a field that holds a Yes/No value for activity rather than allowing it to be deleted.

What to Take Away from This Module

As important as the insertion, updating, and deletion of records is in a data-driven site, you will likely be surprised to see how easily it can be done in Dreamweaver. This product truly has simplified the most repetitive tasks of data access, freeing you to spend more time on the parts of your site that are unique. Although there are other ways to perform these tasks that may become preferable in certain circumstances as you become more adept, these methods take full advantage of the built-in power of Dreamweaver. They should serve you well as you learn.

Module 15 Mastery Check

1. Where can you find the Record Insertion form in the Dreamweaver interface?

2. How does the database know that it is updating or deleting the proper record?

3. What happens after an insertion is complete?

4. What is the purpose of the manual label entry in a data-populated list menu?

5. Rather than deleting a record, it is often more advisable to _____ it.

6. What is a Unique Key column and why is it important?

7. What happens when you update a record?

8. Why should you delete any autonumber fields from the insert record field list?

9. A record identifier passed in the address of a page is known as a _____

10. What is the purpose of a redirect page?

Module 16

User Registration, Login, and Site Security

n a Web application, there is typically a page where users can register a username and password to use each time they log in to the site. There is also typically an access level set for users so that they will see only the parts of the site that they are meant to see. The Web is a stateless environment, so there has to be a way to keep track of users when they visit the site, and also to keep prying eyes away from parts of the site that need to be protected from casual users.

Dreamweaver MX provides built-in functionality to authenticate users and create login sections for your site. There is a submenu on the Server Behaviors menu named User Authentication. On this menu are four different server behaviors that work hand in hand with each other to create an authentication system for your site using a username, password, and an optional access group.

NOTE

User Authentication Server Behaviors are not available for PHP or ASP.NET as part of Dreamweaver MX, but there may be third-party extensions that allow this functionality.

The server behaviors that make up the system are as follows:

- **Log In User** Sets up a login page with username and password and checks the values against a database table

- **Restrict Access To Page** Keeps unauthorized users from accessing a page based on an access group stored in a database table

- **Log Out User**   Effectively kills the session of the user currently logged in by allowing the user to click a "log out" link

- **Check New Username**   Makes sure there are no users by the same name before adding the username to the database

This module introduces these four server behaviors and shows you how to build an authentication system for any site.

CRITICAL SKILL
16.1 # Understand the Concepts of User Logins and Sessions

Session variables were explained in Module 7, but they play an important part of the eFlea site, so we'll do a quick refresher. Session variables are available in all of the server models that Dreamweaver MX supports (ASP, JSP, PHP, ASP.NET, and ColdFusion) and have similar implementations in each. A session is created when a user requests a page with server-side code in it, such as an ASP page. The application server creates a session with a session ID number and keeps track of these numbers internally by storing the information in memory (or using the file system or a database, in some cases) and on the user's machine in a cookie. Every time the user asks for another page, the server looks at the cookie on the user's machine and then checks its memory to see if the user has a current session.

NOTE

Cookies are needed for session management, but the cookie contains only a session ID to identify the user to the server. The username and password information are stored securely in the server's memory. Some server models support sessions without the use of cookies, such as ColdFusion.

Session variables can store pertinent information about a user or about the current session. Because the Web is a stateless environment, session variables play a key part in keeping information "alive" as the user accesses various pages in the site. Although there are other methods of maintaining state, session variables are the easiest and most widely used method. Typically, a user is given an ID number or username that is stored in a database and used when he or she logs in to the site.

The Dreamweaver MX User Authentication server behaviors take care of the details of assigning the session variables. All you have to worry about is where to store the user information. Your database should have a table with user information. Among the columns of information stored about each user should be a username column and a password column. Optionally, you can have an access level column as well, to define the role the user will play in the site. Just be sure to give yourself full administration privileges so you can see the pages you build!

CAUTION

If you are using ColdFusion, you'll have to create an Application.cfm page to use session variables and the User Authentication behaviors. Your login page won't show any errors because of error handling built into the login code, but the code won't work without the Application.cfm page. There is a tech note on the subject at www.macromedia.com/support/ultradev/ts/documents/cfsessionerror.htm or in the online ColdFusion documentation at livedocs.macromedia.com/cfmxdocs/Developing_ColdFusion_MX_Applications_with_CFML/sharedVars5.jsp#1154679.

When the user logs in, the username and password are compared to values in the database. If they match any row in the database table, a session is created for the user. If the login fails, no session is created and the user is either given the boot or given the option to try again.

Before the user can be validated, however, he or she has to exist in the database.

CRITICAL SKILL

16.2 Set Up a Form to Insert a New User

The Web application will need a page where the user can register and get a username and password assigned that he or she will use each time he or she logs in to the site. Also, the page can set an optional access level for the user. The database can assign the access level of the user automatically when he or she registers the first time. This allows the user to see only those pages that have the same access level attached to them. A Web site administrator might have "admin" privileges, whereas a typical user of the site might have "user" privileges. These names are arbitrary names that you set up when you design your site, or they can be numbers.

To add a new user to the database, you'll need a Web form that accomplishes the following:

● Accepts input from two input fields for username and password

● Searches the database for the username so you won't have two identical usernames in the database

Adding a Validate Form Behavior

The two fields are required fields, so you'll have to add a Validate Form behavior to the Submit button. To add this behavior, you'll need to perform the following steps:

1. Click Submit.

2. If the Behaviors panel isn't showing, select it from the Window menu.

3. Click the plus (+) sign in the Behaviors panel.

4. Choose Validate Form from the drop-down list.

5. The Validate Form behavior has a check box for Required. Check this box for each element in turn.

Dreamweaver MX provides some basic form validations, but you can find others on the Macromedia Exchange that provide more functionality, such as checking for length and illegal characters.

TIP

Validating your form elements before submitting them to the database can prevent many errors down the line. Some forms will even validate that an address is valid before allowing any database insert. Other types of validation are for valid numbers, e-mail addresses, ZIP codes, states, or credit card numbers.

Adding the Insert Server Behavior

After the form validation is done and the form is ready to be submitted to the database, you can add an Insert server behavior to the page to insert the values into the database. You accomplish this by clicking the plus (+) sign on the Server Behaviors panel and choosing Insert Record from the drop-down list. This will bring up the next dialog box.

This dialog box allows you to set up your database insert using the form elements that are available on the page. The following fields need to be filled in:

● **Connection**   The database connection for the insert

● **Insert Into Table**   Drop-down list of all tables in the database

- **After Inserting, Go To** Allows you to redirect the user to another page after the insert

- **Get Values From** Drop-down list of forms that are available on the page

- **Form Elements** All form fields should be listed here. You have to set these up one by one by selecting the form element and choosing the appropriate column and appropriate data type underneath the text box.

After completing these steps, you can click OK and the server behavior will be applied to the page. The server behavior will automatically write all of the code to your page to complete the database insert.

Testing for a Duplicate Username

On a standard database insert, you can use the Insert server behavior from the Server Behaviors panel by itself. This insert action will be a little different, however, because you have to first search the database for the username. If it exists, you'll have to send the user back to the registration page to try again. This is accomplished by using the new User Authentication set of server behaviors. There is one called Check New Username, which is exactly what is needed.

NOTE

Even though the Insert server behavior is applied to the page before the Check New Username server behavior, the Insert will occur after the username has been tested against the database for duplicates. Dreamweaver MX automatically places the code in the correct sequence on the page.

In order to use this behavior, the form and Insert server behavior have to be applied to the page already. This server behavior will first check to see that the Insert behavior is in place. If it isn't, you'll see an error message telling you to put an Insert Record behavior on the page first. The Check New Username server behavior looks like this:

The dialog box for the Check New Username prompts you for two parameters:

- **Username Field**   The name of the field that has the username in it
- **If Already Exists, Go To**   Error page to send the user to if the name already exists

This server behavior automatically creates a recordset that will check your database for the username and redirect the user to a failed page if the username already exists. The recordset doesn't show up as a recordset in the Bindings panel; it is specific to this behavior. If you remove the server behavior from the page, the recordset will be removed as well.

Where to Send Failed Attempts

The Check New Username server behavior prompts you with If Already Exists, Go To. Where should you send the user? Your site can have a general error page that handles all errors, or a specific "failed new user" page that will do nothing but display a message to the user if the user has entered a username that already exists. You can place a message on the page: "Username exists. Please go back and choose another." Then put a link on the page using the text "<<< Back" to link back to the page that allows you to add a new user. This way users can see that they have entered a duplicate username and can click the Back link to return and try again.

Another method is to place the text directly on the page where the user has attempted to add the new username. The Check New Username server behavior will append the variable *requsername* to the end of the URL as a parameter so that the page will know there was an error. The text can be displayed on an error condition with an IF statement. This statement is in ASP VBScript, but can easily be adapted to your own language of choice:

```
<%
If (Request("requsername")<>"") Then
     Response.Write("Username exists: Please choose another")
End If
%>
```

The ultimate goal of any Web site is to make the user experience as painless as possible while providing for the best possible content. It's simply easier for the end user to see the error message on the page itself and not have to worry about clicking the Back button or clicking another link to reenter the information.

Progress Check

1. Will the User Authentication server behaviors work if cookies are turned off on the end user's machine?

2. What does the Check New Username server behavior do?

3. Which server behavior is applied to the page first: Check New Username or Insert?

CRITICAL SKILL

16.3 Create a Login Form to Log In a User

After building a registration page, you will also have to build the actual login page for the site. This page will allow the newly inserted user to officially log in and begin to use the site. A login page will typically perform several duties:

● It will check the database for the username/password combination.

● It will retrieve a unique identifier, such as a user ID number, for the person who has just logged in and store it in a session variable so that it is available to all pages the user might go to. In the case of the built-in Dreamweaver MX server behaviors, the username is the unique identifier.

● It will optionally retrieve an access group level for the user so he or she will only be allowed on the pages his or her access level is set for. The access level is typically stored in a session variable as well.

As part of the User Authentication server behaviors, Dreamweaver MX has a Log In User server behavior that will perform these tasks.

---

1. No. Because the User Authentication server behaviors rely on session variables, cookies have to be on.
2. It checks the database to see if the username already exists.
3. The Insert server behavior is applied to the page first.

This server behavior is applied to a page where you've already inserted a couple of form fields for username and password. The parameters for the server behavior should be filled in as follows:

- **Get Input From Form**   Drop-down list of all forms on the page

- **Username Field**   Text field on the page for username

- **Password Field**   Text field on the page for password

- **Validate Using Connection**   The database connection used in the validation

- **Table**   The database table in which the user information is stored

- **Username Column**   Column from the database storing username information

- **Password Column**   Column from the database storing the user password

- **If Log In Succeeds, Go To**   Page to be redirected to upon a successful login

- **Go to Previous URL (If It Exists)**   Allows the user to be redirected back to the page he or she attempted to view and was denied access to

● **If Log In Fails, Go To**   An error page the user is redirected to if the login fails

● **Restrict Access Based On**   Username and Password, or Username, Password, and Access Level

● **Get Level From**   The database column where the access level is retrieved from

Project 16-1 register.asp

The eFlea site will need a place where users can register to allow them to access the site. This project allows you to complete a registration page that will simply allow the user to choose a username and password and then test the values against the values already in the database.

Step by Step

1. Create a new blank page in Dreamweaver MX and save it with the name register.asp (or register.jsp or register.cfm, depending on your server model). It is always a good idea to save the page immediately in Dreamweaver MX so that any behaviors and server behaviors that you use will have the correct path information available.

2. Attach the page to the eFlea template by clicking Modify | Templates | Apply Template To Page. This will bring up the Select Template dialog box in which you can choose the site (eFlea) and the template (eflea_template).

3. Put some text on the page:

   ● **Register for the eFlea Site**

   ● **Choose a Username and Password to log in to the site**

4. Insert a form by clicking Insert | Form.

5. *Without moving your cursor out of the form*, click Insert | Table and choose a three-row, two-column table with 50 percent width and no border.

6. In the first column, place the text **Username** in row 1 and place the text **Password** in row 2.

7. In the second column, place a text field in row 1 by clicking Insert | Form Objects | Text Field. Name the text field **txtUsername** by accessing the Property Inspector.

8. In the second column, place a text field in row 2 by clicking Insert | Form Objects | Text Field. Name the text field **txtPassword** by accessing the Property Inspector.

9. Place a Submit button in row 3 by clicking Insert | Form Objects | Button. The default settings are fine for the button.

10. Click the plus (+) sign on the Server Behaviors panel and choose Insert Record. This will bring up the Insert Record dialog box.

11. The eFlea connection should already be defined for the site, so it should appear in the drop-down box. Choose this connection.

12. The Insert Into Table box should be set to the Users table of the database.

13. After Inserting Go To should be set to myFleas.asp. This is temporary. Later, you'll set this box to the login page.

14. The txtUsername and txtPassword fields should be listed in the Form Elements box. Make sure these point to the database columns that match the input—username and password. When you have this step completed, you can click OK to exit the Insert Record server behavior.

15. Click the plus (+) sign on the Server Behaviors panel again and then choose User Authentication | Check New Username.

16. Make sure the form field in the Check New Username server behavior is set to the txtUsername field.

17. Fill in the redirect page as register.asp. That will redirect the user to this page if a username already exists.

18. If you're feeling spunky, you can put a conditional message on the page and try a little bit of hand-coding in Code view to display the message if the username exists. The message should be "Username Exists: Please Choose Another." The next two tables show the code that can be placed before and after the text in Code view to make it a conditional region on the page.

Application Server	Code to Place Before the Message
ASP/VBScript	`<% if Request("requsername") <> "" Then %>`
ASP/JScript	`<% if(Request("requsername") != "") { %>`
ColdFusion	`<cfif url.requsername NEQ "">`
JSP	`<% if(request.getParameter("requsername") != "") { %>`
Language	Code to Place After the Message
ASP/VBScript	`<% End if %>`
ASP/JScript	`<% } %>`
ColdFusion	`</cfif>`
JSP	`<% } %>`

Project Summary

In this project, you learned how to add a user registration form to a Web page in Dreamweaver MX and also how to attach a Check New Username server behavior to that form. The Check New Username server behavior required the use of an Insert server behavior as well, so you learned how to apply the different server behaviors in the proper sequence.

NOTE

PHP and ASP.NET are not listed because Dreamweaver MX does not support User Authentication server behaviors for these server models.

CRITICAL SKILL
16.4 Implement Page Access Levels

The User Authentication Server behaviors were all designed to work hand in hand. Logging in a user by itself doesn't do anything—you have to use the login information to allow the user to access your other pages. By using the built-in Log In User behavior on the login page for your site, session variables that are set on this page can be retrieved with the Restrict Access To Page server behavior on other pages. In fact, you need to use the Log In User server behavior for the Restrict Access To Page server behavior to even work. With the Log In User server behavior in place on your login page, you can now restrict access to pages in your site based on this login information.

The Restrict Access To Page server behavior can be applied to any or all pages in your site. It works with username alone or with username and access level. A basic site that requires a login might use just the username to restrict users. A site with separate sections for administration, Web users, customers, special customers, or employees might have different access levels for the various pages in the site. If you are not implementing different access levels, your site will basically have two levels of access—anonymous (Web users) and registered (logged in.)

When you choose the server behavior from the menu, you are presented with the following dialog box:

Restrict Access To Page		☒
Restrict Based On: ○ Username and Password		OK
⊙ Username, Password, and Access Level		Cancel
Select Level(s): admin seller buyer	Define...	Help
If Access Denied, Go To: access_denied.asp	Browse...	

There are two radio buttons on the interface that allow you to choose to verify the user with username and password, or username, password, and access level. If you choose the second option, the Select Levels box is made active so that you can choose one or more access groups that are allowed on the page. The Define button allows you to define access groups for the site. These site-wide settings will be available to each page that you want to apply this behavior to. There is also a box labeled If Access Denied, Go To. This is the page to redirect any users that aren't authenticated.

Clicking Define brings up the Define Access Levels dialog box.

This box has the familiar plus and minus buttons on the interface to allow you to add or subtract access levels from the site settings. This box should contain all access levels available to the site.

This behavior can be applied to all pages in the site, one at a time. You can also copy the server behavior directly from the server behavior panel after you've applied it, and then paste it into other pages. By applying it in this way, you have the access levels already set.

If you have any pages that don't need to be restricted, you don't need to use this behavior on them.

CAUTION

If you have any HTML pages in your site, be sure not to attempt to use any server behaviors on those pages—the code won't work unless the page has a recognized server. Many users attempt to apply the Restrict Access To Page server behavior to all of their pages, never realizing that the code will never execute on an HTML page.

Progress Check

1. Where does the username, password, and access group information come from when a user attempts to log in?

2. Does the Restrict Access To Page server behavior use session variables, application variables, or server variables?

3. What is the prerequisite to using the Restrict Access To Page server behavior?

Log Out a User

The Log Out User server behavior closes the module on sessions. What this behavior actually does is kill the current session for the user. If the user has any desire to continue browsing in the site, he or she will have to log in again. The Log Out User server behavior looks like this:

There are two options for the server behavior:

● Log the user out upon page load.

● Log the user out by clicking a link.

The first option is the most basic—it will simply kill the session as the page loads. The second option allows you to set a link on the page that says "Log Out" or something similar. This is handy for intranets and situations where the user might leave the machine so that another person can use the machine and log in under a different username.

---

1. The database
2. Session variables
3. The Log In User server behavior has to be applied to a login page in your site.

After killing the session, you can set an optional page to redirect the user to upon logging out. If you are using the link option of the Log Out User server behavior, this is probably a good idea.

Ask the Expert

Q: **Because session variables don't work if cookies are turned off on the end user's machine, can you use the User Authentication server behaviors in such a situation?**

A: No. You would have to hand-code some additional functionality into your site for such users, or simply display a message that states that cookies must be enabled to access certain features of the site.

One method for authenticating users if they have cookies turned off is to pass a unique ID in the URL variable so that each page that has an access level set up on it can authenticate users using the URL variable instead of a session variable. This is a lot of work, however, because everything would have to be hand-coded. You could conceivably start by using the User Authentication SBs on the pages and then hand-code your additional functionality into the pages, but in a lot of cases hand-coding will cause the server behaviors to stop functioning as server behaviors—meaning that you will no longer be able to edit them from the Server Behaviors panel. The code will still work, but Dreamweaver MX will no longer recognize them as server behaviors that were generated by the program.

Q: **Can I use the session variables that Dreamweaver MX creates for the User Authentication server behaviors for other things?**

A: Yes. The session variables created by Dreamweaver MX are named *MM_Username* and *MM_UserAuthorization*. These variables can be placed into the Bindings panel for easy drag-and-drop functionality, or you can hand-code your script on the page using these variable names. The *MM_Username* variable, for example, can be used to greet the user by username, or it can be used when it is necessary to insert the username into the database for a transaction of some sort. The *MM_UserAuthorization* variable is useful for showing or hiding various sections of pages depending on access level. Some people will have one page that works for all users, but show certain parts only to authorized users. An example might be a button to edit a record that would be shown only to administrators; everyone else would just see the data.

What to Take Away from This Module

In this module, we've given an introduction to the User Authentication server behaviors. We explained how session variables are used to authenticate users on a Web page. Then we showed you how the built-in Dreamweaver MX server behaviors were used to create registration pages and login pages. Also, the Restrict Access To Page server behavior was introduced as a way to keep unauthorized users from accessing a page. Finally, we showed the use of the Log Out User server behavior.

✓ Module 16 Mastery Check

1. Which server models don't contain User Authentication server behaviors?

2. What is a session variable?

3. How does a session variable maintain state?

4. What is the client-side cookie's role in the User Authentication server behaviors?

5. How many form fields are necessary to authenticate a user?

6. Does Dreamweaver MX use a distinct user identification number or a username for its User Authentication server behaviors?

7. Can two users have the same username?

8. Does the Restrict Access To Page server behavior work on an HTML page?

9. If you don't have different access levels defined in your site but want to include a login page, how many levels of access are assumed?

10. Does the Log Out User server behavior remove the user from the database, kill the session, or destroy all the application variables?

11. What are the names of the session variables created by the Dreamweaver MX code when you allow a user to log in?

12. Which Dreamweaver MX behavior allows you to validate the form elements?

13. What are the prerequisites to applying a Check New Username server behavior?

Part IV

Adding Advanced Features to Your Site

Module 17

Extensions and
the Extension Manager

Dreamweaver MX comes with a lot of features out of the box. When you first start up Dreamweaver MX, you may be a little overwhelmed by how much needs to be learned. Once you become familiar with the program, however, you'll likely find that you frequently want it to do more. You might wish that you had your own menu of favorite help files accessible from the program. Or maybe you would like to be able to count how many words are in the document. Or maybe you need a form field validation function. These are examples of Dreamweaver MX extensions that can be downloaded and installed into the program to make the environment more productive.

17.1 Add Functionality to Dreamweaver MX with Extensions

Allowing the user to add new features to programs has been a long-standing tradition in the computer world. Many people build macros in Microsoft Word or Corel WordPerfect that allow them to enhance their work environments. The concept of the macro is taken a step further in Dreamweaver. A majority of the features that you have come to know in the program are completely within the grasp of the user.

For example, when you click Insert | Table, the Table dialog box pops up.

You've probably seen this dialog box 100 or 1,000 times by now. What you may not know is that the dialog box is nothing but an HTML file that is in your Configuration folder. In fact, all of the objects on the Insert bar (or Insert panel, if you are in Dreamweaver classic mode) are located in a folder named Objects. If you know what you're doing, you can go into these folders and modify the files within or create your own. The text fields in the dialog box are nothing more than standard HTML text fields. There is also a corresponding JavaScript file that does the dirty work of inserting the table code into your document.

This is possible because the designers of Dreamweaver and Dreamweaver MX have enabled the entire program with an *application programming interface (API)* that allows the user to build extensions to the program in HTML and JavaScript. Since most Web developers know a thing or two about HTML and JavaScript, the program can be extended using the languages that you already know. This was a stroke of genius that has truly paid off for Macromedia. Dreamweaver is currently the number one environment in the world for building Web applications, partly because of the open nature of the program that allows users to extend the functionality.

When a user creates an HTML file and enables it with JavaScript that ties in with the Dreamweaver API, he or she has created an extension. These extensions can be packaged and shared with other users, or they can exist solely for that user. Dreamweaver MX on my desktop is going to look completely different than Dreamweaver MX on your desktop. You can add whichever features you want to make your own work environment more productive.

Dreamweaver MX Extensions

Dreamweaver has been around since 1997, but Dreamweaver MX is a new product, debuting in May 2002. It combines elements of Dreamweaver, UltraDev, and CF Studio. UltraDev came out in 2000 and went through two versions (1 and 4) before being merged into Dreamweaver MX. Dreamweaver MX is based on the Dreamweaver platform, and anything that you can do in Dreamweaver or UltraDev you can do in Dreamweaver MX. This includes using some of the existing Dreamweaver 4 or UltraDev 4 extensions within the Dreamweaver MX program.

NOTE

There are some incompatibility problems with extensions written for Dreamweaver 4 or UltraDev 4 with Dreamweaver MX. Many UltraDev and some Dreamweaver 4 extensions will not work in Dreamweaver MX.

Dreamweaver extensions include (but aren't limited to) the following types:

- **Objects**   Objects are "things" that you can insert into your document, such as tables, form elements, Flash movies, or characters. In Dreamweaver MX, these are located in the Insert menu or on the Insert bar.

- **Behaviors**   If objects are the nouns, behaviors are the verbs. They perform an action on the page or to an object. These are usually JavaScript functions that are attached automatically to an event of an HTML element.

- **Commands**   Commands are versatile extensions that can do just about anything, and usually perform some sort of code manipulation on the page, such as Clean Up HTML.

- **Floaters**   Floaters are more properly named panels in Dreamweaver MX, and are all located in the Windows menu. These extensions are versatile because they can remain open while you work within Dreamweaver MX, unlike other extensions.

- **Inspectors**   These are the Property Inspectors that appear when something is selected or the cursor is within a section of code on the page.

- **Toolbars**   These are the buttons that reside above your document window. You can add new toolbars or new buttons to existing toolbars.

Most Dreamweaver MX extensions add to the core HTML functionality of the Web page, or add bits of JavaScript to make your page or objects do things. Dreamweaver MX extensions can also allow the user to insert and manipulate server-side code on the page. This code can be in the body of the document, in the head, or even above or below the <html> tags.

Dreamweaver MX extensions that perform server-side code manipulation include the following types:

- **Server behaviors**   These are to server-side code what behaviors are to client-side code. They typically enable an action that the page can execute on the server.

- **Data sources**   These are the things like recordsets, session variables, or JavaBeans that can display some information coming from the server onto the page.

- **Server formats**   These extensions allow you to format the server-side data in a meaningful way, such as adding a dollar sign and decimal point with two decimal places to a number for money formatting.

- **Connections**   These are the files that allow you to connect to a database. They contain the functionality needed by Dreamweaver MX to build a connection to the database.

These extensions are written in a similar fashion to the client-side Dreamweaver extensions, in HTML and JavaScript. Just as you can find the Table object in the Objects folder, you can find the Repeat Region server behavior in the Server Behaviors folder, along with all of the other items on the Server Behaviors menu. The server-side extensions are much more complex, however, and a thorough knowledge of JavaScript is going to be a necessity if you plan to modify any existing extensions or code your own extensions by hand. Also, much of the functionality of the server-side Dreamweaver MX extensions is in files that use a variation of XML syntax, so knowledge of basic XML syntax is good if you want to delve into the world of extension writing.

Progress Check

1. What languages do you need to know to write Dreamweaver and Dreamweaver MX extensions?

2. Which of the following extensions will work in Dreamweaver MX?

   A. Inspectors

   B. Objects

   C. Behaviors

   D. Server behaviors

   E. All of the above

CRITICAL SKILL

17.2 Use the Extension Manager That Comes Packaged with Dreamweaver MX

We've talked about extensions and how they can be built to add functionality to the program, but how do you keep track of them? Dreamweaver MX itself doesn't have any functionality to enable the packaging or installation of new extensions, but Macromedia has created a program that works with Dreamweaver MX, Fireworks, and Flash. It's called the Extension Manager, and it is installed by default with all of those programs.

NOTE

The latest version of the Extension Manager (as of the writing of this book) is 1.5. This version no longer supports Dreamweaver 3 or UltraDev 1.

---

1. HTML, JavaScript, and XML
2. E: all of the above

The Extension Manager

If you open your Macromedia folder on your hard drive, you'll see the Extension Manager folder alongside the Dreamweaver MX folder. If you have other Macromedia programs installed, such as Dreamweaver 4, Flash MX, or UltraDev 4, they will all share this one Extension Manager. The Extension Manager has several uses:

● It allows you to install extensions that you may have downloaded or found on a CD.

● It keeps track of all extensions that are installed by placing them in a list.

● It has a built-in extension packager to allow you to package new extensions.

● It allows you to import your extensions from a previous version, a networked remote computer, or another program.

The Extension Manager can be opened from several places. On a Windows machine, it is located in the Start menu under Macromedia Extension Manager. It will open automatically if you double-click on an extension package (MXP) file or an extension installation (MXI) file. It is also accessible from the Commands menu by clicking Commands | Manage Extensions.

When you open it, you should see a list of all extensions installed on your machine.

Turn extensions on and off   List of installed extensions

Remove extension   Go to Macromedia Exchange   Get help information

On/Off	Installed Extensions	Version	Type	Author
✓	CF Insert-Retrieve ID	1.1.0	Server Behavior	Thomas Muck
✓	CF XHTML Editor	1.1.5	Suite	Massimo Foti
✓	Dynamic Search SQL ASP	0.9.0	Suite	Thomas Muck
✓	Dynamic Search SQL ASP VB	1.0.2	Suite	Thomas Muck
✓	Dynamic Search SQL PHP	1.0.0	Suite	Thomas Muck
✓	Evaluate JavaScript	1.0.1	Floater	Thomas Muck
✓	Horizontal Looper	2.4.0	Server Behavior	Thomas Muck
✓	Live Preview	1.0.0	Other	Thomas Muck, DW Team
✓	QuickLink	1.0.5	Command	Thomas Muck
✓	Recordset Navigation Suite	3.5.5	Suite	Thomas Muck
✓	Send Email	1.0.0	Other	Thomas Muck
✓	Sort Repeat Region	1.6.6	Server Behavior	Thomas Muck
✓	Translated Source Viewer	1.0.1	Floater	Thomas Muck
	UltraDev Shopping Cart II DMX	2.1.1	Server Behavior	Joseph Scavitto

This is a Horizontal Repeat Region Server Behavior. You simply choose the number of rows and columns to display, and this behavior will build a table based on the number of rows and columns you chose. There's also an option to show all records, by clicking the radio button for "All records". It will work with the standard "Go to page" (next, previous,etc.) Server Behaviors. Works with ASP VBScript and JavaScript, JSP, and Cold Fusion-UD4 mode.

Version 2.4.0 works with DW MX.

Apply this Server Behavior by highlighting an area that contains a database column or columns and choose "Horizontal Looper 2" in the Server Behaviors menu. For further information, click the Help button on the extension.

Extension description

The Extension Manager also has these features on the File menu:

- **Install Extension**   Browse to an extension package on your computer.

- **Package Extension**   Package an extension you have written.

- **Submit Extension**   Submit your extension to the Macromedia Exchange.

- **Remove Extension**   Permanently remove an extension.

- **Import Extensions**   Import extensions from another program, such as Dreamweaver or Dreamweaver MX.

- **Go To Macromedia Exchange**   Open your Web browser and go directly to the Exchange.

NOTE

Import Extensions is a handy feature to allow the importation of extensions from other programs, but to utilize it properly you also have to make sure that the extension is compatible with the program you are importing to. Many Dreamweaver 4 and UltraDev 4 extensions do not work in Dreamweaver MX.

Packages

Extension packages contain all the necessary files for an extension. The packages are stored in a special format that can be read only by the Extension Manager. When you install an extension, the extension package is unpacked and the files are installed into Dreamweaver MX.

Along with the files, there is a Macromedia Extension Installation (MXI) file that gives the Extension Manager instructions on where to put the files and what to write to the menus. The Extension Manager reads the MXI file and receives instructions on how to unpack the files, put them into the correct locations within the Dreamweaver MX Configuration folder, and add any menu items that are included in the package.

CRITICAL SKILL
17.3 Download New Extensions

Extension packages can be obtained from a variety of places. You can go directly to the Macromedia Exchange (http://www.macromedia.com/exchange/) and search for extensions there, but that's only the tip of the iceberg. A Web search for "Dreamweaver MX extensions" will point to dozens of other useful sites where you can find extensions. Our site (http://www.dwteam.com/) has several as well.

After downloading an extension, you merely have to double-click on it to install it into Dreamweaver MX.

Project 17-1   Horizontal Looper Extension

To proceed with the project, you'll need to download the Horizontal Looper extension from www.dwteam.com/extensions/. The project shows you how to install an extension into Dreamweaver MX.

Step by Step

1. Go to www.dwteam.com/extensions/ and download the Horizontal Looper extension.

2. Save the file on your computer in a central location so that you'll be able to find it. There is a folder named Downloaded Extensions in the root Dreamweaver MX folder that is a perfect place to store and keep track of third-party extensions.

3. Browse to the folder where you downloaded the extension.

4. Double-click the extension file package. This should bring up the Extension Manager. If it doesn't, you may need to reinstall Dreamweaver MX or the Extension Manager.

5. The first screen you'll see is the Macromedia Extensions Disclaimer licensing agreement. You should read this before proceeding. It tells you, among other things, that the extensions are the property of the person who wrote the extension and that there is no warranty of any kind. In other words, install at your own risk and don't redistribute the extensions.

6. Click Accept to install the extension.

7. If you get any dialog boxes that tell you there is a file installed that is older than the one you are about to install, you can usually click Yes and safely overwrite this file.

8. If you get any dialog boxes that tell you there is a file installed that is newer than the one you are about to install, you should probably click No so as not to overwrite the newer file. It is up to the extension developer to make sure that these shared files don't conflict with each other. The Extension Manager doesn't keep track of different versions of files—only different versions of extensions.

9. You should now see a dialog box that tells you the extension has been installed successfully. Click OK.

10. One thing you will want to do is to read the information available in the Extension Manager after installing the extension. After clicking OK in Step 9, you'll see the information page of the Extension Manager, which lists descriptions of all extensions you've installed. One reason to read this is because the extension may be hard to find in Dreamweaver MX. There are many places where an extension can show up. In this case, the file will show up in the Server Behaviors panel. Armed with that information, you can start Dreamweaver MX and try to apply the extension.

11. If Dreamweaver MX is running, you'll have to shut it down and restart it to be able to use a new extension. This is because Dreamweaver MX loads references to all current extensions into memory when you start it up. When you install a new extension, Dreamweaver MX doesn't know about it until you restart it.

12. Open the Server Behaviors panel and click the plus (+) sign. The new extension Horizontal Looper should be in the menu.

(continued)

Project Summary

This project showed you how easy it is to add an extension to the Dreamweaver environment. After completing the project, you should be comfortable downloading and installing extensions into Dreamweaver MX.

CRITICAL SKILL
17.4 # Use the Server Behavior Builder

You might think that writing your own extension is out of reach. Even if you don't know how to build an extension using HTML and JavaScript using the Dreamweaver MX API, you can still create your own extensions by using a new feature of Dreamweaver MX 4 called the Server Behavior Builder (SBB). All you need to know is the code that you want to insert and a few details about how the SBB works.

Access the Server Behavior Builder

The SBB can be invoked by clicking the plus (+) sign on the Server Behavior panel.

There are two commands in this menu that apply to the SBB:

- **New Server Behavior**   Allows you to create a new server behavior. This is the command that we will concern ourselves with.

- **Edit Server Behaviors**   Allows you to edit an existing server behavior. This command shouldn't be used unless you really know what you're doing. You can easily cause damage to an existing server behavior, which may require you to reinstall Dreamweaver MX.

The SBB does all the work behind the scenes and lets you concentrate on the code that you want to put in the server behavior. The complex details of the JavaScript API are completely hidden when you use the SBB.

Create a New Server Behavior

The hardest part of building a server behavior using the SBB is finalizing the code that makes the behavior. Typically, a server behavior will have one or more variables that you will want to fill in at the time you use it. This might be a recordset name, a page name in your site, or even a form field name. In fact, the best feature of a server behavior is that you can customize the code with parameters to not only make the code reusable, but also give you the ability to insert the block of code with a click and have it appear on your page with your parameters filled in.

For example, if you wanted to make a simple server behavior that redirects a user if a form field isn't filled out, you could start with some VBScript code:

```
<%
If Request.Form(formelement) <> "" Then
  Response.Redirect("somepage.asp")
End If
%>
```

After you've tested the code and you are sure that it works, you should make the code identifiable as *yours*. You can do this by inserting a server-side comment in the script:

```
<% 'start of My First SB
If Request.Form(formelement) <> "" Then
  Response.Redirect("somepage.asp")
End If
%>
```

The reason for doing this is that you want your server behavior to pop up in the Server Behavior panel when you've applied it on the page. But you *don't* want it to pop up if there is a piece of code on the page that looks just like your code but isn't yours. If you make it identifiable to Dreamweaver MX, it will show up only when you apply it.

When the code is finished, and it works, you are ready to go to the next step—opening the Server Behavior Builder. The next project takes you through the creation of a simple server behavior using this sample code.

Project 17-2 Create a Server Behavior

Creating your own server behaviors is easy in Dreamweaver MX. You need to know only two things: the code that you want to apply to the page and where you want to put it. You have the code already from the previous section. Now you need to open the server behavior builder and create the server behavior. You can do this by following the steps in this project.

Step by Step

1. Click the plus sign (+) on the Server Behaviors panel.

2. Click New Server Behavior at the bottom of the menu. That will bring up this dialog box:

If you haven't used the SBB before, the dialog box will suggest a name for your new server behavior—Untitled1. You should change this to something meaningful, such as "My First SB" or "Redirect Empty Form Element." Call it **My First SB** for the sake of this project.

3. You can choose the server model in the dialog box as well, although it should pop up with the current server model in the drop-down list. This is an ASP VBScript server behavior, so make sure that this is the option showing in the drop-down box.

4. There is a check box to allow you to copy an existing server behavior; you should leave this unchecked.

5. Click OK. You'll see this dialog box:

This is where you will insert your code and your parameters for the server behavior. It is sitting there waiting for your input.

6. Click the plus sign to add a new code block. When you click the plus sign, you'll be able to name the new code block.

There will always be a suggested name when the dialog box pops up. In this case, the name is My First SB_block1. You can leave this alone for now. As you become more experienced, you'll develop your own naming conventions. After clicking OK, the Code Block box is filled in with some dummy code:

```
<% Replace this text with the code to insert
when the server behavior is applied %>
```

(continued)

7. Select the text and delete it from the box—your code will go in here.

8. Next, copy your code from the document and paste it into the Code Block box.

    So far, you have a piece of generic code that can be inserted into the document.

9. Here is the part that makes a server behavior more than just a glorified snippet—inserting parameters. The code you want to insert has two parameters—*somepage.asp* and *formelement*. These were the generic placeholders that we used to test the page. To turn these placeholders into parameters, simply select the text that you want to replace.

```
<% 'start of My First SB
If Request.Form(formelement) <> "" Then
  Response.Redirect("somepage.asp")
End If
%>
```

10. Next, click Insert Parameter In Code Block.

```
Insert Parameter in Code Block...
```

    That will bring up this dialog box:

```
Insert Parameter In Code Block                          [x]

A parameter is a placeholder in the code block for information        OK
that will be specified when the behavior is applied.
                                                                   Cancel

    Parameter Name:  Form Element                   [v]           Help
```

11. Fill in the name of the parameter. This should be a "nice" name, because it will be the name that is on the server behavior interface when you apply the server behavior. You can call this one Form Element. Do the same thing for the somepage.asp, giving it a name like Page To Redirect To. Now there are two parameters in the code:

```
<% 'start of My First SB
If Request.Form(@@Form Element@@) <> "" Then
  Response.Redirect("@@Page To Redirect To@@")
End If
%>
```

    The Server Behavior Builder automatically inserts @@ around each of the parameters.

12. The next step is to set the position of the code on the page. The code is inserted into the document in a set position each time. You might want the code to come at the beginning

of the file, or you might want it to come after a recordset is declared. Or, you may even want the code to display something on the page, in which case it would have to go into the body of the document. The Server Behavior Builder gives you a list of different places to insert the code. For this SB, you should choose Above The <html> Tag for the Insert Code drop-down box, and The Beginning Of The File for the Relative Position drop-down box.

Insert Code:	Above the <html> Tag
Relative Position:	Just Above the <html> Tag

The Beginning of the File
Just Before the Recordsets
Just After the Recordsets
Just Above the <html> Tag
Custom Position

13. Click Next to go to the next step—assigning server behavior controls (form fields) for the parameters. This is the easy part. Every parameter that you defined in the previous steps will be displayed in a list in the dialog box. All you have to do is assign a field to accept the user input from the drop-down list of available fields.

Generate Behavior Dialog Box

When this behavior is applied to a document, the behavior's dialog box will appear. Choose which form controls to display in that dialog box.

OK
Cancel
Help

Items in Behavior Dialog Box:

Parameter	Display As
Form Element	Text Field
Page To Redirect To	Text Field

Recordset Menu
Recordset Field Menu

Editable Recordset Menu
Editable Recordset Field Menu

CF Data Source Menu
Connection Menu
Connection Table Menu
Connection Column Menu

Text Field
Dynamic Text Field
URL Text Field
Numeric Text Field

Recordset Fields Ordered List
Text Field Comma Separated List

List Menu
Checkbox
Radio Group

(continued)

The full list of choices for available controls is as follows:

- **Recordset Menu**   A list of recordsets on the page
- **Recordset Field Menu**   A list of recordset fields in the recordset
- **Editable Recordset Menu**   A list of recordsets on the page with an option to type in a recordset name
- **Editable Recordset Field Menu**   A list of recordset fields in the recordset with an option to type in a field instead
- **CF Data Source Menu**   A list of ColdFusion data sources on the page
- **Connection Menu**   A list of connections available in your site
- **Connection Table Menu**   A list of tables available from a chosen connection
- **Connection Column Menu**   A list of columns available from a chosen table
- **Text Field**   A plain text field
- **Dynamic Text Field**   A text field with a lightning bolt icon next to it where you can assign dynamic data to the SB
- **URL Text Field**   A plain text field with a Browse button to allow the user to choose a URL or page from the site
- **Numeric Text Field**   A plain text field that allows only a numeric input
- **Recordset Fields Ordered List**   Complex control that allows you to choose from a list of recordset fields and have them returned to your server behavior as a list
- **Text Field Comma Separated List**   A plain text field that can accept multiple values separated by commas
- **List Menu**   A list menu that has to be set up manually by the developer after being applied to the page
- **Checkbox**   Adds a check box form element to the user interface
- **Radio Group**   Adds a radio group to the interface, but has to be set up manually by the developer

14. For this particular server behavior, choose the Text Field for the Form Field parameter, and choose a URL Text Field for the Page To Redirect To.

15. Click OK; you are finished. The new server behavior can be used in any ASP VBScript site. The finished server behavior looks like this:

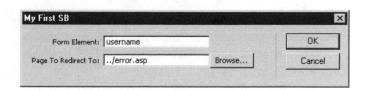

After applying the SB to a page, it will show up in the Server Behavior panel.

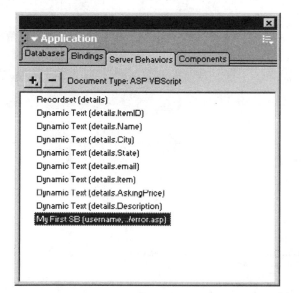

Project Summary

The Server Behavior builder is one of the timesaving features of Dreamweaver MX that can be used by anyone—not just extension writers. This project showed how easy it is to add a new server behavior to the Dreamweaver MX environment.

The Macromedia Exchange

The Macromedia Web site is a great place to look for information about Dreamweaver MX and other Macromedia products. There are numerous help files, updates, demos, and tech notes available. If you ever have a problem with some aspect of Dreamweaver MX, chances are good that there will be a tech note on the subject. A special part of the Macromedia site has been set up for extension developers to upload their extensions so that anyone can download and install them into their own computer. It's called the Exchange, and it's online at http://www.macromedia.com/exchange/.

To use the Exchange, you have to sign up first. Most of the extensions available on the Exchange are free, however. As of this writing there were more than 500 extensions available for Dreamweaver users. Many of these Dreamweaver extensions are fully operational in Dreamweaver MX. Many new server behaviors are becoming available as well.

Most of the extensions on the Exchange were written by third parties, but there are a number written by Macromedia as add-ons to the program. The Dreamweaver command Create Web Page Photo Album, available on the Exchange, is a good example of a Macromedia-written extension that adds more functionality to the program by building upon the existing Create Web Page Photo Album command, which is a standard Commands menu item.

NOTE

Make sure you check the compatibility of extensions before you download. Certain extensions, such as the Web Page Photo Album, are available in Dreamweaver 4 and Dreamweaver MX versions.

To find extensions on the Exchange, you can browse through a list of all the extensions, with handy column headings that allow you to sort by name, author, date, and other groupings.

The list is quite long, but on your first visit it is a good idea to see everything that is available. After you get an idea of what's there, you can go back from time to time and search for extensions that you might need for any given task. There is an advanced search page that will allow you to search the extensions by almost any criteria.

Each extension has its own page with the extension description and download links for the PC and Macintosh. There is also a place where you can rate the extension from 1 to 5. Extensions with the higher ratings are generally a safe bet, but you also shouldn't put much faith in the ratings. The ratings are completely unfiltered and contain random junk in addition to real comments.

You'll notice that some of the extensions have the Macromedia logo next to them—they are Macromedia-approved extensions. This simply means they've undergone more stringent testing and conform to certain Macromedia interface standards.

TIP

All extensions on the Exchange have been tested by Macromedia before being posted, so it is usually a safe bet to install an extension if you find it on the Exchange.

What to Take Away from This Module

In this module, you learned about extensions. Extensions are the Dreamweaver MX equivalent to macros, only much more powerful and far-reaching because they insert code into your Web pages using an API that you can learn how to program in HTML and JavaScript. You've also learned how to create simple extensions with the Server Behavior Builder. Finally, you were given a tour of the Macromedia Exchange, a central repository for extensions.

Ask the Expert

Q: How do I package a server behavior after it's been built so that I can share it with other people or post it on the Exchange?

A: There is an item in the Extension Manager Help menu called Creating and Submitting Extensions, which should put you on the correct path. Also, further information can be found in our other books, *Dreamweaver MX: The Complete Reference* and *Building Dreamweaver 4 and UltraDev 4 Extensions*. The process is fairly simple and requires that you know how to code the Macromedia Extension Installation (MXI) file format. The file is written using a variation of XML and can be easily edited in a text editor such as Notepad or BBEdit. Another option is to use an extension packager program.

A template for building your own MXI file, named Blank.mxi, is located in the \Macromedia\Extension Manager\Samples\Dreamweaver MX folder. Also, when you install a third-party extension, the MXI files are unpacked to the Extensions folder under Configuration. You can look at existing MXI files to see how they are written and easily adapt one for your own extension.

Module 17 Mastery Check

1. What is the three-letter file extension for an extension package for Dreamweaver MX?

2. Where is the Server Behavior Builder accessed from?

3. Can extensions be imported from other machines or other programs?

4. Do all Dreamweaver 4 extensions work with Dreamweaver MX?

5. What about UltraDev 4 extensions?

6. What is the URL of the Macromedia Exchange?

7. Is the Extension Manager a free program or a low-cost add-on?

8. What are some other programs that the Extension Manager works with?

9. Did Macromedia create all of the extensions on the Exchange?

10. Can anyone post an extension on the Exchange?

11. Which of the following are *not* typical extensions to Dreamweaver MX?

   A. Objects

   B. Commands

   C. Macros

   D. Toolbars

   E. Databases

   F. Server behaviors

Module 18

Troubleshooting
Your Site

W e can't leave you without spending some time talking about what is going to go wrong with your site. That's right, even with expert help like this book, you are bound to end up having some trouble. It is the way of the Web. Better to learn how to fix it than worry about it.

Some of these problems you will be able to fix yourself, and some of them you will likely have to contact your ISP or your system administrator about. The key to the successful technical support session, though, is knowing what the problem is and what to ask for. If you are well versed in the common problems developers have, you will be better prepared to avoid them or to have them fixed quickly.

These issues are broken down into two categories:

● Server errors

● Coding errors

CRITICAL SKILL
18.1 # Recognize Common Server Errors

No matter how careful you are, some problems are likely to pop up that you will need to resolve to get your pages working. If you are working with Internet Information Server and ASP, the errors you will receive can be rather confusing and not at all indicative of the true nature of the problem. Here are some of the more common errors that occur and their possible remedies.

Microsoft OLE DB Provider for ODBC Drivers Error '80004005' [Microsoft][ODBC Microsoft Access Driver] Operation Must Use an Updatable Query

80004005 errors usually indicate that your pages are having problems reaching the database. This one is usually because of the write permissions on the Windows NT directories. You can read from databases anywhere on the drive, but to write to them they have to be in a directory to which the IUSR_ user has write permissions. The IUSR_ user is the default user that your visitors access your site under. Speak to your ISP or network administrator about the proper permission to allow users to write to the database on your server; this will usually fix the error.

If this doesn't help, check to make sure you are not using joins in your query. Queries with joins are not updatable.

Error 0156: 80004005 The HTTP Headers Have Already Been Written to the Browser. Changes in HTTP Headers Should Occur Before Page Is Written

Your ASP page is most likely trying to redirect to another location after data has already been written into the HTML response stream. This can occur if programmatic decisions in the body of your page try to send the user to another page after elements of the current page are already on the way to the browser. To prevent this problem, put the following code at the top of your ASP page:

```
Response.Buffer = true
```

Microsoft OLE DB Provider for ODBC Drivers Error '80004005' Data Source Name Not Found and No Default Driver Specified

This error indicates that a data source name (DSN) has not been set up on the server. It is most commonly encountered the first time you upload a site to your remote server. You may have been developing and testing on a computer that has the DSN set up correctly, but you must also set one up on the server machine that maps the correct path to the database (or have your ISP do it for you).

Keep in mind that if you are using an Access database, the database file (.mdb file) must also be uploaded to a directory on the server. This directory may end up being different from the one on your development machine, and the server's DSN will need to be mapped appropriately. The directory needs to have read and write permissions set for the IUSR_*<machine_name>* user, or you will end up getting this 80004005 error.

NOTE

The IUSR_*<machine_name>* user is a special user that IIS sets up to accommodate visitors to your Web site. It represents the default user account that anonymous users will access to be allowed privileges on your server. The actual name of this user depends on the name you have given your computer. For instance, if the computer's name was WWW, this account would be IUSR_WWW.

Microsoft OLE DB Provider for ODBC Drivers Error '80040e14' [Microsoft][ODBC Microsoft Access 97 Driver] Syntax Error in INSERT INTO Statement

This error is often caused by a reserved word used as a column name. Make sure that you do not have a column named "date" or some other reserved word.

Microsoft OLE DB Provider for ODBC Drivers Error '80040e10' [Microsoft][ODBC Microsoft Access 97 Driver] Too Few Parameters. Expected 1

This error usually occurs when a column name in your query does not exist. Make sure that you are using the actual column names rather than alias names and that you have spelled all of your column names properly.

My Script Is Showing Up in the Browser Window Instead of Being Run by the Server

There are a couple of possible causes for this problem, which are illustrated in Figure 18-1.

First, you may have created an ASP page and given it an .html or .htm extension. This can be a common problem in Dreamweaver if you set .html as you default page extension and then save pages without specifying the .asp extension. This can be a stealthy problem because it

File	Edit	View	Favorites	Tools	Help								

Back Forward Stop Refresh Home Search Favorites History Mail Print Edit Discuss Real.com Create Mobil...

Links @ Best of » Address @ http://www.bettergig.com/CDOTest.html ▾ @ Go

< % if (cStr(Request("Submit")) <> "") Then Dim objCDO Set objCDO = Server.CreateObject("CDONTS.NewMail") objCDO.From = "ray@workablesolutions.com" objCDO.To = Request("to") objCDO.CC = "" objCDO.Subject = "Test" objCDO.Body = "test" objCDO.Send() Set objCDO = Nothing Response.Redirect("CDOtest.asp") End If %>

To: [   ] [Submit]

@ Done   🌐 Internet

Figure 18-1 Script error example

may cause your page to display correctly in the browser, but your ASP code is viewable in the source view of the page, exposing what should be secure information. Check the page you are trying to access to see that it has the proper extension.

TIP

It is sometimes wise to set the default extension to .html in your site definition. Many times a site has only a few pages that contain code that need to be processed by the ASP, JSP, or CF engine. Those pages, if given an .asp, .jsp, or .cfm extension, will access the engine and slow performance even though there is no code on them to run. Setting your default to .html in Dreamweaver can help you save regular Web pages as an HTML file. This processes more quickly, but you will have to remember to save your coded pages with the appropriate extension.

Second, you may have hand-written code that is not properly delineated with script tags (such as <% %>). If you have missed tags or mistyped them, portions of your code will be treated as text rather than being sent through the processing engine, and the code will display as text in the user's browser.

Third, it is possible that the mapping in your Web server that tells the server where to run script code has been corrupted. For example, when running ASP on Internet Information Server, the server knows from the .asp file extension that the file needs special handling. It gets instructions on how to process the file from the Applications Settings dialog box in the Web sites properties in IIS. In Figure 18-2, you will see that IIS holds a list of file extensions and the processing libraries that are needed to interpret them. If this list becomes corrupted, or the dynamic link library (DLL) that is referenced is missing or corrupted, the server may either display the ASP file or try to download it to the user's computer. Either one is bad.

To repair this problem, it is usually necessary to reload IIS or PWS on the problem computer. The ASP DLLs will be replaced with the reload, and the files should interpret properly.

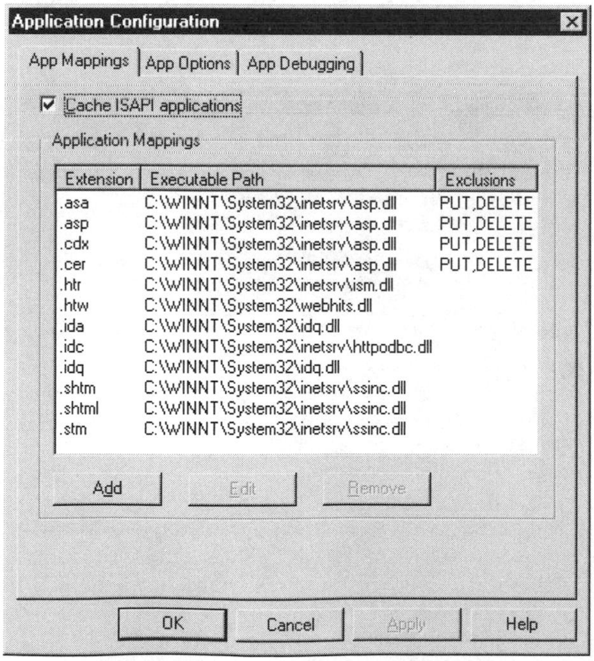

Figure 18-2 IIS File Extension Application Mapping window

CRITICAL SKILL
18.2 Debug Server-Side ASP

Internet Information Server provides a means for debugging server-side VBScript or JScript. To do this, you must enable debugging for the Web site in the Microsoft Management Console. In the properties for the site, choose Configuration on the Home Directory tab (see Figure 18-3) and enable ASP server-side debugging on the App Debugging tab (see Figure 18-4).

In your ASP script, include the debugging keyword appropriate to your server-side language choice immediately before the line where you want the debugger to pause. For VBScript, the keyword is *Stop*:

```
<%   Response.Write "The debugger will start right after this line"
     Stop
     Response.Write "The debugger has paused the page"
%>
```

For JScript, use the *debugger* keyword:

```
<%   Response.Write "The debugger will start right after this line"
     debugger
     Response.Write "The debugger has paused the page"
%>
```

Figure 18-3 IIS home directory configuration palette

When viewed in a browser, the page will pause and allow you to inspect assigned variables before they are passed on.

Those are just a few tips for troubleshooting and debugging script problems. Even if you are not using ASP, these issues should give you some idea of where to look to find what your problem might be. Remember to check permissions for your database, your file extensions, your database connection strings or DSN, and your tags and syntax, and you will eliminate most of the common errors that people encounter.

Progress Check

1. 80004005 errors usually indicate what?

2. When using a DSN connection, the DSN must be defined in what two places?

3. In order for the code on your page to be interpreted properly, it is very important that the page is saved with the proper _____.

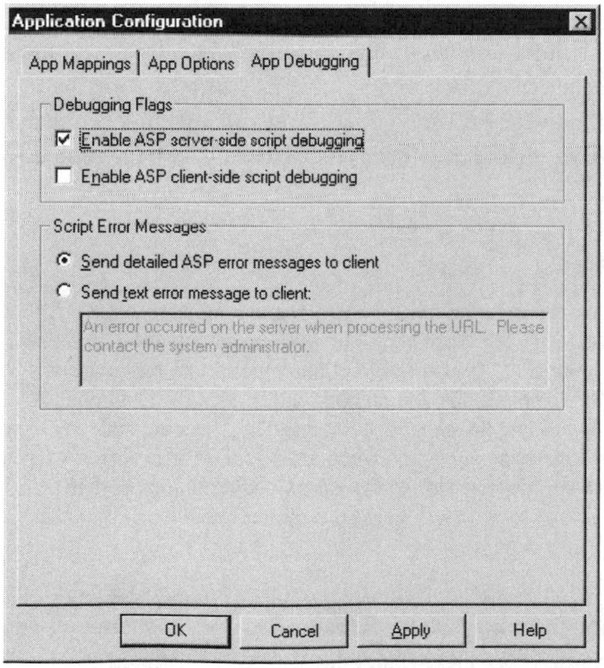

Figure 18-4 IIS application debugging palette

---

1. That your page is having trouble reaching the database
2. On the development machine and on the server
3. Extension (as in .asp, .aspx, .php, .cfm, .jsp, or .html)

Recognize Common Coding Errors

When you are working with Dreamweaver, you are most likely building Web applications that will contain two kinds of code: client-side (most likely JavaScript) and server-side (VBScript, JavaScript; or maybe Java, Cold Fusion, or PHP depending on the server model you are working with). Although each different language will have its own tricks and traps, several debugging techniques apply equally. Consider some general guidelines that will assist you when you start getting errors in your code.

Errors Come in Many Shapes and Sizes

An error can be one of several things. There are three common results when your code contains errors.

An Explicit Error

The explicit error occurs when an attempt to run a page results in a message from the server or the browser that something has gone wrong. Sometimes the code will try to continue running the best it can, and sometimes execution halts. Either way, you have a problem to find and repair.

The good thing about explicit errors is that they usually come with some indication of what went wrong and where it went wrong. They often include a line number that you can reference in your code that approximates the place at which the problem occurred.

NOTE

There is a notable exception to the helpfulness of the line number in an error message when you are dealing with database code and SQL statements. SQL statements are often built and stored in a variable. That variable is then passed into the database. If you have an error in your SQL statement, the line number that is displayed will often refer to the line at which the variable holding the statement is passed in. This can lead you to spend time troubleshooting the database connection when the actual error occurred when an incorrect SQL statement was assigned to the variable several lines earlier.

Nothing Happens

Sometimes an error will expose itself when nothing happens. Most likely this is when you expected something to happen, so the fact that nothing did should tip you off.

A common example is CDO Mail code. Very often, properties are set incorrectly to the CDO Mail object. For instance, CDO requires that a validly formatted e-mail address be used for the sender. If the sender is coming from a database field where no entry has been made or a user does not enter a valid e-mail address, the page will appear to run correctly, but no e-mail will arrive at the expected location. A look through the BadMail folder on Internet Information Server will likely reveal the problem because messages that are sitting there will not have a valid sender's e-mail address. In this case, you have identified the need to more closely monitor the source of the e-mail address because something you expected to happen did not.

The Wrong Thing Happens

The most dangerous kind of error occurs when your code appears to execute correctly, but it generates an incorrect result. This is common with financial applications where a lot of calculation is necessary. A misplaced parenthesis or an incorrect operator can wreak havoc on your results. Unfortunately, when you are dealing with complex mathematics, it is often not readily apparent that the result is something other than what you intended to code.

It is very important that you set up test cases that are manually evaluated and compared against your system's results to see that the results you are getting are in line with your expectations. Knowing exactly what you expect to happen is the only defense against coding errors that execute successfully but are not properly written to achieve the desired result.

Some Debugging Techniques

There are several techniques you can employ to ferret out bugs in your code.

Control Your Testing Environment

This goes back to the discussion in the previous section. It is important to set up a testing environment that is favorable to catching and correcting bugs. It should also include a desired resultset that can be compared with the output of your system. A successful testing plan should include all parts of the system. It must define a set of operations and what the expected outcome of those operations is so that anomalies in the system will be apparent as you test.

Simplify Your Code

If you are having trouble with a section of your code, your best hope is to isolate the lines that are causing the error. Software systems are complex enough now that the actual error could exist in one of any number of ancillary functions or in any line of pages of code. Two techniques will help you isolate the offending code.

First, reduce complex operations to their most basic components. Returning to the CDO Mail example, if you are trying to send a mail message with numerous recipients, file attachments, and a complex, variable-based message body, you are more likely to mask your error than if you use only the basic elements of the e-mail message: a sender, a recipient, and a simple message. Reducing your code to these basics and getting it to work will provide you with a platform on which you can rebuild the complexities that are required for your application. Continue to test as you add each piece. You will have found your error when you try to add some piece of functionality that causes the operation to fail.

Second, make use of watch points to identify where you are in the structure of your code. For example, if your client-side code contains several functions, you can use a JavaScript alert to identify where you are in the code. This is extremely useful to find out what branches of your code are being called. In a complex *SWITCH* statement, you could place the following line inside a branch of the section that you expect your code to fire:

```
Alert("Made it this far")
```

At the point at which your code hit that section (if it actually did), the alert box would appear, informing you that your expected result had occurred. Clicking OK would allow your code to continue. If that alert box never appeared, you would know that the correct section of code was not firing. This would help you isolate the specific commands that are causing the trouble.

This can be more difficult to do with server-side code. The message box commands that are usually available to you are not present in server-side versions of the language, because even if they were to run, the alert or message box would appear on the running machine, the server, and be of no use to you. It is possible to apply the same idea, though, by using a response object of some kind to write text to the browser at various times during program execution.

This can be extremely useful when troubleshooting complex SQ statements. Sometimes SQL statements that are built up within your application contain very minor, easy-to-fix syntax errors, but since you do not see the completed SQL statement (it is generated dynamically from the choices your user makes) you have no way of knowing the problem exists. You can use a response object to write a text version of the SQL command out to the browser during testing that will allow you to identify the problem and fix it.

Keep an Open Mind

Always keep an open mind toward the problem you are having and toward its possible solutions. Remember that errors are common, and it is expected that you will need to test and debug your code. Allow for the fact that the error could be your fault and could be staring you in the face. But also allow for the fact that the problem could be a bug inherent to the platform you are using and may require the help of a technical support professional from the vendor company.

The solution could be a simple syntax fix, or it could be a reworking of a section of code because of poor design or implementation. The one and only goal here is code that is as error free as possible. Whatever steps get you to that goal as efficiently as possible are the steps you should take.

Improvise

No matter how well you have planned your site, you must retain the ability to improvise when the need arises. Be willing to try a new approach or to rewrite a section if a technique you are trying just isn't working. Doggedly trying to force something that "should work" to adhere to your will does not work well with computers. There is often more than one way to accomplish something, and you will do well to remain willing to try a different way when your preferred method just isn't cutting it.

CRITICAL SKILL
18.4 Avoid Common Coding Errors

Following are some common coding errors that you can look out for. They are not specific to any language, but should apply equally to all platforms to some degree.

- **Using improper variable names**   Make sure that you use the correct variable names, especially in a weakly typed language like VBScript. A language that does not require you to declare a variable before it is used will simply create a new and different variable if you mistype a variable name. For instance, if you have a variable called *strName* and you want to set its value to "Ray," but you accidentally type **strNane = "Ray"**, you will suddenly have a variable called *strNane* with that information in it, and your program will not respond as you expect when you ask it for the value in *strName*.

- **Using improper function names**   Closely related is the mistaken use of functions that do not exist, or calling the wrong function during an operation.

- **Using braces improperly**   If the language you are using requires braces—{ and } —make sure they are in the right place and are properly balanced (meaning that opening braces have appropriate closing braces).

- **Leaving quotes off of strings**   If you are assigning strings to variables, they must be enclosed in quotes or they will be treated as variable names.

- **Confusing operators**   For instance, you must use the assignment operator (=) for assigning a variable and the comparison operator (==) when comparing two values.

- **Using incorrect object names**   It is important to refer to objects correctly, especially when referencing the document object model. For instance, refer to document.form1.textbox.value, not to window.form1.textbox.value.

- **Using incorrect case**   Especially with JavaScript, which is a case-sensitive language, you must watch your case. The variable *A*, for instance, is entirely different than the variable *a*, and they cannot be substituted for each other.

- **Incorrect query formatting**   When building SQL statements, you should also watch for a couple of things, such as using single quotes (not double quotes) around your strings but not around your numbers and knowing how your database platform likes to see dates.

Project 18-1 Learning to Debug

You will be better prepared to handle many of the bugs you are likely to encounter if you have seen a few of them in action. This project guides you through a simple JavaScript routine and highlights the errors that are received as we introduce mistakes into the code.

Project Goals

By the end of this project, you will

- Understand how common client-side coding errors can occur
- Learn to recognize the cause of common errors
- Learn some techniques for debugging your code

Step by Step

1. To complete this project, you will need a text editor and a browser open on your computer. (You can use Dreamweaver if you are comfortable with switching back and forth into its code editor.) Create a new file in your text editor and type the following code:

```
!DOCTYPE HTML PUBLIC "-//W3C//DTD HTML 4.0 Transitional//EN">>
<html>
<head>
<title> Debugging Test </title>
</head>
<body>
<script language"Javacript">
<!--var a
if (3==3){
document.write("The numbers are the same");
}
//-->>
</script>
</body>
</html>
```

2. This is a very simple HTML page that checks to see if 3 is equivalent to 3 (which it always will be) and, if so, displays a message in the browser that says the numbers are the same. Save this file as debugtest.html in a folder on your computer. Open a browser and choose File | Open. Navigate to this page on your hard drive and select it so that your browser opens the page. Because 3 is equivalent to 3, the message should appear in your browser as shown here:

```
Debugging Test - Microsoft Internet Explorer
File   Edit   View   Favorites   Tools   Help
Back  -     -           Search    Favorites    History
Links    Customize Links     Free Hotmail     Windows
Address    C:\DBug.html                                    Go

The numbers are the same




Done                                                My Computer
```

3. Now, start to introduce some errors into the code to see how it reacts. First, remove the closing brace from the *if* statement, like this:

```
if (3==3){
document.write("The numbers are the same");
```

4. Save the page and refresh your browser, and you will receive an error message. The good thing is that this error message is fairly descriptive and even tells you what line to look on. This illustrates the importance of watching your syntax carefully.

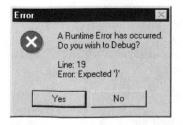

(continued)

5. Next, after replacing the }, change one of the 3s to a 4, like this:

```
if (3==4){
```

6. Now, you know that 3 is not equivalent to 4, but consider this in the context that you may have just mistyped it or you are actually checking variables against each other that should be, as far as you know, equivalent to one another. Save the file and refresh your browser. This time you will not get the message, you will get a blank browser screen, but you expected that.

7. You can use the alert box technique discussed earlier to help in a situation like this when you are trying to debug an *if...then* statement. Add the following alert box to your code:

```
if (3==4){
alert("Made it this far!");
document.write("The numbers are the same");
}
```

8. This alert box will run if the code makes it inside the braces of the *if* statement. This is particularly useful when the *if* statement has *else* branches to find out which branch is running. As it is, the alert box in this code will not fire, so you know that your expression is not evaluating as true (because 3 is not equivalent to 4). Change the 4 back to a 3, save your page and refresh the browser, and the alert box will fire, letting you know that part of the code is firing. After you click OK on the alert box, the message will display in your browser.

9. Next, replace the 3, but change the == (double equal sign) to = (single equal sign):

```
if (3=3){
```

10. Save the page and refresh your browser. You will get an error message stating that you can't set a value to a number. This illustrates the difference between the = and the == operators in JavaScript. The = operator attempts to set the right side value to the object or variable on the left side. If it cannot do so, this error is thrown. Luckily, you were trying to perform an operation that is not allowed anyway, so you were given an error. Try it a different way.

11. You will notice that the code prepared a variable called *a* that has not been used yet. Change your code to the following to incorporate the variable:

```
<!--var a
if (a==3){
alert("Made it this far!");
document.write("The numbers are the same");
}
//-->>
```

12. Save your page and refresh the browser. The code will execute fine, but because the variable *a* has not been assigned a value, it is certainly not equivalent to 3, and the alert box and message are not displayed. This is a good example of nothing happening, as was discussed earlier. You may expect code within the *if* statement to execute, and when it doesn't you will go looking for the reason. The reason is that a value that you expected to be set was not. The alert box is very helpful because the fact that it did not run alerts you that the problem begins before the code that you want to execute is ever reached. Although you may have started looking for a problem inside that code, this method saves you from the trouble until you are sure that the code is even running.

13. As a good illustration of the wrong thing happening, make one more change to your code. Change the == operator to an = and see what happens when you save the page and refresh:

```
<!--var a
if (a=3){
alert("Made it this far!");
document.write("The numbers are the same");
}
//-->>
```

14. You may be surprised to see that the page fires the alert box and displays the message. This is because, rather than checking for the value of *a* as the == operator does, the = operator attempted to assign the value 3 to the variable *a*. Because this is a legal operation and the code was able to make this assignment, the *if* statement executed. The trouble is, rather than checking a value that should have already existed, the code is changing the values, leaving you with two problems: inappropriately executed code and a change value in variable *a*. These types of errors are extremely dangerous and difficult to track. Check your operators carefully.

Project Summary

There is no better way to prepare for a job like debugging than to actually experience it firsthand. This project has presented you with some common error messages and their resolutions. Although you will not remember everything that was covered, the fact that you have seen it before will be a great help when you run across errors like this in your own code.

Progress Check

1. True or False: The variable *a* is the same as the variable *A* in JavaScript.

2. Which operator is used in JavaScript to compare two values?

3. What technique can be used to allow you to isolate the problem you are having?

What to Take Away from This Module

Programming Web applications is a rewarding experience, precisely because it is not easy to do. Between server setup issues and coding mistakes, you are likely to end up having to troubleshoot some part of every program you write. Avoiding some of the more obvious traps discussed in this module will save you a lot of headaches and allow you to spend your time on more important issues.

✓ *Module 18 Mastery Check*

1. What does balancing braces refer to?

2. What are three common forms that an error can take?

3. The common HTTP headers error can be solved with what line of code?

4. Leaving the <% and %> delimiters out of your ASP code will cause what problem?

5. Which of the three types of errors discussed in this module is the most dangerous?

6. The variables A and a are not the same in JavaScript because JavaScript is a _____ language.

7. What two steps can you take to simplify your code when troubleshooting?

8. What common errors often result in the error "Operation must use an updatable query"?

9. Most errors can be classified into what two categories?

10. What two common issues should you keep in mind when formatting your queries?

---

1. False
2. == (double equal sign)
3. Simplify your code

Part V

Appendixes

Appendix A

Mastery Check Answers

Module 1: Dreamweaver MX: Your Connection to the Internet

1. The series of numbers that are assigned to every host on the Internet is known as an
   _____.

   IP Address

2. Which of the following is the scripting language that you would use with the ASP server model?

   A. Visual Basic Script

   B. Perl

   C. C++

   D. JavaScript

   E. Tcl/Tk

   F. Java

     A and **D** are correct.

3. The protocol used to send mail over the Internet is _____.

   SMTP

4. What features of Cold Fusion make it a popular choice for those with experience building static Web pages?

   Based on a series of tags, much like HTML.

5. What is the protocol that is used to provide communications for the World Wide Web?

   HTTP

6. A collection of HTML documents that are related to one another and need to be displayed together form a _____.

   Web site

7. What type of server provides a place to post your pages for review before they go live?

   A. A Testing server

   B. A Staging server

   C. An Interim server

   D. A Push server

     B is the correct answer.

8. **Which protocol is responsible for making sure that all of the packets of a Web transmission have arrived?**

   A. Transmission Control Protocol

   B. File Transfer Protocol

   C. Internet Protocol

   D. Hypertext Transmission Protocol

   A is the correct answer.

9. **Name three server-side languages that could be deployed on a Linux Server.**

   PHP, ColdFusion, JSP, ASP (using a third-party variant)

10. **What programming language is supported by JSP?**

   Java

Module 2: The Dreamweaver MX Environment

1. **What are the three prongs of Dreamweaver's approach to Web page construction?**

   Typing in the design window, using objects to insert code, and hand-coding in the Code View window

2. **What are the three parts of the implementation of a behavior?**

   An object, action, and an event

3. **What is the main purpose of an object?**

   To accept input from the user and place the appropriate HTML into the page

4. **Many of Dreamweaver's features, such as objects, behaviors, and commands, are made available on _____.**

   Panel groups and panels

5. **What are the four views available on the Dreamweaver Site Panel?**

   Local View, Remote View, Testing Server, and Map View

6. **The _____ provides a way to view and select the page hierarchy as you edit your pages.**

   Tag Selector

7. **_____ Mode allows you to draw tables and cells on your page.**

   Layout

8. **Extensions that place javascript actions onto your page are known as** _____

Behaviors

9. **What is the purpose of the Download Indicator?**

It gives you a pretty good idea of the average download time your users will experience.

10. **You can test your page at different screen sizes using the** _____

Window Size Pop-Up Menu

Module 3: Creating a Web Page

1. **What are the legal characters that you can use in a Web page name?** _____

Letters, numbers, underscores, and dash characters. Spaces are legal, but not recommended.

2. **Which of the following are deprecated by the W3C?**

A. CSS

B. <font> tags

C. <table> tags

D. <b> tags

E. ASP

F. Java

B and **D** are the correct answers.

3. **The two most widely used image formats are _____ and _____.**

GIF and JPG

4. **Which image format is better for photos and which format is better for graphics?**

JPG is better for photos; GIF is better for graphics.

5. **What are the tags used for tables, table rows, table headings, and table cells?**

<table>, <tr>, <th>, <td>

6. **Dreamweaver includes a special mode that allows you to draw complex table structures on your page. It is called** _____.

Layout view

7. **A transparent graphic used to keep table cells at the proper width is called a** _____.

Spacer image

8. **What is a newer graphic format that shows great promise but is not yet supported in all browsers?**

PNG

9. **Dreamweaver will open with a new Untitled Page created for you. What is the first thing you should do before working with this page?**

A. Name it.

B. Save it.

C. Add a background image.

D. Put a table on it.

E. Switch to Layout view.

B is the correct answer.

10. **For what reason are sections of code indented in Code view?**

For readability.

Module 4: Creating a Web Site

1. **What setting in Dreamweaver's Site Definition panel can be used to increase performance during development?**

The auto-refresh setting

2. **True or False. You should always set your default page extension to the server model you are using for the site.**

False

3. **Dreamweaver's Check Links feature can identify pages that have no other pages linked to them. These pages are known as _____.**

Orphaned files

4. **A graphical representation of the site can be viewed using the _____.**

Site map

5. **To put a file means what?**

To upload your file from the local machine to the remote server

6. **What is the purpose of site synchronization?**

To keep the local version of your site consistent with the remote version of your site. Synchronization can go both ways—synchronize local site or synchronize remote site.

7. **How is the site panel expanded and collapsed?**

   The site panel has a button on the far right end that allows you to expand and collapse the panel.

8. **True or false: Check-in and check-out allows Dreamweaver users to lock files from being edited by other programs.**

   False. It only locks against other Dreamweaver users.

9. **True or false: It is a good idea to edit remote files directly.**

   False. It is never a good idea to edit production files directly. Always test locally and debug before uploading to a remote server.

10. **The .lck files created by Dreamweaver are used by which feature?**

    Check-in/check-out

11. **True or false: Get and put are only available from the Site panel.**

    False. It is also available from the Site menu in Dreamweaver or from the Document toolbar.

12. **True or false: Dynamic pages like ASP, CFM, or PHP can be browsed in a browser from the file system, like c:\inetpub\wwwroot\mypage.asp.**

    False. They must be browsed through the application server, as in http://127.0.0.1/mypage.asp.

Module 5: Adding Content to Your Site

1. **What three methods can be used to apply a template to a page?**

   Create the page from the template initially, apply a template to an existing page, drop a template onto a page from the Assets panel

2. **When exporting a page design from Fireworks to Dreamweaver, the Fireworks graphic is divided into portions called _____.**

   Slices

3. **An image that responds to a user's mouse contacting it is known as a _____.**

   Rollover image

4. **What happens to existing content when a template is applied to a page?**

   It can be either deleted or moved to a single editable region of the template

5. **A combination of what three things is used to create pages in Dreamweaver?**

   Text, assets, and Dreamweaver objects

A

6. **When creating slices in Fireworks, the programs will automatically name them for you. You can change the assigned names on the _____.**

   Properties Inspector

7. **When creating a Dreamweaver template, you will identify a content area known as an _____.**

   Editable Region

8. **Templates are used primarily to give your site a _____.**

   Consistent look and feel

9. **Creating a simple page in Dreamweaver is done with a combination of what?**

   Text, Assets, and Dreamweaver Objects

10. **If a link on your page leads to a page outside your site, you should make sure to use what?**

    Fully Qualified Path, like http://www.somewhere.com

Module 6: Planning the Site

1. **Will the Site Map feature of Dreamweaver work without a home page?**

   No. The Site Map needs a home page on which to base its diagram, and you will be prompted to create one if it does not exist.

2. **How are design notes stored in Dreamweaver?**

   They are stored as XML files with a .mno file extension in the _notes folder under your site root.

3. **Does Dreamweaver's Find/Replace work outside the site you are currently working on?**

   Yes. It can search through any directory on your computer.

4. **Do all the files in your Site Window show up in the Site Map?**

   No. The pages have to be linked in some way to the other files in the Site Map.

5. **What is a regular expression?**

   A regular expression is a pattern that identifies character combinations within text.

6. **Name two site design no-nos.**

   Tiled graphics that obscure the text; light-colored text on light-colored backgrounds.

7. **What are some questions that you need answered about your target audience?**

   Do they have computers?; how much time do they spend on the Web?; what browsers do they use?; and how do they hear about Web sites?

8. **What collaboration features help make sure that team members do not overwrite each other's work?**

   Check-In/Check-Out.

9. **Page load times should be limited to about _____ on a 56K modem.**

   10 to 20 seconds

10. **What is a translator?**

    An extension that causes code to be displayed in a friendly format in Design view

Module 7: Essential Language Components

1. **What do letters in ASP, JSP, PHP, and CFML stand for?**

   Active Server Pages, Java Server Pages, Personal Home Page, and ColdFusion Markup Language

2. **What does the query string do?**

   Allows you to pass variables in name/value pairs in the URL

3. **Which of the following languages are case-sensitive: Java, VBScript, JavaScript, CFML, PHP, C#?**

   Java, JavaScript, PHP, and C#

4. **Which languages have typed variables of the languages mentioned?**

   Java and C#

5. **Can a server retrieve a cookie that was set by another Web site?**

   No, it can only access cookies that it set itself

6. **Can PHP be run on a Windows server?**

   Yes

7. **Can ColdFusion be run on a Linux server?**

   Yes

8. **What database does Dreamweaver MX allow you to use with PHP?**

   MySQL

9. **Which of the following server technologies allows you to send e-mail using the core language components: PHP, ASP, ColdFusion?**

   ColdFusion and PHP

10. **True or false: Sessions in ASP require that cookies be present on the client machine.**

    True. Cookies are a requirement.

11. **What does EJB stands for?**

    Enterprise Java Beans

12. **True or false: Always use the root user when accessing a MySQL database from a Web application.**

    False. You should never use the root user from a Web application.

13. **True or false: ASP pages work without change in ASP.NET.**

    False. ASP.NET is a completely new environment and requires a relearning of basic Web application development.

14. **What is the string concatenation character in PHP?**

    The dot (.) is the string concatenation character.

15. **True or false: PHP can run natively on the Macintosh.**

    True. As of Mac OSX, PHP will run on the Macintosh operating system.

Module 8: Creating a Database

1. **What is the autonumber data type designed to do?**

   Provide a unique identification number to each new record added to a table

2. **Which data type forces all numbers to a two-decimal-place representation?**

   Currency

3. **Which normal form holds that no duplicate information is allowed in the database?**

   The third normal form

4. **What types of table relationships are there?**

   One-to-one; one-to-many; many-to-many

5. **What is special about a primary key?**

   It has been arbitrarily designated as the primary key from the list of available candidate keys

6. **What data type is used to provide a unique ID for a record in Microsoft Access?**

   Autonumber

7. **You can have the database enter a value for you using what property?**

   Default value

8. **To keep from overwriting data while updating the features of an Access database, it is best to** _____**.**

   Temporarily shut down your site

9. **True or False: It is wise to store as much information as possible in a field, separating the data by commas if necessary.**

   False. Each field should contain only one item of data.

10. **How would you define a one-to-many relationship?**

    A one-to-many relationship means that one record in one table can relate to many records in another table.

11. **What number on currency would be equivalent to a primary key—the denomination or the serial number—and why?**

    The serial number, because each serial number is unique

12. **How does a many-to-many relationship work in a typical database?**

    It works using three tables—the two tables that you want to relate, and a third table containing lookup values (primary keys) for the other two tables.

13. **What type of form field is typically used to display yes/no answers?**

    A check box

Module 9: Choosing Your Database and Connecting to It

1. **What is meant by a local database connection?**

   Connection to a database on your local machine rather than on your remote server

2. **What do the letters ADO stand for, and what is the significance of ADO for ASP developers?**

   ActiveX Data Objects. This is the primary connection method that is used to create recordsets and other forms of data access for ASP developers.

3. **What do the letters ODBC stand for, and what is ODBC's purpose?**

   Open Database Connectivity. It is an agreed-upon standard method of defining a database connection on a Windows machine.

4. **Where is the connection information for your site located in the Dreamweaver MX environment?**

   Dreamweaver MX stores the information in a special folder in your Web site named Connections.

5. **How does Dreamweaver MX communicate with the database?**

   Dreamweaver MX uses HTTP to connect to the database through a special file on the server that queries the database for information about that database.

6. **What database does Dreamweaver MX allow you to use for PHP development?**

   Dreamweaver MX allows only the use of MySQL for PHP development.

7. **True or false: Microsoft Access will handle thousands of simultaneous users.**

   False. MS Access is useful for a handful of simultaneous users before moving up to SQL Server.

8. **Which of the following database servers are available for free: Oracle, PostgreSQL, DB2, MySQL?**

   MySQL and PostgreSQL

9. **True or false: The database panel in Dreamweaver MX allows you to create databases.**

   False. It allows you to create connections to a database.

10. **How does Dreamweaver MX make a connection to a database?**

    Through HTTP, like a Web page

11. **True or false: ColdFusion MX uses ODBC drivers natively.**

    False. ColdFusion MX uses JDBC drivers, but can connect to ODBC through a bridge.

Module 10: A SQL Primer

1. **Name the four essential parts of a basic *Select* statement.**

   The *Select* keyword, an * or list of fields, the *From* keyword, and a table or tables from which the data is to be queried

2. **What is the definition of an expression in the context of SQL?**

   Anything that returns a value, such as 2 + 2 or variable1 * variable2

3. **What are the three types of action queries discussed in this module?**

   Insert, Update, and Delete queries

4. **What function would you use to return the total of all of the payments made by a certain customer?**

   The SUM function

5. **What type of join returns only those records that have matching data in two tables?**

   An inner join

6. **When you will need to filter your data by a value provided by the user of the application at run time, what will you use in your SQL statement?**

   A variable

7. **Name two types of subqueries discussed in this module.**

   The In Statement and the Embedded Select Statement

8. **+, *, and / are examples of _____ .**

   Operators

9. **What does the acronym SQL stand for?**

   Structured Query Language

10. **Sum and Avg are examples of _____ .**

    SQL Functions

Module 11: Displaying Your Data

1. **What feature of Dreamweaver MX allows you to edit your pages while viewing real data from your database?**

   Live Data view

2. **What server behavior can be used to display more than one record at a time on your page?**

   Repeat Region

3. **What feature of Dreamweaver makes it particularly suited for team development?**

   The fact that design and data are kept separate

4. **Additional server behaviors are available where?**

   On the Macromedia Exchange and a variety of locations around the Web

5. **How can you tell that a portion of your page is included in a Repeat Region?**

   It will be indicated by a small tab labeled "repeat"

6. **List three steps to getting a recordset on your page.**

   Define a connection, create a basic SQL statement, filter the selection to get just the records you need

7. **What are the three position indicators supplied by Dreamweaver for your recordsets?**

   First Record Index, Last Record Index, and Total Fields

8. **You can quickly preview a page in a browser by pressing what hotkey?**

   F12

9. **Dreamweaver makes it easy to scroll through your recordset with which set of Server Behaviors?**

   The Move To Record server behaviors

10. **A set of results sent by a database in response to a query is known as a _____.**

    Recordset

Module 12: Searching Your Data

1. **What is the purpose of a form on a Web page?**

   It allows the user to enter some text that can be sent to the server for processing.

2. **What are the two primary attributes of the <form> tag that you need to change to adapt a Web form to your own application, and what settings do these two attributes reflect?**

   The *method* attribute needs to be set to *POST* to allow the form data to be sent to the action page. The *action* attribute needs to be set to the page that performs some sort of action on the incoming form data.

3. **Can you enter SQL in the simple recordset dialog box?**

   No. You need to use the advanced dialog box.

4. **What is the default value used for in the Recordset dialog box when you add a variable to the SQL statement?**

   The default value is used by the Web page when the user enters no value. In a search situation, you can use the wildcard character % when doing text searches to allow all matches.

5. **What is the reason to HTML encode or URL encode a string of data entered by a user when displaying it on a Web page?**

   By using HTML or URL encoding on the text entered by a user, you can be reasonably certain that special characters and scripts aren't sent to the browser.

6. **Which method allows for more data to be passed: GET or POST?**

   POST allows an unlimited amount of data to be posted.

7. **Which method works better for search forms and why?**

   GET allows the search criteria to become part of the URL so that the link can be copied/pasted and saved or shared.

8. What are two advantages to using the Advanced recordset dialog box in Dreamweaver MX?

Allows you to query more than one table, allows you to specify your own variable names, allows finer control of parameters, allows you to specify default values, and forces you to work with and learn SQL.

9. What is the wildcard character in SQL?

The % character

10. Which SQL keyword(s) is used to sort a recordset?

ORDER BY

11. True or False: Client-side form validation is foolproof.

False. It can be turned off by a user.

12. The Repeat Region is applied to which element on the page to create a typical search results page?

It is applied to the <tr> tag in a table.

Module 13: Recordset Navigation

1. What is the difference between a server behavior and an Application Object?

An Application Object usually consists of several server behaviors applied at once.

2. What is the purpose of the master-detail page set?

The master page allows you to display summaries of many records that each link to a separate detail page that displays more detailed information about a record.

3. What is required before you can apply a Master-Detail Page Set Application Object?

A recordset is required showing all fields necessary for the details page.

4. What are two reasons for using a Show Region server behavior?

To show an area of the page if the recordset is empty, or to show an area of the page if the recordset is not empty

5. Can you edit an Application Object after you apply it?

No. Application Objects are made up of various HTML and server-side code. To edit an Application Object, you have to edit each of the individual parts that make up the object. In some cases, this means editing dozens of different elements.

6. **What is the purpose of the query string (URL) variable in the link to the details page from the results page?**

The query string variable is usually the primary key of a table in the database, and is the best way to locate one specific record in a database table to be displayed on a detail page.

7. **What does the Recordset Navigation Status Application Object do?**

The Recordset Navigation Status object shows the record numbers for the records that are being shown on the page, along with the total records figure. The text looks like "Records {rsSearch_first} to {rsSearch_last} of {rsSearch_total}."

8. **Can you create Master-Detail page sets manually?**

Yes

9. **How do you manually create a link to a detail page from a master page?**

Apply a Go To Detail Page server behavior to a field on the master page, passing the unique ID of the record.

10. **What does the Recordset Navigation Bar application object do?**

It creates a set of First, Previous, Next, and Last links to navigate through your recordset.

11. **How can you create the same effect manually using Server Behaviors?**

You can manually apply Move To First Record, Move To Previous Record, Move To Next Record, and Move To Last Record to some text or images on the page.

12. **How do you show alternative text if there are no results on a result page using Dreamweaver MX?**

Add a Show Region If Recordset Is Not Empty to the database results display, add alternate text to another region on the page, and add a Show Region If Recordset Is Empty server behavior to that region.

Module 14: Creating Dynamic Form Objects

1. **What panel allows you to bind data to a form field?**

Bindings panel

2. **What form element is populated with labels and values?**

List menus (select fields)

3. Why should you always use the Server Behaviors panel to create dynamic check boxes?

Because dragging the field from the Bindings panel will fail to provide the criteria to determine when the check box should appear checked

4. A check box is designed to provide answers to questions that have how many possible responses?

Two

5. Radio button groups are identified by what two things?

The name of the button and its value

6. How should radio buttons be named?

All buttons in a group should have the same name.

7. If you have a list of four multiple choice questions with one possible answer, should you use radio buttons or check boxes?

Radio buttons

8. If you have a list of four multiple choice questions with more than one possible answer, should you use radio buttons or check boxes?

Check boxes

9. What purpose does the static option serve in a list menu?

To give the user directions

10. What are hidden fields used for?

To pass values in the form that you don't want the user to see or be able to modify

Module 15: Inserting, Updating, and Deleting Data

1. Where can you find the Record Insertion form in the Dreamweaver interface?

On the Application tab of the Insert bar

2. How does the database know that it is updating or deleting the proper record?

By identifying the record using a column that is guaranteed to be unique

3. What happens after an insertion is complete?

The user is redirected to a page of the developer's choice.

4. What is the purpose of the manual label entry in a data-populated list menu?

To provide a visual clue to the end user that a selection needs to be made

5. **Rather than deleting a record, it is often more advisable to _____ it.**

   Deactivate

6. **What is a Unique Key column and why is it important?**

   A column that is guaranteed unique for every record in the items table so that the database knows when it locates a certain itemID, it is updating or deleting the proper record

7. **What happens when you update a record?**

   Changes are written to the database in place of what was originally there.

8. **Why should you delete any autonumber fields from the insert record field list?**

   Because you cannot insert data into an autonumber field

9. **A record identifier passed in the address of a page is known as a _____**

   URL parameter

10. **What is the purpose of a redirect page?**

    To provide a location to send a user to after a procedure has completed

Module 16: User Registration, Login, and Site Security

1. **Which server models don't contain User Authentication server behaviors?**

   PHP and ASP.NET

2. **What is a session variable?**

   A special variable that maintains state for a user when going from page to page.

3. **How does a session variable maintain state?**

   A session variable maintains state by keeping a cookie stored on the user's machine with a session ID number that corresponds to a session ID number in the memory of the server. Note that some application servers use other methods to store session variables, such as the file system.

4. **What is the client-side cookie's role in the User Authentication server behaviors?**

   A client-side cookie stores the session id number so that the server can keep track of the session.

5. **How many form fields are necessary to authenticate a user?**

   You need two fields: username and password.

6. **Does Dreamweaver MX use a distinct user identification number or a username for its User Authentication server behaviors?**

   Username

7. **Can two users have the same username?**

   It is possible, but it is not as easy to maintain. You are advised to have unique usernames when you plan your site.

8. **Does the Restrict Access To Page server behavior work on an HTML page?**

   No, the page has to be served from an application server.

9. **If you don't have different access levels defined in your site but want to include a login page, how many levels of access are assumed?**

   Two access levels: authenticated and anonymous Web users

10. **Does the Log Out User server behavior remove the user from the database, kill the session, or destroy all the application variables?**

    It kills the session.

11. **What are the names of the session variables created by the Dreamweaver MX code when you allow a user to log in?**

    MM_Username and *MM_UserAuthorization*

12. **Which Dreamweaver MX behavior allows you to validate the form elements?**

    Validate Form

13. **What are the prerequisites to applying a Check New Username server behavior?**

    You need to have a form with a username field, a submit button, and an Insert server behavior on the page.

Module 17: Extensions and the Extension Manager

1. **What is the three letter file extension for an extension package for Dreamweaver MX?**

   .mxp

2. **Where is the Server Behavior Builder accessed from?**

   The Server Behavior panel

3. **Can extensions be imported from other machines or other programs?**

   Yes

4. **Do all Dreamweaver 4 extensions work with Dreamweaver MX?**

   No, there are incompatibility problems with some Dreamweaver 4 extensions.

5. **What about UltraDev 4 extensions?**

   No, there are incompatibility problems with some UltraDev 4 extensions.

6. **What is the URL of the Macromedia Exchange?**

   www.macromedia.com/exchange

7. **Is the Extension Manager a free program or a low-cost add-on?**

   Free with Dreamweaver, Fireworks, or Flash, or a free download by itself

8. **What are some other programs that the Extension Manager works with?**

   Flash 5, Flash MX, Fireworks, UltraDev, Dreamweaver 4, and others

9. **Did Macromedia create all of the extensions on the Exchange?**

   No, most extensions are created by third-party developers.

10. **Can anyone post an extension on the Exchange?**

    Yes

11. **Which of the following are *not* typical extensions to Dreamweaver MX?**

    A. Objects

    B. Commands

    C. Macros

    D. Toolbars

    E. Databases

    F. Server behaviors

       C and **E** are the correct answers.

Module 18: Troubleshooting Your Site

1. **What does balancing braces refer to?**

   Making sure that all of the opening braces have the appropriate closing braces in your code

2. **What are three common forms that an error can take?**

   An explicit error, nothing happens, and the wrong thing happens

3. **The common HTTP headers error can be solved with what line of code?**

   Response.buffer = True

4. **Leaving the <% and %> delimiters out of you ASP code will cause what problem?**

The code will display as text in the browser instead of executing.

5. **Which of the three types of errors discussed in this module is the most dangerous?**

When the wrong thing happens, because you are often unaware that the result was incorrect

6. **The variables A and a are not the same in JavaScript because JavaScript is a _____ language.**

Case-sensitive

7. **What two steps can you take to simplify your code when troubleshooting?**

Reduce complex procedures to their most basic parts, and use watch points to identify where you are in your code.

8. **What common errors often result in the error "Operation must use an updatable query"?**

Improper permissions to the database folder, and trying to update a joined query

9. **Most errors can be classified into what two categories?**

Server Errors and Coding Errors

10. **What two common issues should you keep in mind when formatting your queries?**

Using single quotes around strings, and the way in which your database wants dates formatted.

Appendix B

Additional Resources

The Macromedia community is large, with newsgroups, tutorials, extensions, and other resources available all over the Web. Some of the available resources are listed as follows, but it is by no means an exhaustive list. There are new sites popping up daily providing more and more content for the Web developer.

Studio MX

Dreamweaver MX is a part of Studio MX, which is an integrated suite of applications that allow you to create dynamic Web applications. In addition to Dreamweaver MX, the suite contains Freehand, Fireworks MX, Flash MX, and a developmental edition of ColdFusion MX (for the PC version only). If you haven't purchased Dreamweaver yet, you should look into getting it as part of the entire suite of applications. Flash MX will allow you to create animations, forms, interfaces, menus, and other types of interactive content simply not possible with HTML. Fireworks MX will allow you to create layouts and images for your Web site with round-trip editing between Dreamweaver and Fireworks.

Information on Studio MX can be found at **http://www.macromedia.com/software/studio/**.

Community

The Macromedia forums are a great place to get questions answered in a timely fashion. They are located in two places—on the Web at the following address:

- **http://www.macromedia.com/support/forums/**

and from your newsreader interface (Outlook Express or similar newsreader):

- **news://forums.macromedia.com/**

The forums are broken down by product, and for popular products they are broken down even further. There is a Dreamweaver general discussion forum, a Dreamweaver application development forum, and a Dreamweaver extensions forum. You'll find many of the top Dreamweaver experts in the forums posting answers to common (and not-so-common) questions.

Books

The release of Dreamweaver MX has unleashed a whole slew of new books on the market. At last count, there were 49 Dreamweaver MX books listed on Amazon.com. Your best bet at finding a book that expands on the content from the Beginner's Guide is to browse through the books at your local bookstore. We would recommend the following books:

- ***Dreamweaver MX: The Complete Reference***

  by Ray West, Tom Muck
  ISBN: 0072195142 (McGraw-Hill/Osborne)

- ***The Joy of Dreamweaver MX: Recipes for Data-Driven Web Sites***

  by Paul Newman
  ISBN: 0072224649 (McGraw-Hill/Osborne)

Sites

Support sites for Dreamweaver are popping up daily. It seems that everyone with a copy of Dreamweaver is eager to share his or her knowledge with the rest of the community. There are some very good supports sites and some poor ones. Here are some of the best of the current sites:

- **www.macromedia.com/desdev**   Macromedia's designer and developer center is one of the best places to go to learn about the products.

- **www.macromedia.com/support/dreamweaver/**   Macromedia's online support site features technotes that relate to Dreamweaver.

- **www.dwteam.com**   The Dreamweaver Team consists of some of the top experts in the Dreamweaver community.

- **www.mxzone.com**   The "zones" are a fixture in the Dreamweaver community. They feature content posted by people all over the world.

- **www.dwfaq.com**   More than just an FAQ site, dwfaq also features many tutorials and products from some of the top names in the field.

Magazines

MXinSite is a magazine devoted to Macromedia's Studio MX. There are many in-depth articles about Dreamweaver MX and the other products in the suite. Information is available at **www.mxinsite.com**.

Computer Arts is a magazine from the UK that is more focused on the design aspects of Web development, but frequently features content about Dreamweaver MX and the other Studio MX products. Information is available at **www.computerarts.co.uk**.

Conventions

Computer conferences are a good place to learn about the products and technologies that relate to Web development. Most conferences span two or three days and offer a wide variety of content.

The annual TODCON (The Other Dreamweaver Conference) is devoted to Dreamweaver and other Macromedia products. TODCON is more than just a conference—it is a community event attended by many of the top Dreamweaver experts and community members. Information is available at **www.todcon.org**.

Devcon is a Macromedia-sponsored annual event that was once heavily geared toward ColdFusion developers. Since Macromedia's acquisition of Allaire, the focus of the conference has shifted and now features other Macromedia technologies, such as Dreamweaver and Flash. Information can be found on the Macromedia Web site.

Thunder Lizard also holds many conferences throughout the year, such as Macromedia Web World and Webbuilder. Information on Thunder Lizard conferences can be found at **www.ftpconferences.com/thunderlizard/**.

Index

INTERNATIONAL CONTACT INFORMATION

AUSTRALIA
McGraw-Hill Book Company Australia Pty. Ltd.
TEL +61-2-9900-1800
FAX +61-2-9878-8881
http://www.mcgraw-hill.com.au
books-it_sydney@mcgraw-hill.com

CANADA
McGraw-Hill Ryerson Ltd.
TEL +905-430-5000
FAX +905-430-5020
http://www.mcgraw-hill.ca

**GREECE, MIDDLE EAST, & AFRICA
(Excluding South Africa)**
McGraw-Hill Hellas
TEL +30-1-656-0990-3-4
FAX +30-1-654-5525

MEXICO (Also serving Latin America)
McGraw-Hill Interamericana Editores S.A. de C.V.
TEL +525-117-1583
FAX +525-117-1589
http://www.mcgraw-hill.com.mx
fernando_castellanos@mcgraw-hill.com

SINGAPORE (Serving Asia)
McGraw-Hill Book Company
TEL +65-863-1580
FAX +65-862-3354
http://www.mcgraw-hill.com.sg
mghasia@mcgraw-hill.com

SOUTH AFRICA
McGraw-Hill South Africa
TEL +27-11-622-7512
FAX +27-11-622-9045
robyn_swanepoel@mcgraw-hill.com

SPAIN
McGraw-Hill/Interamericana de España, S.A.U.
TEL +34-91-180-3000
FAX +34-91-372-8513
http://www.mcgraw-hill.es
professional@mcgraw-hill.es

**UNITED KINGDOM, NORTHERN,
EASTERN, & CENTRAL EUROPE**
McGraw-Hill Education Europe
TEL +44-1-628-502500
FAX +44-1-628-770224
http://www.mcgraw-hill.co.uk
computing_neurope@mcgraw-hill.com

ALL OTHER INQUIRIES Contact:
Osborne/McGraw-Hill
TEL +1-510-549-6600
FAX +1-510-883-7600
http://www.osborne.com
omg_international@mcgraw-hill.com

Designed for people. Not clocks.

People learn at their own pace. That's why our Beginner's Guides provide a systematic pedagogy. Real-world examples from seasoned trainers teach the critical skills needed to master a tool or technology.

Osborne Beginner's Guides: Essential Skills—Made Easy

Solaris 9 Administration: A Beginner's Guide
Paul A. Watters, Ph.D.
ISBN: 0-07-222317-0

UNIX System Administration: A Beginner's Guide
Steve Maxwell
ISBN: 0-07-219486-3

Dreamweaver MX: A Beginner's Guide
Ray West & Tom Muck
ISBN: 0-07-222366-9

HTML: A Beginner's Guide, Second Edition
Wendy Willard
ISBN: 0-07-222644-7

Java 2: A Beginner's Guide, Second Edition
Herbert Schildt
ISBN: 0-07-222588-2

UML: A Beginner's Guide
Jason Roff
ISBN: 0-07-222460-6

Windows XP Professional: A Beginner's Guide
Martin S. Matthews
ISBN: 0-07-222608-0

Networking: A Beginner's Guide, Third Edition
Bruce Hallberg
ISBN: 0-07-222563-7

Linux Administration: A Beginner's Guide, Third Edition
Steve Graham
ISBN: 0-07-222562-9

Red Hat Linux Administration: A Beginner's Guide
Narender Muthyala
ISBN: 0-07-222631-5

Windows .NET Server 2003: A Beginner's Guide
Martin S. Matthews
ISBN: 0-07-219309-3

9 proven learning features:

1 Modules
2 Critical Skills
3 Step-by-Step Tutorials
4 Ask the Experts
5 Progress Checks
6 Annotated Syntax
7 Mastery Checks
8 Projects
9 Network Blueprints

OSBORNE DELIVERS RESULTS!

OSBORNE
www.osborne.com

Complete References

Herbert Schildt
0-07-213485-2

Jeffery R. Shapiro
0-07-213381-3

Chris H. Pappas & William
H. Murray, III
0-07-212958-1

Herbert Schildt
0-07-213084-9

Ron Ben-Natan & Ori Sasson
0-07-222394-4

Arthur Griffith
0-07-222405-3

For the answers to everything related to your technology, drill as deeply as you please into our Complete Reference series. Written by topical authorities, these comprehensive resources offer a full range of knowledge, including extensive product information, theory, step-by-step tutorials, sample projects, and helpful appendixes.

OSBORNE
www.osborne.com

For more information on these and other Osborne books, visit our Web site at www.osborne.com